Divorce

C.G.T. Canadian Legal Forms Ltd
Burnaby, B.C. / service@CanadaForms.com

> **NOTICE:**
>
> THIS PRODUCT IS NOT INTENDED TO PROVIDE LEGAL ADVICE. IT CONTAINS GENERAL INFORMATION FOR EDUCATIONAL PURPOSES ONLY. PLEASE CONSULT A LAWYER IN ALL LEGAL MATTERS. THIS PRODUCT WAS NOT NECESSARILY PREPARED BY A PERSON LICENSED TO PRACTICE LAW IN YOUR PROVINCE.

Divorce

© Copyright 2002 C.G.T. Canadian Legal Forms LTD

P.O. Box 82664

Burnaby, B.C. V5C 5W4

service@CanadaForms.com

All rights reserved.

1 2 3 4 5 6 7 8 9 10

This publication is designed to provide accurate and authoritative information in regard to subject matter covered. It is sold with the understanding that neither the publisher nor author is engaged in rendering legal, accounting, or other professional services. If legal advice or other expert assistance is required, the services of a competent professional should be sought.

Divorce

Table of Contents

Introduction 7

1   Do You Need a Lawyer? 9

2   Preparing For Divorce 17

3   How Property is Divided—Who Gets What? 31

4   Alimony, Custody, and Support 43

5   Preparing the Paperwork For Court 53

6   Getting On With Your Life 85

Glossary of Useful Terms 91

Appendix A: Addresses To Write To For
            Marriage Certificates 95

Appendix B: The Divorce Act 97

Appendix C: Comparative Analysis of
            Family Property Legislation 159

Appendix D: Child Support Tables 173

Index 241

Introduction

Divorce doesn't have to be expensive and painful. Whether you are considering a divorce, or have already started a legal separation, there are ways to control the costs and emotions when partners agree to part. *Divorce* provides a step-by-step strategy for working through an uncontested divorce, even when children are involved.

By taking steps now, you can confidently resolve your divorce. An undefended divorce enables you to customize your divorce settlement to best suit your family's needs without interference from expensive lawyers or legal professionals.

You will also find important information about how to divide and preserve your assets when you are both a marriage and business partner with your spouse. Discover how to come to an agreement on dividing assets, assigning debts, setting reasonable support amounts, and having achievable, post-divorce goals. This book will also help you prepare and survive an undefended divorce without suffering a crushing financial defeat.

Do you really want a divorce?

Before you start divorce proceedings, make certain you want a divorce. No marriage is without its occasional problems. There are a number of things you can do to assure yourself that you are making the correct decision.

Don't act hastily. Never rush into a divorce. Make certain you have given your problems adequate time to work themselves out. Anger and feelings do change over time. With patience, you and your spouse may be able to resolve your difficulties and enjoy a happy marriage.

Seek professional help. Can a psychologist, psychiatrist, social worker, or marriage counselor help you and your spouse improve your relationship? These professionals can act as mediators because they more clearly see the reasons for your conflict and offer valuable suggestions for overcoming your problem. Don't forget, these professionals have counseled many other couples who have shared precisely the same problems.

There are basically three types of mediation:

1. *Open mediation.* Everything that is said may be quoted by any of the parties involved and should it become necessary, in reporting recommendations to the court.

2. *Closed mediation.* Everything that is said remains confidential. The mediator cannot make recommendations to the court. Closed mediation is not preferable because should this type of mediation fail, the parties must start the divorce process all over again.

3. *Collaborative mediation.* Here the spouses and lawyer(s) involved agree to try to resolve the issues out of court. Should this type of mediation fail however, the parties can proceed to litigate only with new lawyers. This can be quite costly and time consuming.

Should mediation fail, a final attempt may be made by submitting to arbitration. Both parties agree in advance to abide by whatever decision the neutral arbitrator, who is paid by the couple, makes. In effect, the arbitrator who may have both psychological and legal training, imposes his/her solution upon the couple. However, either party may still appeal an arbitration ruling to the court.

Try a separation. Rather than jump from marriage straight into divorce, why not try a trial separation? Living apart from your spouse allows you to realistically assess the importance of your spouse in your life. You can simply agree to live apart for a while or file for a legal separation. Obtaining a legal separation and living apart for at least one year is often the least burdensome method for obtaining a divorce.

Do You Need a Lawyer?

1

Do You Need a Lawyer?

A divorce is one of the most important events in life. It can affect you emotionally, financially and, of course, legally. Your divorce will legally resolve important rights and obligations concerning:

- financial support
- division of property
- custody and visitation of your minor children

While these are certainly vital issues, the law on these points is not overly complicated and is reasonably uniform among the different provinces. Considerably more complex is the process for obtaining a divorce. But this too is simplified with the aid of this book and perhaps some information from your local divorce court.

Will you need a lawyer to handle your divorce? To answer the question ask yourself the following four questions:

1. *Is your divorce defended or undefended?*

If you and your spouse agree that you should divorce, you have an undefended divorce. A defended divorce requires the services of a lawyer, as you must litigate whether you are entitled to a divorce as a matter of law.

Divorce

You and your spouse may both agree about the divorce but disagree on other issues, such as how your property will be divided or who will have custody of your children. These disagreements mean the divorce is still defended, and you will most likely need a lawyer to litigate these issues in court. Even if the divorce is undefended, there may be procedural issues that are best resolved with the help of a lawyer. Such issues could include the amount of spousal or child support, division of property, and service of process.

> You definitely need a lawyer if your spouse has abandoned you, is avoiding being served, or otherwise cannot be found. Because your spouse will not sign the paperwork, the divorce is considered defended.

2. *Do you have minor children?*

The most important issues in a divorce concern the welfare of your minor children. These include child support, custody and visitation rights. Because these issues are so important, the court will be quite concerned with their resolution and that what has been decided is, in fact, in the best interest of your minor children. Because the rights of your children are paramount, it is wise to have an attorney review provisions concerning your children—even if you and your spouse are in agreement. An experienced divorce lawyer can guide you to a settlement that a court will approve as fair and in the best interests of the children.

3. *Do you have minimal and easily divided property?*

If your divorce is nothing more than deciding who gets the dog or some furniture, you and your spouse can resolve these questions on your own without a lawyer. If you own considerable property, you will want a lawyer to make certain you receive your fair share, and that you understand existing liabilities and taxation.

Chapter 1

4. *Do you need or expect future support from your spouse?*

If you will be financially dependent upon your spouse you may need a lawyer to help you negotiate equitable support as well as make the obligation binding through valid support agreements.

Alimony and spousal support are becoming less common as more husbands and wives pursue independent careers today. Still, if you have questions about whether you are entitled to alimony—or what a proper support amount should be—you'll need a lawyer's advice.

You probably do not need a lawyer if:

- you and your spouse want the divorce and agree on the division of property
- you have no minor children
- your marital or separately owned property is minimal
- you are not seeking alimony or spousal support

If you meet these criteria, ask yourself whether you are comfortable handling your own divorce—completing the paperwork and representing yourself should you have to appear in court. To help you decide, it might be a good idea to visit a divorce court and watch the proceedings. If you are comfortable, why not try?

Other factors may also influence your decision on whether to hire a lawyer. If your situation has unusual complications or your spouse has a lawyer, consider representation.

> Should you reach a point where you no longer feel comfortable representing yourself, you can always hire a lawyer—or consult a lawyer about a particular aspect of the divorce that may be causing you difficulty.

Advantages of using a lawyer

Whether or not you think you need a lawyer, retaining a lawyer does offer you several advantages:

- You can let your lawyer handle all the details while you get on with your life with less concern over legal matters.

- A lawyer will give you added protection—particularly in areas where you may not now see the need for protection.

- The judge and court clerk will prefer to work with your lawyer. Since your lawyer knows the procedures, your case can be processed more efficiently.

- A lawyer can be emotionally supportive during the divorce. It can be comforting to have a lawyer to turn to for objectivity when your feelings cloud clear thinking.

> Your lawyer can be a buffer between you and your spouse and resolve some of the more emotionally charged issues.

Advantages of representing yourself

There are corresponding benefits to handling your own divorce without a lawyer.

- **You save legal fees.** A simple defended divorce can cost $1,000 or more. Fees can become astronomical in large, defended cases. Attorneys charge between $150 and $500 an hour for their time, so a fee can quickly climb for even the smallest case.

- **Your divorce may be less adversarial.** Lawyers can bring an adversarial atmosphere to a case that may be resolved more quickly and smoothly in an informal atmosphere involving only you and your spouse.

- **Your case may move faster without a lawyer.** Your lawyer may be busy with other cases, causing needless delays that you can avoid by personally taking charge of your case.

- **Without a lawyer the judge may give you more leeway**. However this can't always be counted on.

Of course, you can compromise and hire a lawyer on an hourly basis who will not formally represent you, but who will answer questions that may arise. You will save on legal fees, but still have available to you the professional assistance you need. Many readers of this book have discovered this is an ideal way to proceed.

Finding a lawyer

Many lawyers handle divorce cases and quite a few specialize in family law. It will not be difficult to find a lawyer to handle your divorce, but you may have to interview several lawyers before you find one that makes you feel comfortable and can handle your divorce efficiently and economically. How can you find such a lawyer?

- Seek referrals from friends or family members who have gone through a divorce.

- Call the lawyer referral service of your local bar association.

- Ask your family lawyer for a referral. You may have used a real estate lawyer or bankruptcy lawyer, for example, who may also know of a good divorce lawyer.

- Look through the telephone book. Divorce lawyers frequently advertise their specialty.

- Ask the clerk of your local divorce court for the names of the more active divorce lawyers in your area. Similarly, the various social service agencies may be an excellent referral source.

Once you have a number of names, set up interviews with four or five lawyers. When interviewing the lawyer, ask these questions:

- How long has the lawyer been in practice?

- What percentage of his or her cases are divorce?
- Does the lawyer generally represent the husband, the wife or both?
- Who will actually handle the case, and will associates be involved?
- What will be the general strategy for the case, and how long will it take?
- What approximate outcome might be expected?
- Approximately how much will it cost, and how is the fee to be paid?

Since an important objective is to save money on legal fees, here are a few ways to keep legal fees to a minimum:

- Don't hire a divorce lawyer solely because the lawyer has a prominent reputation. A lesser-known lawyer may be equally effective at a fraction of the cost.
- Use your time with the lawyer efficiently. Be concise on the phone and limit your phone calls. The same rule applies to office visits.
- Give information to your lawyer's secretary whenever possible. It will save expensive time.
- Do the routine work (deliver papers, etc.) yourself.

It may be that after you talk to several lawyers, or even retain one, you will decide you can handle or complete the divorce on your own—or perhaps with a lawyer as an occasional advisor.

As you can see, this book is not necessarily intended to replace your lawyer. It's designed to help you decide if you need one and also to work more effectively with your lawyer should one be retained.

Preparing For Divorce

Preparing For Divorce

Grounds for divorce

You or your spouse may want a divorce, but that does not mean you can automatically obtain a divorce. You must satisfy the legalities or "legal grounds" that are considered justification for the divorce.

Years ago these laws were much more strict and it was much more difficult to obtain a divorce. All provinces today recognize only one ground for divorce—marriage breakdown. This means neither party necessarily did anything wrong but that the couple simply has irreconcilable differences and no longer wish to remain married. There are only three ways to prove marriage breakdown:

> Attitudes about divorce have changed and with it most laws have been liberalized.

1. **Live separate and apart for at least one uninterrupted year**

    This usually begins with a written contract called a *legal separation*. A legal separation is a document signed by both husband and wife in which they agree to live apart. This contract must be freely undertaken—free from fraud, misrepresentation, coercion, duress, or undue influence. Both parties must be of sound mind and clearly understand the nature and consequences of their acts—they must act in good faith. Even if the contract is fair, obtaining legal advice prevents either party from later claiming that he/she did not really understand the contract.

> Some provinces require that the parties obtain independent legal advice prior to signing the Separation Agreement.

The Separation Agreement asserts that each party will:

- be free from the other's control and authority
- live apart as if unmarried
- refrain from harassing or molesting the other during this period

Additionally, the Separation Agreement usually contains provisions for:

- financial arrangements, including tax consequences
- spousal support
- child support, including child care
- visitation rights called "Access"
- division of property, including the disposition of the family home
- payment of debts
- maintenance of insurance
- disposition of assets
- terms of the agreement

One of the advantages of using a Separation Agreement is that it provides much of the framework for the divorce. It provides the spouses an opportunity to work out their issues and come to terms with custody, support, and access. By the time they are ready to divorce, the procedure is much smoother and faster.

Not all separation occurs by mutual consent or through physical relocation. Either spouse may have been deserted without cause by the other or may have been living under the same roof, leading completely independent lives including separate bedrooms, separate meals, and shopping trips. They may have had no sexual or social relations with each other. In other words, they failed to share a common home life.

The parties do not have to wait the full 12 months before starting the divorce proceedings. They must, however, be separated at the time the divorce proceedings begin. The Divorce Judgment itself will only be granted after 12 months have elapsed.

While the time requirement must be 12 uninterrupted months, the parties are allowed to attempt reconciliation. They may live together and have sexual relations during this period, for a maximum 90 days, without jeopardizing the 12 months. These 90 days of cohabitation do not have to be consecutive. Should the parties exceed the ninety-day period, the 12 months would restart from the point where they resume their separation.

If the spouses manage to reconcile, the Separation Agreement is cancelled. Should they break up again, a new Separation Agreement must be created.

> To avoid the problem of defining a genuine reconciliation, many Separation Agreements will be tied to a specific number of consecutive days of reconciliation.

2. Adultery

Even in an undefended divorce, you must prove adultery to the court. To be able to prove that your spouse committed adultery, you must be able to produce evidence and also prove that your spouse had the opportunity to do so. The evidence does not have to include eyewitness testimony or photographs but may instead be based upon circumstantial evidence—evidence that indicates adultery probably occurred. For example, two people

Divorce

staying overnight in a hotel or in one another's apartment are presumed to have had sexual relations together.

> Private investigators are often hired to collect adulterous evidence.

Adultery can be grounds for divorce even if it was not the initial cause of the separation or if it occurred during the period of separation. You cannot use your own adultery to obtain a divorce nor can you conspire to commit adultery just to receive a divorce. You will be asked to swear in court that you did not do so.

The three easiest ways to prove adultery are:

a) The spouse and partner admit to adultery in court. This is commonly accomplished through a sworn affidavit.

b) Have a lawyer interview the adulterous spouse in the presence of a court reporter. The court reporter records the questions and answers verbatim and the transcript of the conversation is submitted to the court and will be read by the judge

c) Appear in court yourself with or without your spouse and partner. Call witnesses and present evidence to establish the adultery.

3. Cruelty

Cruelty may be mental, physical, or both. Each case must be decided upon its own circumstances and conditions. Courts try to use common sense and average person standards to decide whether behavior is cruel or simply the result of mutual incompatibility. Cruelty goes far beyond incompatibility. Cruelty must be of such a nature as to make continued living together intolerable. Therefore, there is a heavy burden of proof placed upon the person using cruelty as grounds for divorce.

> There is no standard legal definition of cruelty.

Chapter 2

Common elements that help define cruelty:

- fear
- jealousy
- physical abuse
- domination
- hypercriticism
- denial of sexual service
- abnormal sex acts
- cruelty to a child or pet
- restriction of freedom
- refusal to interact
- accusations
- complaints
- derision
- desire to inflict suffering
- transmitting venereal disease

> Unlike adultery, which is inferred from the facts, you must prove that cruelty actually occurred. In order to establish your cruelty-based divorce case, it is best to have a detailed list of times and places where the cruelty occurred. Eyewitnesses and medical professionals can be invaluable for corroborating your story. You may use affidavits, witnesses, and court appearances, as you would in adultery, to prove your case.

Getting organized

Divorce can become quite complicated financially and legally—particularly when couples have considerable wealth. To resolve your financial matters fairly, you and your advisors need your complete financial and legal picture.

Organize and have ready:

- deeds and mortgages on real estate
- pension and other retirement plans
- life insurance policies
- last will and testament, codicils and any testamentary trusts
- pre-nuptial or post-nuptial agreements
- divorce decrees and property agreements
- savings and checking accounts
- wills or trusts where you are a beneficiary or grantor
- ownership interests in any closely-held business, including corporate or partnership documents and financial statements of each business
- notes or evidence of obligations due you
- notes or evidence of obligations you owe others
- tax returns for the last three years
- leases
- outstanding major contracts
- inventory of valuable personal assets (antiques, jewelry, art)
- titles, registration and appraisals on any autos, boats, planes or other vehicles

Chapter 2

- lawsuits or evidence concerning contemplated suits against third parties
- lawsuits, judgments or potential claims against yourself
- malpractice or liability insurance
- applications for credit or loans issued within the prior five years

You will, of course, want the same information from your spouse. If you or your spouse own a business, you'll want to review:

- copies of any notes or loans between yourself and your business
- corporate obligations to which you are a guarantor
- life insurance policies maintained by the company
- financial statements of the business
- tax returns of the business

Make certain every important asset you and/or your spouse own is accounted for. It's remarkably easy to overlook valuable assets unless you systematically review this asset inventory:

- cash on hand
- checking and savings accounts
- cash value life insurance
- motor vehicles
- residential real estate
- investment real estate
- stocks or bonds in publicly-owned corporations
- certificates of deposit
- money market funds
- stocks or equities in any closed corporations, partnerships or other business entities

- notes or mortgages receivable
- savings bonds
- accounts receivable
- boats, airplanes or other recreational vehicles
- options to acquire property
- leases or leasehold interests
- art, jewelry and antiques
- beneficial interests in trusts
- revocable trusts to which you are a grantor
- licenses or franchise rights
- retirement accounts
- tax refunds due
- actual or potential claims against third parties
- inheritances and future interests
- safe deposit box inventory
- copyrights, trademarks or patents

Estimate the approximate value of each item as closely as possible. Indicate how each asset is titled (singly in your name, jointly with spouse, in trust, etc.). Also specify your percentage ownership in assets owned with others. Finally, list liens or encumbrances against each asset to determine the equity to be protected. Repeat this exercise for your liabilities:

- mortgages
- tax liabilities
- notes on car loans
- unsecured loans

- other secured installment loans
- charge account balances
- credit card balances
- alimony or child support from previous marriages
- business debts guaranteed
- other guaranteed debts
- outstanding judgments
- potential or threatened claims

Finally, project ahead—over the next year or two—so you anticipate inheritances, other windfalls, or even financial problems that should be factored into the divorce agreement.

> Compile your records so that you fully understand every facet of your finances as well as your spouse's.

Safeguard your assets before divorce

With approaching dissolution of the marriage, one or both spouses may try to hide assets from the other. One spouse, for instance, may sell stocks or bonds, or withdraw savings and claim the proceeds were spent or lost. Divorce courts, of course, see such tactics daily and severely penalize the spouse suspected of such conduct. Don't let that be you. Play fair and you'll come out further ahead. That doesn't necessarily mean your spouse will be as honest. Your goal must be to protect marital assets until they can be equitably divided by the court or an agreement reached.

- Remove all jewelry, artwork and other valuable but movable objects to a secure place beyond the reach of your spouse. Do give your spouse a complete inventory of what was taken so you can't be accused of concealing marital assets.

- Place all cash, securities, stocks, bonds and notes or mortgages due you in a secure place. If these assets are in your joint names, notify your stock broker or transfer agent not to put through any transfers without your written consent.

- If you and your spouse hold joint insurance policies, then draw down any cash value for safekeeping.

- Does your spouse own real estate in his or her name only? You'll need your lawyer to file in court for a restraining order preventing transfer of the property. You may instead file a *Lis Pendens* against the property. This puts any prospective buyer on notice of your claim to the property. This effectively encumbers the property so you don't lose your rights to it even if it is sold.

- Business interests are best protected by a restraining order preventing your spouse from transferring his or her interest. You may also seek a restraining order against the corporate entity itself, thus preventing actions out of the ordinary course of business that may dissipate the value of the business.

- Empty checking accounts and savings accounts that your spouse can sign on. Escrow these funds pending the divorce.

Timing is the key to asset protection when a divorce looms on the horizon. Don't wait for your spouse to act first—there may then be very few assets left to protect. There are several ways one or both spouses in a divorce can play "hide and seek" with property:

> When you prepare the list of assets that you and your spouse own, also record serial numbers and other means of identification.

- **Relocate property to a safer locale.** This may mean transferring assets to offshore havens where privacy is assured.

- **Camouflage ownership.** Did one spouse "sell" an interest in a business for cash or other consideration of little value? Fraudulent transfers of assets—particularly business interests—are notoriously common in a divorce. The defrauded spouse can attempt to prove it a fraudulent transfer, but such an effort can be quite difficult and expensive.

- **Delay receiving income.** Income may be inheritances or assets from other sources until the divorce is final. An accommodating employer may assist by deferring salary increases, bonuses or commissions until the divorce is over. Substantial income can also be secreted in defined-benefit pension plans. These hidden payments may be as much as 100 percent of the person's income.

Divorce courts award a disproportionately large share of assets to the innocent spouse when the other spouse is believed to have secreted assets. For example, if your spouse can prove that you transferred cash to an offshore bank, the court may well award your spouse equal or greater amounts of other marital assets. As you can see, it matters little that courts can't attach some assets when they can divide others.

> Endless possibilities abound in a divorce for one or both parties to hide assets or income. Such actions may seem smart, but in practice you'll be in an even better position by remaining honest.

How Property is Divided— Who Gets What?

3

How Property is Divided— Who Gets What?

Dividing property by agreement

This book assumes that you and your spouse will reach agreement on the division of marital assets and liabilities, and there will thus be no need for the court to divide the property.

If you have minimal property, you and your spouse may simply divide it with no formality. If you have more substantial assets, you will want a written agreement. Judges nearly always go along with the property agreement of the spouses if it is generally fair, and the judge is convinced the agreement was freely entered into by both spouses with no fraud or coercion.

How do courts divide property when the spouses cannot agree?

Equitable distribution

Although spouses may themselves agree upon the division of their property and may even draft a contract to that effect, in cases where no agreement is possible, the court attempts to equitably divide the marital property. The court normally allows individually owned property, including gifts and inheritances brought into the marriage, to remain with the owner. However, the value of any property except the family home, acquired during the marriage, must be divided equally. To understand the theory of asset division, you must first understand that the law views marriage as an equal business partnership. The law then divides property into two categories: personal property and marital property. *Marital property* is anything acquired jointly, or by either spouse, during the marriage. *Personal property* is from one of two sources:

1) property that each spouse owned individually before the marriage and retained in his or her name after the marriage

2) property that each spouse received as a gift or inheritance either before or during the marriage

Court-ordered payments to equalize property values may often be made over a period of years—with interest—sometimes accruing on the outstanding balance.

> The right to any specific property is not guaranteed—only the right to specific payments of dollar amounts.

As with assets, liabilities either spouse has incurred prior to the marriage remain a separate obligation. While the parties may agree to keep separate debts incurred during the marriage, these provisions do not bind creditors. Be certain that marital bills are discharged or indemnified against you should you go through a divorce.

How do you best protect your personal property upon marriage? Start by listing your property when you marry. Clearly stipulate that it is to remain separate property thereafter. Similarly, keep separate any gifts or inheritances you receive during your marriage. These assets will then always remain yours.

A petition to divide property need not wait until divorce proceedings begin. Either spouse may petition for a division of property upon separation. This would enable the spouses to retain exclusive possession of the family home, and establish custody and financial relief. This should not be undertaken without the advice of a lawyer. Should the spouses eventually decide to divorce, the only remaining issue would be the actual grounds for divorce as everything else has been decided.

How to deal with specific assets

The family home

The *family home* or the matrimonial home is the last place the spouses normally lived prior to their separation. Should the family home be acquired during the marriage, it will be valued at the current market value on one of the following dates:

- the date of the separation
- the date one spouse files an application to the court to equalize the property because the property is or will be devalued
- The date the other spouses dies

Suppose the family home was owned by one of the spouses prior to the marriage. In that case the spouses would only share in the increased market value (if any) of the home. The spouses would be allowed to deduct the original value of the home on the date of the marriage.

For example, suppose John owned a home free and clear valued at $200,000 on the date of the marriage. After 10 years, the current market value of the home is $250,000. Should John separate from his spouse at that time, the home, for purposes of property distribution, would be valued at $50,000 only—the difference between its value at the time of separation and its value on the date of the marriage. Therefore, each spouse would receive $25,000 when the home is sold.

It's important to remember that you are dealing with the equity in the house—not the fair market value of the home. If the home is worth $200,000 but has a $150,000 mortgage, then the equity shared by you and your spouse is only $50,000. It is that amount you must focus on when negotiating your settlement.

During the marriage, both spouses have an equal right to live in the family home even if one spouse owns the home. Neither spouse can be forced out without a court order.

> The home cannot be sold or mortgaged without the consent of both spouses.

Pension and profit-sharing plans

What happens in divorce to retirement funds you or your spouse accumulated? There are some general guidelines to follow in determining which of these assets are subject to division in a divorce.

Less than half of those with private pension plans are entitled to have their spouse receive a survivor's pension. Of this group, a divorced or separated spouse may not be entitled to be considered the surviving spouse if no spouse had been paid prior to separation.

Canada pensions

Workers contribute to the *Canada Pension Plan* just like any other pension plan. It provides some protection against disability, death, and loss of income. One of the features of this plan is survivor benefits. Survivor's benefits include:

- death benefit
- survivor's pension
- children's benefit

Your pension credits build up as you continue to pay into the Plan. When you apply for a benefit, Canada Pension Plan uses these credits to calculate your entitlement. Generally, the more credits you have, the higher your Canada Pension Plan benefit will be.

The Canada Pension Plan recognizes that in a legal marriage or common-law relationship, both spouses or common-law partners share in the building of their assets and entitlements. Among these are Canada Pension Plan pension credits. When a relationship ends, the Canada Pension Plan pension credits which the couple built up during the time they lived together can be divided equally between them. This division is called "credit splitting." Credits can be split even if one spouse or common-law partner did not pay into the Canada Pension Plan.

> Canada Pension Plan keeps a record of your "pensionable" earnings, and the contributions you make over the years. These become your "Canada Pension Plan pension credits."

Generally, the credits of one person, the lower earner, are increased and the credits of the other, the higher earner, are reduced by the same amount. The longer you and your former spouse or common-law partner were together, and the bigger the difference between your earnings while you were together, the greater the exchange of credits will be. If your "pensionable" earnings and your spouse's or common-law partner's were the same while you were together, there would be nothing to exchange. So a credit split would not be done.

In a case where both spouses or common-law partners are already receiving a Canada Pension Plan benefit and both benefits would be reduced, then the credit split would not be done.

Cohabitation

Most of the time, "cohabiting" in a conjugal (married) relationship means living together. But sometimes people who are still in a relationship have to live apart for a time, for instance, because of illness or work. In such a case, you and your spouse or common-law partner would still be considered as cohabiting.

> Canada Pension Plan splits only the credits for the time you cohabited, and works in calendar years.

Working in "calendar years" means dealing with complete years from January to December. In calculating a credit split, Canada Pension Plan:

- includes the whole calendar year for the year you began living together
- does not include any of the calendar year for the year the relationship ended

Normally, the more you as an individual earn and contribute to the Canada Pension Plan over the years, the greater the number of "credits" you will have. The more credits you have, the higher the benefit will be (when you become entitled). But credit splitting between former spouses or common-law partners means that for the period they lived together, Canada Pension Plan credits can be "equalized."

Splitting credits with a former spouse or common-law partner is generally to your advantage if you were the lower wage earner during your years together. It would increase your Canada Pension Plan credits, meaning that you would get a larger benefit when you become eligible (or if you are getting one now). It is also to your advantage if you have never been a wage earner. In this case, credit splitting could give you Canada Pension Plan credits which you have never had before. These new credits could make you eligible for your own Canada Pension Plan benefits.

> Credit splitting is generally to your disadvantage if you were the higher wage earner. It would reduce your credits, meaning you could get a smaller benefit when you become eligible (or if you are getting one now).

Is credit splitting optional?

Since January 1, 1987, once Canada Pension Plan has the necessary information about your legal divorce or annulment, your Canada Pension Plan pension credits must be split, unless there is a valid spousal or common-law union agreement signed in Saskatchewan, Quebec, or British Columbia. But, if you are separated or have left a common-law relationship, there may be a credit split only if you (or your former spouse or common-law partner) choose to apply for it. In these cases only (not in cases of divorce or annulment) the applicant can ask to withdraw the application within 60 days of being notified of the credit split. Pension laws are very complicated. Therefore, you should consult with a lawyer if these issues apply to your situation

Professional licensure

Academic diplomas and professional licenses may be considered marital assets. This is particularly true when one spouse helped put the other through school to become a professional. Most valuable are the licenses to practice high-income professions—such as medicine, dentistry, and law. The Ph.D. is also an asset the courts are likely to attach a value to.

> A divorce court may determine that professional status is a marital asset worth $1 million or more. To balance outcomes, the court may leave the spouse with professional status very little in other marital assets.

Other assets to consider

If you have prepared a thorough list of assets before you negotiated your Separation Agreement, you will be less likely to overlook some of these less visible assets:

- inheritances due
- options to acquire property
- claims or lawsuits against third parties

Dividing debts and liabilities

If there are bills incurred by you and your spouse, they must be divided along with your assets. A bill may stand in the name of one spouse, but that doesn't mean the other spouse can't agree to pay it or share in its payment as part of the divorce agreement.

You must realize that orders of the court or your agreement concerning division of debts do not affect your creditors. Whoever was originally liable on a debt remains liable for the debt even if the other spouse agrees to pay it. If your spouse agrees to pay one of your debts and fails to, you can sue your spouse, but your creditor can still sue you.

> The creditor's recourse is against the spouse who owes the money—not the spouse who agreed to assume the debt.

Bear this in mind when dividing liabilities. Make certain your spouse has the financial responsibility to pay the debts he or she agrees to pay. If you believe your spouse may default, try to obtain security to ensure his or her payments. You may take a mortgage on any real estate or personal property (a car or boat) conveyed to your spouse. You may require your spouse to escrow funds to ensure payment.

Good credit is an asset worth protecting during a divorce. Unfortunately, you can easily lose your good credit, either because your spouse ran up big bills on your charge accounts and credit cards or through your own inability to cope with finances amidst the turmoil and expense of divorce.

Three timely steps can protect you from whatever your spouse may do to injure your credit:

1) **Immediately notify everyone you have charge privileges with that you will no longer be responsible for debts incurred by your spouse.** Send the notice by registered mail so there can be no question of its receipt.

2) **Destroy all credit cards you and your spouse share.** Never assume you have no liability on credit cards that stand only in your spouse's name. You may have signed and guaranteed the credit application years earlier.

3) **Publish your disclaimer.** By publishing your disclaimer of liability you are putting third parties on notice that you are not responsible for any of your spouse's debts incurred after you publish such notice. Check the laws in your province and follow the procedures carefully.

Alimony, Custody, and Support

4

Alimony, Custody, and Support

Spousal support

Laws and practices concerning spousal support have changed enormously over the past two decades. All spouses have a legal obligation to support themselves to the best of their abilities. Support is determined on a case-by-case basis. The courts take into account all relevant factors such as the length of the marriage, the needs of the spouses, ability to pay, the length of time for which support should be awarded, lump sum payments, earning ability, and many other factors. When will a court consider spousal support?

> Neither spouse is entitled automatically to receive support.

- when the wife spent nearly all her marital years at home raising the family
- when the wife must continue to remain at home to properly care for the children
- when the wife is ill, unemployable or has no special skills
- when the husband has high earnings or earnings potential

The length of the marriage certainly plays a role in the court's decision.

However, current thinking is that even a short marriage, if it interrupted the wife's career, can significantly hurt her future earning capacity. To remedy this, lump sum payments for retraining are sometimes awarded in addition to periodic support payments. Occasionally lump sum payments may be allowed instead of periodic payments, but this usually means the spouse will receive less money in total. The two primary advantages of a lump sum payment are:

1) the security of receiving the money all at once

2) the money is tax-free (periodic support payments are taxable)

Lump sum payments may be an especially attractive solution when the husband has a history of nonpayment or when there is a fear of reduced ability to earn in the future. Courts are even willing to re-examine previous support orders in the light of changing circumstances, in order that those orders remain fair and just.

Unless so ordered by the court, support does not automatically stop when the wife cohabits or remarries—the estate of the payer is responsible for maintaining support payments even after the payer's death. Provisions for termination may include payments for a specific number of years—usually until the youngest child reaches a certain age, or until the wife can complete her education or a training program to make herself employable. Support can also be awarded during the separation phase of the marriage.

> The courts pay particular attention to the current and future consequences of a woman leaving the workforce or working part-time to assume the traditional role of wife and mother in the marriage.

The court is required to distribute the marital resources as fairly as possible on order to remedy the economic hardships of the broken marriage. Although less common, a husband may also petition the court for support from his wife. The same standards apply.

Health coverage

Related to spousal support is the issue of continued health coverage for a spouse. This is a major problem for many divorcing couples, as a spouse may no longer be covered under the other spouse's insurance. Health insurance plans usually allowed continued coverage as long as the spouses are not divorced. Should the likelihood of a divorce increase, the spouse who will not be covered should prepare alternative coverage well in advance of the final divorce.

Child custody

The most emotional part of your divorce will involve the custody decision. It is also the most important. If you have children the court will compel you and your ex-spouse to maintain as harmonious a relationship as possible because your joint cooperation is vital to the well-being of your children.

In the past there was a strong presumption that the mother would make the best custodial parent. That was because the mother was the homemaker and natural caretaker of the children while the husband was the breadwinner. This presumption was particularly true with younger children and especially with daughters. Fathers, in the past, could only hope for custody by convincing the court that the mother was unfit to care for the children. This usually meant that the mother was a substance abuser or otherwise unsuitable because of psychological or behavioral problems that would be injurious to the children.

In more recent years the presumption weakened that the mother was the best custodian of the children. Courts now consider both parents to have equal rights to custody and "what's in the best interests of the children" when deciding upon the custodial parent.

Courts generally consider six separate issues when deciding child custody issues:

- the love, affection and emotional ties between the child and the parties, other members of the family who live with the child, and the persons involved in the care and upbringing of the child

- the length of time the child has lived in a stable home environment

- the views and preferences of the child, where these can be reasonably ascertained

- the ability and willingness of each applicant to provide the child with guidance and education, the necessities of life, and any special needs of the child.

- any plans proposed for the care and upbringing of the child

- any blood or adoptive relationship with a party

The court does not take into account a parent's past conduct unless it affects that person's ability to act as a parent. The court also has the right to order a psychiatric evaluation of that parent.

Types of custody

Before we proceed further it is important to understand the different types of custody. *Sole custody* means that the custodial parent has both physical custody or possession of the child and legal custody or sole authority to make all decisions concerning the child. This type of custody, with the non-custodial parent only having visitation rights, remains the most common arrangement.

> Historically, sole custody was the usual form of custody.

In recent years the concept of *joint custody* has gained in popularity. This means that both parents have an equal say in the decision-making and upbringing of the child. That is, they *share* legal custody. The child may also spend equal time living with each parent, or the custodial parent may continue to have sole physical custody.

Joint physical custody of the children can also be provided for. Under this type of custody, each parent has exclusive physical custody for alternating periods—which may, for example, be certain days, weeks or months per year. While it seems a fair arrangement, many courts and psychologists believe this is harmful to the stability of the child, who loses his or her sense of "home." This arrangement is also called *shared parenting*.

Another possibility is *split custody*. Here both the husband and wife each gain custody of one or more children. In essence, the family becomes divided. Courts understandably frown on this because it means not only separation of one's parents but also separation from siblings.

In deciding custody, more and more courts are determining which parent is the more active caregiver. That is, whom does the child most rely upon for day-to-day care? Courts believe continuing the primary caregiver as custodian provides the child the most stability.

Access

Related to the issue of custody is the matter of *access* or *visitation*. Access rights can be broad or specific. They may simply be agreements for "reasonable" access or they can include detailed plans of days, pickup and delivery times, and specific locations. The parent denied physical custody of the child has the right to reasonable visitation with the child. The only exception is if the parent is abusive or behaves in a way that can be harmful to the child.

The frequency and duration of visitation must be carefully worked out with your spouse. The more frequent the visits, the closer the relationship between child and non-custodial parent. Therefore, the most liberal and flexible visitation arrangement possible is encouraged.

> While you and your spouse may agree on custody and visitation, this is always subject to review and modification by the court.

When considering the terms of visitation, the court will generally favor a fixed or detailed visitation schedule rather than rely on vague terms such as "reasonable visitation," which can only invite disagreement when the spouses are not getting along. You can, however, build some flexibility into your agreement as long as you stay close to the standard of what a court may consider reasonable.

What factors will the court consider when evaluating whether your agreement is in the best interests of your children?

- age and sex of the child
- the capability and willingness of each parent to provide the child's needs
- the bond between the child and each parent
- the desires of the child (if an older child)
- the desires of the parents
- the health of all parties
- the effect on the child of moving

Additionally, the court will more willingly grant joint custody when:

- the parents can cooperate and make decisions together
- the relationship between the child and each parent is reasonably balanced
- both parents enthusiastically welcome joint custody

Child support

The obligation of the parent to support a child is basic and one strongly enforced by the courts. Most judges look closest at this issue, realizing it is here where the agreement may be inequitable and not adequately provide for

Chapter 4

the minor child. Note that while parents have the option to modify the *Child Support Guidelines* (see Appendix D), judges do not. Judges are bound by those guidelines.

> If you and your spouse choose a support amount that is less than the guidelines, you will have to justify the amount to the court.

Obviously, the goal is to provide the children with as much support as possible and at the same time leave the obligated parent with sufficient income to live in reasonable style. Achieving these two objectives is seldom easy. Most often the obligated spouse (usually the husband) does not have sufficient income to adequately support both himself and his children. Courts are not obligated to accept child support agreements between spouses. All children have the right to receive support until age 16 and may continue to receive support until age 18 if unable to fend for themselves. All provinces have passed their own legislation establishing guidelines for spousal and child support.

> Support orders may be modified but the applicant must prove the need to do so.

What the court considers in awarding support:

- the number of children and their ages. Courts may award less support when you have teenage children with some earning power of their own

- whether the custodial spouse has any earning capability and can contribute to the support of the children

- the health or special needs of the children

- the income of the obligated spouse as well as his earnings potential

- the assets or wealth of the obligated spouse

- other financial responsibilities of the obligated spouse, including support obligations from a prior marriage

Preparing the Paperwork For Court

Preparing the Paperwork For Court

No two divorces are identical, of course. If you have considerable property or lack confidence that you can adequately pursue your own divorce, you should seek the advice of a lawyer.

General requirements

Legal documents must be prepared following certain rather uniform procedures and standards. These instructions apply to all documents in your divorce, whether filed in Court or not.

1) All information should be neatly typed, double spaced, on 81/2" x 11" white paper (some provinces still use 81/2" x 14" legal bond paper; check with the Clerk of your Court). Each page should be numbered. Photocopies may be submitted to the Court as original documents. You should also use photocopies as worksheets. All copies of documents submitted to the Court must be printed on one side only. Some Courts also require a "blue backer." Check with the Clerk of your Court.

2) Make certain that all documents are properly completed, signed and notarized, where required.

3) File original documents with the Court. Make at least two additional copies for your files and an additional copy for your spouse.

Preparing your divorce documents

Each province sets its own procedures for processing divorce cases. Counties within a province may also adopt slightly different procedures than those followed in other counties. The process described in this book follows the more common procedures found in most provinces.

Specific province requirements

Each province has a slightly different format and wording that it uses on its Court papers and to caption documents. Unless you comply with local rules, the Court Clerk will not accept your documents for filing. Be sure to check with the Clerk of Court for help in obtaining the proper forms as well the caption requirements in your area before filing any documents. Every caption includes:

1) the name of the Court

2) the name of the parties

3) the title or heading of the document

4) the Court file number

The documents you will need

Before submitting your documents to the Court, it is always a good idea to have the Clerk of the Court review them. An incomplete or incorrect form will delay the process of obtaining your divorce. The various documents needed to actually process the divorce in Ontario, for example, are the following:

- Joint Petition for Divorce
- Motion Record
- Index
- Notice of Motion

- Joint Affidavit
- Waiver of Financial Statements
- Divorce Judgment
- Certificate of Divorce

Proof of Marriage

The first step is to obtain a copy of your *Marriage Registration Certificate*. This is your proof that you are legally married. This should be filed in the Divorce Court before you submit your Petition. *(see Appendix A)*

If your Marriage Certificate is in a foreign language you may have it translated, but it must be done so under oath and the certificate must be attached. If you need this service, then seek the advice of a lawyer who can recommended a translator.

The Joint Petition for Divorce

This is your application for an undefended divorce based upon meeting the separation requirements. You should include in the *Joint Petition* everything you and your spouse mutually agreed to include in your *Divorce Judgment* including support. This form requests information about:

- The grounds for divorce—should be separation.
- Reconciliation—if any, should have been unsuccessful.
- Details of the marriage—includes simple questions about date of birth and birthplace.
- Residence—asks about the current residence of your and your spouse.
- Children—name, birth date, school, grade, and person with whom the child lives. Are the educational needs of the children being met? If no children of this marriage, so indicate. Also petition for custody or joint custody.
- Other Court proceedings—list any other Court proceedings involving your marriage or your children.

Sample Ontario Joint Petition for Divorce

Court File No._____

ONTARIO SUPERIOR COURT OF JUSTICE

HUSBAND

(Court Seal)

and

WIFE

JOINT PETITION FOR DIVORCE

Date_____ Issued by_____
                                                                           Local registrar

Address of court office

State precisely everything you want the court to include in the judgment. Everything you want to include must have been agreed to by both spouses. If you want to include provisions of a separation agreement in the judgement, refer to the specific provisions to be included.

JOINT PETITION

1. The husband and wife jointly seek:

    (a) a divorce;

    (b) under the Divorce Act,

    (i)

GROUNDS FOR DIVORCE — SEPARATION

2. The spouses have lived separate and apart since_____.
                                                                                                            Date

The spouses have resumed cohabitation during the following periods in an unsuccessful attempt at reconciliation:

If none, state "none".   Date(s) of cohabitation

RECONCILIATION

3. There is no possibility of reconciliation of the spouses.

4. The following efforts to reconcile have been made:

State details. Where no efforts have been made, state "none".

DETAILS OF MARRIAGE

Where possible, copy the information from the marriage certificate.

5. Date of marriage:_____

6. Place of marriage:_____
   (City, town, or municipality, province or state, country)

7. Wife's surname immediately before marriage:_____

8. Wife's surname at birth:_____

9. Husband's surname immediately before marriage:_____

10. Husband's surname at birth:_____

11. Marital status of husband at time of marriage:_____
    (Never married, divorced, or widower)

12. Marital status of wife at time of marriage:_____
    (Never married, divorced, or widow)

13. Wife's birthplace:_____
    (City, town, or municipality, province or state, country)

14. Wife's birthdate:_____

15. Husband's birthplace:_____
    (City, town, or municipality, province or state, country)

16. Husband's birthdate:_____

Check one of (a), (b), or (c) and complete as required.

17. (a) [ ] A certificate of [ ] the marriage [ ] the registration of the marriage of the spouses has been filed with the court

    (b) [ ] It is impossible to obtain a certificate of the marriage or its registration because:

    (c) [ ] A certificate of the marriage or its registration will be filed before this action is set down for trial or a motion is made for judgment.

...Œ

...municipality, province or state, country)

...(Date)

...municipality, province or state, country)

...(Date)

...resided in Ontario for at least one year ...eeding.

N

...rriage as defined by the Divorce Act:

| | Person with whom child lives and
...ear | length of time child has lived there

Be sure that this paragraph agrees with the claim under 1. above.

The children ordinarily reside in:_____
(City, town, or municipality, province or state, country)

23. (a) The spouses seek an order on consent for custody or joint custody of the following children on the following terms:

    Name of child   Terms of the order

Divorce

Check appropriate box. Strike out if not applicable.

(b) The spouses are not seeking an order for custody and
    [ ] are content that a previous order for custody remain in force
    [ ] are attempting to obtain an order for custody in another proceeding full particulars of which are as follows:

State name of court, court file number, and particulars of the order or proceeding.

Be sure that this paragraph agrees with the claim under 1. above or strike out if inapplicable.

(c) The spouses seek an order on consent for access (visiting arrangements) to the following children on the following terms:

Name of child   **Terms of the order**

State details such as days of the week, hours of visit, and place of access.

24. (a) The following are the existing visiting arrangements (access) for the spouse who does not have the children living with him or her:

60

Chapter 5

Check appropriate box.

(b) The existing visiting arrangements (access) are:
[ ] satisfactory   [ ] not satisfactory

If not satisfactory, give reasons and describe how the arrangements should be changed.

25. The order sought in paragraph 23 is in the best interests of the children for the following reasons:

26. The following material changes in the circumstances of the spouses are expected to affect the children, their custody, and the visiting arrangements (access) in the future:

...ses for support for the children are as follows:

	Paid by	**Paid for**
	(Husband or wife)	*(Name of child)*

...ot being honoured.

...ements for the children should be as follows:

	To be paid by	**To be paid for**
	(Husband or wife)	*(Name of child)*

(weekly, monthly, etc.)

Check appropriate box.

If not being met, state particulars.

28. The education needs of the children:
[ ] are being met   [ ] are not being met.

61

Divorce

OTHER COURT PROCEEDINGS

State the name of the court, the court file number, the kind of order the court was asked to make, and what order, if any, the court made. If the proceeding is not yet completed, state its current status.

29. The following are all other court proceedings with reference to the marriage or any child of the marriage:

DOMESTIC CONTRACTS AND FINANCIAL ARRANGEMENTS

Indicate whether the contract or arrangement is now in effect, and if support payments are not being paid in full, state the amount that has not been paid.

30. The spouses have entered into the following domestic contracts and other written or oral financial arrangements:

Date   Nature of contract or arrangement   Status

NO COLLUSION

31. There has been no collusion in relation to this divorce proceeding.

DECLARATION OF SPOUSES

32. (a) I have read and understand this petition for divorce. The statements in it are true, to the best of my knowledge, information, and belief.
    (b) I understand that I have the right to seek independent legal advice concerning this proceeding and to retain my own separate counsel.
    (c) I understand that I may lose my right to make a claim for division of property after the divorce if I do not make the claim at this time.

Date_____ _____
                                                    (Signature of husband)

Date_____ _____
                                                    (Signature of wife)

- Domestic contracts and financial arrangements—describe all oral or written contracts that the spouses are involved in.

- No collusion—the Court must believe that neither party used fraud, coercion or threat in preparing the petition.

- Declaration of spouses—spouses affirm their rights and understanding of the divorce proceeding.

Joint Affidavit

This affidavit is sufficient providing it includes:

- The grounds for divorce. This should be limited to a one-year separation. Include the date the spouses have lived separate and apart from each other.

- Describe efforts, if any, to reconcile.

- The *Certificate of Marriage* marked as *Exhibit A*. Describe efforts to obtain certificate if unavailable.

- Indicate how many children there are, if any, and their names and dates of birth.

- State the details of current and future custody and access arrangements for each child if there is any change from the arrangements stated in the petition. Explain why these arrangements are in the best interests of the children.

- Explain the support arrangements that have been made. This should include the amount paid, how often paid, who will pay, and the child for whom the payments are being made.

- Indicate the total cost of payments and whether father or mother will make the support payments.

- Indicate whether there are any other Court proceedings involving the marriage or the children.

- Describe the status of any oral or written contracts that the spouses currently are involved in.

Sample Ontario Joint Affidavit

Court File No._____

ONTARIO SUPERIOR COURT OF JUSTICE

BETWEEN:

Type in name of husband.

_____ (HUSBAND)

-and-

Type in name of wife.

_____ (WIFE)

JOINT AFFIDAVIT

Name of husband
City, town Municipality or county
Name of wife
City, town Municipality or county

We,_____ (Husband),
of the_____ in the_____
_____ and_____ (Wife),
of the_____, in the
_____, MAKE OATH AND SAY AS FOLLOWS:

1. We are the husband and wife described above and as such have knowledge of the matters to which we hereinafter depose.

2. We are jointly petitioning for divorce on the grounds that we have lived separate and apart since the_____ day of_____, 20_____.

3. There is no possibility of our reconciliation. The following efforts to reconcile have taken place:

Set out particulars. If no efforts to reconcile have been made, state "None".

4. The particulars of our marriage as contained in the Certificate of Marriage are true. Attached hereto and marked as Exhibit "A" is a true copy of the Marriage Certificate.

...n for Divorce, filed, that relates to details of

...).

Birthdate

en) have lived with the_____
e to do so.

_____
(address)

stody where the_____
times:

described in Petition.

8. This arrangement is in the best interests of the child(ren) for the following reasons:

Chapter 5

9. The arrangements we have made for support are as follows:

Amount paid	Time period (weekly, monthly)	Paid by (husband or wife)	Paid for (name of child)

10. We have agreed that the support arrangements for the child(ren) should be as set out above based on the financial statements, filed, and the budgets of the children. We agree that the child(ren) cost approximately $_____ per month and, based on our earnings, we agree that the_____ should pay $_____ to the_____.

Type in "father" or "mother" as appropriate.
Type in "father" or "mother" as appropriate.

11. The educational needs of the children are being met.

12. The following are all other court proceedings with reference to the marriage or any child(ren) of the marriage:

Set out particulars. If none, state "None."

13. We have entered into the following domestic contracts and other written or oral financial arrangements:

Set out particulars. If none, state "None."

Date	Nature of contract or arrangement	Status

...erstanding or arrangement to which we are ...of subverting the administration of justice, ...g the Court.

...spousal support have been settled. We do ...we are aware that a claim for a division of

_____
_____
_____
_____
_____

20_____.   )
)   _____
)

_____
A Commissioner for taking Affidavits.

- An acknowledgement by the spouses that they have not in any way attempted to subvert the administration of justice, fabricate or suppress evidence, or deceive the Court.

- Indicate the husband's present address.

- Explain how this is known, e.g., through "personal knowledge."

- Indicate the wife's present address.

- Explain how this is known, e.g., through "personal knowledge."

- Signatures of both spouses, which are acknowledged by a lawyer, notary, or commissioner for taking affidavits.

While it may take a month to obtain your *Divorce Judgment*, it is important to note that if your affidavit sets out any other grounds besides a one-year separation, or if both spouses fail to agree upon custody, support, or property issues, the judge will probably require a trial.

The Motion Record and Index

This is simply a collection of all the documents that you will submit to the Court. They should be arranged by date. It should contain a table of contents listing the title, date and page number of each form. Be sure to include a copy of the *Petition for Divorce*. Do not include the original. You will need to include a cardboard backer (usually light blue) which may be obtained from your local stationery supply store. *The Motion Record* identifies the *petitioning spouse* and the *responding spouse* and serves as a binder for all the forms that are filed with the Court.

Notice of Motion

The *Notice of Motion* contains a record of all the evidence. It contains photocopies of the original documents in the following order:

- An index or table of contents listing the page number of all forms

- The *Notice of Motion*

- A photocopy of the *Petition for Divorce*

- The *Financial Statement*, unless waived by both spouses

- The *Order for Substituted Service*, if applicable

- A photocopy of the Order waiving service on each person named in the petition, if applicable

- Photocopies of all other orders related to the divorce hearing

- The *Petitioner's Affidavit*

- The *Respondent's Affidavit*, if applicable

- *Blue Backer*. This may be purchased at stationery or office supply stores

Sample Ontario Notice of Motion

Court File No._____

ONTARIO SUPERIOR COURT OF JUSTICE

BETWEEN:

                                HUSBAND

-and-

                                WIFE

NOTICE OF MOTION

The motion is for default judgment in accordance with the petition.
The grounds for the motion are that the spouses jointly petitioned for divorce.
The following documentary evidence will be relied on:
1. the petition
2. the certificate of marriage or the registration of marriage filed in this action
3. the affidavits of the husband and wife petitioner dated_____
(List any other)

The petitioners intend to present oral evidence at the hearing of the motion.
(Delete if not applicable)

Date_____
Names, addresses, and telephone numbers of petitioners.

Make a complete photocopy of these records for your files. Then staple everything together down the left side of the binder to form a book. When you submit the *Motion Record* to the Court, you may also file your *Support Deduction Order* and *Support Deduction Order Information Form*, if you have not already done so.

At this point you are ready to submit your documents to the Court. Call the Court Clerk for information regarding current fees, return envelopes, and to obtain an application for a *Divorce Judgment*, which must be signed by a judge. Have the Clerk of the Court look over your documents to see that they are in order—before you submit them to the Court.

Depending upon your province, you will have to wait a certain number of days after the judge signs the *Divorce Judgment* to apply for your *Certificate of Divorce.*

Financial statements

If there are going to be support payments of any kind, each spouse must complete a financial statement. Its purpose is to allow the Court to determine the reasonableness of the agreement—and whether child support is fair and equitable given the financial circumstances of the parties. The *Financial Statement* is a complete summary of each spouse's income, including benefits received, an actual and proposed weekly, monthly, and yearly budget for housing, food, clothing, transportation, health and medical care. The spouse also deducts taxes, the cost of insurance, and debts. Assets such as land, vehicles, savings, securities, insurance, accounts receivable and other business interests must all be disclosed. A copy of the most recent tax return and tax assessment notice should be attached top this form.

Waiver of Financial Statements

If there are no support payments to be made, it is not necessary to submit individual financial statements. Simply complete the *Joint Waiver of Financial Statements* by entering the date, name, address, and phone number of each spouse.

Sample Ontario Waiver of Financial Statements

> Court File No._____
>
> **ONTARIO SUPERIOR COURT OF JUSTICE**
>
> BETWEEN:
>
> HUSBAND
>
> -and-
>
> WIFE
>
> **WAIVER OF FINANCIAL STATEMENTS**
>
> The husband and the wife waive financial statements in respect of claims made in this action for support under the Divorce Act.
>
> Date:_____   Date:_____
> _____   _____
> *Signature of wife*   *Signature of husband*
>
> Wife's name_____   Husband's name_____
> Address:_____   Address:_____
> _____   _____
> _____   _____
> Tel. No:_____   Tel. No:_____

Support Deduction Order

This form is used by the Court to order that regular support payments be deducted by the paying spouse's employer and paid directly to the appropriate agency which, in turn, pays the receiving spouse. The payments are made in accordance with the information listed on the *Support Deduction Order Information Form*, which is attached to the *Support Deduction Order*.

Support Deduction Order Information Form

- name and address of Court

- enter an "X" next to box marked "FINAL" under "Type of Support or Order"

- enter Court file number, the names of the petitioning spouse, and the name of the respondent spouse. The Court will fill in the date.

- provide the name, birthday, gender, and address of the person paying the support

- provide the name, birthday, gender, and address of the person receiving the support

- enter the name and address of the employer of the person paying the support

- if the person paying the support has additional sources of income, check the appropriate box

- enter the name of the person who is obligated to pay the support

- complete matrix

- complete cost of living, arrears, and termination of support sections

Chapter 5

Sample Ontario Support Deduction Order

English

Name of Court_____
Location_____

SUPPORT DEDUCTION ORDER
INFORMATION FORM
Family Responsibility and Support Arrears Enforcement Act

Note: Please print.
Leave shaded areas blank,
the court will fill them in.

Type of Support Order Interim [ ] Final [ ] **Form 2**   Court file no.

FAMILY RESPONSIBILITY OFFICE (F.R.O.) FILE INFORMATION
Family Support Plan Regional Office_____ F.R.O. Case Number (if known) | | | | | | | |

1. **INFORMATION ON PARTIES**
   Payor name_____ Birthdate | Day | Month | Year | Sex [ ] M [ ] F
   Payor address_____
   Street and Number   Town/City   Province   Postal code
   Recipient name_____ Birthdate | Day | Month | Year | Sex [ ] M [ ] F
   Payor address_____
   Street and Number   Town/City   Province   Postal code

2. **INFORMATION ON PAYOR'S EMPLOYER(S) AND OTHER INCOME SOURCE(S)**
   Employer/Income source name_____ Telephone_____
   Payroll office address_____
   Street and Number   Town/City   Province   Postal code
   [ ] Additional income source information attached.
   [ ] Payor not receiving periodic payments as explained in the Family Support Plan Act.
   [ ] Recipient does not know.

3. **SUPPORT ORDER INFORMATION**
   The attached support deduction order relates to a support order which says that:
   _____ is required to pay support for the following persons:
   Payor name
   (Court will change this list if necessary)

Name	Birthdate day month year	Amount payable	Frequency of payments	Payments to begin Day month year
Spouse a.	/ /	$		/ /
Other Dependants b.	/ /	$		/ /
c.	/ /	$		/ /
d.	/ /	$		/ /
e.	/ /	$		/ /

Is the support order a variation of a previous support order? [ ] Yes [ ] No

4. **COST OF LIVING ADJUSTMENTS** [ ] None provided
   Support is indexed in accordance with [ ] s 34(5) of the Family Law Act OR [ ] as per attached
   Or [ ] as follows_____

5. **ARREARS** (Complete if applicable)
   Arrears are fixed at $_____ as of the _____ day of _____ 20___
   To be paid as follows (if applicable): _____

6. **TERMINATION OF SUPPORT** (Complete if previously ordered support is terminated by this order)
   Support is terminated for the following persons
   for _____ on the _____ day of _____ 20___
   for _____ on the _____ day of _____ 20___

NOTE: (gray area above) this area is for Court use only

French

SUPPORT DEDUCTION ORDER
ORDONNANCE DE RETENUE DES ALIMENTS
Family Responsibility and Support Arrears Enforcement Act, 1996
Loi de 1996 sur les obligations familiales et l'execution des arriérés d'aliments

Formule 1   Court file no./N de dossier du tribunal

_____
Judge/*Juge*

_____
Date

Applicant/Petitioner/Plaintiff
Requérant/Demandeur

Respondent/Defendant
Intimé/Défendeur

...ICE DE RETENUE DES ALIMENTS
...nt of support on a periodic basis at regular
...sement d'aliments sur une base périodique
...n 3.1(3) of the Family Responsibility and
...aragraphe 3.1(3) de la *Loi de 1996 sur les*
...s:

1. THIS COURT ORDERS THAT_____ pay support as set out in
   LE TRIBUNAL ORDONNE que   verse les aliments tel qu'il
   the attached information form.
   est énoncé dans la formule de renseignements ci-jointe.

2. THIS COURT ORDERS that any income source that receives notice of this support deduction
   LE TRIBUNAL ORDONNE que toute source de revenu qui reçoit avis de la présente ordonnance
   order make payments to the Director of the Family Responsibility Office in respect of the
   fasse des versements au directeur du Régime des obligations alimentaires envers la famille
   payor out of money owed by the income source to the payor.
   à l'égard du payeur à même l'argent que la source de revenu doit au payeur.

_____
Signature of Judge, Registrar, or Clerk of the Court
Signature du juge, ou du greffier du tribunal

71

Divorce Judgment

Call the Clerk of the Court to find out how many copies of the *Divorce Judgment* and self-addressed stamped envelopes need to be filed with the Court. A *Judgment of Divorce* may be granted based upon the documents filed or the judge may request it be amended or corrected. The date it takes effect depends upon which of the two occurs. Should a change in the filed document need to take place, the date of the judgment will be the date the amended document is filed with the Court registrar. If all is in order, the *Divorce Judgment* is usually mailed to you about a month after you file. This judgment is recognized and enforced in every province.

Certificate of Divorce

The Court typically completes this form

Affidavit (No Appeal)

One spouse must swear that there is neither an appeal pending from this divorce nor an extension of time in which to appeal. 31 days after receiving your *Divorce Judgment*, complete and file the *Certificate of Divorce* and the *Affidavit of No Appeal* with the Clerk of the Court and you will receive a *Certificate of Divorce*—valid everywhere in Canada.

Please Note: Forms shown and listed may vary from one province to another. Please contact your local Clerk of Court for exact requirement of your Provincial Court.

Chapter 5

Sample Ontario Divorce Judgement

Court File No._____

ONTARIO SUPERIOR COURT OF JUSTICE

THE HONOURABLE _____ 20____
(day and date judgment given)

BETWEEN:

                                                  HUSBAND

-and-

(Court Seal)   WIFE

DIVORCE JUDGMENT

THIS MOTION made jointly by the spouses for judgment for divorce was heard this day at
_____
                   (place)

The spouses jointly petitioned for divorce.
    ON READING the petition, the notice of motion for judgment, the affidavit dated
_____ of the husband and the wife
           (date)
filed in support of the motion and

(add any other material filed)

(names of spouses)
_____
_____
_____
(date)

_____ percent per year
_____

hich postjudgment interest is payable.

Family Support Plan paragraph here.

(In a judgment that provides for payment of support, set out the last known address of the support creditor and debtor.)

THE SPOUSES ARE NOT FREE TO REMARRY UNTIL THIS JUDGMENT TAKES EFFECT, AT WHICH TIME A CERTIFICATE OF DIVORCE MAY BE OBTAINED FROM THIS COURT. IF AN APPEAL IS TAKEN IT MAY DELAY THE DATE WHEN THIS JUDGMENT TAKES EFFECT.

Sample British Columbia Statement of Claim

No.:_____

Registry:_____

IN THE SUPREME COURT OF BRITISH COLUMBIA
RE: A JOINT ACTION FOR DIVORCE BROUGHT BY

WIFE,

AND

HUSBAND

STATEMENT OF CLAIM — FAMILY LAW PROCEEDING

The wife and husband must complete Parts A, B, C, and D of the statement of claim, leaving out those paragraphs that are not relevant and making changes and additions if necessary. The wife and husband must only complete Parts E to I if a claim is made appropriate to those parts.

If a paragraph is not completed, the remaining paragraphs must not be renumbered. If a paragraph is added, it must be given a decimal subnumber (such as 7.1, 7.2) or be continued numerically after paragraph 36.

PART A: PARTICULARS OF PARTIES

1. The wife is _____
   (name and address)
2. The wife was born on _____
   (date of birth)
3. The husband is _____
   (name and address)
4. The husband was born on _____
   (date of birth)
5. The wife has ordinarily been resident in British Columbia since _____
   (date)
6. The husband has ordinarily been resident in British Columbia since _____
   (date)

...who is joined in the action.)

...NSHIP OF PARTIES

_____ at _____
(date) *(city, province)*

...efined by the *Family Relations Act* (give ...s of the plaintiff and defendant as spouses).

...ion on _____.

_____
(date of separation)
...ch other by an order made on _____

...LDREN

...y the *Divorce Act* (Canada) are:

Person with whom child resides

_____
_____
_____
_____

OR

(b) The parties are parents as defined by the *Family Relations Act* and the children of the parties are:

Name   Birth date   Person with whom child resides

_____
_____
_____

OR

Chapter 5

(c) There are no children of the marriage as defined by the *Divorce Act* (Canada).

OR

(d) The parties are not the parents of any children as defined by the *Family Relations Act*.

PART D: OTHER PROCEEDINGS AND AGREEMENTS

14. (a) The particulars and status of any other proceeding between or any agreement between the parties with respect to a separation between the parties, or to the support or maintenance of a party or of a child of the party, or with respect to the division of property of the parties, are as follows *(set out particulars and status)*:

OR

(b) There has been no other proceeding or agreement between the parties with respect to a separation between the parties, or to the support or maintenance of a party or of a child of a party, or with respect to the division of property of the parties.

PART E: DIVORCE

[Complete this part if the husband and wife jointly seek an order of divorce from each other.]

15. There has been a breakdown in the marriage as defined by the *Divorce Act* (Canada) the particulars of which are as follows *(refer to specific sections of the Divorce Act [Canada])*:

16. (a) The surname of the wife immediately before marriage was _____.
    (b) The surname of the wife at birth was _____.
17. (a) The surname of the husband immediately before marriage was _____.
    (b) The surname of the husband at birth was _____.
18. The marital status of the wife at the time of marriage was _____.
19. The marital status of the husband at the time of marriage was _____.

...is proceeding. There has been no condonation
...ed.
...ge has been filed.
...te of the marriage or a certificate of the
out reasons):

...icate of registration of the marriage will be
...rial or an application is made for an order of
a certificate at this time).

PART F: CUSTODY, GUARDIANSHIP, AND ACCESS

[Complete this part if an order in relation to the custody of, guardianship of, or access to children is sought.]

23. The children for whom an order of custody, guardianship, or access is sought are *(set out names)*:

Name	Birth date	Person with whom child resides
_____	_____	_____
_____	_____	_____
_____	_____	_____
_____	_____	_____

24. (a) The children in respect of whom such claim is made have been habitually resident in British Columbia since _____.
         (date)
    OR
    (b) The grounds of jurisdiction under section 44 of the *Family Relations Act* are *(set out particulars)*:

25. The wife and husband seek such orders under:
    (a) the *Divorce Act* (Canada),
    (b) the *Family Relations Act*, or
    (c) both.

26. The particulars of the past, present, and proposed care of the children are as follows *(set out particulars)*:

PART G: SUPPORT OR MAINTENANCE
[Complete this part if the wife or husband seeks an order for support or maintenance.]

27. The wife/husband seeks an order for spousal support or maintenance under:
    (a) the *Divorce Act* (Canada),
    (b) the *Family Relations Act*, or
    (c) both.

28. The wife/husband seeks an order for child support or maintenance under:
    (a) the *Divorce Act* (Canada),
    (b) the *Family Relations Act*, or
    (c) both.

...d and of the children in care of the wife/
...income statement, an expense statement, and
...in which that financial position is set out:
...at.

...is document.

...sband and of the children in care of the
...iculars)*:

...ther spouse set out her/his financial

...nd is as follows *(set out particulars)*:

PART H: PROPERTY
[Complete this part if the wife or husband seeks an order in respect of family assets.]

31. (a) The wife and husband seek an order for equal division of family assets.
    OR
    (b) The wife/husband seeks a reapportionment of family assets on the following grounds *(set out particulars)*:

32. (a) The assets owned by each of the parties are set out in a property statement that:
    (i) will be served with this document.
    OR
    (ii) will be served after service of this document.
OR
(b) The assets owned by each of the parties are *(set out particulars)*:

33. The legal description of land in which the wife/husband claims an interest is *(set out legal description)*:

PART I: OTHER RELIEF
[Complete this part if the wife or husband seeks other relief.]

34. The wife/husband seeks a change of name under the *Name Act* on the granting of a divorce order *(set out particulars)*:

35. The wife/husband seeks the following relief under the *Family Relations Act* *(set out any other orders sought under the* Family Relations Act, *the sections of the Act under which the orders are sought, and the particulars)*:

...onal relief *(set out particulars)*:

SUMMARY OF RELIEF SOUGHT
(Set out the relief claimed by reference to each part of the statement of claim and any claim for costs.)

Sample British Columbia Registrar's Certificate of Pleadings

No.:_____

Registry:_____

IN THE SUPREME COURT OF BRITISH COLUMBIA

RE: A JOINT APPLICATION FOR DIVORCE BROUGHT BY

WIFE,

AND

HUSBAND

REGISTRAR'S CERTIFICATE OF PLEADINGS

I DO HEREBY CERTIFY that the pleadings, documents, and procedures in this cause are correct and in order.

DATED at _____, in the Province of British Columbia this _____ day of _____, 200___.

_____
District Registrar

---

name and birth date of each child of the

Date of birth
_____
_____
_____
_____

_____ shall have joint/sole custody of the
_____

_____ shall be the sole guardian of the
with the _____.

_____ (Payor) having been found to
_____ (Recipient)
$_____

_____ (Payor) shall pay to the
cipient) the sum of $_____ per month
_____
_____
ommencing _____ 1, 200___, and
continuing for so long as the child is a "child of the marriage" as defined in the *Divorce Act* (Canada).

BY THE COURT

_____
District Registrar

Chapter 5

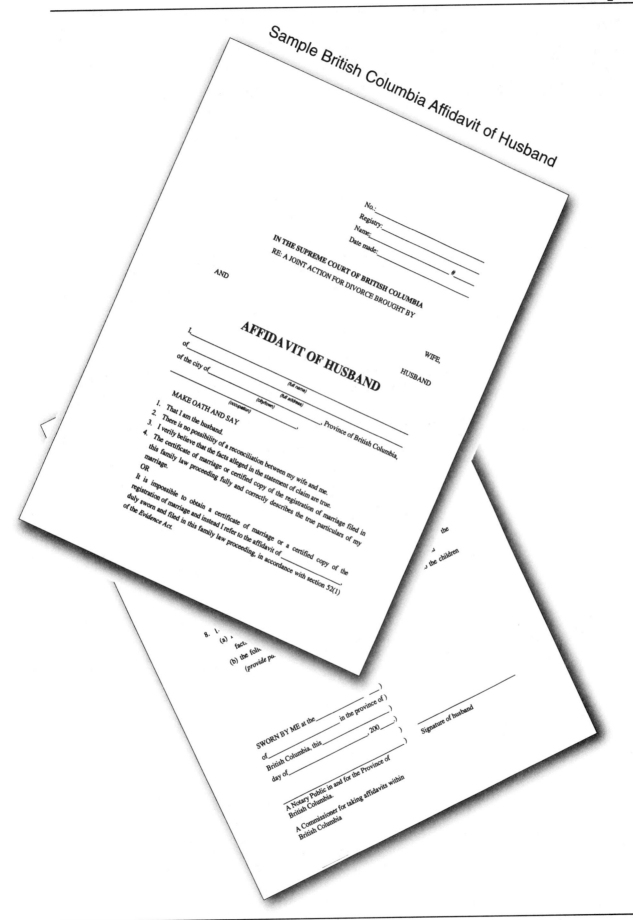

Sample British Columbia Affidavit of Husband

Divorce

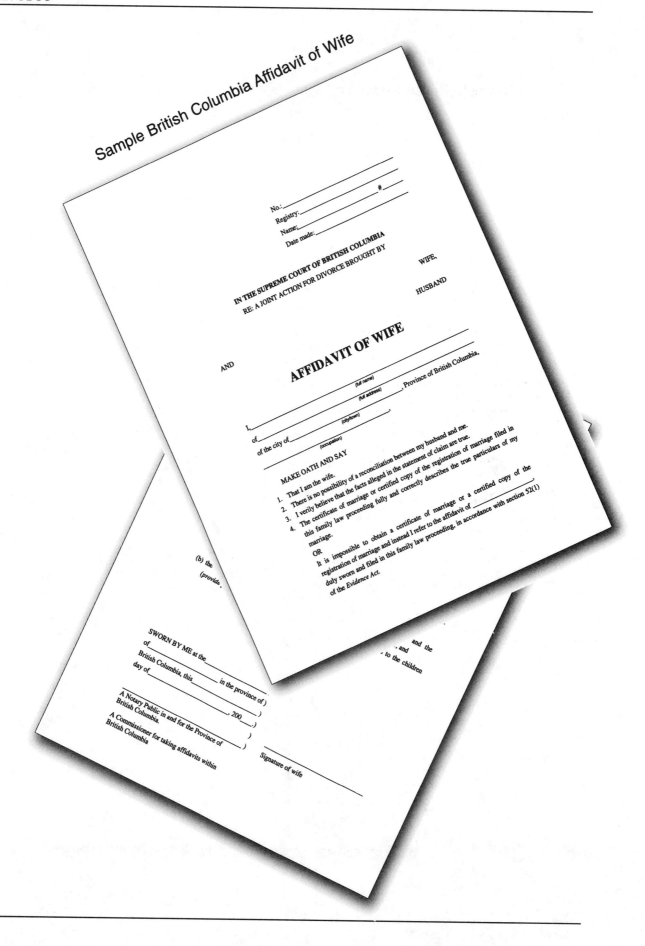

Sample British Columbia Child Support Fact Sheet

No.:_____

Registry:_____

IN THE SUPREME COURT OF BRITISH COLUMBIA
RE: A JOINT ACTION FOR DIVORCE BROUGHT BY

                                      WIFE,

AND

                                  HUSBAND

CHILD SUPPORT FACT SHEET
(Section numbers refer to federal and provincial child support guidelines
[the "child support guidelines"])

The following information respecting child support is provided by _____, the wife, and _____, the husband in this proceeding, and includes each of the supplementary child support fact sheets that are applicable to that party.

1. Payor_____ Age_____
   Birth date_____ Province of residence_____
2. Recipient_____ Age_____
   Birth date_____ Province of residence_____
3. Date of marriage_____
   Place of marriage_____
4. Date of separation_____
5. Children

Name	Age	Birth date	Reside with Payor	Recipient

...clude a claim for a child support order? ____
_____
_____;
is required: Recipient's annual guideline
source of income:_____
...ealing with support of children:

...children:

...y): $_____
...er available medical and dental insurance

SWORN BY ME at the_____)
of_____ in the province of)
British Columbia, this_____)
day of_____, 200____.)   Signature of wife
_____)
_____)
_____)   Signature of husband
A Notary Public in and for the Province of
British Columbia.
A Commissioner for taking affidavits within
British Columbia

Sample British Columbia Order With Child

No.:_____

Registry:_____

IN THE SUPREME COURT OF BRITISH COLUMBIA
RE: A JOINT APPLICATION FOR DIVORCE BROUGHT BY

_____ WIFE,

AND

_____ HUSBAND

ORDER
(with children)

BEFORE A JUDGE OF THE COURT) _____day, the_____day
) of_____, 200___

THIS PROCEEDING coming before me as a joint application for divorce without an oral hearing, and on reading the affidavits and other documents filed:

THIS COURT ORDERS that:

1. Subject to section 12 of the *Divorce Act* (Canada), the applicants,_____ and _____, who were married at _____, in the Province of _____ on the _____day of _____, _____ (year) are divorced from each other, the divorce to take effect on the thirty-first day after the date of this order.

Sample British Columbia Order Without Child

No.:_____

Registry:_____

IN THE SUPREME COURT OF BRITISH COLUMBIA
RE: A JOINT ACTION FOR DIVORCE BROUGHT BY

_____ WIFE,

AND

_____ HUSBAND

ORDER
(without children)

BEFORE A JUDGE OF THE COURT) _____day, the_____day
) of_____, 200___

THIS PROCEEDING coming before me as a joint application for divorce without an oral hearing, and on reading the affidavits and other documents filed:

THIS COURT ORDERS that:

1. Subject to section 12 of the *Divorce Act* (Canada), the applicants, _____ and _____, who were married at _____, in the Province of _____, on the_____day of _____, _____ (year) are divorced from each other, the divorce to take effect on the thirty-first day after the date of this order.

BY THE COURT

_____
District Registrar

Chapter 5

Sample British Columbia Praecipe

No.:_____

Registry:_____

IN THE SUPREME COURT OF BRITISH COLUMBIA
RE: A JOINT ACTION FOR DIVORCE BROUGHT BY

WIFE,

AND

HUSBAND

PRAECIPE

REQUIRED: A CERTIFICATE OF DIVORCE
ENCLOSED:
1. An entered copy of the divorce order
2. A certificate of divorce

DATED at the_____, in the Province of British Columbia, this_____day of_____, 200___.

_____
Signature of wife (or husband)

TRIAL
_____.

OWLEDGEMENTS

this joint writ of summons and statement of

e independently of the other,

esented by a lawyer of his or her own choice,

iired by the other to seek a divorce or to sign

_____, in the Province of British
_____, 200___, the wife and
summons and statement of claim are true.

_____
Signature of wife

_____
Signature of husband

Sample British Columbia Certificate of Divorce

No.:_____

Registry:_____

IN THE SUPREME COURT OF BRITISH COLUMBIA

CERTIFICATE OF DIVORCE

This is to certify that_____and_____, who were married at_____on_____, were divorced under the *Divorce Act* (Canada) by an order on this Court which took effect and dissolved the marriage on_____.

Given under my hand and Seal of this Court this_____day of_____200___.

_____
District Registrar

Getting On With Your Life

Getting On With Your Life

Your divorce decree makes you a single person once again. You are free to live your own life without interference from your spouse except for those obligations in your divorce agreement or court decree. Your province may require you to wait a period of time before you can marry again.

Post-divorce checklist

Once divorced, there are some basic steps you and your spouse must take so you can separate as cleanly as possible—financially and legally:

1. Obtain from the court certified copies of your final divorce decree. You'll need this to transfer property, divide bank accounts, etc.

2. Exchange personal and household property as soon as possible after the divorce. Jewelry, tools, furnishings, etc. that are due you may otherwise disappear no matter what your agreement says.

3. Close any remaining joint checking accounts and savings accounts, but first verify balances and insist upon bank checks so you are certain the check representing your share is, in fact, a good check.

4. Joint credit accounts should be formally closed. However, this action should have been taken when you first decided upon the divorce. Estimate and pro-rate utility bills if you don't have a final balance.

Divorce

Destroy all joint charge cards or surrender them to the credit card company. Also notify them that you no longer have responsibility for your ex-spouse's debts. Finally, establish a new account solely in your name, and with a change of address, if applicable.

5. Similarly, notify lenders owed joint loans. If your spouse is responsible for paying the entire loan under the divorce agreement, then request a release from the obligation. This is generally not granted unless the lender is comfortable with the collateral or your spouse's creditworthiness alone.

   If you do remain bound on the loan, and your spouse indemnified you for losses under the loan, then ask the lender for immediate notice should your spouse default in payments. You can then take timely legal action against your spouse, as well as intervene with the lender, before the lender looks to your assets for satisfaction of the debt.

6. Will you and your spouse change title on any cars, boats, airplanes or recreational vehicles? Change their registration, license plates and insurance, and transfer title with a bill of sale.

7. Review your insurance policies. Direct changes of beneficiary to your insurance company or agent who administers your policies. Review all policies including accident and health, disability, homeowners, and insurance on children.

8. If real estate is to change hands, you'll need your attorney to convey the property. If the real estate has a mortgage against it, you may need to notify the mortgage holder. But where the property is simply being transferred from you and your spouse as joint owners to one of you singly, no consent by the bank is normally required.

9. Will you and your spouse file a joint tax return for the year or will you file separately? Caution: To file jointly, you must be married on the last day of the tax year. For liability reasons, it's best to file separately.

> If you do file jointly, decide beforehand who will pay the taxes due or be entitled to the refund.

10. Check what needs to be done with your last will and testament. Some provinces automatically revoke wills upon divorce, others only upon remarriage, and in still other provinces, neither divorce nor remarriage have an effect upon a prior will. It's safest to prepare a new will. Preparing your own will is not difficult. The *Last Will and Testament* book by C.G.T. Canadian Legal Forms LTD is ideal for that purpose.

Visitation / access rights

Divorce never completely ends the relationship between spouses with children. Just as the father (or non-custodial parent) typically has the obligation to pay child support, he also has the right to reasonable visitation or access with his children. And just as child support may not be honored by the non-custodial parent, visitation may be denied or frustrated by the mother (or custodial parent). The custodial parent cannot deny visitation simply because she is upset with her ex-spouse—or even because the ex-spouse failed to make child support payments.

Should one spouse deny visitation to the other in violation of the court decree, the spouse in violation of the court decree can be held in contempt and the court can even order the suspension of support until visitation is duly restored.

Parents are reminded that their children also have certain rights in a divorce—and one of these rights is the opportunity to maintain as close a relationship as possible with each parent.

Glossary of Useful Terms

A

Action

A court proceeding or lawsuit.

Affidavit

A written statement of facts, sworn to be true under oath before a notary public.

Agreement

An understanding and intention between the parties with respect to their relative rights and duties.

Allegations

The assertions or claims made in a pleading against the other party in a lawsuit.

Alimony

A lump sum or periodic payments made to a divorced spouse by a former spouse for maintenance or support. Alimony (Maintenance or Spousal Support) may be temporary or permanent.

Answer (Response)

The defendant's legal response to a complaint or petition.

Appearance

The voluntary submission by a defendant to a court's jurisdiction. The appearance can be made in person or by filing an answer, response or an appearance and waiver.

Award

A formal order by the court giving a party the right to compensation.

C-D

Cause of Action
The grounds upon which a suit is maintained.

Complaint (Petition)
The first document filed in court by one party (plaintiff, petitioner) stating the grievance against the other party.

Contested Divorce
When the court decides issues which have not been resolved by the parties.

Custodial Parent
The parent with whom the child(ren) resides.

Decree (Final Judgment)
The final court order dissolving the marriage.

Default Judgment
Where the defendant (respondent) fails to answer an allegation or make an appearance in the case; the court will give judgment to plaintiff (petitioner) based on the relief sought.

Defendant (Respondent)
The person defending against or denying the claim.

Divorce (Dissolution of Marriage)
The termination of a marriage by the courts through the powers given to them by the state.

Domicile (Residence)
Where a person lives and intends to reside.

E-M

Equitable Distribution

The equitable, but not necessarily equal, division of property acquired during the marriage. This is defined according to provincial law.

Grounds

The legal reasons for the granting of a divorce.

Joint Legal Custody

Where the parents share the responsibilities and major decisions of the child(ren). Usually one parent is awarded physical custody.

Joint Physical Custody

Both parents share the physical custody of the child over alternating periods of time (also called shared parenting or co-parenting).

Jointly Owned Property

Property owned together.

Jurisdiction

The legal right by which a partucilar judge has the power to hear a case. The court must have subject matter jurisdiction and personal jurisdiction to grant a divorce.

Legal Separation

A court order used as the basis for support, allowing the parties to live separate and apart even though they are still married to each other.

Marital Property

Property acquired by persons while married and divided by the court upon divorce (dissolution of marriage).

P-W

Pleading
Any document filed with the court which seeks action by the court.

Pre-nuptial Agreement
A contract entered into by people about to enter marriage. This agreement helps resolve issues of support, property distribution, or inheritance upon divorce. This is also called a pre-marriage agreement.

Primary Caregiver
The parent who has provided most of the daily care to a child—a determination often used in awarding custody.

Separate Property
The property that is not owned by both of the parties but owned individually. This may, nevertheless, be divided by the court.

Service of Process
The delivery of a summons informing the defendant (respondent) of a lawsuit.

Sole Custody
One parent is given physical custody of the child, along with the right to make all major decisions regarding the child.

Summons
A document which informs that a lawsuit has been filed against you.

Waiver
A document which intentionally or voluntarily relinquishes a person's right.

Appendix A

ADDRESSES TO WRITE TO FOR MARRIAGE AND BIRTH CERTIFICATES

You will need a certificate as proof of a valid marriage in many of the proceedings described in this book. The following addresses show where to write to.

PROVINCE	ADDRESS
Alberta	Alberta Vital Statistics no longer provides certificates. Contact your local Alberta Registry private agent to order the certificate.
British Columbia	Division of Vital Statistics 818 Fort Street Victoria, BC V8W 1H8 (payable to Minister of Finance)
Manitoba	Vital Statistics 254 Portage Avenue Main Floor Winnipeg, MB R3C 0B6
New Brunswick	Registrar General of Vital Statistics Department of Health & Community Services P.O. Box 6000 Fredericton, NB E3B 5H1
Newfoundland	Vital Statistics Division Department of Health Confederation Building P.O. Box 8700 St. John's, NF A1B 4J6
Northwest Territories	Registrar of Vital Statistics Department of Justice Government of the Northwest Territories P.O. Box 1320 Yellowknife, NT X1A 2L9
Nova Scotia	Vital Statistics Department of Health Provincial Building P.O. Box 157 1523 Hollis Street Halifax, NS B3J 2M9

Divorce

Ontario	Office of the Registrar General P.O. Box 4600 189 Red River Road Thunder Bay, ON P7B 6L8 (payable to Treasurer of Ontario)
Prince Edward Island	Director of Vital Statistics Department of Health and Social Services P.O. Box 2000 Charlottetown, PE C1A 7N8
Quebec	Ministère de la Justice Registre du reference 300 boul. Jean-Lesage, RC-20 Quebec City, QC G1K 8K6 (Birth and marriage certificates are issued by the Civil Archives of the judicial district where the event was registered. Contact the above address for a list of the 32 offices in Quebec.)
Saskatchewan	Division of Vital Statistics Department of Health 1919 Rose Street Regina, SK S4P 3V7
Yukon	Vital Statistics Department of Health and Human Resources P.O. Box 2703 Whitehorse, YT Y1A 2C6

Appendix B
The Divorce Act

Divorce Act (R.S. 1985, c. 3 (2nd Supp.))
Disclaimer: These documents are not the official versions.
Source: http://laws.justice.gc.ca/en/D-3.4/text.html
Updated to April 30, 2001

Subject: Family

Divorce Act
R.S., 1985, c. 3 (2nd Supp.)

An Act respecting divorce and corollary relief

[1986, c. 4, assented to
13th February, 1986]

SHORT TITLE

Short title   **1.** This Act may be cited as the Divorce Act.

INTERPRETATION

Definitions   **2.** (1) In this Act,

"age of majority" *« majeur »*

"age of majority", in respect of a child, means the age of majority as determined by the laws of the province where the child ordinarily resides, or, if the child ordinarily resides outside of Canada, eighteen years of age;

"appellate court" *«cour d'appel»*

Divorce

"appellate court", in respect of an appeal from a court, means the court exercising appellate jurisdiction with respect to that appeal;

"applicable guidelines" *« lignes directrices applicables »*

"applicable guidelines" means

>   (*a*) where both spouses or former spouses are ordinarily resident in the same province at the time an application for a child support order or a variation order in respect of a child support order is made, or the amount of a child support order is to be recalculated pursuant to section 25.1, and that province has been designated by an order made under subsection (5), the laws of the province specified in the order, and

>   (*b*) in any other case, the Federal Child Support Guidelines;

"child of the marriage" *«enfant à charge»*

"child of the marriage" means a child of two spouses or former spouses who, at the material time,

>   (*a*) is under the age of majority and who has not withdrawn from their charge, or

>   (*b*) is the age of majority or over and under their charge but unable, by reason of illness, disability or other cause, to withdraw from their charge or to obtain the necessaries of life;

"child support order" *« ordonnance alimentaire au profit d'un enfant »*

"child support order" means an order made under subsection 15.1(1);

"corollary relief proceeding" *« action en mesures accessoires »*

"corollary relief proceeding" means a proceeding in a court in which either or both former spouses seek a child support order, a spousal support order or a custody order;

"court" *«tribunal»*

"court", in respect of a province, means

>   (*a*) for the Province of Ontario, the Superior Court of Justice,

>   (*a.1*) for the Province of Prince Edward Island or Newfoundland, the trial division of the Supreme Court of the Province,

>   (*b*) for the Province of Quebec, the Superior Court,

Appendix B

(*c*) for the Provinces of Nova Scotia and British Columbia, the Supreme Court of the Province,

(*d*) for the Province of New Brunswick, Manitoba, Saskatchewan or Alberta, the Court of Queen's Bench for the Province, and

(*e*) for the Yukon Territory or the Northwest Territories, the Supreme Court of the territory, and in Nunavut, the Nunavut Court of Justice, and includes such other court in the province the judges of which are appointed by the Governor General as is designated by the Lieutenant Governor in Council of the province as a court for the purposes of this Act;

"custody" *«garde»*

"custody" includes care, upbringing and any other incident of custody;

"custody order" *«ordonnance de garde»*

"custody order" means an order made under subsection 16(1);

"divorce proceeding" *« action en divorce »*

"divorce proceeding" means a proceeding in a court in which either or both spouses seek a divorce alone or together with a child support order, a spousal support order or a custody order;

"Federal Child Support Guidelines" *« lignes directrices fédérales sur les pensions alimentaires pour enfants »*

"Federal Child Support Guidelines" means the guidelines made under section 26.1;

"provincial child support service" *« service provincial des aliments pour enfants »*

"provincial child support service" means any service, agency or body designated in an agreement with a province under subsection 25.1(1);

"spousal support order" *« ordonnance alimentaire au profit d'un époux »*

"spousal support order" means an order made under subsection 15.2(1);

"spouse" *«époux»*

"spouse" means either of a man or woman who are married to each other;

"support order" *« ordonnance alimentaire »*

"support order" means a child support order or a spousal support order;

"variation order" *«ordonnance modificative»*

"variation order" means an order made under subsection 17(1);

"variation proceeding" *«action en modification»*

"variation proceeding" means a proceeding in a court in which either or both former spouses seek a variation order.

Child of the marriage

(2) For the purposes of the definition "child of the marriage" in subsection (1), a child of two spouses or former spouses includes

(*a*) any child for whom they both stand in the place of parents; and

(*b*) any child of whom one is the parent and for whom the other stands in the place of a parent.

Term not restrictive

(3) The use of the term "application" to describe a proceeding under this Act in a court shall not be construed as limiting the name under which and the form and manner in which that proceeding may be taken in that court, and the name, manner and form of the proceeding in that court shall be such as is provided for by the rules regulating the practice and procedure in that court.

Idem

(4) The use in section 21.1 of the terms "affidavit" and "pleadings" to describe documents shall not be construed as limiting the name that may be used to refer to those documents in a court and the form of those documents, and the name and form of the documents shall be such as is provided for by the rules regulating the practice and procedure in that court.

Provincial child support guidelines

(5) The Governor in Council may, by order, designate a province for the purposes of the definition "applicable guidelines" in subsection (1) if the laws of the province establish comprehensive guidelines for the determination of child support that deal with the matters referred to in section 26.1. The order shall specify the laws of the province that constitute the guidelines of the province.

Amendments included

(6) The guidelines of a province referred to in subsection (5) include any amendments made to them from time to time.

R.S., 1985, c. 3 (2nd Supp.), s. 2, c. 27 (2nd Supp.), s. 10; 1990, c. 18, s. 1; 1992, c. 51, s. 46; 1997, c. 1, s. 1; 1998, c. 30, ss. 13(F), 15(E); 1999, c. 3, s. 61.

JURISDICTION

Jurisdiction in divorce proceedings

    3. (1) A court in a province has jurisdiction to hear and determine a divorce proceeding if either spouse has been ordinarily resident in the province for at least one year immediately preceding the commencement of the proceeding.

Jurisdiction where two proceedings commenced on different days

    (2) Where divorce proceedings between the same spouses are pending in two courts that would otherwise have jurisdiction under subsection (1) and were commenced on different days and the proceeding that was commenced first is not discontinued within thirty days after it was commenced, the court in which a divorce proceeding was commenced first has exclusive jurisdiction to hear and determine any divorce proceeding then pending between the spouses and the second divorce proceeding shall be deemed to be discontinued.

Jurisdiction where two proceedings commenced on same day

    (3) Where divorce proceedings between the same spouses are pending in two courts that would otherwise have jurisdiction under subsection (1) and were commenced on the same day and neither proceeding is discontinued within thirty days after it was commenced, the Federal Cour—Trial Division has exclusive jurisdiction to hear and determine any divorce proceeding then pending between the spouses and the divorce proceedings in those courts shall be transferred to the Federal Court—Trial Division on the direction of that Court.

Jurisdiction in corollary relief proceedings

    4. (1) A court in a province has jurisdiction to hear and determine a corollary relief proceeding if

    (*a*) either former spouse is ordinarily resident in the province at the commencement of the proceeding; or

    (*b*) both former spouses accept the jurisdiction of the court.

Jurisdiction where two proceedings commenced on different days

    (2) Where corollary relief proceedings between the same former spouses and in respect of the same matter are pending in two courts that would otherwise have jurisdiction under subsection (1) and were commenced on different days and the

proceeding that was commenced first is not discontinued within thirty days after it was commenced, the court in which a corollary relief proceeding was commenced first has exclusive jurisdiction to hear and determine any corollary relief proceeding then pending between the former spouses in respect of that matter and the second corollary relief proceeding shall be deemed to be discontinued.

Jurisdiction where two proceedings commenced on same day

(3) Where proceedings between the same former spouses and in respect of the same matter are pending in two courts that would otherwise have jurisdiction under subsection (1) and were commenced on the same day and neither proceeding is discontinued within thirty days after it was commenced, the Federal Court–Trial Division has exclusive jurisdiction to hear and determine any corollary relief proceeding then pending between the former spouses in respect of that matter and the corollary relief proceedings in those courts shall be transferred to the Federal Court–Trial Division on the direction of that Court.

R.S., 1985, c. 3 (2nd Supp.), s. 4; 1993, c. 8, s. 1.

Jurisdiction in variation proceedings

5. (1) A court in a province has jurisdiction to hear and determine a variation proceeding if

(*a*) either former spouse is ordinarily resident in the province at the commencement of the proceeding; or

(*b*) both former spouses accept the jurisdiction of the court.

Jurisdiction where two proceedings commenced on different days

(2) Where variation proceedings between the same former spouses and in respect of the same matter are pending in two courts that would otherwise have jurisdiction under subsection (1) and were commenced on different days and the proceeding that was commenced first is not discontinued within thirty days after it was commenced, the court in which a variation proceeding was commenced first has exclusive jurisdiction to hear and determine any variation proceeding then pending between the former spouses in respect of that matter and the second variation proceeding shall be deemed to be discontinued.

Jurisdiction where two proceedings commenced on same day

(3) Where variation proceedings between the same former spouses and in respect of the same matter are pending in two courts that would otherwise have jurisdiction under subsection (1) and were commenced on the same day and neither proceeding is

discontinued within thirty days after it was commenced, the Federal Court-Trial Division has exclusive jurisdiction to hear and determine any variation proceeding then pending between the former spouses in respect of that matter and the variation proceedings in those courts shall be transferred to the Federal Court-Trial Division on the direction of that Court.

Transfer of divorce proceeding where custody application

6. (1) Where an application for an order under section 16 is made in a divorce proceeding to a court in a province and is opposed and the child of the marriage in respect of whom the order is sought is most substantially connected with another province, the court may, on application by a spouse or on its own motion, transfer the divorce proceeding to a court in that other province.

Transfer of corollary relief proceeding where custody application

(2) Where an application for an order under section 16 is made in a corollary relief proceeding to a court in a province and is opposed and the child of the marriage in respect of whom the order is sought is most substantially connected with another province, the court may, on application by a former spouse or on its own motion, transfer the corollary relief proceeding to a court in that other province.

Transfer of variation proceeding where custody application

(3) Where an application for a variation order in respect of a custody order is made in a variation proceeding to a court in a province and is opposed and the child of the marriage in respect of whom the variation order is sought is most substantially connected with another province, the court may, on application by a former spouse or on its own motion, transfer the variation proceeding to a court in that other province.

Exclusive jurisdiction

(4) Notwithstanding sections 3 to 5, a court in a province to which a proceeding is transferred under this section has exclusive jurisdiction to hear and determine the proceeding.

Exercise of jurisdiction by judge

7. The jurisdiction conferred on a court by this Act to grant a divorce shall be exercised only by a judge of the court without a jury.

DIVORCE

Divorce

8. (1) A court of competent jurisdiction may, on application by either or both spouses, grant a divorce to the spouse or spouses on the ground that there has been a breakdown of their marriage.

Breakdown of marriage

(2) Breakdown of a marriage is established only if

(*a*) the spouses have lived separate and apart for at least one year immediately preceding the determination of the divorce proceeding and were living separate and apart at the commencement of the proceeding; or

(*b*) the spouse against whom the divorce proceeding is brought has, since celebration of the marriage,

    (*i*) committed adultery, or

    (*ii*) treated the other spouse with physical or mental cruelty of such a kind as to render intolerable the continued cohabitation of the spouses.

Calculation of period of separation

(3) For the purposes of paragraph (2)(a),

(*a*) spouses shall be deemed to have lived separate and apart for any period during which they lived apart and either of them had the intention to live separate and apart from the other; and

(*b*) a period during which spouses have lived separate and apart shall not be considered to have been interrupted or terminated

    (*i*) by reason only that either spouse has become incapable of forming or having an intention to continue to live separate and apart or of continuing to live separate and apart of the spouse's own volition, if it appears to the court that the separation would probably have continued if the spouse had not become so incapable, or

    (*ii*) by reason only that the spouses have resumed cohabitation during a period of, or periods totalling, not more than ninety days with reconciliation as its primary purpose.

Appendix B

Duty of legal adviser

9. (1) It is the duty of every barrister, solicitor, lawyer or advocate who undertakes to act on behalf of a spouse in a divorce proceeding

(*a*) to draw to the attention of the spouse the provisions of this Act that have as their object the reconciliation of spouses, and

(*b*) to discuss with the spouse the possibility of the reconciliation of the spouses and to inform the spouse of the marriage counselling or guidance facilities known to him or her that might be able to assist the spouses to achieve a reconciliation, unless the circumstances of the case are of such a nature that it would clearly not be appropriate to do so.

Idem

(2) It is the duty of every barrister, solicitor, lawyer or advocate who undertakes to act on behalf of a spouse in a divorce proceeding to discuss with the spouse the advisability of negotiating the matters that may be the subject of a support order or a custody order and to inform the spouse of the mediation facilities known to him or her that might be able to assist the spouses in negotiating those matters.

Certification

(3) Every document presented to a court by a barrister, solicitor, lawyer or advocate that formally commences a divorce proceeding shall contain a statement by him or her certifying that he or she has complied with this section.

Duty of court — reconciliation

10. (1) In a divorce proceeding, it is the duty of the court, before considering the evidence, to satisfy itself that there is no possibility of the reconciliation of the spouses, unless the circumstances of the case are of such a nature that it would clearly not be appropriate to do so.

Adjournment

(2) Where at any stage in a divorce proceeding it appears to the court from the nature of the case, the evidence or the attitude of either or both spouses that there is a possibility of the reconciliation of the spouses, the court shall

(*a*) adjourn the proceeding to afford the spouses an opportunity to achieve a reconciliation; and

(*b*) with the consent of the spouses or in the discretion of the court, nominate (*i*) a person with experience or training in marriage counselling or guidance, or

(*ii*) in special circumstances, some other suitable person, to assist the spouses to achieve a reconciliation.

Resumption

(3) Where fourteen days have elapsed from the date of any adjournment under subsection (2), the court shall resume the proceeding on the application of either or both spouses.

Nominee not competent or compellable

(4) No person nominated by a court under this section to assist spouses to achieve a reconciliation is competent or compellable in any legal proceedings to disclose any admission or communication made to that person in his or her capacity as a nominee of the court for that purpose.

Evidence not admissible

(5) Evidence of anything said or of any admission or communication made in the course of assisting spouses to achieve a reconciliation is not admissible in any legal proceedings.

Duty of court — bars

11. (1) In a divorce proceeding, it is the duty of the court

(*a*) to satisfy itself that there has been no collusion in relation to the application for a divorce and to dismiss the application if it finds that there was collusion in presenting it;

(*b*) to satisfy itself that reasonable arrangements have been made for the support of any children of the marriage, having regard to the applicable guidelines, and, if such arrangements have not been made, to stay the granting of the divorce until such arrangements are made; and

(*c*) where a divorce is sought in circumstances described in paragraph 8(2)(b), to satisfy itself that there has been no condonation or connivance on the part of the spouse bringing the proceeding, and to dismiss the application for a divorce if that spouse has condoned or connived at the act or conduct complained of unless, in the opinion of the court, the public interest would be better served by granting the divorce.

Revival

(2) Any act or conduct that has been condoned is not capable of being revived so as to constitute a circumstance described in paragraph 8(2)(b).

Condonation

(3) For the purposes of this section, a continuation or resumption of cohabitation during a period of, or periods totalling, not more than ninety days with reconciliation as its primary purpose shall not be considered to constitute condonation.

Definition of "collusion"

(4) In this section, "collusion" means an agreement or conspiracy to which an applicant for a divorce is either directly or indirectly a party for the purpose of subverting the administration of justice, and includes any agreement, understanding or arrangement to fabricate or suppress evidence or to deceive the court, but does not include an agreement to the extent that it provides for separation between the parties, financial support, division of property or the custody of any child of the marriage.

R.S., 1985, c. 3 (2nd Supp.), s. 11; 1997, c. 1, s. 1.1.

Effective date generally

12. (1) Subject to this section, a divorce takes effect on the thirty-first day after the day on which the judgment granting the divorce is rendered.

Special circumstances

(2) Where, on or after rendering a judgment granting a divorce,

(*a*) the court is of the opinion that by reason of special circumstances the divorce should take effect earlier than the thirty-first day after the day on which the judgment is rendered, and

(*b*) the spouses agree and undertake that no appeal from the judgment will be taken, or any appeal from the judgment that was taken has been abandoned, the court may order that the divorce takes effect at such earlier time as it considers appropriate.

Effective date where appeal

(3) A divorce in respect of which an appeal is pending at the end of the period referred to in subsection (1), unless voided on appeal, takes effect on the expiration of the time fixed by law for instituting an appeal from the decision on that appeal or any subsequent appeal, if no appeal has been instituted within that time.

Divorce

Certain extensions to be counted

(4) For the purposes of subsection (3), the time fixed by law for instituting an appeal from a decision on an appeal includes any extension thereof fixed pursuant to law before the expiration of that time or fixed thereafter on an application instituted before the expiration of that time.

No late extensions of time for appeal

(5) Notwithstanding any other law, the time fixed by law for instituting an appeal from a decision referred to in subsection (3) may not be extended after the expiration of that time, except on an application instituted before the expiration of that time.

Effective date where decision of Supreme Court of Canada

(6) A divorce in respect of which an appeal has been taken to the Supreme Court of Canada, unless voided on the appeal, takes effect on the day on which the judgment on the appeal is rendered.

Certificate of divorce

(7) Where a divorce takes effect in accordance with this section, a judge or officer of the court that rendered the judgment granting the divorce or, where that judgment has been appealed, of the appellate court that rendered the judgment on the final appeal, shall, on request, issue to any person a certificate that a divorce granted under this Act dissolved the marriage of the specified persons effective as of a specified date.

Conclusive proof

(8) A certificate referred to in subsection (7), or a certified copy thereof, is conclusive proof of the facts so certified without proof of the signature or authority of the person appearing to have signed the certificate.

Legal effect throughout Canada

13. On taking effect, a divorce granted under this Act has legal effect throughout Canada.

Marriage dissolved

14. On taking effect, a divorce granted under this Act dissolves the marriage of the spouses.

Appendix B

COROLLARY RELIEF

Interpretation

Definition of "spouse"

15. In sections 15.1 to 16, "spouse" has the meaning assigned by subsection 2(1), and includes a former spouse.

R.S., 1985, c. 3 (2nd Supp.), s. 15; 1997, c. 1, s. 2.

Child Support Orders

Child support order

15.1 (1) A court of competent jurisdiction may, on application by either or both spouses, make an order requiring a spouse to pay for the support of any or all children of the marriage.

Interim order

(2) Where an application is made under subsection (1), the court may, on application by either or both spouses, make an interim order requiring a spouse to pay for the support of any or all children of the marriage, pending the determination of the application under subsection (1).

Guidelines apply

(3) A court making an order under subsection (1) or an interim order under subsection (2) shall do so in accordance with the applicable guidelines.

Terms and conditions

(4) The court may make an order under subsection (1) or an interim order under subsection (2) for a definite or indefinite period or until a specified event occurs, and may impose terms, conditions or restrictions in connection with the order or interim order as it thinks fit and just.

Court may take agreement, etc., into account

(5) Notwithstanding subsection (3), a court may award an amount that is different from the amount that would be determined in accordance with the applicable guidelines if the court is satisfied

(*a*) that special provisions in an order, a judgment or a written agreement respecting the financial obligations of the spouses, or the division or transfer of their property, directly or indirectly benefit a child, or that special provisions have otherwise been made for the benefit of a child; and

(*b*) that the application of the applicable guidelines would result in an amount of child support that is inequitable given those special provisions.

Reasons

(6) Where the court awards, pursuant to subsection (5), an amount that is different from the amount that would be determined in accordance with the applicable guidelines, the court shall record its reasons for having done so.

Consent orders

(7) Notwithstanding subsection (3), a court may award an amount that is different from the amount that would be determined in accordance with the applicable guidelines on the consent of both spouses if it is satisfied that reasonable arrangements have been made for the support of the child to whom the order relates.

Reasonable arrangements

(8) For the purposes of subsection (7), in determining whether reasonable arrangements have been made for the support of a child, the court shall have regard to the applicable guidelines. However, the court shall not consider the arrangements to be unreasonable solely because the amount of support agreed to is not the same as the amount that would otherwise have been determined in accordance with the applicable guidelines.

1997, c. 1, s. 2.

Spousal Support Orders

Spousal support order

15.2 (1) A court of competent jurisdiction may, on application by either or both spouses, make an order requiring a spouse to secure or pay, or to secure and pay, such lump sum or periodic sums, or such lump sum and periodic sums, as the court thinks reasonable for the support of the other spouse.

Interim order

(2) Where an application is made under subsection (1), the court may, on application by either or both spouses, make an interim order requiring a spouse to secure

or pay, or to secure and pay, such lump sum or periodic sums, or such lump sum and periodic sums, as the court thinks reasonable for the support of the other spouse, pending the determination of the application under subsection (1).

Terms and conditions

(3) The court may make an order under subsection (1) or an interim order under subsection (2) for a definite or indefinite period or until a specified event occurs, and may impose terms, conditions or restrictions in connection with the order as it thinks fit and just.

Factors

(4) In making an order under subsection (1) or an interim order under subsection (2), the court shall take into consideration the condition, means, needs and other circumstances of each spouse, including

    (*a*) the length of time the spouses cohabited;

    (*b*) the functions performed by each spouse during cohabitation; and

    (*c*) any order, agreement or arrangement relating to support of either spouse.

Spousal misconduct

(5) In making an order under subsection (1) or an interim order under subsection (2), the court shall not take into consideration any misconduct of a spouse in relation to the marriage.

Objectives of spousal support order

(6) An order made under subsection (1) or an interim order under subsection (2) that provides for the support of a spouse should

    (*a*) recognize any economic advantages or disadvantages to the spouses arising from the marriage or its breakdown;

    (*b*) apportion between the spouses any financial consequences arising from the care of any child of the marriage over and above any obligation for the support of any child of the marriage;

    (*c*) relieve any economic hardship of the spouses arising from the breakdown of the marriage; and

    (*d*) in so far as practicable, promote the economic self-sufficiency of each spouse within a reasonable period of time.

1997, c. 1, s. 2.

Priority

Priority to child support

15.3 (1) Where a court is considering an application for a child support order and an application for a spousal support order, the court shall give priority to child support in determining the applications.

Reasons

(2) Where, as a result of giving priority to child support, the court is unable to make a spousal support order or the court makes a spousal support order in an amount that is less than it otherwise would have been, the court shall record its reasons for having done so.

Consequences of reduction or termination of child support order

(3) Where, as a result of giving priority to child support, a spousal support order was not made, or the amount of a spousal support order is less than it otherwise would have been, any subsequent reduction or termination of that child support constitutes a change of circumstances for the purposes of applying for a spousal support order, or a variation order in respect of the spousal support order, as the case may be.

1997, c. 1, s. 2.

Custody Orders

Order for custody

16. (1) A court of competent jurisdiction may, on application by either or both spouses or by any other person, make an order respecting the custody of or the access to, or the custody of and access to, any or all children of the marriage.

Interim order for custody

(2) Where an application is made under subsection (1), the court may, on application by either or both spouses or by any other person, make an interim order respecting the custody of or the access to, or the custody of and access to, any or all children of the marriage pending determination of the application under subsection (1).

Application by other person

(3) A person, other than a spouse, may not make an application under subsection (1) or (2) without leave of the court.

Appendix B

Joint custody or access

(4) The court may make an order under this section granting custody of, or access to, any or all children of the marriage to any one or more persons.

Access

(5) Unless the court orders otherwise, a spouse who is granted access to a child of the marriage has the right to make inquiries, and to be given information, as to the health, education and welfare of the child.

Terms and conditions

(6) The court may make an order under this section for a definite or indefinite period or until the happening of a specified event and may impose such other terms, conditions or restrictions in connection therewith as it thinks fit and just.

Order respecting change of residence

(7) Without limiting the generality of subsection (6), the court may include in an order under this section a term requiring any person who has custody of a child of the marriage and who intends to change the place of residence of that child to notify, at least thirty days before the change or within such other period before the change as the court may specify, any person who is granted access to that child of the change, the time at which the change will be made and the new place of residence of the child.

Factors

(8) In making an order under this section, the court shall take into consideration only the best interests of the child of the marriage as determined by reference to the condition, means, needs and other circumstances of the child.

Past conduct

(9) In making an order under this section, the court shall not take into consideration the past conduct of any person unless the conduct is relevant to the ability of that person to act as a parent of a child.

Maximum contact

(10) In making an order under this section, the court shall give effect to the principle that a child of the marriage should have as much contact with each spouse as is consistent with the best interests of the child and, for that purpose, shall take into consideration the willingness of the person for whom custody is sought to facilitate such contact.

Divorce

Variation, Rescission or Suspension of Orders

Order for variation, rescission or suspension

17. (1) A court of competent jurisdiction may make an order varying, rescinding or suspending, prospectively or retroactively,

(*a*) a support order or any provision thereof on application by either or both former spouses; or

(*b*) a custody order or any provision thereof on application by either or both former spouses or by any other person.

Application by other person

(2) A person, other than a former spouse, may not make an application under paragraph (1)(b) without leave of the court.

Terms and conditions

(3) The court may include in a variation order any provision that under this Act could have been included in the order in respect of which the variation order is sought.

Factors for child support order

(4) Before the court makes a variation order in respect of a child support order, the court shall satisfy itself that a change of circumstances as provided for in the applicable guidelines has occurred since the making of the child support order or the last variation order made in respect of that order.

Factors for spousal support order

(4.1) Before the court makes a variation order in respect of a spousal support order, the court shall satisfy itself that a change in the condition, means, needs or other circumstances of either former spouse has occurred since the making of the spousal support order or the last variation order made in respect of that order, and, in making the variation order, the court shall take that change into consideration.

Factors for custody order

(5) Before the court makes a variation order in respect of a custody order, the court shall satisfy itself that there has been a change in the condition, means, needs or other circumstances of the child of the marriage occurring since the making of the custody order or the last variation order made in respect of that order, as the case may be, and, in making the variation order, the court shall take into consideration only the best interests of the child as determined by reference to that change.

Conduct

(6) In making a variation order, the court shall not take into consideration any conduct that under this Act could not have been considered in making the order in respect of which the variation order is sought.

Guidelines apply

(6.1) A court making a variation order in respect of a child support order shall do so in accordance with the applicable guidelines.

Court may take agreement, etc., into account

(6.2) Notwithstanding subsection (6.1), in making a variation order in respect of a child support order, a court may award an amount that is different from the amount that would be determined in accordance with the applicable guidelines if the court is satisfied

> (*a*) that special provisions in an order, a judgment or a written agreement respecting the financial obligations of the spouses, or the division or transfer of their property, directly or indirectly benefit a child, or that special provisions have otherwise been made for the benefit of a child; and

> (*b*) that the application of the applicable guidelines would result in an amount of child support that is inequitable given those special provisions.

Reasons

(6.3) Where the court awards, pursuant to subsection (6.2), an amount that is different from the amount that would be determined in accordance with the applicable guidelines, the court shall record its reasons for having done so.

Consent orders

(6.4) Notwithstanding subsection (6.1), a court may award an amount that is different from the amount that would be determined in accordance with the applicable guidelines on the consent of both spouses if it is satisfied that reasonable arrangements have been made for the support of the child to whom the order relates.

Reasonable arrangements

(6.5) For the purposes of subsection (6.4), in determining whether reasonable arrangements have been made for the support of a child, the court shall have regard to the applicable guidelines. However, the court shall not consider the arrangements to be unreasonable solely because the amount of support agreed to is not the same as the amount that would otherwise have been determined in accordance with the applicable guidelines.

Objectives of variation order varying spousal support order

(7) A variation order varying a spousal support order should

(*a*) recognize any economic advantages or disadvantages to the former spouses arising from the marriage or its breakdown;

(*b*) apportion between the former spouses any financial consequences arising from the care of any child of the marriage over and above any obligation for the support of any child of the marriage;

(*c*) relieve any economic hardship of the former spouses arising from the breakdown of the marriage; and

(*d*) in so far as practicable, promote the economic self-sufficiency of each former spouse within a reasonable period of time.

(8) [Repealed, 1997, c. 1, s. 5]

Maximum contact

(9) In making a variation order varying a custody order, the court shall give effect to the principle that a child of the marriage should have as much contact with each former spouse as is consistent with the best interests of the child and, for that purpose, where the variation order would grant custody of the child to a person who does not currently have custody, the court shall take into consideration the willingness of that person to facilitate such contact.

Limitation

(10) Notwithstanding subsection (1), where a spousal support order provides for support for a definite period or until a specified event occurs, a court may not, on an application instituted after the expiration of that period or the occurrence of the event, make a variation order for the purpose of resuming that support unless the court is satisfied that

(*a*) a variation order is necessary to relieve economic hardship arising from a change described in subsection (4.1) that is related to the marriage; and

(*b*) the changed circumstances, had they existed at the time of the making of the spousal support order or the last variation order made in respect of that order, as the case may be, would likely have resulted in a different order.

Copy of order

(11) Where a court makes a variation order in respect of a support order or a custody order made by another court, it shall send a copy of the variation order, certified by a judge or officer of the court, to that other court.

R.S., 1985, c. 3 (2nd Supp.), s. 17; 1997, c. 1, s. 5.

Variation order by affidavit, etc.

17.1 Where both former spouses are ordinarily resident in different provinces, a court of competent jurisdiction may, in accordance with any applicable rules of the court, make a variation order pursuant to subsection 17(1) on the basis of the submissions of the former spouses, whether presented orally before the court or by means of affidavits or any means of telecommunication, if both former spouses consent thereto.

1993, c. 8, s. 2.

Provisional Orders

Definitions

18. (1) In this section and section 19,

"Attorney General" *«procureur général»*

"Attorney General", in respect of a province, means

(*a*) for the Yukon Territory, the member of the Council of the Yukon Territory designated by the Commissioner of the Yukon Territory,

(*b*) for the Northwest Territories, the member of the Council of the Northwest Territories designated by the Commissioner of the Northwest Territories,

(*b.1*) for Nunavut, the member of the Executive Council of Nunavut designated by the Commissioner of Nunavut, and

(c) for the other provinces, the Attorney General of the province, and includes any person authorized in writing by the member or Attorney General to act for the member or Attorney General in the performance of a function under this section or section 19;

"provisional order" *«ordonnance conditionnelle»*

"provisional order" means an order made pursuant to subsection (2).

Provisional order

(2) Notwithstanding paragraph 5(1)(a) and subsection 17(1), where an application is made to a court in a province for a variation order in respect of a support order and

(a) the respondent in the application is ordinarily resident in another province and has not accepted the jurisdiction of the court, or both former spouses have not consented to the application of section 17.1 in respect of the matter, and

(b) in the circumstances of the case, the court is satisfied that the issues can be adequately determined by proceeding under this section and section 19, the court shall make a variation order with or without notice to and in the absence of the respondent, but such order is provisional only and has no legal effect until it is confirmed in a proceeding under section 19 and, where so confirmed, it has legal effect in accordance with the terms of the order confirming it.

Transmission

(3) Where a court in a province makes a provisional order, it shall send to the Attorney General for the province

(a) three copies of the provisional order certified by a judge or officer of the court;

(b) a certified or sworn document setting out or summarizing the evidence given to the court; and

(c) a statement giving any available information respecting the identification, location, income and assets of the respondent.

Idem

(4) On receipt of the documents referred to in subsection (3), the Attorney General shall send the documents to the Attorney General for the province in which the respondent is ordinarily resident.

Appendix B

Further evidence

(5) Where, during a proceeding under section 19, a court in a province remits the matter back for further evidence to the court that made the provisional order, the court that made the order shall, after giving notice to the applicant, receive further evidence.

Transmission

(6) Where evidence is received under subsection (5), the court that received the evidence shall forward to the court that remitted the matter back a certified or sworn document setting out or summarizing the evidence, together with such recommendations as the court that received the evidence considers appropriate.

R.S., 1985, c. 3 (2nd Supp.), s. 18; 1993, c. 8, s. 3, c. 28, s. 78.

Transmission

19. (1) On receipt of any documents sent pursuant to subsection 18(4), the Attorney General for the province in which the respondent is ordinarily resident shall send the documents to a court in the province.

Procedure

(2) Subject to subsection (3), where documents have been sent to a court pursuant to subsection (1), the court shall serve on the respondent a copy of the documents and a notice of a hearing respecting confirmation of the provisional order and shall proceed with the hearing, in the absence of the applicant, taking into consideration the certified or sworn document setting out or summarizing the evidence given to the court that made the provisional order.

Return to Attorney General

(3) Where documents have been sent to a court pursuant to subsection (1) and the respondent apparently is outside the province and is not likely to return, the court shall send the documents to the Attorney General for that province, together with any available information respecting the location and circumstances of the respondent.

Idem

(4) On receipt of any documents and information sent pursuant to subsection (3), the Attorney General shall send the documents and information to the Attorney General for the province of the court that made the provisional order.

Right of respondent

(5) In a proceeding under this section, the respondent may raise any matter that might have been raised before the court that made the provisional order.

Further evidence

(6) Where, in a proceeding under this section, the respondent satisfies the court that for the purpose of taking further evidence or for any other purpose it is necessary to remit the matter back to the court that made the provisional order, the court may so remit the matter and adjourn the proceeding for that purpose.

Order of confirmation or refusal

(7) Subject to subsection (7.1), at the conclusion of a proceeding under this section, the court shall make an order

(*a*) confirming the provisional order without variation;

(*b*) confirming the provisional order with variation; or

(*c*) refusing confirmation of the provisional order.

Guidelines apply

(7.1) A court making an order under subsection (7) in respect of a child support order shall do so in accordance with the applicable guidelines.

Further evidence

(8) The court, before making an order confirming the provisional order with variation or an order refusing confirmation of the provisional order, shall decide whether to remit the matter back for further evidence to the court that made the provisional order.

Interim order for support of children

(9) Where a court remits a matter pursuant to this section in relation to a child support order, the court may, pending the making of an order under subsection (7), make an interim order in accordance with the applicable guidelines requiring a spouse to pay for the support of any or all children of the marriage.

Interim order for support of spouse

(9.1) Where a court remits a matter pursuant to this section in relation to a spousal support order, the court may make an interim order requiring a spouse to secure or pay, or to secure and pay, such lump sum or periodic sums, or such lump sum and periodic sums, as the court thinks reasonable for the support of the other spouse, pending the making of an order under subsection (7).

Terms and conditions

(10) The court may make an order under subsection (9) or (9.1) for a definite or indefinite period or until a specified event occurs, and may impose terms, conditions or restrictions in connection with the order as it thinks fit and just.

Provisions applicable

(11) Subsections 17(4), (4.1) and (6) to (7) apply, with such modifications as the circumstances require, in respect of an order made under subsection (9) or (9.1) as if it were a variation order referred to in those subsections.

Report and filing

(12) On making an order under subsection (7), the court in a province shall

(*a*) send a copy of the order, certified by a judge or officer of the court, to the Attorney General for that province, to the court that made the provisional order and, where that court is not the court that made the support order in respect of which the provisional order was made, to the court that made the support order;

(*b*) where an order is made confirming the provisional order with or without variation, file the order in the court; and

(*c*) where an order is made confirming the provisional order with variation or refusing confirmation of the provisional order, give written reasons to the Attorney General for that province and to the court that made the provisional order.

R.S., 1985, c. 3 (2nd Supp.), s. 19; 1993, c. 8, s. 4; 1997, c. 1, s. 7.

Definition of "court"

20. (1) In this section, "court", in respect of a province, has the meaning assigned by subsection 2(1) and includes such other court having jurisdiction in the province as is designated by the Lieutenant Governor in Council of the province as a court for the purposes of this section.

Legal effect throughout Canada

(2) Subject to subsection 18(2), an order made under any of sections 15.1 to 17 or subsection 19(7), (9) or (9.1) has legal effect throughout Canada.

Enforcement

(3) An order that has legal effect throughout Canada pursuant to subsection (2) may be

(*a*) registered in any court in a province and enforced in like manner as an order of that court; or

(*b*) enforced in a province in any other manner provided for by the laws of that province, including its laws respecting reciprocal enforcement between the province and a jurisdiction outside Canada.

Variation of orders

(4) Notwithstanding subsection (3), a court may only vary an order that has legal effect throughout Canada pursuant to subsection (2) in accordance with this Act.

R.S., 1985, c. 3 (2nd Supp.), s. 20; 1997, c. 1, s. 8.

Assignment of order

20.1 (1) A support order may be assigned to

(*a*) any minister of the Crown for Canada designated by the Governor in Council;

(*b*) any minister of the Crown for a province, or any agency in a province, designated by the Lieutenant Governor in Council of the province;

(*c*) any member of the Council of the Yukon Territory, or any agency in the Yukon Territory, designated by the Commissioner of the Yukon Territory;

(*d*) any member of the Council of the Northwest Territories, or any agency in the Northwest Territories, designated by the Commissioner of the Northwest Territories; or

(*e*) any member of the Legislative Assembly of Nunavut, or any agency in Nunavut, designated by the Commissioner of Nunavut.

Rights

(2) A minister, member or agency referred to in subsection (1) to whom an order is assigned is entitled to the payments due under the order, and has the same right to be notified of, and to participate in, proceedings under this Act to vary, rescind, suspend or enforce the order as the person who would otherwise be entitled to the payments.

1993, c. 28, s. 78; 1997, c. 1, s. 9; 1998, c. 15, s. 23.

APPEALS

Appeal to appellate court

21. (1) Subject to subsections (2) and (3), an appeal lies to the appellate court from any judgment or order, whether final or interim, rendered or made by a court under this Act.

Restriction on divorce appeals

(2) No appeal lies from a judgment granting a divorce on or after the day on which the divorce takes effect.

Restriction on order appeals

(3) No appeal lies from an order made under this Act more than thirty days after the day on which the order was made.

Extension

(4) An appellate court or a judge thereof may, on special grounds, either before or after the expiration of the time fixed by subsection (3) for instituting an appeal, by order extend that time.

Powers of appellate court

(5) The appellate court may

(*a*) dismiss the appeal; or

(*b*) allow the appeal and

(*i*) render the judgment or make the order that ought to have been rendered or made, including such order or such further or other order as it deems just, or

(*ii*) order a new hearing where it deems it necessary to do so to correct a substantial wrong or miscarriage of justice.

Procedure on appeals

(6) Except as otherwise provided by this Act or the rules or regulations, an appeal under this section shall be asserted, heard and decided according to the ordinary procedure governing appeals to the appellate court from the court rendering the judgment or making the order being appealed.

GENERAL

Definition of "spouse"

21.1 (1) In this section, "spouse" has the meaning assigned by subsection 2(1) and includes a former spouse.

Affidavit re removal of barriers to religious remarriage

(2) In any proceedings under this Act, a spouse (in this section referred to as the "deponent") may serve on the other spouse and file with the court an affidavit indicating

(*a*) that the other spouse is the spouse of the deponent;

(*b*) the date and place of the marriage, and the official character of the person who solemnized the marriage;

(*c*) the nature of any barriers to the remarriage of the deponent within the deponent's religion the removal of which is within the other spouse's control;

(*d*) where there are any barriers to the remarriage of the other spouse within the other spouse's religion the removal of which is within the deponent's control, that the deponent

(i) has removed those barriers, and the date and circumstances of that removal, or

(*ii*) has signified a willingness to remove those barriers, and the date and circumstances of that signification;

(*e*) that the deponent has, in writing, requested the other spouse to remove all of the barriers to the remarriage of the deponent within the deponent's religion the removal of which is within the other spouse's control;

(*f*) the date of the request described in paragraph (*e*); and

(*g*) that the other spouse, despite the request described in paragraph (*e*), has failed to remove all of the barriers referred to in that paragraph.

Powers of court where barriers not removed

(3) Where a spouse who has been served with an affidavit under subsection (2) does not

(*a*) within fifteen days after that affidavit is filed with the court or within such longer period as the court allows, serve on the deponent and file with the court an affidavit indicating that all of the barriers referred to in paragraph (2)(e) have been removed, and

Appendix B

(*b*) satisfy the court, in any additional manner that the court may require, that all of the barriers referred to in paragraph (2)(e) have been removed, the court may, subject to any terms that the court considers appropriate,

(*c*) dismiss any application filed by that spouse under this Act, and

(*d*) strike out any other pleadings and affidavits filed by that spouse under this Act.

Special case

(4) Without limiting the generality of the court's discretion under subsection (3), the court may refuse to exercise its powers under paragraphs (3)(c) and (d) where a spouse who has been served with an affidavit under subsection (2)

(*a*) within fifteen days after that affidavit is filed with the court or within such longer period as the court allows, serves on the deponent and files with the court an affidavit indicating genuine grounds of a religious or conscientious nature for refusing to remove the barriers referred to in paragraph (2)(e); and

(*b*) satisfies the court, in any additional manner that the court may require, that the spouse has genuine grounds of a religious or conscientious nature for refusing to remove the barriers referred to in paragraph (2)(e).

Affidavits

(5) For the purposes of this section, an affidavit filed with the court by a spouse must, in order to be valid, indicate the date on which it was served on the other spouse.

Where section does not apply

(6) This section does not apply where the power to remove the barrier to religious remarriage lies with a religious body or official.

1990, c. 18, s. 2.

Recognition of foreign divorce

22. (1) A divorce granted, on or after the coming into force of this Act, pursuant to a law of a country or subdivision of a country other than Canada by a tribunal or other authority having jurisdiction to do so shall be recognized for all purposes of determining the marital status in Canada of any person, if either former spouse was ordinarily resident in that country or subdivision for at least one year immediately preceding the commencement of proceedings for the divorce.

Idem

(2) A divorce granted, after July 1, 1968, pursuant to a law of a country or subdivision of a country other than Canada by a tribunal or other authority having jurisdiction to do so, on the basis of the domicile of the wife in that country or subdivision determined as if she were unmarried and, if she was a minor, as if she had attained the age of majority, shall be recognized for all purposes of determining the marital status in Canada of any person.

Other recognition rules preserved

(3) Nothing in this section abrogates or derogates from any other rule of law respecting the recognition of divorces granted otherwise than under this Act.

Provincial laws of evidence

23. (1) Subject to this or any other Act of Parliament, the laws of evidence of the province in which any proceedings under this Act are taken, including the laws of proof of service of any document, apply to such proceedings.

Presumption

(2) For the purposes of this section, where any proceedings are transferred to the Federal Court–Trial Division under subsection 3(3) or 5(3), the proceedings shall be deemed to have been taken in the province specified in the direction of the Court to be the province with which both spouses or former spouses, as the case may be, are or have been most substantially connected.

Proof of signature or office

24. A document offered in a proceeding under this Act that purports to be certified or sworn by a judge or an officer of a court shall, unless the contrary is proved, be proof of the appointment, signature or authority of the judge or officer and, in the case of a document purporting to be sworn, of the appointment, signature or authority of the person before whom the document purports to be sworn.

Definition of "competent authority"

25. (1) In this section, "competent authority", in respect of a court, or appellate court, in a province means the body, person or group of persons ordinarily competent under the laws of that province to make rules regulating the practice and procedure in that court.

Rules

(2) Subject to subsection (3), the competent authority may make rules applicable to any proceedings under this Act in a court, or appellate court, in a province, including, without limiting the generality of the foregoing, rules

(a) regulating the practice and procedure in the court, including the addition of persons as parties to the proceedings;

(b) respecting the conduct and disposition of any proceedings under this Act without an oral hearing;

(b.1) respecting the application of section 17.1 in respect of proceedings for a variation order;

(c) regulating the sittings of the court;

(d) respecting the fixing and awarding of costs;

(e) prescribing and regulating the duties of officers of the court;

(f) respecting the transfer of proceedings under this Act to or from the court; and

(g) prescribing and regulating any other matter considered expedient to attain the ends of justice and carry into effect the purposes and provisions of this Act.

Exercise of power

(3) The power to make rules for a court or appellate court conferred by subsection (2) on a competent authority shall be exercised in the like manner and subject to the like terms and conditions, if any, as the power to make rules for that court conferred on that authority by the laws of the province.

Not statutory instruments

(4) Rules made pursuant to this section by a competent authority that is not a judicial or quasi-judicial body shall be deemed not to be statutory instruments within the meaning and for the purposes of the Statutory Instruments Act.

R.S., 1985, c. 3 (2nd Supp.), s. 25; 1993, c. 8, s. 5.

Agreements with provinces

25.1 (1) With the approval of the Governor in Council, the Minister of Justice may, on behalf of the Government of Canada, enter into an agreement with a province authorizing a provincial child support service designated in the agreement to (*a*) assist courts in the province in the determination of the amount of child support; and

(*b*) recalculate, at regular intervals, in accordance with the applicable guidelines, the amount of child support orders on the basis of updated income information.

Effect of recalculation

(2) Subject to subsection (5), the amount of a child support order as recalculated pursuant to this section shall for all purposes be deemed to be the amount payable under the child support order.

Liability

(3) The former spouse against whom a child support order was made becomes liable to pay the amount as recalculated pursuant to this section thirty-one days after both former spouses to whom the order relates are notified of the recalculation in the manner provided for in the agreement authorizing the recalculation.

Right to vary

(4) Where either or both former spouses to whom a child support order relates do not agree with the amount of the order as recalculated pursuant to this section, either former spouse may, within thirty days after both former spouses are notified of the recalculation in the manner provided for in the agreement authorizing the recalculation, apply to a court of competent jurisdiction for an order under subsection 17(1).

Effect of application

(5) Where an application is made under subsection (4), the operation of subsection (3) is suspended pending the determination of the application, and the child support order continues in effect.

Withdrawal of application

(6) Where an application made under subsection (4) is withdrawn before the determination of the application, the former spouse against whom the order was made becomes liable to pay the amount as recalculated pursuant to this section on the day on which the former spouse would have become liable had the application not been made.

1997, c. 1, s. 10; 1999, c. 31, s. 74(F).

Regulations

26. (1) The Governor in Council may make regulations for carrying the purposes and provisions of this Act into effect and, without limiting the generality of the foregoing, may make regulations (*a*) respecting the establishment and operation of a central registry of divorce proceedings in Canada; and

(*b*) providing for uniformity in the rules made pursuant to section 25.

Regulations prevail

(2) Any regulations made pursuant to subsection (1) to provide for uniformity in the rules prevail over those rules.

Guidelines

26.1 (1) The Governor in Council may establish guidelines respecting the making of orders for child support, including, but without limiting the generality of the foregoing, guidelines

(*a*) respecting the way in which the amount of an order for child support is to be determined;

(*b*) respecting the circumstances in which discretion may be exercised in the making of an order for child support;

(*c*) authorizing a court to require that the amount payable under an order for child support be paid in periodic payments, in a lump sum or in a lump sum and periodic payments;

(*d*) authorizing a court to require that the amount payable under an order for child support be paid or secured, or paid and secured, in the manner specified in the order;

(*e*) respecting the circumstances that give rise to the making of a variation order in respect of a child support order;

(*f*) respecting the determination of income for the purposes of the application of the guidelines;

(*g*) authorizing a court to impute income for the purposes of the application of the guidelines; and

(*h*) respecting the production of income information and providing for sanctions when that information is not provided.

Principle

(2) The guidelines shall be based on the principle that spouses have a joint financial obligation to maintain the children of the marriage in accordance with their relative abilities to contribute to the performance of that obligation.

Definition of "order for child support"

(3) In subsection (1), "order for child support" means

(a) an order or interim order made under section 15.1;

(b) a variation order in respect of a child support order; or

(c) an order or an interim order made under section 19.

1997, c. 1, s. 11.

Fees

27. (1) The Governor in Council may, by order, authorize the Minister of Justice to prescribe a fee to be paid by any person to whom a service is provided under this Act or the regulations.

Agreements

(2) The Minister of Justice may, with the approval of the Governor in Council, enter into an agreement with the government of any province respecting the collection and remittance of any fees prescribed pursuant to subsection (1).

Review and report

28. The Minister of Justice shall undertake a comprehensive review of the provisions and operation of the Federal Child Support Guidelines and the determination of child support under this Act and shall cause a report on the review to be laid before each House of Parliament within five years after the coming into force of this section.

R.S., 1985, c. 3 (2nd Supp.), s. 28; 1997, c. 1, s. 12.

29. to **31.** [Repealed, 1997, c. 1, s. 12]

TRANSITIONAL PROVISIONS

Proceedings based on facts arising before commencement of Act

32. Proceedings may be commenced under this Act notwithstanding that the material facts or circumstances giving rise to the proceedings or to jurisdiction over the proceedings occurred wholly or partly before the day on which this Act comes into force.

Appendix B

Divorce Act, R.S. 1970, c. D-8

Proceedings commenced before commencement of Act

33. Proceedings commenced under the Divorce Act, chapter D-8 of the Revised Statutes of Canada, 1970, before the day on which this Act comes into force and not finally disposed of before that day shall be dealt with and disposed of in accordance with that Act as it read immediately before that day, as though it had not been repealed.

Variation and enforcement of orders previously made

34. (1) Subject to subsection (1.1), any order made under subsection 11(1) of the Divorce Act, chapter D-8 of the Revised Statutes of Canada, 1970, including any order made pursuant to section 33 of this Act, and any order to the like effect made corollary to a decree of divorce granted in Canada before July 2, 1968 or granted on or after that day pursuant to subsection 22(2) of that Act may be varied, rescinded, suspended or enforced in accordance with sections 17 to 20, other than subsection 17(10), of this Act as if

(*a*) the order were a support order or custody order, as the case may be; and

(*b*) in subsections 17(4), (4.1) and (5), the words "or the last order made under subsection 11(2) of the Divorce Act, chapter D-8 of the Revised Statutes of Canada, 1970, varying that order" were added immediately before the words "or the last variation order made in respect of that order".

Combined orders

(1.1) Where an application is made under subsection 17(1) to vary an order referred to in subsection (1) that provides a single amount of money for the combined support of one or more children and a former spouse, the court shall rescind the order and treat the application as an application for a child support order and an application for a spousal support order.

Enforcement of interim orders

(2) Any order made under section 10 of the Divorce Act, chapter D-8 of the Revised Statutes of Canada, 1970, including any order made pursuant to section 33 of this Act, may be enforced in accordance with section 20 of this Act as if it were an order made under subsection 15.1(1) or 15.2(1) or section 16 of this Act, as the case may be.

Assignment of orders previously made

(3) Any order for the maintenance of a spouse or child of the marriage made under section 10 or 11 of the Divorce Act, chapter D-8 of the Revised Statutes of Canada, 1970, including any order made pursuant to section 33 of this Act, and any order to the like effect made corollary to a decree of divorce granted in Canada before July 2, 1968 or

granted on or after that day pursuant to subsection 22(2) of that Act may be assigned to any minister, member or agency designated pursuant to section 20.1.

R.S., 1985, c. 3 (2nd Supp.), s. 34; 1997, c. 1, s. 14.

Procedural laws continued

35. The rules and regulations made under the Divorce Act, chapter D-8 of the Revised Statutes of Canada, 1970, and the provisions of any other law or of any rule, regulation or other instrument made thereunder respecting any matter in relation to which rules may be made under subsection 25(2) that were in force in Canada or any province immediately before the day on which this Act comes into force and that are not inconsistent with this Act continue in force as though made or enacted by or under this Act until they are repealed or altered by rules or regulations made under this Act or are, by virtue of the making of rules or regulations under this Act, rendered inconsistent with those rules or regulations.

Divorce Act, R.S. 1985, c. 3 (2nd Supp.)

Variation and enforcement of support orders previously made

35.1 (1) Subject to subsection (2), any support order made under this Act before the coming into force of this section may be varied, rescinded, suspended or enforced in accordance with sections 17 to 20 as if the support order were a child support order or a spousal support order, as the case may be.

Combined orders

(2) Where an application is made under subsection 17(1) to vary a support order made under this Act before the coming into force of this section that provides for the combined support of one or more children and a former spouse, the court shall rescind the order and treat the application as an application for a child support order and an application for a spousal support order.

Assignment of orders previously made

(3) Any support order made under this Act before the coming into force of this section may be assigned to any minister, member or agency designated pursuant to section 20.1.

1997, c. 1, s. 15.

Appendix B

COMMENCEMENT

Commencement

*36. This Act shall come into force on a day to be fixed by proclamation.

*[Note: Act in force June 1, 1986, see SI/86-70.]

RELATED PROVISIONS

-- R.S., 1985, c. 27 (2nd Supp.), s. 11:

Transitional: proceedings

"11. Proceedings to which any of the provisions amended by the schedule apply that were commenced before the coming into force of section 10 shall be continued in accordance with those amended provisions without any further formality."

-- 1990, c. 18, s. 3:

Application of amendments

"3. Subsection 2(4) and section 21.1 of the Divorce Act, as enacted by this Act, apply in respect of proceedings commenced under the Divorce Act either before or after the coming into force of this Act."

-- 1993, c. 8, ss. 19(1), (2):

Transitional

19. (1) Sections 4 and 17.1 and subsection 18(2) of the Divorce Act, as enacted by sections 1, 2 and 3, respectively, of this Act, apply only to corollary relief proceedings commenced under the Divorce Act after the coming into force of those sections.

Idem

(2) Subsections 19(2) and (7) of the Divorce Act, as enacted by section 4 of this Act, apply to corollary relief proceedings commenced under the Divorce Act before or after the coming into force of that section.

-- 1998, c. 30, s. 10:

Transitional – proceedings

10. Every proceeding commenced before the coming into force of this section and in respect of which any provision amended by sections 12 to 16 applies shall be taken up and continued under and in conformity with that amended provision without any further formality.

Consolidated Statutes and Regulations
Enabling statute: Divorce Act
Disclaimer: These documents are not the official versions.
Source: http://laws.justice.gc.ca/en/D-3.4/SOR-97-175/91301.html
Updated to April 30, 2001

Federal Child Support Guidelines

SOR/97-175
Registration 8 April, 1997

DIVORCE ACT
Federal Child Support Guidelines

P.C. 1997-469 8 April, 1997

His Excellency the Governor General in Council, on the recommendation of the Minister of Justice, pursuant to section 26.1a of the Divorce Act, hereby establishes the annexed Federal Child Support Guidelines.
a S.C. 1997, c. 1, s. 11b R.S., c. 3 (2nd Supp.)

FEDERAL CHILD SUPPORT GUIDELINES
OBJECTIVES

Objectives

1. The objectives of these Guidelines are

(*a*) to establish a fair standard of support for children that ensures that they continue to benefit from the financial means of both spouses after separation;

(*b*) to reduce conflict and tension between spouses by making the calculation of child support orders more objective;

(*c*) to improve the efficiency of the legal process by giving courts and spouses guidance in setting the levels of child support orders and encouraging settlement;

Appendix B

and

(*d*) to ensure consistent treatment of spouses and children who are in similar circumstances.

INTERPRETATION

Definitions

2. (1) The definitions in this subsection apply in these Guidelines.

"Act" *« Loi »*

"Act" means the Divorce Act. *(Loi)*

"child" *« enfant »*

"child" means a child of the marriage. *(enfant)*

"income" *« revenu »*

"income" means the annual income determined under sections 15 to 20. *(revenu)*

"order assignee" *« cessionnaire de la créance alimentaire »*

"order assignee" means a minister, member or agency referred to in subsection 20.1(1) of the Act to whom a child support order is assigned in accordance with that subsection. *(cessionnaire de la créance alimentaire)*

"spouse" *« époux »*

"spouse" has the meaning assigned by subsection 2(1) of the Act, and includes a former spouse. (époux)

"table" *« table »*

"table" means a federal child support table set out in Schedule I. *(table)*

Income Tax Act

(2) Words and expressions that are used in sections 15 to 21 and that are not defined in this section have the meanings assigned to them under the *Income Tax Act.*

Most current information

(3) Where, for the purposes of these Guidelines, any amount is determined on the basis of specified information, the most current information must be used.

Application of Guidelines

(4) In addition to child support orders, these Guidelines apply, with such modifications as the circumstances require, to

(a) interim orders under subsections 15.1(2) and 19(9) of the Act;

(b) orders varying a child support order;

(c) orders referred to in subsection 19(7) of the Act; and

(d) recalculations under paragraph 25.1(1)(b) of the Act.

Recalculations

(5) For greater certainty, the provisions of these Guidelines that confer a discretionary power on a court do not apply to recalculations under paragraph 25.1(1)(b) of the Act by a provincial child support service.

AMOUNT OF CHILD SUPPORT

Presumptive rule

3. (1) Unless otherwise provided under these Guidelines, the amount of a child support order for children under the age of majority is

(*a*) the amount set out in the applicable table, according to the number of children under the age of majority to whom the order relates and the income of the spouse against whom the order is sought; and

(*b*) the amount, if any, determined under section 7.

Child the age of majority or over

(2) Unless otherwise provided under these Guidelines, where a child to whom a child support order relates is the age of majority or over, the amount of the child support order is

(*a*) the amount determined by applying these Guidelines as if the child were under the age of majority; or

(*b*) if the court considers that approach to be inappropriate, the amount that it considers appropriate, having regard to the condition, means, needs and other circumstances of the child and the financial ability of each spouse to contribute to the support of the child.

Appendix B

Applicable table

(3) The applicable table is

(*a*) if the spouse against whom an order is sought resides in Canada,

> (*i*) the table for the province in which that spouse ordinarily resides at the time the application for the child support order, or for a variation order in respect of a child support order, is made or the amount is to be recalculated under section 25.1 of the Act,
>
> (*ii*) where the court is satisfied that the province in which that spouse ordinarily resides has changed since the time described in subparagraph, the table for the province in which the spouse ordinarily resides at the time of determining the amount of support, or
>
> (*iii*) where the court is satisfied that, in the near future after determination of the amount of support, that spouse will ordinarily reside in a given province other than the province in which the spouse ordinarily resides at the time of that determination, the table for the given province; and

(*b*) if the spouse against whom an order is sought resides outside of Canada, or if the residence of that spouse is unknown, the table for the province where the other spouse ordinarily resides at the time the application for the child support order or for a variation order in respect of a child support order is made or the amount is to be recalculated under section 25.1 of the Act. SOR/97-563, s. 1.

Incomes over $150,000

4. Where the income of the spouse against whom a child support order is sought is over $150,000, the amount of a child support order is

(*a*) the amount determined under section 3; or

(*b*) if the court considers that amount to be inappropriate,

> (*i*) in respect of the first $150,000 of the spouse's income, the amount set out in the applicable table for the number of children under the age of majority to whom the order relates;
>
> (*ii*) in respect of the balance of the spouse's income, the amount that the court considers appropriate, having regard to the condition, means, needs and other circumstances of the children who are entitled to support and the financial ability of each spouse to contribute to the support of the children; and

(*iii*) the amount, if any, determined under section 7.

Spouse in place of a parent

5. Where the spouse against whom a child support order is sought stands in the place of a parent for a child, the amount of a child support order is, in respect of that spouse, such amount as the court considers appropriate, having regard to these Guidelines and any other parent's legal duty to support the child.

Medical and dental insurance

6. In making a child support order, where medical or dental insurance coverage for the child is available to either spouse through his or her employer or otherwise at a reasonable rate, the court may order that coverage be acquired or continued.

Special or extraordinary expenses

7. (1) In a child support order the court may, on either spouse's request, provide for an amount to cover all or any portion of the following expenses, which expenses may be estimated, taking into account the necessity of the expense in relation to the child's best interests and the reasonableness of the expense in relation to the means of the spouses and those of the child and to the family's spending pattern prior to the separation:

(*a*) child care expenses incurred as a result of the custodial parent's employment, illness, disability or education or training for employment;

(*b*) that portion of the medical and dental insurance premiums attributable to the child;

(*c*) health-related expenses that exceed insurance reimbursement by at least $100 annually, including orthodontic treatment, professional counselling provided by a psychologist, social worker, psychiatrist or any other person, physiotherapy, occupational therapy, speech therapy and prescription drugs, hearing aids, glasses and contact lenses;

(*d*) extraordinary expenses for primary or secondary school education or for any other educational programs that meet the child's particular needs;

(*e*) expenses for post-secondary education; and

(*f*) extraordinary expenses for extracurricular activities.

Sharing of expense

(2) The guiding principle in determining the amount of an expense referred to in subsection (1) is that the expense is shared by the spouses in proportion to their

respective incomes after deducting from the expense, the contribution, if any, from the child.

Subsidies, tax deductions, etc.

(3) In determining the amount of an expense referred to in subsection (1), the court must take into account any subsidies, benefits or income tax deductions or credits relating to the expense, and any eligibility to claim a subsidy, benefit or income tax deduction or credit relating to the expense. SOR/2000-337, s. 1; SOR/2000-390, s. 1(F).

Split custody

8. Where each spouse has custody of one or more children, the amount of a child support order is the difference between the amount that each spouse would otherwise pay if a child support order were sought against each of the spouses.

Shared custody

9. Where a spouse exercises a right of access to, or has physical custody of, a child for not less than 40 per cent of the time over the course of a year, the amount of the child support order must be determined by taking into account

(*a*) the amounts set out in the applicable tables for each of the spouses;

(*b*) the increased costs of shared custody arrangements; and

(*c*) the conditions, means, needs and other circumstances of each spouse and of any child for whom support is sought.

Undue hardship

10. (1) On either spouse's application, a court may award an amount of child support that is different from the amount determined under any of sections 3 to 5, 8 or 9 if the court finds that the spouse making the request, or a child in respect of whom the request is made, would otherwise suffer undue hardship.

Circumstances that may cause undue hardship

(2) Circumstances that may cause a spouse or child to suffer undue hardship include the following:

(*a*) the spouse has responsibility for an unusually high level of debts reasonably incurred to support the spouses and their children prior to the separation or to earn a living;

(*b*) the spouse has unusually high expenses in relation to exercising access to a child;

(c) the spouse has a legal duty under a judgment, order or written separation agreement to support any person;

(d) the spouse has a legal duty to support a child, other than a child of the marriage, who is

    (i) under the age of majority, or

    (ii) the age of majority or over but is unable, by reason of illness, disability or other cause, to obtain the necessaries of life; and

(e) the spouse has a legal duty to support any person who is unable to obtain the necessaries of life due to an illness or disability.

Standards of living must be considered

(3) Despite a determination of undue hardship under subsection (1), an application under that subsection must be denied by the court if it is of the opinion that the household of the spouse who claims undue hardship would, after determining the amount of child support under any of sections 3 to 5, 8 or 9, have a higher standard of living than the household of the other spouse.

Standards of living test

(4) In comparing standards of living for the purpose of subsection (3), the court may use the comparison of household standards of living test set out in Schedule II.

Reasonable time

(5) Where the court awards a different amount of child support under subsection (1), it may specify, in the child support order, a reasonable time for the satisfaction of any obligation arising from circumstances that cause undue hardship and the amount payable at the end of that time.

Reasons

(6) Where the court makes a child support order in a different amount under this section, it must record its reasons for doing so.

ELEMENTS OF A CHILD SUPPORT ORDER

Form of payments

11. The court may require in a child support order that the amount payable under the order be paid in periodic payments, in a lump sum or in a lump sum and periodic payments.

Security

12. The court may require in the child support order that the amount payable under the order be paid or secured, or paid and secured, in the manner specified in the order.

Information to be specified in order

13. A child support order must include the following information:

(*a*) the name and birth date of each child to whom the order relates;

(*b*) the income of any spouse whose income is used to determine the amount of the child support order;

(*c*) the amount determined under paragraph 3(1)(a) for the number of children to whom the order relates;

(*d*) the amount determined under paragraph 3(2)(b) for a child the age of majority or over;

(*e*) the particulars of any expense described in subsection 7(1), the child to whom the expense relates, and the amount of the expense or, where that amount cannot be determined, the proportion to be paid in relation to the expense; and

(*f*) the date on which the lump sum or first payment is payable and the day of the month or other time period on which all subsequent payments are to be made.

VARIATION OF CHILD SUPPORT ORDERS

Circumstances for variation

14. For the purposes of subsection 17(4) of the Act, any one of the following constitutes a change of circumstances that gives rise to the making of a variation order in respect of a child support order:

(*a*) in the case where the amount of child support includes a determination made in accordance with the applicable table, any change in circumstances that would result in a different child support order or any provision thereof;

(*b*) in the case where the amount of child support does not include a determination made in accordance with a table, any change in the condition, means, needs or other circumstances of either spouse or of any child who is entitled to support; and

(c) in the case of an order made before May 1, 1997, the coming into force of section 15.1 of the Act, enacted by section 2 of chapter 1 of the Statutes of Canada, (1997). SOR/97-563, s. 2; SOR/2000-337, s. 2.

INCOME

Determination of annual income

15. (1) Subject to subsection (2), a spouse's annual income is determined by the court in accordance with sections 16 to 20.

Agreement

(2) Where both spouses agree in writing on the annual income of a spouse, the court may consider that amount to be the spouse's income for the purposes of these Guidelines if the court thinks that the amount is reasonable having regard to the income information provided under section 21.

Calculation of annual income

16. Subject to sections 17 to 20, a spouse's annual income is determined using the sources of income set out under the heading "Total income" in the T1 General form issued by the Canada Customs and Revenue Agency and is adjusted in accordance with Schedule III. SOR/2000-337, s. 3.

Pattern of income

17. (1) If the court is of the opinion that the determination of a spouse's annual income under section 16 would not be the fairest determination of that income, the court may have regard to the spouse's income over the last three years and determine an amount that is fair and reasonable in light of any pattern of income, fluctuation in income or receipt of a non-recurring amount during those years.

Non-recurring losses

(2) Where a spouse has incurred a non-recurring capital or business investment loss, the court may, if it is of the opinion that the determination of the spouse's annual income under section 16 would not provide the fairest determination of the annual income, choose not to apply sections 6 and 7 of Schedule III, and adjust the amount of the loss, including related expenses and carrying charges and interest expenses, to arrive at such amount as the court considers appropriate. SOR/2000-337, s. 4.

Shareholder, director or officer

18. (1) Where a spouse is a shareholder, director or officer of a corporation and the court is of the opinion that the amount of the spouse's annual income as determined under section 16 does not fairly reflect all the money available to the spouse for the payment of child support, the court may consider the situations described in section 17 and determine the spouse's annual income to include

(*a*) all or part of the pre-tax income of the corporation, and of any corporation that is related to that corporation, for the most recent taxation year; or

(*b*) an amount commensurate with the services that the spouse provides to the corporation, provided that the amount does not exceed the corporation's pre-tax income.

Adjustment to corporation's pre-tax income

(2) In determining the pre-tax income of a corporation for the purposes of subsection (1), all amounts paid by the corporation as salaries, wages or management fees, or other payments or benefits, to or on behalf of persons with whom the corporation does not deal at arm's length must be added to the pre-tax income, unless the spouse establishes that the payments were reasonable in the circumstances.

Imputing income

19. (1) The court may impute such amount of income to a spouse as it considers appropriate in the circumstances, which circumstances include the following:

(*a*) the spouse is intentionally under-employed or unemployed, other than where the under-employment or unemployment is required by the needs of a child of the marriage or any child under the age of majority or by the reasonable educational or health needs of the spouse;

(*b*) the spouse is exempt from paying federal or provincial income tax;

(*c*) the spouse lives in a country that has effective rates of income tax that are significantly lower than those in Canada;

(*d*) it appears that income has been diverted which would affect the level of child support to be determined under these Guidelines;

(*e*) the spouse's property is not reasonably utilized to generate income;

(*f*) the spouse has failed to provide income information when under a legal obligation to do so;

(g) the spouse unreasonably deducts expenses from income;

(h) the spouse derives a significant portion of income from dividends, capital gains or other sources that are taxed at a lower rate than employment or business income or that are exempt from tax; and

(i) the spouse is a beneficiary under a trust and is or will be in receipt of income or other benefits from the trust.

Reasonableness of expenses

(2) For the purpose of paragraph (1)(g), the reasonableness of an expense deduction is not solely governed by whether the deduction is permitted under the Income Tax Act. SOR/2000-337, s. 5.

Non-resident

20. Where a spouse is a non-resident of Canada, the spouse's annual income is determined as though the spouse were a resident of Canada.

INCOME INFORMATION

Obligation of applicant

21. (1) A spouse who is applying for a child support order and whose income information is necessary to determine the amount of the order must include the following with the application:

(a) a copy of every personal income tax return filed by the spouse for each of the three most recent taxation years;

(b) a copy of every notice of assessment and reassessment issued to the spouse for each of the three most recent taxation years;

(c) where the spouse is an employee, the most recent statement of earnings indicating the total earnings paid in the year to date, including overtime or, where such a statement is not provided by the employer, a letter from the spouse's employer setting out that information including the spouse's rate of annual salary or remuneration;

(d) where the spouse is self-employed, for the three most recent taxation years

(i) the financial statements of the spouse's business or professional practice, other than a partnership, and (*ii*) a statement showing a breakdown of all salaries, wages, management fees or other payments or benefits paid to, or on behalf of, persons or corporations with whom the spouse does not deal at arm's length;

(*e*) where the spouse is a partner in a partnership, confirmation of the spouse's income and draw from, and capital in, the partnership for its three most recent taxation years;

(*f*) where the spouse controls a corporation, for its three most recent taxation years

(*i*) the financial statements of the corporation and its subsidiaries, and

(*ii*) a statement showing a breakdown of all salaries, wages, management fees or other payments or benefits paid to, or on behalf of, persons or corporations with whom the corporation, and every related corporation, does not deal at arm's length;

(*g*) where the spouse is a beneficiary under a trust, a copy of the trust settlement agreement and copies of the trust's three most recent financial statements; and

(*h*) in addition to any income information that must be included under paragraphs (c) to (g), where the spouse receives income from employment insurance, social assistance, a pension, workers compensation, disability payments or any other source, the most recent statement of income indicating the total amount of income from the applicable source during the current year, or if such a statement is not provided, a letter from the appropriate authority stating the required information.

Obligation of respondent

(2) A spouse who is served with an application for a child support order and whose income information is necessary to determine the amount of the order, must, within 30 days after the application is served if the spouse resides in Canada or the United States or within 60 days if the spouse resides elsewhere, or such other time limit as the court specifies, provide the court, as well as the other spouse or the order assignee, as the case may be, with the documents referred to in subsection (1).

Special expenses or undue hardship

(3) Where, in the course of proceedings in respect of an application for a child support order, a spouse requests an amount to cover expenses referred to in subsection 7(1) or pleads undue hardship, the spouse who would be receiving the amount of child support must, within 30 days after the amount is sought or undue hardship is pleaded if the spouse resides in Canada or the United States or within 60 days if the spouse resides elsewhere, or such other time limit as the court specifies, provide the court and the other spouse with the documents referred to in subsection (1).

Income over $150,000

(4) Where, in the course of proceedings in respect of an application for a child support order, it is established that the income of the spouse who would be paying the amount of child support is greater than $150,000, the other spouse must, within 30 days after the income is established to be greater than $150,000 if the other spouse resides in Canada or the United States or within 60 days if the other spouse resides elsewhere, or such other time limit as the court specifies, provide the court and the spouse with the documents referred to in subsection (1).

Making of rules not precluded

(5) Nothing in this section precludes the making of rules by a competent authority, within the meaning of section 25 of the Act, respecting the disclosure of income information that is considered necessary for the purposes of the determination of an amount of a child support order. SOR/2000-337, s. 6.

Failure to comply

22. (1) Where a spouse fails to comply with section 21, the other spouse may apply

    (*a*) to have the application for a child support order set down for a hearing, or move for judgment; or

    (*b*) for an order requiring the spouse who failed to comply to provide the court, as well as the other spouse or order assignee, as the case may be, with the required documents.

Costs of the proceedings

(2) Where a court makes an order under paragraph (1)(a) or (b), the court may award costs in favour of the other spouse up to an amount that fully compensates the other spouse for all costs incurred in the proceedings.

Adverse inference

23. Where the court proceeds to a hearing on the basis of an application under paragraph 22(1)(a), the court may draw an adverse inference against the spouse who failed to comply and impute income to that spouse in such amount as it considers appropriate.

Appendix B

Failure to comply with court order

24. Where a spouse fails to comply with an order issued on the basis of an application under paragraph 22(1)(b), the court may

(*a*) strike out any of the spouse's pleadings;

(*b*) make a contempt order against the spouse;

(*c*) proceed to a hearing, in the course of which it may draw an adverse inference against the spouse and impute income to that spouse in such amount as it considers appropriate; and

(*d*) award costs in favour of the other spouse up to an amount that fully compensates the other spouse for all costs incurred in the proceedings.

Continuing obligation to provide income information

25. (1) Every spouse against whom a child support order has been made must, on the written request of the other spouse or the order assignee, not more than once a year after the making of the order and as long as the child is a child within the meaning of these Guidelines, provide that other spouse or the order assignee with

(*a*) the documents referred to in subsection 21(1) for any of the three most recent taxation years for which the spouse has not previously provided the documents;

(*b*) as applicable, any current information, in writing, about the status of any expenses included in the order pursuant to subsection 7(1); and

(*c*) as applicable, any current information, in writing, about the circumstances relied on by the court in a determination of undue hardship.

Below minimum income

(2) Where a court has determined that the spouse against whom a child support order is sought does not have to pay child support because his or her income level is below the minimum amount required for application of the tables, that spouse must, on the written request of the other spouse, not more than once a year after the determination and as long as the child is a child within the meaning of these Guidelines, provide the other spouse with the documents referred to in subsection 21(1) for any of the three most recent taxation years for which the spouse has not previously provided the documents.

Obligation of receiving spouse

(3) Where the income information of the spouse in favour of whom a child support order is made is used to determine the amount of the order, the spouse must, not

more than once a year after the making of the order and as long as the child is a child within the meaning of these Guidelines, on the written request of the other spouse, provide the other spouse with the documents and information referred to in subsection (1).

Information requests

(4) Where a spouse or an order assignee requests information from the other spouse under any of subsections (1) to (3) and the income information of the requesting spouse is used to determine the amount of the child support order, the requesting spouse or order assignee must include the documents and information referred to in subsection (1) with the request.

Time limit

(5) A spouse who receives a request made under any of subsections (1) to (3) must provide the required documents within 30 days after the request's receipt if the spouse resides in Canada or the United States and within 60 days after the request's receipt if the spouse resides elsewhere.

Deemed receipt

(6) A request made under any of subsections (1) to (3) is deemed to have been received 10 days after it is sent.

Failure to comply

(7) A court may, on application by either spouse or an order assignee, where the other spouse has failed to comply with any of subsections (1) to (3)

(*a*) consider the other spouse to be in contempt of court and award costs in favour of the applicant up to an amount that fully compensates the applicant for all costs incurred in the proceedings; or

(*b*) make an order requiring the other spouse to provide the required documents to the court, as well as to the spouse or order assignee, as the case may be.

Unenforceable provision

(8) A provision in a judgment, order or agreement purporting to limit a spouse's obligation to provide documents under this section is unenforceable. SOR/97-563, s. 3(E).

Provincial child support services

26. A spouse or an order assignee may appoint a provincial child support service to act on their behalf for the purposes of requesting and receiving income information under

Appendix B

any of subsections 25(1) to (3), as well as for the purposes of an application under subsection 25(7).

COMING INTO FORCE

Coming into force

Consolidated Statutes and Regulations
Enabling statute: Divorce Act
P.C. 1997-469 8 April, 1997
Disclaimer: These documents are not the official versions (more).
Source: http://laws.justice.gc.ca/en/D-3.4/SOR-97-175/91440.html
Updated to April 30, 2001

27. These Guidelines come into force on May 1, 1997.

SCHEDULE I

(Subsection 2(1))

FEDERAL CHILD SUPPORT TABLES

Notes:

1. The federal child support tables set out the amount of monthly child support payments for each province on the basis of the annual income of the spouse ordered to pay child support (the "support payer") and the number of children for whom a table amount is payable. Refer to these Guidelines to determine whether special measures apply.

2. There is a threshold level of income below which no amount of child support is payable. Child support amounts are specified for incomes up to $150,000 per year. Refer to section 4 of these Guidelines to determine the amount of child support payments for support payers with annual incomes over $150,000.

3. Income is set out in the tables in intervals of $1,000. Monthly amounts are determined by adding the basic amount and the amount calculated by multiplying the applicable percentage by the portion of the income that exceeds the lower amount within that interval of income.

Divorce

Example:

Province: British Columbia
Number of children: 2
Annual income of support payer: $33,760
Basic amount: $480
Percentage: 1.20%
Lower amount of the income interval: $33,000

The amount of monthly child support is calculated as follows:

$480 + [1.2% _ ($33,760 - 33,000)]
$480 + [1.2/100 _ $760]
$480 + [0.012 _ $760]
$480 + $9.12 = $489.12

4. There are separate tables for each province. The amounts vary from one province to another because of differences in provincial income tax rates. The tables are in the following order:

    (a) Ontario

    (b) Quebec

    (c) Nova Scotia

    (d) New Brunswick

    (e) Manitoba

    (f) British Columbia

    (g) Prince Edward Island

    (h) Saskatchewan

    (i) Alberta

    (j) Newfoundland

    (k) Yukon

    (l) Northwest Territories

    (m) Nunavut

5. The amounts in the tables are based on economic studies of average spending on children in families at different income levels in Canada. They are calculated on the basis

that child support payments are no longer taxable in the hands of the receiving parent and no longer deductible by the paying parent. They are calculated using a mathematical formula and generated by a computer program.

6. The formula referred to in note 5 sets support amounts to reflect average expenditures on children by a spouse with a particular number of children and level of income. The calculation is based on the support payer's income. The formula uses the basic personal amount for non-refundable tax credits to recognize personal expenses, and takes other federal and provincial income taxes and credits into account. Federal Child Tax benefits and Goods and Services Tax credits for children are excluded from the calculation. At lower income levels, the formula sets the amounts to take into account the combined impact of taxes and child support payments on the support payer's limited disposable income.

Consolidated Statutes and Regulations
Enabling statute: Divorce Act
P.C. 1997-469 8 April, 1997
 Section 27
Disclaimer: These documents are not the official versions (more).
Source: http://laws.justice.gc.ca/en/D-3.4/SOR-97-175/91752.html
Updated to April 30, 2001

SCHEDULE II

(Subsection 10(4))

COMPARISON OF HOUSEHOLD STANDARDS OF LIVING TEST

Definitions

  1. The definitions in this section apply in this Schedule.

"average tax rate" [Repealed, SOR/2000-337, s. 7]

"child" *« enfant »*

"child" means a child of the marriage or a child who

  (*a*) is under the age of majority; or

  (*b*) is the age of majority or over but is unable, by reason of illness, disability or other cause to obtain the necessaries of life. (enfant) "household" *« ménage »*

"household" means a spouse and any of the following persons residing with the spouse

> (*a*) any person who has a legal duty to support the spouse or whom the spouse has a legal duty to support;
>
> (*b*) any person who shares living expenses with the spouse or from whom the spouse otherwise receives an economic benefit as a result of living with that person, if the court considers it reasonable for that person to be considered part of the household; and
>
> (*c*) any child whom the spouse or the person described in paragraph (a) or (b) has a legal duty to support. *(ménage)*

"taxable income" *« revenu imposable »*

"taxable income" means the annual taxable income determined using the calculations required to determine "Taxable Income" in the T1 General form issued by the Canada Customs and Revenue Agency. *(revenu imposable)*

Test

> 2. The comparison of household standards of living test is as follows:

STEP 1

> Establish the annual income of each person in each household by applying the formula

$$A - B$$

where

A is the person's income determined under sections 15 to 20 of these Guidelines, and

B is the federal and provincial taxes payable on the person's taxable income.

Where the information on which to base the income determination is not provided, the court may impute income in the amount it considers appropriate.

STEP 2

> Adjust the annual income of each person in each household by
>
> (*a*) deducting the following amounts, calculated on an annual basis:
>
>> (*i*) any amount relied on by the court as a factor that resulted in a

determination of undue hardship, except any amount attributable to the support of a member of the household that is not incurred due to a disability or serious illness of that member,

>   (*ii*) the amount that would otherwise be payable by the person in respect of a child to whom the order relates, if the pleading of undue hardship was not made,
>
>>   (A) under the applicable table, or
>>
>>   (B) as is considered by the court to be appropriate, where the court considers the table amount to be inappropriate,
>
>   (*iii*) any amount of support that is paid by the person under a judgment, order or written separation agreement, except
>
>>   (A) an amount already deducted under subparagraph, and
>>
>>   (B) an amount paid by the person in respect of a child to whom the order referred to in subparagraph (ii) relates; and

(*b*) adding the following amounts, calculated on an annual basis:

>   (*i*) any amount that would otherwise be receivable by the person in respect of a child to whom the order relates, if the pleading of undue hardship was not made,
>
>>   (A) under the applicable table, or
>>
>>   (B) as is considered by the court to be appropriate, where the court considers the table amount to be inappropriate,
>
>   (*ii*) any amount of child support that the person has received for any child under a judgment, order or written separation agreement.

STEP 3

Add the amounts of adjusted annual income for all the persons in each household to determine the total household income for each household.

STEP 4

Determine the applicable low-income measures amount for each household based on the following:

(LOW-INCOME MEASURES)

Household Size	Low-income Measures Amount
One person	
1 adult	$10,382
Two persons	
2 adults	$14,535
1 adult and 1 child	$14,535
Three persons	
3 adults	$18,688
2 adults and 1 child	$17,649
1 adult and 2 children	$17,649
Four persons	
4 adults	$22,840
3 adults and 1 child	$21,802
2 adults and 2 children	$20,764
1 adult and 3 children	$20,764
Five persons	
5 adults	$26,993
4 adults and 1 child	$25,955
3 adults and 2 children	$24,917
2 adults and 3 children	$23,879
1 adult and 4 children	$23,879
Six persons	
6 adults	$31,145
5 adults and 1 child	$30,108
4 adults and 2 children	$29,070
3 adults and 3 children	$28,031
2 adults and 4 children	$26,993
1 adult and 5 children	$26,993

Seven persons
7 adults	$34,261
6 adults and 1 child	$33,222
5 adults and 2 children	$32,184
4 adults and 3 children	$31,146
3 adults and 4 children	$30,108
2 adults and 5 children	$29,070
1 adult and 6 children	$29,070

Eight persons
8 adults	$38,413
7 adults and 1 child	$37,375
6 adults and 2 children	$36,337
5 adults and 3 children	$35,299
4 adults and 4 children	$34,261
3 adults and 5 children	$33,222
2 adults and 6 children	$32,184
1 adult and 7 children	$32,184

STEP 5

Divide the household income amount (Step 3) by the low-income measures amount (Step 4) to get a household income ratio for each household.

STEP 6

Compare the household income ratios. The household that has the higher ratio has the higher standard of living.

SOR/97-563, ss. 10, 11; SOR/2000-337, s. 7.

SCHEDULE III
(Section 16)
ADJUSTMENTS TO INCOME

Employment expenses

1. Where the spouse is an employee, the spouse's applicable employment expenses described in the following provisions of the Income Tax Act are deducted:

(*a*) [Repealed, SOR/2000-337, s. 8]

(b) paragraph 8(1)(d) concerning expenses of teacher's exchange fund contribution;

(c) paragraph 8(1)(e) concerning expenses of railway employees;

(d) paragraph 8(1)(f) concerning sales expenses;

(e) paragraph 8(1)(g) concerning transport employee's expenses;

(f) paragraph 8(1)(h) concerning travel expenses;

(f.1) paragraph 8(1)(h.1) concerning motor vehicle travel expenses;

(g) paragraph 8(1) concerning dues and other expenses of performing duties;

(h) paragraph 8(l)(j) concerning motor vehicle and aircraft costs;

(i) paragraph 8(1)(l.1) concerning Canada Pension Plan contributions and Employment Insurance Act premiums paid in respect of another employee who acts as an assistant or substitute for the spouse;

(j) paragraph 8(1)(n) concerning salary reimbursement;

(k) paragraph 8(1)(o) concerning forfeited amounts;

(l) paragraph 8(1)(p) concerning musical instrument costs; and

(m) paragraph 8(1)(q) concerning artists' employment expenses.

Child support

2. Deduct any child support received that is included to determine total income in the T1 General form issued by the Canada Customs and Revenue Agency.

Spousal support

3. (1) To calculate income for the purpose of determining an amount under an applicable table, deduct the spousal support received from the other spouse.

Special or extraordinary expenses

(2) To calculate income for the purpose of determining an amount under section 7 of these Guidelines, deduct the spousal support paid to the other spouse.

Appendix B

Social assistance

    4. Deduct any amount of social assistance income that is not attributable to the spouse.

Dividends from taxable Canadian corporations

    5. Replace the taxable amount of dividends from taxable Canadian corporations received by the spouse by the actual amount of those dividends received by the spouse.

Capital gains and capital losses

    6. Replace the taxable capital gains realized in a year by the spouse by the actual amount of capital gains realized by the spouse in excess of the spouse's actual capital losses in that year.

Business investment losses

    7. Deduct the actual amount of business investment losses suffered by the spouse during the year.

Carrying charges

    8. Deduct the spouse's carrying charges and interest expenses that are paid by the spouse and that would be deductible under the Income Tax Act.

Net self-employment income

    9. Where the spouse's net self-employment income is determined by deducting an amount for salaries, benefits, wages or management fees, or other payments, paid to or on behalf of persons with whom the spouse does not deal at arm's length, include that amount, unless the spouse establishes that the payments were necessary to earn the self-employment income and were reasonable in the circumstances.

Additional amount

    10. Where the spouse reports income from self-employment that, in accordance with sections 34.1 and 34.2 of the Income Tax Act, includes an additional amount earned in a prior period, deduct the amount earned in the prior period, net of reserves.

Capital cost allowance for property

11. Include the spouse's deduction for an allowable capital cost allowance with respect to real property.

Partnership or sole proprietorship income

12. Where the spouse earns income through a partnership or sole proprietorship, deduct any amount included in income that is properly required by the partnership or sole proprietorship for purposes of capitalization.

Employee stock options with a Canadian-controlled private corporation

13. (1) Where the spouse has received, as an employee benefit, options to purchase shares of a Canadian-controlled private corporation and has exercised those options during the year, add the difference between the value of the shares at the time the options are exercised and the amount paid by the spouse for the shares and any amount paid to acquire the options to purchase the shares, to the income for the year in which the options are exercised.

Disposal of shares

(2) If the spouse has disposed of the shares during a year, deduct from the income for that year the difference determined under subsection (1).

SOR/97-563, ss. 12 to 14; SOR/2000-337, ss. 8 to 11, 12(E).

Appendix C

Comparative Analysis of Family Property Legislation

Since the Ontario Family Law Reform Act was passed in 1978, each of the other provinces has passed a new family property statute.

There is no uniformity to the legislation and thus tremendous potential for conflict of laws. All number references are to sections of the statute. This is an overview; for full text, please refer to the proper statute.

There is no uniformity to the legislation and thus tremendous potential for conflict of laws. All number references are to sections of the statute. This is an overview; for full text, please refer to the proper statute.

ALBERTA

Statute

The Matrimonial Property Act

Intent

Unstated

Jurisdiction

Supreme or District Court (1)

Who may apply

A spouse, if habitual residence of both spouses, or last joint habitual residence was Alberta; or a party to a divorce petition issued in Alberta. (5)

When may order be made

If a decree nisi or declaration of nullity or a judgement of judicial separation is made; if spouses have been living separate and apart for at least one year before application, or less if there is no possibility of reconciliation; or if the defendant spouse transfers or dissipates property or intends to do so.

May be commenced not later than two years after decree nisi, declaration of annulment or judgment of judicial separation, etc. (6).

Property included

All property owned by both spouses and by each of them (7.1).

Property excluded

Market value of property at time of marriage or acquisition, whichever is later, acquired by third-party gift, inheritance, damages for tort, insurance proceeds; or acquired before the marriage (7.2).

Basic entitlement

Just and equitable distribution, considering: contribution (including that of a home-maker or parent); income, earning capacity, liabilities, obligations, property and other financial resources; duration of marriage; date of acquisition; agreement; previous gifts or transfers; previous distribution between spouses; prior order; tax liability as a result of transfer or sale; dissipation of property; "any fact or circumstance that is relevant." (8)

Power of Court

Partition, sale, transfer, division, order for payment, declaration re-title; order for charging, security, imposing trust, variation of prior order, "any other order that in the opinion of the Court is necessary." (9)

Date of Valuation

Not specifically stated, but probably the date of trial.

Effect of Agreement

Overrides statutory property rights; must contain written acknowledgment made before a lawyer. (37, 38) Non-reviewable if valid.

BRITISH COLUMBIA

Statute or Source

Family Relations Act

Intent

Unstated

Jurisdiction

Supreme Court

Who may apply

Spouse or former spouse.

When may application be made

Within two years of an order for dissolution of marriage, judicial separation or declaring the marriage to be null and void (1).

Property included

"Family assets," i.e, property owned by one or both spouses and ordinarily used by a spouse or a minor child of either spouse for a family purpose. Includes a right of a spouse under an annuity or a pension, home ownership or retirement savings plan or "a right share or interest of a spouse *in a venture* to which money or moneys worth was directly or indirectly contributed by or on behalf of the other spouse." (45.3)

Property excluded

Property owned by one spouse to the exclusion of the other and used primarily for business purposes where the spouse who does not own the property made no direct or indirect contribution to the acquisition of the property by the other spouse or to the operation of the business; but an indirect contribution includes savings through effective management of household or child-rearing responsibilities by the spouse who holds no interest in the property. (46)

Basic entitlement

An undivided half interest in family assets as a tenant–in–common.

Powers of Court

Determine any matter respecting the ownership right of possession or division of property and make such orders as are necessary, reasonable or ancillary to give effect to the determination, etc.; and interim orders. (53)

Judicial discretion to create unequal sharing where provisions for division of property in accordance with a basic entitlement or under a marriage agreement would be unfair. (51)

Date of Valuation

Unstated.

Effect of Agreement

Parties may contract for management of family assets or other property during marriage or ownership in or division of family assets or other property during marriage or on the making of an order for dissolution of marriage, judicial separation, or declaration of nullity of marriage; this includes separation agreements, but apparently parties cannot contract in respect of support obligations. (48)

Apparently, marriage agreements override statutory property rights.

MANITOBA

Statute

The Marital Property Act

Intent

To provide for presumption in the event of the break-down of the marriage of equal sharing of the family and commercial assets of the parties of the marriage acquired by them during the marriage.

Jurisdiction

Queen's Bench or County Court

Who may apply

Spouses whether married before or after coming into force of the Act if the habitual residence of both spouses is in Manitoba or, where each of the spouses has a different habitual residence if the last common habitual residence of the spouses was in Manitoba. (2) The Act does not apply to spouses who were living separate and apart from each other on May 6, 1977, unless those spouses after that date resumed cohabitation for a period of more than 90 days. (2.4)

When may application be made

Any time up to 60 days after granting of decree absolute of divorce or decree of nullity or, as against estate, within six months after date of death. (18)

Property included

Assets

Property excluded

Any article of personal apparel. Assets acquired after separation, while married to a former spouse or while unmarried, or disposed of by spousal agreement.

Appendix C

Basic entitlement

Equal sharing of assets where spouses made a separation agreement in writing, an order for judicial separation, where spouses have been living separate and apart for a continuous period of at least six months, where Court has pronounced a decree absolute of divorce or decree of nullity or proceedings for same have been commenced, or where the other spouse has committed an act amounting to dissipation of assets.

Powers of Court

Unequal division of family assets if equal division would be grossly unfair or unconscionable having regard to any extraordinary financial or other circumstances of the spouses or the extraordinary nature or value of any of their assets.

Unequal division of commercial assets if equal division would be clearly inequitable having regard to any circumstances the Court deems relevant. (13)

Accounting and division of assets valued at fair market value, with payment made by lump sum or installments or by transfer, conveyance or delivery of asset(s) or any combination of this.

Date of valuation

Date as agreed by spouses and in the absence of agreement the date when they last cohabited or where the application results from dissipation of assets, the date of the application to Court for an accounting and division.

Effect of agreement

Overrides statutory property rights.

NEW BRUNSWICK

Statute

Marital Property Act

Intent

Equal sharing of marital property, subject to equitable considerations and equal sharing of marital debts (2).

Jurisdiction

Court of Queen's Bench

Who may apply

A Spouse (married person); a person whose marriage is declared a nullity shall be deemed to have been a spouse during the period between the purported solemnization of marriage and the declaration of nullity (3).

When may order be made

Where a decree nisi of divorce is pronounced, or the marriage is declared a nullity or the spouses are living separate and apart and there is no reasonable prospect of the resumption of cohabitation, or the marriage is broken down, and there is no reasonable prospect of reconciliation whether or not the spouses are living separate and apart. The application must be made not later than 60 days after a spouse ceases to be a spouse by reason of a divorce or declaration of nullity (3).

Property included

Marital property which includes family assets and property owned by one or both spouses that is not a family asset and acquired while the spouses cohabited (1).

Property excluded

A business asset; property that was a gift from one spouse to the other including income from that property; property that was a gift from any other person to one spouse including income from that property; property that represents the proceeds of disposition of property that was not a family asset and that was not acquired while the spouses cohabited or in contemplation of marriage, or insurance proceeds from that property; property acquired by one spouse after cessation of cohabitation and that was acquired through the disposition of property that would have been marital property had the disposition not occurred (1).

Basic entitlement

Equal sharing of marital property.

Powers of Court

Partition, sale, payment out of proceeds of sale, transfer of property to or in trust for a child, posting of security, ancillary orders (10).

Unequal division of marital property on equitable grounds (7).

Division of property of either spouse that is not marital property on equitable grounds (8).

Fair and equitable division of marital debts taking into account any tax consequences that may arise from the division of property (9).

Date of valuation

Overrides Statutory property rights (40).

Effect of agreement

May be disregarded by the Court in matter involving the welfare of a child (38).

May be disregarded by the Court if it was made before the Act came into force and not made in contemplation of the Act or if it was entered into without independent legal advice, if the agreement would be inequitable in all the circumstances (41).

NEWFOUNDLAND

Statute

The Matrimonial Property Act

Intent

To reform the law with respect to matrimonial property in order to recognize the contribution made by each spouse to a marriage, give a one-half interest in the matrimonial home to each spouse, provide for the deferred sharing of most other property acquired during the marriage and provide for judicial discretion in sharing business assets built up by a spouse during the marriage.

Jurisdiction

Unified Family Court, Trial Division of the Supreme Court or the District Court (2.1).

Who may apply

A spouse, but not persons who have received a Decree Absolute of divorce or in relation to matrimonial assets provided for in a Separation Agreement before July 1, 1980 (2.3, 19).

When may order be made

Where divorce petition is filed, and marriage is declared a nullity, spouses have been separated and there is no reasonable prospect of the resumption of cohabitation or one of the spouses has died (19).

"Matrimonial Assets" which includes all real and personal property acquired by either or both spouses during the marriage, and "Business Assets" meaning property primarily used or held for or in connection with a commercial, business, investment or other income or profit-producing purpose (16).

Property excluded

Gifts, inheritances, trusts, or settlements received by one spouse from a person other than the other spouse and any appreciation in value of them during the marriage; personal injury awards except that portion that represents compensation for economic loss; personal effects; property exempted under a marriage contract or separation agreement; family heirlooms; and real and personal property acquired after separation.

Basic entitlement

Equal division of matrimonial assets. Sharing of business assets where one spouse has contributed work money or money's worth in respect of the acquisition, management, maintenance, operation or improvement of the business asset of the other spouse (19, 27).

Powers of Court

Order—equal division of matrimonial assets or unequal division if satisfied that a division of these assets in equal shares would be grossly unjust or unconscionable, (20). Order—title to specific property be transferred to or held in trust for a spouse; partition or sale; payment be made out of proceeds of sale; transfer property to or held in trust for a child; order security; order of payment; make declaratory orders as to ownership or right of possession; all necessary interim orders (24, 25).

Date of valuation

Unstated

Effect of agreement

Varies or excludes the application of this Act (41)

NOVA SCOTIA

Statute or source

Married Persons Property Act, 1978

Intent

Value of property to be divided equally between spouses on termination of marriage. (2, 6)

Jurisdiction

Trial Division of Supreme Court. (3)

Who may apply

Married persons both resident in the province at the time of termination of the marriage. (4)

When may application be made

On termination of marriage by death; application for divorce or annulment; after separation agreement; or upon determination that marriage has terminated. (7)

Property included

Real or personal property or any interest therein, wheresoever situate. (3, 4)

Property excluded

Property of spouse who has been living apart at least 3 years before Act comes into force, or where there is separation agreement; legacy, bequest, gift; property acquired before marriage. (3, 5)

Basic entitlement

Equal sharing. (9)

Powers of Court

Valuation and distribution of property, except that the spouse in whose name an asset is shall have the right to retain that asset as part of the share in the value of the property of the marriage, if not interfering with other's share. No power to make unequal division. (9)

Date of valuation

Date of termination of marriage. (7)

Effect of agreement

Overrides statute. If valid as contract, nonreviewable.

PRINCE EDWARD ISLAND

Statute

Family Law Reform Act.

Intent

Unstated.

Jurisdiction

Family Division of Supreme Court. (2)

Who may apply

Spouse. (5)

When application may be made

After separation, or in connection with divorce or annulment. (5)

Property included

Real or personal property or any interest therein. (4)

Property excluded

Net value of the equity of any property acquired by either spouse prior to date of marriage. (5)

Basic entitlement

Equal division of family assets, i.e., matrimonial home and property owned by one dr both spouses and ordinarily used . . . while residing together for household, educational, recreational, social and aesthetic purposes, except excluded property. (4)

Powers of the Court

Unequal division of family assets based on equitable considerations. (5)

Sharing of non-family assets based on contribution (9), or on equitable considerations (5).

Transfer of title, partition or sale, payment from proceeds of sale, transfer to trust for spouse or child, posting of security, ancillary orders. (7)

Date of valuation

Unstated. Implicitly, family assets at date of hearing, non-family assets at date of separation.

Effect of agreement

Overrides statutory property rights. (3) May be disregarded by Court in matter involving welfare of a child. (55) May be disregarded by Court as to provision for support or waiver of support if result is unconscionable, if dependent spouse qualifies for public support, or if there has been default in payment of support under the agreement. (19)

QUEBEC

Statute

Quebec Civil Code, principally Articles 462.1 to 462.17, 482, 483, 485, 495, 500, 503, 504, 505, 514, 517, 524.1 and 607.1 to 607.11; in force January 1, 1991

Appendix C

Intent

(a) recognize that both spouses contribute to the family's wealth, whatever their spousal and parental assignments are during the marriage;

(b) . . . permit dissolutions to be completed as efficiently as possible...

(c) [minimize post-divorce financial interaction] by giving each an immediate financial stake when the marriage is terminated.

"The object of this bill is to favour economic equity and to underline the character of marriage as a partnership"

Jurisdiction

Superior Court

Who may apply

Spouse; no provision for common-law relationships.

When may application be made

Subsequent to separation, divorce or annulment of marriage

Property included

Principal residence, secondary residence, household furniture, motor vehicles used for family travel, benefits accrued during marriage under a retirement plan, QPP pension plan

Property excluded

Business assets, and apparently all other property excluded

Basic entitlement

Equal sharing of the included property, called the entitlement   "family patrimony"

Powers of Court

Order payment in currency in installments spread over a period of not more than ten years; transfer of no more than half value of a pension plan; transfer other property as parties may agree; award ownership of property, particularly the family residence. Judicial discretion not to divide pension equally, considering brevity of marriage, waste of property by one spouse, or bad faith

Date of valuation

Date of institution of proceedings for separation, divorce or annulment

Effect of agreement

These rights cannot be renounced by spouses married agreement subsequent to July 1, 1989.

Note—These rights could be renounced by spouses married prior to July 1, 1989, if they did so by or before December 31, 1990.

These provisions do not apply to parties who separated prior to 1989, and settled the consequences of their separation by agreement in writing; or to spouses who instituted proceedings for separation, divorce or annulment prior to May 15, 1989.

SASKATCHEWAN

Statute

The Matrimonial Property Act

Intent

To recognize that child care, household management and financial provision are the joint and mutual responsibilities of spouses . . . that entitles each spouse to an equal distribution of the matrimonial property . . . (2)

Jurisdiction

Court of Queen's Bench, District Court or Unified Family Court

Who may apply

Spouse (1)

When may application be made

Apparently, any time, by a *spouse* (not former spouse); or within six months of a grant of probate or administration for estate of a deceased spouse.

Property included

Any real or personal property whatsoever, viz. "matrimonial property."

Property excluded

Fair market value of property at time of marriage owned by a spouse before marriage or acquired by a spouse before marriage by third party gift or inheritance.

Award or settlement of damages; insurance proceeds; property acquired after decree nisi, declaration of nullity, or a judgment of judicial separation; property exchanged for these; appreciation on or income from these.

Basic entitlement

"... Subject to any exceptions, exemptions and equitable considerations mentioned in this Act, order that matrimonial property or its value be distributed equally between the spouses."

Power of Court

Include or exclude any property from "matrimonial property." (23.4) If satisfied that it would be unfair and inequitable to make an equal distribution of matrimonial property or its value, refuse to order any distribution, order that all the matrimonial property be vested in one spouse; or make any other order that it considers fair and equitable. (21.2)

Partition, sale, transfer, lump sum, installments vesting, any other necessary order etc. (26)

Date of valuation

Unstated

Effect of agreement

If in writing, signed, witnessed; and if each spouse has independently acknowledged the nature and effect of the contract, overrides statutory property rights. (38)

Appendix D
Child Support Tables

Instructions for Simplified Federal Child Support Tables 174

Alberta..179

British Columbia 186

Manitoba 193

New Brunswick..200

Newfoundland...207

Nova Scotia 214

Ontario 221

Prince Edward Island 227

Saskatchewan 234

Divorce

FEDERAL CHILD SUPPORT AMOUNTS : SIMPLIFIED TABLES
MONTANTS FÉDÉRAUX DE PENSIONS ALIMENTAIRES POUR ENFANTS : TABLES SIMPLIFIÉES

How to use the simplified federal child support tables

NOTE: This document provides general information only. If you want more information contact the Department of Justice Canada. This is not a legal document. You may wish to consult a lawyer for advice on how this relates to your personal situation.

The Federal Child Support Guidelines include the rules for calculating the amount of child support, as well as a table of awards for each province and territory.

This sheet provides basic information to show how the Federal Child Support Guidelines apply in most cases. The Guidelines make the calculation of child support fair, predictable and consistent.

[**Note:** In certain cases, the amount of child support a court orders may be different from the amount shown on the tables because:

- there are special or extraordinary expenses (such as childcare; health expenses over $100 a year; education; extra-curricular activities);

- the court finds that the amounts determined by using the Guidelines cause undue hardship;

- parents have shared custody or access to the child at least 40% of the time;

- parents have split custody (each parent has at least one child in his or her custody);

- a child is the age of majority (18 or 19 years of age, depending on the province or territory) or over and has an ongoing need for support;

Comment utiliser les tables fédérales simplifiées de pensions alimentaires pour enfants

NOTA : Le présent document n'est fourni qu'à titre d'information. Pour plus de renseignements, veuillez communiquer avec le ministère de la Justice du Canada. Ce document n'a aucune valeur juridique. Il pourrait être bon de consulter un avocat pour savoir comment il s'applique à votre situation personnelle.

Les lignes directrices fédérales sur les pensions alimentaires pour enfants comportent les règles à suivre pour le calcul de la pension alimentaire pour enfants, ainsi qu'une table des montants d'ordonnances alimentaires pour chaque province et territoire.

Le présent document montre comment s'appliquent, dans la plupart des cas, les Lignes directrices fédérales sur les pensions alimentaires pour enfants. Grâce à ces lignes directrices, le calcul de ces pensions est juste, prévisible et uniforme.

[**Nota :** le montant de l'ordonnance de pension alimentaire pour enfants rendue par un tribunal peut être différent de celui indiqué dans les tables:

- s'il y a des dépenses spéciales ou extra-ordinaires (tels les frais de garde, les dépenses reliées à la santé de plus de 100 $ par année, l'éducation, les frais reliés aux activités para-scolaires);

- si le tribunal estime que les montants déterminés en utilisant les Lignes directrices occasionne des difficultés excessives;

- si les parents ont la garde partagée de l'enfant ou y ont accès au moins 40 % du temps;

- si les parents ont la garde exclusive (chaque parent a au moins un enfant sous sa garde);

- si l'enfant est majeur (s'il a 18 ou 19 ans, selon la province ou le territoire) et continue à avoir besoin d'une aide financière;

Note: This table shows amounts of child support based on income to the nearest $100. There is a mathematical formula for calculating specific child support amounts between the $100 levels. For more information, please contact the Department of Justice.
Nota: La présente table indique le montant de la pension alimentaire pour enfants à verser d'après le revenu (aux 100 $ près). Il existe une formule mathématique pour calculer le montant exact de la pension alimentaire pour enfants dans le cas des revenus qui se situent entre les tranches de 100 $. Pour plus de renseignements, veuillez communiquer avec le ministère de la Justice.

Appendix D

FEDERAL CHILD SUPPORT AMOUNTS : SIMPLIFIED TABLES
MONTANTS FÉDÉRAUX DE PENSIONS ALIMENTAIRES POUR ENFANTS : TABLES SIMPLIFIÉES

- the person paying support has an income of more than $150,000 a year;

- special provisions have been made for the child in an order or agreement.]

THE FOLLOWING STEPS WILL HELP YOU USE THE TABLES:

STEP 1

Do the Federal Child Support Guidelines apply to you?

As of May 1, 1997, the Federal Child Support Guidelines apply to:

- parents who want to change an existing child support order obtained under the *Divorce Act;*

- parents who will pay or receive child support further to a new child support order made under the *Divorce Act.*

There may be exceptions -- See Step 3.

STEP 2

What is the total annual income, before taxes, of the person who is paying, or will pay, child support?

Annual income is the money a person earns from employment and self-employment and income from investments. This includes all sources of income identified in your tax return (for example: salary, wages, commissions, UI, social assistance). If you are unsure, a T4 slip or Revenue Canada Assessment may give you an indication of annual income.

- si le parent qui paie la pension alimentaire a un revenu annuel de plus de 150 000 $;

- si des dispositions spéciales ont été prises pour l'enfant dans une ordonnance ou une entente.]

LES ÉTAPES SUIVANTES VOUS AIDERONT À UTILISER LES TABLES :

ÉTAPE 1

Les Lignes directrices fédérales sur les pensions alimentaires pour enfants, s'appliquent-elles à vous?

À compter du 1er mai 1997, les Lignes directrices fédérales sur les pensions alimentaires pour enfants seront applicables :

- aux parents qui veulent modifier une ordonnance de pension alimentaire pour enfants déjà rendue en vertu de la *Loi sur le divorce;*

- aux parents qui paieront ou recevront une pension alimentaire pour enfants conformément à une nouvelle ordonnance de pension alimentaire pour enfants qui sera rendue en vertu de la *Loi sur le divorce.*

Il pourrait y avoir des exceptions -- voir l'étape 3.

ÉTAPE 2

Quel est le revenu annuel total, avant impôts, de la personne qui paie ou aura à payer la pension alimentaire pour enfants?

Le revenu annuel comprend l'argent qu'une personne tire d'un emploi ou d'un travail autonome ainsi que les revenus de placements, c'est-à-dire les revenus de toutes provenances, inscrits dans votre déclaration de revenus (par ex., traitement, salaire, commissions, prestations d'assurance-emploi ou d'aide sociale). Dans le doute, le feuillet T4 ou l'avis de cotisation de Revenu Canada peut fournir une indication du revenu annuel.

Note: This table shows amounts of child support based on income to the nearest $100. There is a mathematical formula for calculating specific child support amounts between the $100 levels. For more information, please contact the Department of Justice.

Nota: La présente table indique le montant de la pension alimentaire pour enfants à verser d'après le revenu (aux 100 $ près). Il existe une formule mathématique pour calculer le montant exact de la pension alimentaire pour enfants dans le cas des revenus qui se situent entre les tranches de 100 $. Pour plus de renseignements, veuillez communiquer avec le ministère de la Justice.

Divorce

FEDERAL CHILD SUPPORT AMOUNTS : SIMPLIFIED TABLES
MONTANTS FÉDÉRAUX DE PENSIONS ALIMENTAIRES POUR ENFANTS : TABLES SIMPLIFIÉES

STEP 3

Which tables apply to your situation?

1. **Both parents live in the same province or territory.**

If the province or territory *does not have* its own guidelines for cases under the *Divorce Act*, use the federal tables for that province or territory.

However, if the province or territory *does have* its own child support guidelines, these guidelines will apply to cases under the *Divorce Act*.

2. **The person paying support lives in a different province or territory from the person receiving support.**

In this case, use the federal tables for the province or territory in which the person paying support lives.

3. **The person paying support lives outside Canada or the address is unknown.**

In this case, use the federal tables for the province or territory in which the person with custody of the child or children lives.

STEP 4

How much child support should be paid?

Once you have found the table you need to use, the amount of child support will be listed under the income level you identified in Step 2 and the number of children for whom you are determining child support.

ÉTAPE 3

Quelle table s'applique à vous?

1. **Les deux parents habitent dans la même province ou le même territoire.**

Si votre province ou territoire ne dispose pas de ses propres lignes directrices sur les pensions alimentaires pour enfants pour les cas régis par la *Loi sur le divorce*, utilisez les lignes directrices fédérales pour cette province ou ce territoire.

Toutefois, si la province ou le territoire dispose de ses propres lignes directrices, celles-ci s'appliqueront aux cas régis par la *Loi sur le divorce*.

2. **La personne qui paie la pension alimentaire et celle qui la reçoit n'habitent pas dans la même province ou le même territoire.**

Dans ce cas, utilisez la table fédérale applicable à la province ou au territoire où réside la personne qui paie la pension alimentaire.

3. **La personne qui paie la pension alimentaire habite à l'extérieur du Canada, ou son lieu de résidence est inconnu.**

Dans ce cas, utilisez la table fédérale applicable à la province ou au territoire où réside la personne ayant la garde de l'enfant ou des enfants.

ÉTAPE 4

Quel doit être le montant de la pension alimentaire à verser?

Après avoir déterminé la table que vous devez utiliser, le montant de la pension alimentaire apparaîtra sous le niveau de revenu que vous avez établi à l'étape 2 et le nombre d'enfants pour lesquels vous déterminez le montant de la pension alimentaire.

Note: This table shows amounts of child support based on income to the nearest $100. There is a mathematical formula for calculating specific child support amounts between the $100 levels. For more information, please contact the Department of Justice.

Nota: La présente table indique le montant de la pension alimentaire pour enfants à verser d'après le revenu (aux 100 $ près). Il existe une formule mathématique pour calculer le montant exact de la pension alimentaire pour enfants dans le cas des revenus qui se situent entre les tranches de 100 $. Pour plus de renseignements, veuillez communiquer avec le ministère de la Justice.

Appendix D

FEDERAL CHILD SUPPORT AMOUNTS : SIMPLIFIED TABLES
MONTANTS FÉDÉRAUX DE PENSIONS ALIMENTAIRES POUR ENFANTS : TABLES SIMPLIFIÉES

EXAMPLE (Step 4) / EXEMPLE (Étape 4)
Ontario

Income/ Revenu ($)	Monthly Award/ Paiement mensuel ($) No. of Children/ N^{bre} d'enfants			
	1	2	3	4
33200	291	483	637	738
33300	291	484	639	741
33400	292	486	640	743
33500	293	487	642	746
33600	294	488	643	748
33700	295	489	645	751
33800	296	491	647	753
33900	296	492	648	756

Note: This table is an example only. Please be sure you refer to the tables for the province or territory where the person paying support lives. The table amounts were calculated on the basis that child support payments are no longer taxable in the hands of the receiving parent nor deductible by the paying parent.

Nota : Cette table est un exemple. Veuillez vous référer à la table de la province ou du territoire où réside la personne qui doit payer la pension alimentaire pour enfants. Les montants de pensions alimentaires pour enfants, figurant dans les tables, tiennent compte du fait que ces pensions ne sont plus imposables pour les parents qui les reçoivent ni déductibles pour les parents qui les paient.

For example, let's say the person who is paying support lives in Ontario, has an income of $33,700 a year and has two children. The amount of child support would be $489 each month.

These tables cover one to four children. If you require the tables for five or more children, please get in touch with the Department of Justice Canada.

STEP 5

Can the amount be adjusted?

The amount of child support may be adjusted to recognize special expenses for the child or to prevent financial hardship for a parent or child in extraordinary circumstances.

For more information contact the Department of Justice Canada.

Voici, par exemple, la marche à suivre dans le cas d'une personne qui doit payer une pension alimentaire pour deux enfants, qui réside en Ontario et qui a un revenu annuel de 33 700 $. Le montant mensuel de la pension alimentaire pour enfants sera de 489 $.

Ces tables indiquent les montants de pensions alimentaires pour un à quatre enfants. Si vous désirez obtenir les tables pour cinq enfants ou plus, veuillez communiquer avec le ministère de la Justice du Canada.

ÉTAPE 5

Le montant peut-il être ajusté?

Le montant de la pension alimentaire pour enfants peut-être ajusté pour tenir compte des dépenses spéciales devant être engagées pour l'enfant, ou pour éviter d'occasionner des difficultés excessives à un parent ou à un enfant dans des circonstances exceptionnelles.

Pour plus d'information, veuillez communiquer avec le ministère de la Justice du Canada.

Note: This table shows amounts of child support based on income to the nearest $100. There is a mathematical formula for calculating specific child support amounts between the $100 levels. For more information, please contact the Department of Justice.

Nota: La présente table indique le montant de la pension alimentaire pour enfants à verser d'après le revenu (aux 100 $ près). Il existe une formule mathématique pour calculer le montant exact de la pension alimentaire pour enfants dans le cas des revenus qui se situent entre les tranches de 100 $. Pour plus de renseignements, veuillez communiquer avec le ministère de la Justice.

FEDERAL CHILD SUPPORT AMOUNTS : SIMPLIFIED TABLES
MONTANTS FÉDÉRAUX DE PENSIONS ALIMENTAIRES POUR ENFANTS : TABLES SIMPLIFIÉES

> The Department of Justice Canada has a toll-free number for information on the Guidelines. On request, we would be pleased to send you more detailed information as it becomes available. Call 1-888-373-2222. In the National Capital Region, call 946-2222. The Department of Justice Canada's Internet address is: http://canada.justice.gc.ca
>
> Le ministère de la Justice du Canada offre un service d'information sans frais sur les Lignes directrices. Nous nous ferons un plaisir de vous envoyer sur demande, des renseignements plus détaillés au fur et à mesure qu'ils seront disponibles. Composez le 1-888-373-2222. Dans la Région de la capitale nationale, faites le 946-2222. L'adresse Internet du ministère de la Justice du Canada est : http://canada.justice.gc.ca

Note: This table shows amounts of child support based on income to the nearest $100. There is a mathematical formula for calculating specific child support amounts between the $100 levels. For more information, please contact the Department of Justice.

Nota: La présente table indique le montant de la pension alimentaire pour enfants à verser d'après le revenu (aux 100 $ près). Il existe une formule mathématique pour calculer le montant exact de la pension alimentaire pour enfants dans le cas des revenus qui se situent entre les tranches de 100 $. Pour plus de renseignements, veuillez communiquer avec le ministère de la Justice.

Appendix D

ALBERTA

FEDERAL CHILD SUPPORT AMOUNTS : SIMPLIFIED TABLES
MONTANTS FÉDÉRAUX DE PENSIONS ALIMENTAIRES POUR ENFANTS : TABLES SIMPLIFIÉES

1997

Income/ Revenu ($)	Monthly Award/ Paiement mensuel ($) No. of Children/ N^{bre} d'enfants				Income/ Revenu ($)	Monthly Award/ Paiement mensuel ($) No. of Children/ N^{bre} d'enfants				Income/ Revenu ($)	Monthly Award/ Paiement mensuel ($) No. of Children/ N^{bre} d'enfants				Income/ Revenu ($)	Monthly Award/ Paiement mensuel ($) No. of Children/ N^{bre} d'enfants			
	1	2	3	4		1	2	3	4		1	2	3	4		1	2	3	4
6700	0	0	0	0	12000	109	169	191	213	17300	142	256	348	394	22600	200	343	457	550
6800	0	0	0	0	12100	109	172	194	217	17400	143	258	350	398	22700	201	344	459	553
6900	0	0	0	1	12200	110	175	197	220	17500	144	260	352	402	22800	202	346	461	555
7000	2	3	4	5	12300	110	177	200	224	17600	145	261	354	405	22900	203	347	463	557
7100	5	7	8	10	12400	111	180	203	227	17700	146	263	356	409	23000	204	349	465	559
7200	9	11	13	15	12500	111	182	206	230	17800	147	264	358	413	23100	205	350	467	562
7300	12	14	17	19	12600	111	185	209	234	17900	148	266	360	417	23200	206	352	469	564
7400	15	18	21	24	12700	112	187	212	237	18000	149	268	363	420	23300	207	353	471	566
7500	19	22	25	28	12800	112	190	215	241	18100	150	269	365	424	23400	208	355	472	569
7600	22	26	29	33	12900	112	193	218	244	18200	151	271	367	428	23500	209	356	474	571
7700	25	29	33	37	13000	113	195	221	247	18300	152	273	369	432	23600	210	358	476	573
7800	29	33	37	42	13100	113	198	224	251	18400	154	274	371	435	23700	211	359	478	576
7900	32	37	42	46	13200	114	200	227	254	18500	155	276	373	439	23800	212	361	480	578
8000	35	40	46	51	13300	114	203	230	258	18600	156	277	375	443	23900	213	362	482	580
8100	38	44	50	56	13400	114	206	233	261	18700	157	279	377	447	24000	214	364	484	582
8200	42	48	54	60	13500	115	208	236	265	18800	158	281	379	450	24100	215	365	486	585
8300	45	52	58	65	13600	115	210	239	268	18900	159	282	381	454	24200	216	367	488	587
8400	48	55	62	69	13700	116	211	242	271	19000	160	284	383	458	24300	217	368	490	589
8500	52	59	66	74	13800	116	212	245	275	19100	161	286	385	462	24400	218	370	492	592
8600	55	63	71	78	13900	116	213	248	278	19200	162	287	387	465	24500	219	372	494	594
8700	58	66	75	83	14000	117	214	251	282	19300	164	289	389	469	24600	220	373	496	596
8800	62	70	79	87	14100	117	215	254	285	19400	165	291	391	473	24700	221	375	498	598
8900	65	74	83	92	14200	118	216	257	288	19500	166	292	393	476	24800	222	376	500	601
9000	68	78	87	97	14300	118	217	260	292	19600	167	294	395	478	24900	223	378	502	603
9100	72	81	91	101	14400	119	218	263	295	19700	168	295	397	481	25000	223	379	504	605
9200	75	85	95	106	14500	119	220	266	299	19800	169	297	399	483	25100	224	381	505	608
9300	78	89	100	110	14600	120	221	269	302	19900	170	299	401	486	25200	225	382	507	610
9400	81	93	104	115	14700	120	222	272	306	20000	171	300	404	488	25300	226	384	509	612
9500	85	96	108	119	14800	121	223	275	309	20100	172	302	406	490	25400	227	385	511	615
9600	88	100	112	124	14900	121	224	278	312	20200	173	304	408	493	25500	228	387	513	617
9700	91	104	116	128	15000	122	225	281	316	20300	175	305	410	495	25600	229	388	515	619
9800	95	107	120	133	15100	122	226	284	319	20400	176	307	412	498	25700	230	390	517	621
9900	98	111	124	138	15200	123	227	287	323	20500	177	308	414	500	25800	231	391	519	624
10000	101	115	128	142	15300	123	228	290	326	20600	178	310	416	502	25900	232	393	521	626
10100	102	118	132	146	15400	125	229	293	329	20700	179	312	418	505	26000	233	394	523	628
10200	102	120	135	149	15500	125	231	296	333	20800	180	313	420	507	26100	234	395	525	630
10300	102	123	138	153	15600	126	232	299	336	20900	181	315	422	510	26200	235	397	526	632
10400	103	126	141	156	15700	127	234	302	340	21000	182	317	424	512	26300	236	398	528	635
10500	103	129	144	160	15800	128	235	305	343	21100	183	318	426	514	26400	237	400	530	637
10600	104	131	147	164	15900	129	236	308	347	21200	185	320	428	517	26500	238	401	532	639
10700	104	134	151	167	16000	130	238	311	350	21300	186	321	430	519	26600	239	402	534	641
10800	104	137	154	171	16100	131	239	314	353	21400	187	323	432	521	26700	239	404	535	643
10900	105	140	157	174	16200	131	241	317	357	21500	188	325	434	524	26800	240	405	537	645
11000	105	142	160	178	16300	132	242	320	360	21600	189	326	436	526	26900	241	407	539	647
11100	105	145	163	182	16400	133	244	323	364	21700	190	328	438	529	27000	242	408	541	650
11200	106	148	166	185	16500	134	245	326	367	21800	191	330	440	531	27100	243	410	543	652
11300	106	151	170	189	16600	135	246	329	370	21900	192	331	442	533	27200	244	411	544	654
11400	107	153	173	192	16700	136	248	332	374	22000	193	333	445	536	27300	245	412	546	656
11500	107	156	176	196	16800	137	249	335	377	22100	194	335	447	538	27400	246	414	548	658
11600	107	159	179	199	16900	138	251	338	381	22200	196	336	449	541	27500	247	415	550	660
11700	108	162	182	203	17000	139	252	341	384	22300	197	338	451	543	27600	248	417	552	662
11800	108	164	185	206	17100	140	254	344	388	22400	198	339	453	545	27700	248	418	553	664
11900	109	167	188	210	17200	141	255	346	391	22500	199	341	455	548	27800	249	419	555	667

Note: This table shows amounts of child support based on income to the nearest $100. There is a mathematical formula for calculating specific child support amounts between the $100 levels. For more information, please contact the Department of Justice.

Nota: La présente table indique le montant de la pension alimentaire pour enfants à verser d'après le revenu (aux 100 $ près). Il existe une formule mathématique pour calculer le montant exact de la pension alimentaire pour enfants dans le cas des revenus qui se situent entre les tranches de 100 $. Pour plus de renseignements, veuillez communiquer avec le ministère de la Justice.

Divorce

ALBERTA
1997

FEDERAL CHILD SUPPORT AMOUNTS : SIMPLIFIED TABLES
MONTANTS FÉDÉRAUX DE PENSIONS ALIMENTAIRES POUR ENFANTS : TABLES SIMPLIFIÉES

Income/Revenu ($)	Monthly Award/Paiement mensuel ($) No. of Children/N^{bre} d'enfants				Income/Revenu ($)	Monthly Award/Paiement mensuel ($) No. of Children/N^{bre} d'enfants				Income/Revenu ($)	Monthly Award/Paiement mensuel ($) No. of Children/N^{bre} d'enfants				Income/Revenu ($)	Monthly Award/Paiement mensuel ($) No. of Children/N^{bre} d'enfants			
	1	2	3	4		1	2	3	4		1	2	3	4		1	2	3	4
27900	250	421	557	669	33200	292	486	641	768	38500	335	552	726	868	43800	379	621	815	973
28000	251	422	559	671	33300	293	487	642	770	38600	335	553	727	870	43900	380	622	816	975
28100	252	424	561	673	33400	294	488	644	771	38700	336	554	729	872	44000	381	624	818	977
28200	253	425	563	675	33500	295	490	646	773	38800	337	556	731	874	44100	382	625	820	979
28300	254	426	564	677	33600	295	491	647	775	38900	338	557	732	876	44200	382	626	821	981
28400	255	428	566	679	33700	296	492	649	777	39000	339	558	734	878	44300	383	628	823	983
28500	256	429	568	681	33800	297	493	650	779	39100	339	559	736	880	44400	384	629	825	985
28600	257	431	570	684	33900	298	494	652	781	39200	340	561	737	881	44500	385	630	826	987
28700	257	432	572	686	34000	298	496	653	783	39300	341	562	739	883	44600	386	631	828	989
28800	258	433	573	688	34100	299	497	655	784	39400	342	563	740	885	44700	387	633	830	991
28900	259	435	575	690	34200	300	498	657	786	39500	343	565	742	887	44800	387	634	831	993
29000	260	436	577	692	34300	301	499	658	788	39600	344	566	744	889	44900	388	635	833	995
29100	261	438	579	694	34400	302	501	660	790	39700	344	567	745	891	45000	389	637	835	997
29200	262	439	581	696	34500	302	502	661	792	39800	345	568	747	893	45100	390	638	837	999
29300	263	440	582	699	34600	303	503	663	794	39900	346	570	749	895	45200	391	639	838	1001
29400	264	442	584	701	34700	304	504	664	796	40000	347	571	750	897	45300	392	641	840	1003
29500	265	443	586	703	34800	305	505	666	797	40100	348	572	752	899	45400	393	642	842	1005
29600	266	445	588	705	34900	306	507	668	799	40200	349	574	754	901	45500	393	643	843	1007
29700	266	446	589	707	35000	306	508	669	801	40300	349	575	755	903	45600	394	645	845	1009
29800	267	447	591	708	35100	307	509	671	803	40400	350	576	757	905	45700	395	646	847	1011
29900	268	448	592	710	35200	308	510	672	805	40500	351	578	759	907	45800	396	647	848	1013
30000	268	449	593	712	35300	309	512	674	807	40600	352	579	760	909	45900	397	648	850	1015
30100	269	451	595	713	35400	309	513	675	809	40700	353	580	762	911	46000	397	650	851	1017
30200	270	451	596	715	35500	310	514	677	810	40800	354	581	764	913	46100	398	651	853	1019
30300	271	452	598	717	35600	311	515	679	812	40900	354	583	765	915	46200	399	652	855	1020
30400	271	453	599	718	35700	312	516	680	814	41000	355	584	767	917	46300	400	653	856	1022
30500	272	455	601	720	35800	313	518	682	816	41100	356	585	769	919	46400	401	655	858	1024
30600	273	456	602	722	35900	313	519	683	818	41200	357	587	771	921	46500	401	656	860	1026
30700	273	457	603	723	36000	314	520	685	820	41300	358	588	772	923	46600	402	657	861	1028
30800	274	458	605	725	36100	315	521	687	822	41400	359	589	774	925	46700	403	658	863	1030
30900	275	459	606	727	36200	316	523	688	824	41500	360	591	776	927	46800	404	660	865	1032
31000	276	460	608	729	36300	317	524	690	826	41600	360	592	777	929	46900	405	661	866	1034
31100	276	461	609	730	36400	317	525	691	827	41700	361	593	779	931	47000	405	662	868	1036
31200	277	462	611	732	36500	318	527	693	829	41800	362	595	781	933	47100	406	664	869	1038
31300	278	463	612	734	36600	319	528	695	831	41900	363	596	782	935	47200	407	665	871	1040
31400	278	465	613	735	36700	320	529	696	833	42000	364	597	784	937	47300	408	666	873	1042
31500	279	466	615	737	36800	321	530	698	835	42100	365	599	786	939	47400	409	667	874	1044
31600	280	467	616	739	36900	322	532	700	837	42200	365	600	787	941	47500	409	669	876	1046
31700	281	468	618	740	37000	322	533	701	839	42300	366	601	789	943	47600	410	670	878	1048
31800	281	469	619	742	37100	323	534	703	841	42400	367	603	791	945	47700	411	671	879	1050
31900	282	470	621	744	37200	324	535	705	843	42500	368	604	793	947	47800	412	672	881	1052
32000	283	471	622	745	37300	325	537	706	845	42600	369	605	794	949	47900	413	674	883	1054
32100	284	472	624	747	37400	326	538	708	847	42700	370	606	796	951	48000	413	675	884	1055
32200	284	474	625	749	37500	326	539	709	849	42800	371	608	798	953	48100	414	676	886	1057
32300	285	475	627	751	37600	327	540	711	851	42900	371	609	799	955	48200	415	677	887	1059
32400	286	476	628	753	37700	328	542	713	853	43000	372	610	801	957	48300	416	679	889	1061
32500	287	477	630	755	37800	329	543	714	854	43100	373	612	803	959	48400	417	680	891	1063
32600	287	479	631	757	37900	330	544	716	856	43200	374	613	804	961	48500	417	681	892	1065
32700	288	480	633	758	38000	330	546	718	858	43300	375	614	806	963	48600	418	683	894	1067
32800	289	481	635	760	38100	331	547	719	860	43400	376	616	808	965	48700	419	684	896	1069
32900	290	482	636	762	38200	332	548	721	862	43500	376	617	809	967	48800	420	685	897	1071
33000	291	483	638	764	38300	333	549	722	864	43600	377	618	811	969	48900	421	686	899	1073
33100	291	485	639	766	38400	334	551	724	866	43700	378	620	813	971	49000	421	688	901	1075

Note: This table shows amounts of child support based on income to the nearest $100. There is a mathematical formula for calculating specific child support amounts between the $100 levels. For more information, please contact the Department of Justice.

Nota: La présente table indique le montant de la pension alimentaire pour enfants à verser d'après le revenu (aux 100 $ près). Il existe une formule mathématique pour calculer le montant exact de la pension alimentaire pour enfants dans le cas des revenus qui se situent entre les tranches de 100 $. Pour plus de renseignements, veuillez communiquer avec le ministère de la Justice.

Appendix D

ALBERTA
1997

FEDERAL CHILD SUPPORT AMOUNTS : SIMPLIFIED TABLES
MONTANTS FÉDÉRAUX DE PENSIONS ALIMENTAIRES POUR ENFANTS : TABLES SIMPLIFIÉES

Income/ Revenu ($)	Monthly Award/ Paiement mensuel ($) No. of Children/ N^{bre} d'enfants				Income/ Revenu ($)	Monthly Award/ Paiement mensuel ($) No. of Children/ N^{bre} d'enfants				Income/ Revenu ($)	Monthly Award/ Paiement mensuel ($) No. of Children/ N^{bre} d'enfants				Income/ Revenu ($)	Monthly Award/ Paiement mensuel ($) No. of Children/ N^{bre} d'enfants			
	1	2	3	4		1	2	3	4		1	2	3	4		1	2	3	4
49100	422	689	902	1077	54400	466	758	991	1181	59700	510	826	1078	1285	65000	550	888	1158	1380
49200	423	690	904	1079	54500	467	759	992	1183	59800	511	827	1080	1286	65100	550	889	1160	1381
49300	424	691	906	1081	54600	468	760	994	1185	59900	512	828	1081	1288	65200	551	890	1161	1383
49400	425	693	907	1083	54700	469	761	996	1187	60000	512	829	1083	1290	65300	552	891	1163	1385
49500	425	694	909	1085	54800	470	763	997	1189	60100	513	830	1084	1292	65400	553	892	1164	1387
49600	426	695	911	1087	54900	470	764	999	1191	60200	514	832	1086	1294	65500	553	893	1166	1388
49700	427	697	912	1089	55000	471	765	1001	1193	60300	515	833	1087	1296	65600	554	895	1167	1390
49800	428	698	914	1091	55100	472	767	1002	1195	60400	515	834	1089	1297	65700	555	896	1169	1392
49900	429	699	916	1093	55200	473	768	1004	1197	60500	516	835	1090	1299	65800	555	897	1170	1394
50000	430	701	917	1095	55300	474	769	1006	1199	60600	517	836	1092	1301	65900	556	898	1171	1395
50100	430	702	919	1097	55400	475	770	1007	1201	60700	518	838	1093	1303	66000	557	899	1173	1397
50200	431	703	921	1099	55500	475	772	1009	1203	60800	519	839	1095	1305	66100	557	900	1174	1399
50300	432	704	922	1100	55600	476	773	1011	1205	60900	519	840	1097	1306	66200	558	901	1176	1400
50400	433	706	924	1102	55700	477	774	1012	1207	61000	520	841	1098	1308	66300	559	902	1177	1402
50500	434	707	926	1104	55800	478	776	1014	1209	61100	521	842	1100	1310	66400	559	904	1179	1404
50600	435	708	927	1106	55900	479	777	1016	1211	61200	522	844	1101	1312	66500	560	905	1180	1406
50700	435	710	929	1108	56000	480	778	1017	1213	61300	522	845	1103	1314	66600	561	906	1182	1407
50800	436	711	931	1110	56100	480	780	1019	1215	61400	523	846	1104	1316	66700	562	907	1183	1409
50900	437	712	932	1112	56200	481	781	1021	1217	61500	524	847	1106	1317	66800	562	908	1185	1411
51000	438	714	934	1114	56300	482	782	1022	1219	61600	525	848	1107	1319	66900	563	909	1186	1413
51100	439	715	936	1116	56400	483	783	1024	1221	61700	525	850	1109	1321	67000	564	910	1188	1415
51200	440	716	937	1118	56500	484	785	1026	1222	61800	526	851	1110	1323	67100	565	912	1189	1416
51300	440	717	939	1120	56600	485	786	1027	1224	61900	527	852	1112	1325	67200	565	913	1191	1418
51400	441	719	941	1122	56700	485	787	1029	1226	62000	528	853	1113	1326	67300	566	914	1192	1420
51500	442	720	942	1124	56800	486	789	1030	1228	62100	529	854	1115	1328	67400	567	915	1194	1422
51600	443	721	944	1126	56900	487	790	1032	1230	62200	529	856	1117	1330	67500	568	916	1195	1423
51700	444	723	946	1128	57000	488	791	1034	1232	62300	530	857	1118	1332	67600	568	917	1197	1425
51800	445	724	947	1130	57100	489	792	1035	1234	62400	531	858	1120	1334	67700	569	919	1198	1427
51900	445	725	949	1132	57200	490	794	1037	1236	62500	532	859	1121	1336	67800	570	920	1200	1429
52000	446	726	951	1134	57300	490	795	1039	1238	62600	532	860	1123	1337	67900	571	921	1201	1430
52100	447	728	952	1136	57400	491	796	1040	1240	62700	533	862	1124	1339	68000	571	922	1203	1432
52200	448	729	954	1138	57500	492	798	1042	1242	62800	534	863	1126	1341	68100	572	923	1204	1434
52300	449	730	956	1140	57600	493	799	1044	1244	62900	535	864	1127	1343	68200	573	924	1206	1436
52400	450	732	957	1142	57700	494	800	1045	1246	63000	535	865	1129	1345	68300	574	926	1207	1438
52500	450	733	959	1144	57800	495	802	1047	1248	63100	536	866	1130	1346	68400	574	927	1209	1439
52600	451	734	961	1146	57900	495	803	1049	1250	63200	537	868	1132	1348	68500	575	928	1210	1441
52700	452	736	962	1148	58000	496	804	1050	1252	63300	538	869	1133	1350	68600	576	929	1212	1443
52800	453	737	964	1150	58100	497	805	1052	1254	63400	539	870	1135	1352	68700	577	930	1213	1445
52900	454	738	966	1152	58200	498	807	1054	1256	63500	539	871	1136	1354	68800	577	931	1215	1446
53000	455	739	967	1154	58300	499	808	1055	1258	63600	540	872	1138	1355	68900	578	933	1216	1448
53100	455	741	969	1156	58400	500	809	1057	1260	63700	541	873	1139	1357	69000	579	934	1218	1450
53200	456	742	971	1158	58500	500	811	1059	1262	63800	541	874	1141	1359	69100	580	935	1219	1452
53300	457	743	972	1160	58600	501	812	1060	1264	63900	542	876	1142	1361	69200	580	936	1221	1453
53400	458	745	974	1161	58700	502	813	1062	1266	64000	543	877	1144	1362	69300	581	937	1222	1455
53500	459	746	976	1163	58800	503	815	1064	1268	64100	543	878	1145	1364	69400	582	938	1224	1457
53600	460	747	977	1165	58900	504	816	1065	1270	64200	544	879	1147	1366	69500	583	940	1225	1459
53700	460	748	979	1167	59000	505	817	1067	1272	64300	545	880	1148	1368	69600	583	941	1227	1461
53800	461	750	981	1169	59100	505	818	1069	1274	64400	546	881	1150	1369	69700	584	942	1228	1462
53900	462	751	982	1171	59200	506	820	1070	1276	64500	546	882	1151	1371	69800	585	943	1230	1464
54000	463	752	984	1173	59300	507	821	1072	1277	64600	547	883	1153	1373	69900	586	944	1231	1466
54100	464	754	986	1175	59400	508	822	1073	1279	64700	548	884	1154	1374	70000	586	945	1233	1468
54200	465	755	987	1177	59500	509	823	1075	1281	64800	548	886	1155	1376	70100	587	947	1234	1469
54300	465	756	989	1179	59600	509	824	1077	1283	64900	549	887	1157	1378	70200	588	948	1236	1471

Note: This table shows amounts of child support based on income to the nearest $100. There is a mathematical formula for calculating specific child support amounts between the $100 levels. For more information, please contact the Department of Justice.

Nota: La présente table indique le montant de la pension alimentaire pour enfants à verser d'après le revenu (aux 100 $ près). Il existe une formule mathématique pour calculer le montant exact de la pension alimentaire pour enfants dans le cas des revenus qui se situent entre les tranches de 100 $. Pour plus de renseignements, veuillez communiquer avec le ministère de la Justice.

Divorce

ALBERTA

FEDERAL CHILD SUPPORT AMOUNTS : SIMPLIFIED TABLES
MONTANTS FÉDÉRAUX DE PENSIONS ALIMENTAIRES POUR ENFANTS : TABLES SIMPLIFIÉES

1997

Income/ Revenu ($)	Monthly Award/ Paiement mensuel ($) No. of Children/ N^{bre} d'enfants				Income/ Revenu ($)	Monthly Award/ Paiement mensuel ($) No. of Children/ N^{bre} d'enfants				Income/ Revenu ($)	Monthly Award/ Paiement mensuel ($) No. of Children/ N^{bre} d'enfants				Income/ Revenu ($)	Monthly Award/ Paiement mensuel ($) No. of Children/ N^{bre} d'enfants			
	1	2	3	4		1	2	3	4		1	2	3	4		1	2	3	4
70300	589	949	1237	1473	75600	628	1011	1317	1567	80900	668	1072	1396	1661	86200	708	1134	1475	1754
70400	589	950	1239	1475	75700	629	1012	1318	1569	81000	669	1074	1397	1662	86300	708	1135	1477	1756
70500	590	951	1240	1476	75800	630	1013	1320	1570	81100	670	1075	1399	1664	86400	709	1136	1478	1758
70600	591	952	1242	1478	75900	631	1014	1321	1572	81200	670	1076	1400	1666	86500	710	1138	1480	1760
70700	592	954	1243	1480	76000	631	1015	1323	1574	81300	671	1077	1402	1668	86600	711	1139	1481	1762
70800	592	955	1245	1482	76100	632	1016	1324	1576	81400	672	1078	1403	1669	86700	711	1140	1483	1763
70900	593	956	1246	1484	76200	633	1018	1326	1577	81500	673	1079	1405	1671	86800	712	1141	1484	1765
71000	594	957	1248	1485	76300	634	1019	1327	1579	81600	673	1081	1406	1673	86900	713	1142	1486	1767
71100	595	958	1249	1487	76400	634	1020	1329	1581	81700	674	1082	1408	1675	87000	714	1143	1487	1769
71200	595	959	1251	1489	76500	635	1021	1330	1583	81800	675	1083	1409	1677	87100	714	1145	1489	1770
71300	596	961	1252	1491	76600	636	1022	1332	1584	81900	676	1084	1411	1678	87200	715	1146	1490	1772
71400	597	962	1254	1492	76700	637	1023	1333	1586	82000	676	1085	1412	1680	87300	716	1147	1492	1774
71500	598	963	1255	1494	76800	637	1025	1334	1588	82100	677	1086	1414	1682	87400	717	1148	1493	1776
71600	598	964	1257	1496	76900	638	1026	1336	1590	82200	678	1088	1415	1684	87500	717	1149	1495	1777
71700	599	965	1258	1498	77000	639	1027	1337	1592	82300	679	1089	1417	1685	87600	718	1150	1496	1779
71800	600	966	1260	1499	77100	640	1028	1339	1593	82400	679	1090	1418	1687	87700	719	1152	1498	1781
71900	601	968	1261	1501	77200	640	1029	1340	1595	82500	680	1091	1420	1689	87800	720	1153	1499	1783
72000	601	969	1263	1503	77300	641	1030	1342	1597	82600	681	1092	1421	1691	87900	720	1154	1501	1785
72100	602	970	1264	1505	77400	642	1032	1343	1599	82700	681	1093	1423	1692	88000	721	1155	1502	1786
72200	603	971	1266	1507	77500	643	1033	1345	1600	82800	682	1095	1424	1694	88100	722	1156	1504	1788
72300	604	972	1267	1508	77600	643	1034	1346	1602	82900	683	1096	1426	1696	88200	723	1157	1505	1790
72400	604	973	1269	1510	77700	644	1035	1348	1604	83000	684	1097	1427	1698	88300	723	1159	1507	1792
72500	605	975	1270	1512	77800	645	1036	1349	1606	83100	684	1098	1429	1700	88400	724	1160	1508	1793
72600	606	976	1272	1514	77900	646	1037	1351	1607	83200	685	1099	1430	1701	88500	725	1161	1510	1795
72700	607	977	1273	1515	78000	646	1039	1352	1609	83300	686	1100	1432	1703	88600	726	1162	1511	1797
72800	607	978	1275	1517	78100	647	1040	1354	1611	83400	687	1102	1433	1705	88700	726	1163	1513	1799
72900	608	979	1276	1519	78200	648	1041	1355	1613	83500	687	1103	1435	1707	88800	727	1164	1514	1800
73000	609	980	1278	1521	78300	649	1042	1357	1615	83600	688	1104	1436	1708	88900	728	1166	1516	1802
73100	610	982	1279	1523	78400	649	1043	1358	1616	83700	689	1105	1438	1710	89000	729	1167	1517	1804
73200	610	983	1281	1524	78500	650	1044	1360	1618	83800	690	1106	1439	1712	89100	729	1168	1519	1806
73300	611	984	1282	1526	78600	651	1046	1361	1620	83900	690	1107	1441	1714	89200	730	1169	1520	1808
73400	612	985	1284	1528	78700	652	1047	1363	1622	84000	691	1109	1442	1715	89300	731	1170	1522	1809
73500	613	986	1285	1530	78800	652	1048	1364	1623	84100	692	1110	1444	1717	89400	732	1171	1523	1811
73600	613	987	1287	1531	78900	653	1049	1366	1625	84200	693	1111	1445	1719	89500	732	1173	1525	1813
73700	614	989	1288	1533	79000	654	1050	1367	1627	84300	693	1112	1447	1721	89600	733	1174	1526	1815
73800	615	990	1290	1535	79100	655	1051	1369	1629	84400	694	1113	1448	1723	89700	734	1175	1528	1816
73900	616	991	1291	1537	79200	655	1053	1370	1631	84500	695	1114	1450	1724	89800	735	1176	1529	1818
74000	616	992	1293	1538	79300	656	1054	1372	1632	84600	696	1116	1451	1726	89900	735	1177	1531	1820
74100	617	993	1294	1540	79400	657	1055	1373	1634	84700	696	1117	1453	1728	90000	736	1178	1532	1822
74200	618	994	1296	1542	79500	658	1056	1375	1636	84800	697	1118	1454	1730	90100	737	1180	1534	1823
74300	619	996	1297	1544	79600	658	1057	1376	1638	84900	698	1119	1456	1731	90200	738	1181	1535	1825
74400	619	997	1299	1546	79700	659	1058	1378	1639	85000	699	1120	1457	1733	90300	738	1182	1537	1827
74500	620	998	1300	1547	79800	660	1060	1379	1641	85100	699	1121	1459	1735	90400	739	1183	1538	1829
74600	621	999	1302	1549	79900	661	1061	1381	1643	85200	700	1123	1460	1737	90500	740	1184	1540	1831
74700	622	1000	1303	1551	80000	661	1062	1382	1645	85300	701	1124	1462	1739	90600	741	1185	1541	1832
74800	622	1001	1305	1553	80100	662	1063	1384	1646	85400	702	1125	1463	1740	90700	741	1187	1543	1834
74900	623	1002	1306	1554	80200	663	1064	1385	1648	85500	702	1126	1465	1742	90800	742	1188	1544	1836
75000	624	1004	1308	1556	80300	664	1065	1387	1650	85600	703	1127	1466	1744	90900	743	1189	1546	1838
75100	625	1005	1309	1558	80400	664	1067	1388	1652	85700	704	1128	1468	1746	91000	744	1190	1547	1839
75200	625	1006	1311	1560	80500	665	1068	1390	1654	85800	705	1129	1469	1747	91100	744	1191	1549	1841
75300	626	1007	1312	1561	80600	666	1069	1391	1655	85900	705	1131	1471	1749	91200	745	1192	1550	1843
75400	627	1008	1314	1563	80700	667	1070	1393	1657	86000	706	1132	1472	1751	91300	746	1194	1552	1845
75500	628	1009	1315	1565	80800	667	1071	1394	1659	86100	707	1133	1474	1753	91400	747	1195	1553	1847

Note: This table shows amounts of child support based on income to the nearest $100. There is a mathematical formula for calculating specific child support amounts between the $100 levels. For more information, please contact the Department of Justice.

Nota: La présente table indique le montant de la pension alimentaire pour enfants à verser d'après le revenu (aux 100 $ près). Il existe une formule mathématique pour calculer le montant exact de la pension alimentaire pour enfants dans le cas des revenus qui se situent entre les tranches de 100 $. Pour plus de renseignements, veuillez communiquer avec le ministère de la Justice.

Appendix D

ALBERTA
1997

FEDERAL CHILD SUPPORT AMOUNTS : SIMPLIFIED TABLES
MONTANTS FÉDÉRAUX DE PENSIONS ALIMENTAIRES POUR ENFANTS : TABLES SIMPLIFIÉES

Income/ Revenu ($)	Monthly Award/ Paiement mensuel ($) No. of Children/ N^{bre} d'enfants				Income/ Revenu ($)	Monthly Award/ Paiement mensuel ($) No. of Children/ N^{bre} d'enfants				Income/ Revenu ($)	Monthly Award/ Paiement mensuel ($) No. of Children/ N^{bre} d'enfants				Income/ Revenu ($)	Monthly Award/ Paiement mensuel ($) No. of Children/ N^{bre} d'enfants			
	1	2	3	4		1	2	3	4		1	2	3	4		1	2	3	4
91500	747	1196	1555	1848	*96800*	787	1258	1634	1942	*102100*	827	1319	1714	2036	*107400*	867	1381	1793	2130
91600	748	1197	1556	1850	*96900*	788	1259	1636	1944	*102200*	828	1321	1715	2038	*107500*	867	1382	1794	2132
91700	749	1198	1558	1852	*97000*	789	1260	1637	1946	*102300*	828	1322	1716	2039	*107600*	868	1383	1796	2133
91800	750	1199	1559	1854	*97100*	789	1261	1639	1947	*102400*	829	1323	1718	2041	*107700*	869	1385	1797	2135
91900	750	1201	1561	1855	*97200*	790	1262	1640	1949	*102500*	830	1324	1719	2043	*107800*	870	1386	1799	2137
92000	751	1202	1562	1857	*97300*	791	1263	1642	1951	*102600*	831	1325	1721	2045	*107900*	870	1387	1800	2139
92100	752	1203	1564	1859	*97400*	792	1265	1643	1953	*102700*	831	1326	1722	2047	*108000*	871	1388	1802	2140
92200	753	1204	1565	1861	*97500*	792	1266	1645	1954	*102800*	832	1328	1724	2048	*108100*	872	1389	1803	2142
92300	753	1205	1567	1862	*97600*	793	1267	1646	1956	*102900*	833	1329	1725	2050	*108200*	872	1390	1805	2144
92400	754	1206	1568	1864	*97700*	794	1268	1648	1958	*103000*	834	1330	1727	2052	*108300*	873	1392	1806	2146
92500	755	1208	1570	1866	*97800*	795	1269	1649	1960	*103100*	834	1331	1728	2054	*108400*	874	1393	1808	2147
92600	756	1209	1571	1868	*97900*	795	1270	1651	1962	*103200*	835	1332	1730	2055	*108500*	875	1394	1809	2149
92700	756	1210	1573	1870	*98000*	796	1272	1652	1963	*103300*	836	1333	1731	2057	*108600*	875	1395	1811	2151
92800	757	1211	1574	1871	*98100*	797	1273	1654	1965	*103400*	837	1335	1733	2059	*108700*	876	1396	1812	2153
92900	758	1212	1576	1873	*98200*	798	1274	1655	1967	*103500*	837	1336	1734	2061	*108800*	877	1397	1814	2155
93000	759	1213	1577	1875	*98300*	798	1275	1657	1969	*103600*	838	1337	1736	2062	*108900*	878	1399	1815	2156
93100	759	1215	1579	1877	*98400*	799	1276	1658	1970	*103700*	839	1338	1737	2064	*109000*	878	1400	1817	2158
93200	760	1216	1580	1878	*98500*	800	1277	1660	1972	*103800*	840	1339	1739	2066	*109100*	879	1401	1818	2160
93300	761	1217	1582	1880	*98600*	801	1279	1661	1974	*103900*	840	1340	1740	2068	*109200*	880	1402	1820	2162
93400	762	1218	1583	1882	*98700*	801	1280	1663	1976	*104000*	841	1342	1742	2070	*109300*	881	1403	1821	2163
93500	762	1219	1585	1884	*98800*	802	1281	1664	1978	*104100*	842	1343	1743	2071	*109400*	881	1404	1823	2165
93600	763	1220	1586	1885	*98900*	803	1282	1666	1979	*104200*	843	1344	1745	2073	*109500*	882	1406	1824	2167
93700	764	1222	1588	1887	*99000*	804	1283	1667	1981	*104300*	843	1345	1746	2075	*109600*	883	1407	1826	2169
93800	765	1223	1589	1889	*99100*	804	1284	1669	1983	*104400*	844	1346	1748	2077	*109700*	884	1408	1827	2170
93900	765	1224	1591	1891	*99200*	805	1286	1670	1985	*104500*	845	1347	1749	2078	*109800*	884	1409	1829	2172
94000	766	1225	1592	1893	*99300*	806	1287	1672	1986	*104600*	846	1349	1751	2080	*109900*	885	1410	1830	2174
94100	767	1226	1594	1894	*99400*	807	1288	1673	1988	*104700*	846	1350	1752	2082	*110000*	886	1411	1832	2176
94200	768	1227	1595	1896	*99500*	807	1289	1675	1990	*104800*	847	1351	1754	2084	*110100*	887	1413	1833	2178
94300	768	1229	1597	1898	*99600*	808	1290	1676	1992	*104900*	848	1352	1755	2086	*110200*	887	1414	1835	2179
94400	769	1230	1598	1900	*99700*	809	1291	1678	1993	*105000*	849	1353	1757	2087	*110300*	888	1415	1836	2181
94500	770	1231	1600	1901	*99800*	810	1293	1679	1995	*105100*	849	1354	1758	2089	*110400*	889	1416	1838	2183
94600	771	1232	1601	1903	*99900*	810	1294	1681	1997	*105200*	850	1356	1760	2091	*110500*	890	1417	1839	2185
94700	771	1233	1603	1905	*100000*	811	1295	1682	1999	*105300*	851	1357	1761	2093	*110600*	890	1418	1841	2186
94800	772	1234	1604	1907	*100100*	812	1296	1684	2001	*105400*	852	1358	1763	2094	*110700*	891	1420	1842	2188
94900	773	1236	1606	1908	*100200*	813	1297	1685	2002	*105500*	852	1359	1764	2096	*110800*	892	1421	1844	2190
95000	774	1237	1607	1910	*100300*	813	1298	1687	2004	*105600*	853	1360	1766	2098	*110900*	893	1422	1845	2192
95100	774	1238	1609	1912	*100400*	814	1300	1688	2006	*105700*	854	1361	1767	2100	*111000*	893	1423	1847	2194
95200	775	1239	1610	1914	*100500*	815	1301	1690	2008	*105800*	855	1363	1769	2101	*111100*	894	1424	1848	2195
95300	776	1240	1612	1916	*100600*	816	1302	1691	2009	*105900*	855	1364	1770	2103	*111200*	895	1425	1850	2197
95400	777	1241	1613	1917	*100700*	816	1303	1693	2011	*106000*	856	1365	1772	2105	*111300*	896	1427	1851	2199
95500	777	1243	1615	1919	*100800*	817	1304	1694	2013	*106100*	857	1366	1773	2107	*111400*	896	1428	1853	2201
95600	778	1244	1616	1921	*100900*	818	1305	1696	2015	*106200*	858	1367	1775	2109	*111500*	897	1429	1854	2202
95700	779	1245	1618	1923	*101000*	819	1307	1697	2016	*106300*	858	1368	1776	2110	*111600*	898	1430	1856	2204
95800	780	1246	1619	1924	*101100*	819	1308	1699	2018	*106400*	859	1370	1778	2112	*111700*	899	1431	1857	2206
95900	780	1247	1621	1926	*101200*	820	1309	1700	2020	*106500*	860	1371	1779	2114	*111800*	899	1432	1859	2208
96000	781	1248	1622	1928	*101300*	821	1310	1702	2022	*106600*	861	1372	1781	2116	*111900*	900	1434	1860	2209
96100	782	1250	1624	1930	*101400*	822	1311	1703	2024	*106700*	861	1373	1782	2117	*112000*	901	1435	1862	2211
96200	783	1251	1625	1931	*101500*	822	1312	1705	2025	*106800*	862	1374	1784	2119	*112100*	902	1436	1863	2213
96300	783	1252	1627	1933	*101600*	823	1314	1706	2027	*106900*	863	1375	1785	2121	*112200*	902	1437	1865	2215
96400	784	1253	1628	1935	*101700*	824	1315	1708	2029	*107000*	864	1377	1787	2123	*112300*	903	1438	1866	2217
96500	785	1254	1630	1937	*101800*	825	1316	1709	2031	*107100*	864	1378	1788	2124	*112400*	904	1439	1868	2218
96600	786	1255	1631	1939	*101900*	825	1317	1711	2032	*107200*	865	1379	1790	2126	*112500*	905	1441	1869	2220
96700	786	1256	1633	1940	*102000*	826	1318	1712	2034	*107300*	866	1380	1791	2128	*112600*	905	1442	1871	2222

Note: This table shows amounts of child support based on income to the nearest $100. There is a mathematical formula for calculating specific child support amounts between the $100 levels. For more information, please contact the Department of Justice.

Nota: La présente table indique le montant de la pension alimentaire pour enfants à verser d'après le revenu (aux 100 $ près). Il existe une formule mathématique pour calculer le montant exact de la pension alimentaire pour enfants dans le cas des revenus qui se situent entre les tranches de 100 $. Pour plus de renseignements, veuillez communiquer avec le ministère de la Justice.

Divorce

ALBERTA
1997

FEDERAL CHILD SUPPORT AMOUNTS : SIMPLIFIED TABLES
MONTANTS FÉDÉRAUX DE PENSIONS ALIMENTAIRES POUR ENFANTS : TABLES SIMPLIFIÉES

Income/ Revenu ($)	Monthly Award/ Paiement mensuel ($) No. of Children/ N^{bre} d'enfants				Income/ Revenu ($)	Monthly Award/ Paiement mensuel ($) No. of Children/ N^{bre} d'enfants				Income/ Revenu ($)	Monthly Award/ Paiement mensuel ($) No. of Children/ N^{bre} d'enfants				Income/ Revenu ($)	Monthly Award/ Paiement mensuel ($) No. of Children/ N^{bre} d'enfants			
	1	2	3	4		1	2	3	4		1	2	3	4		1	2	3	4
112700	906	1443	1872	2224	118000	946	1505	1952	2317	123300	986	1566	2031	2411	128600	1025	1628	2110	2505
112800	907	1444	1874	2225	118100	947	1506	1953	2319	123400	986	1568	2033	2413	128700	1026	1629	2112	2507
112900	908	1445	1875	2227	118200	947	1507	1955	2321	123500	987	1569	2034	2415	128800	1027	1631	2113	2509
113000	908	1446	1877	2229	118300	948	1508	1956	2323	123600	988	1570	2036	2417	128900	1028	1632	2115	2510
113100	909	1448	1878	2231	118400	949	1509	1958	2325	123700	989	1571	2037	2418	129000	1028	1633	2116	2512
113200	910	1449	1880	2232	118500	950	1510	1959	2326	123800	989	1572	2039	2420	129100	1029	1634	2118	2514
113300	911	1450	1881	2234	118600	950	1512	1961	2328	123900	990	1573	2040	2422	129200	1030	1635	2119	2516
113400	911	1451	1883	2236	118700	951	1513	1962	2330	124000	991	1575	2042	2424	129300	1031	1636	2121	2517
113500	912	1452	1884	2238	118800	952	1514	1964	2332	124100	992	1576	2043	2425	129400	1031	1637	2122	2519
113600	913	1453	1886	2240	118900	953	1515	1965	2333	124200	992	1577	2045	2427	129500	1032	1639	2124	2521
113700	914	1455	1887	2241	119000	953	1516	1967	2335	124300	993	1578	2046	2429	129600	1033	1640	2125	2523
113800	914	1456	1889	2243	119100	954	1517	1968	2337	124400	994	1579	2048	2431	129700	1034	1641	2127	2525
113900	915	1457	1890	2245	119200	955	1519	1970	2339	124500	995	1580	2049	2433	129800	1034	1642	2128	2526
114000	916	1458	1892	2247	119300	956	1520	1971	2340	124600	995	1582	2051	2434	129900	1035	1643	2130	2528
114100	917	1459	1893	2248	119400	956	1521	1973	2342	124700	996	1583	2052	2436	130000	1036	1644	2131	2530
114200	917	1460	1895	2250	119500	957	1522	1974	2344	124800	997	1584	2054	2438	130100	1037	1646	2133	2532
114300	918	1462	1896	2252	119600	958	1523	1976	2346	124900	998	1585	2055	2440	130200	1037	1647	2134	2533
114400	919	1463	1898	2254	119700	959	1524	1977	2348	125000	998	1586	2057	2441	130300	1038	1648	2136	2535
114500	920	1464	1899	2255	119800	959	1526	1979	2349	125100	999	1587	2058	2443	130400	1039	1649	2137	2537
114600	920	1465	1901	2257	119900	960	1527	1980	2351	125200	1000	1589	2060	2445	130500	1040	1650	2139	2539
114700	921	1466	1902	2259	120000	961	1528	1982	2353	125300	1001	1590	2061	2447	130600	1040	1651	2140	2541
114800	922	1467	1904	2261	120100	962	1529	1983	2355	125400	1001	1591	2063	2448	130700	1041	1653	2142	2542
114900	923	1469	1905	2263	120200	962	1530	1985	2356	125500	1002	1592	2064	2450	130800	1042	1654	2143	2544
115000	923	1470	1907	2264	120300	963	1531	1986	2358	125600	1003	1593	2066	2452	130900	1043	1655	2145	2546
115100	924	1471	1908	2266	120400	964	1533	1988	2360	125700	1004	1594	2067	2454	131000	1043	1656	2146	2548
115200	925	1472	1910	2268	120500	965	1534	1989	2362	125800	1004	1596	2069	2456	131100	1044	1657	2148	2549
115300	926	1473	1911	2270	120600	965	1535	1991	2363	125900	1005	1597	2070	2457	131200	1045	1658	2149	2551
115400	926	1474	1913	2271	120700	966	1536	1992	2365	126000	1006	1598	2072	2459	131300	1046	1660	2151	2553
115500	927	1476	1914	2273	120800	967	1537	1994	2367	126100	1007	1599	2073	2461	131400	1046	1661	2152	2555
115600	928	1477	1916	2275	120900	968	1538	1995	2369	126200	1007	1600	2075	2463	131500	1047	1662	2154	2556
115700	929	1478	1917	2277	121000	968	1540	1997	2371	126300	1008	1601	2076	2464	131600	1048	1663	2155	2558
115800	929	1479	1919	2278	121100	969	1541	1998	2372	126400	1009	1603	2078	2466	131700	1049	1664	2157	2560
115900	930	1480	1920	2280	121200	970	1542	2000	2374	126500	1010	1604	2079	2468	131800	1049	1665	2158	2562
116000	931	1481	1922	2282	121300	971	1543	2001	2376	126600	1010	1605	2081	2470	131900	1050	1667	2160	2564
116100	932	1483	1923	2284	121400	971	1544	2003	2378	126700	1011	1606	2082	2471	132000	1051	1668	2161	2565
116200	932	1484	1925	2286	121500	972	1545	2004	2379	126800	1012	1607	2084	2473	132100	1052	1669	2163	2567
116300	933	1485	1926	2287	121600	973	1547	2006	2381	126900	1013	1608	2085	2475	132200	1052	1670	2164	2569
116400	934	1486	1928	2289	121700	974	1548	2007	2383	127000	1013	1610	2087	2477	132300	1053	1671	2166	2571
116500	935	1487	1929	2291	121800	974	1549	2009	2385	127100	1014	1611	2088	2479	132400	1054	1672	2167	2572
116600	935	1488	1931	2293	121900	975	1550	2010	2386	127200	1015	1612	2090	2480	132500	1055	1674	2169	2574
116700	936	1490	1932	2294	122000	976	1551	2012	2388	127300	1016	1613	2091	2482	132600	1055	1675	2170	2576
116800	937	1491	1934	2296	122100	977	1552	2013	2390	127400	1016	1614	2093	2484	132700	1056	1676	2172	2578
116900	938	1492	1935	2298	122200	977	1554	2015	2392	127500	1017	1615	2094	2486	132800	1057	1677	2173	2579
117000	938	1493	1937	2300	122300	978	1555	2016	2394	127600	1018	1617	2096	2487	132900	1058	1678	2175	2581
117100	939	1494	1938	2301	122400	979	1556	2018	2395	127700	1019	1618	2097	2489	133000	1058	1679	2176	2583
117200	940	1495	1940	2303	122500	980	1557	2019	2397	127800	1019	1619	2098	2491	133100	1059	1681	2178	2585
117300	941	1497	1941	2305	122600	980	1558	2021	2399	127900	1020	1620	2100	2493	133200	1060	1682	2179	2587
117400	941	1498	1943	2307	122700	981	1559	2022	2401	128000	1021	1621	2101	2494	133300	1061	1683	2181	2588
117500	942	1499	1944	2309	122800	982	1561	2024	2402	128100	1022	1622	2103	2496	133400	1061	1684	2182	2590
117600	943	1500	1946	2310	122900	983	1562	2025	2404	128200	1022	1624	2104	2498	133500	1062	1685	2184	2592
117700	944	1501	1947	2312	123000	983	1563	2027	2406	128300	1023	1625	2106	2500	133600	1063	1686	2185	2594
117800	944	1502	1949	2314	123100	984	1564	2028	2408	128400	1024	1626	2107	2502	133700	1063	1688	2187	2595
117900	945	1504	1950	2316	123200	985	1565	2030	2409	128500	1025	1627	2109	2503	133800	1064	1689	2188	2597

Note: This table shows amounts of child support based on income to the nearest $100. There is a mathematical formula for calculating specific child support amounts between the $100 levels. For more information, please contact the Department of Justice.

Nota: La présente table indique le montant de la pension alimentaire pour enfants à verser d'après le revenu (aux 100 $ près). Il existe une formule mathématique pour calculer le montant exact de la pension alimentaire pour enfants dans le cas des revenus qui se situent entre les tranches de 100 $. Pour plus de renseignements, veuillez communiquer avec le ministère de la Justice.

Appendix D

ALBERTA
1997

FEDERAL CHILD SUPPORT AMOUNTS : SIMPLIFIED TABLES
MONTANTS FÉDÉRAUX DE PENSIONS ALIMENTAIRES POUR ENFANTS : TABLES SIMPLIFIÉES

Income/ Revenu ($)	Monthly Award/ Paiement mensuel ($) No. of Children/ N^{bre} d'enfants				Income/ Revenu ($)	Monthly Award/ Paiement mensuel ($) No. of Children/ N^{bre} d'enfants				Income/ Revenu ($)	Monthly Award/ Paiement mensuel ($) No. of Children/ N^{bre} d'enfants				Income/ Revenu ($)	Monthly Award/ Paiement mensuel ($) No. of Children/ N^{bre} d'enfants			
	1	2	3	4		1	2	3	4		1	2	3	4		1	2	3	4
133900	1065	1690	2190	2599	138000	1096	1738	2251	2672	142100	1126	1785	2313	2744	146200	1157	1833	2374	2817
134000	1066	1691	2191	2601	138100	1096	1739	2253	2673	142200	1127	1787	2314	2746	146300	1158	1834	2376	2818
134100	1066	1692	2193	2602	138200	1097	1740	2254	2675	142300	1128	1788	2316	2748	146400	1159	1836	2377	2820
134200	1067	1693	2194	2604	138300	1098	1741	2256	2677	142400	1129	1789	2317	2749	146500	1159	1837	2379	2822
134300	1068	1695	2196	2606	138400	1099	1742	2257	2679	142500	1129	1790	2319	2751	146600	1160	1838	2380	2824
134400	1069	1696	2197	2608	138500	1099	1744	2259	2680	142600	1130	1791	2320	2753	146700	1161	1839	2382	2826
134500	1069	1697	2199	2610	138600	1100	1745	2260	2682	142700	1131	1792	2322	2755	146800	1162	1840	2383	2827
134600	1070	1698	2200	2611	138700	1101	1746	2262	2684	142800	1132	1794	2323	2756	146900	1162	1841	2385	2829
134700	1071	1699	2202	2613	138800	1102	1747	2263	2686	142900	1132	1795	2325	2758	147000	1163	1843	2386	2831
134800	1072	1700	2203	2615	138900	1102	1748	2265	2687	143000	1133	1796	2326	2760	147100	1164	1844	2388	2833
134900	1072	1702	2205	2617	139000	1103	1749	2266	2689	143100	1134	1797	2328	2762	147200	1165	1845	2389	2834
135000	1073	1703	2206	2618	139100	1104	1751	2268	2691	143200	1135	1798	2329	2764	147300	1165	1846	2391	2836
135100	1074	1704	2208	2620	139200	1105	1752	2269	2693	143300	1135	1799	2331	2765	147400	1166	1847	2392	2838
135200	1075	1705	2209	2622	139300	1105	1753	2271	2695	143400	1136	1801	2332	2767	147500	1167	1848	2394	2840
135300	1075	1706	2211	2624	139400	1106	1754	2272	2696	143500	1137	1802	2334	2769	147600	1168	1850	2395	2841
135400	1076	1707	2212	2625	139500	1107	1755	2274	2698	143600	1138	1803	2335	2771	147700	1168	1851	2397	2843
135500	1077	1709	2214	2627	139600	1108	1756	2275	2700	143700	1138	1804	2337	2772	147800	1169	1852	2398	2845
135600	1078	1710	2215	2629	139700	1108	1758	2277	2702	143800	1139	1805	2338	2774	147900	1170	1853	2400	2847
135700	1078	1711	2217	2631	139800	1109	1759	2278	2703	143900	1140	1806	2340	2776	148000	1171	1854	2401	2849
135800	1079	1712	2218	2633	139900	1110	1760	2280	2705	144000	1141	1808	2341	2778	148100	1171	1855	2403	2850
135900	1080	1713	2220	2634	140000	1111	1761	2281	2707	144100	1141	1809	2343	2780	148200	1172	1857	2404	2852
136000	1081	1714	2221	2636	140100	1111	1762	2283	2709	144200	1142	1810	2344	2781	148300	1173	1858	2406	2854
136100	1081	1716	2223	2638	140200	1112	1763	2284	2710	144300	1143	1811	2346	2783	148400	1174	1859	2407	2856
136200	1082	1717	2224	2640	140300	1113	1764	2286	2712	144400	1144	1812	2347	2785	148500	1174	1860	2409	2857
136300	1083	1718	2226	2641	140400	1114	1766	2287	2714	144500	1144	1813	2349	2787	148600	1175	1861	2410	2859
136400	1084	1719	2227	2643	140500	1114	1767	2289	2716	144600	1145	1815	2350	2788	148700	1176	1862	2412	2861
136500	1084	1720	2229	2645	140600	1115	1768	2290	2718	144700	1146	1816	2352	2790	148800	1177	1864	2413	2863
136600	1085	1721	2230	2647	140700	1116	1769	2292	2719	144800	1147	1817	2353	2792	148900	1177	1865	2415	2864
136700	1086	1723	2232	2648	140800	1117	1770	2293	2721	144900	1147	1818	2355	2794	149000	1178	1866	2416	2866
136800	1087	1724	2233	2650	140900	1117	1771	2295	2723	145000	1148	1819	2356	2795	149100	1179	1867	2418	2868
136900	1087	1725	2235	2652	141000	1118	1773	2296	2725	145100	1149	1820	2358	2797	149200	1180	1868	2419	2870
137000	1088	1726	2236	2654	141100	1119	1774	2298	2726	145200	1150	1822	2359	2799	149300	1180	1869	2421	2872
137100	1089	1727	2238	2656	141200	1120	1775	2299	2728	145300	1150	1823	2361	2801	149400	1181	1871	2422	2873
137200	1090	1728	2239	2657	141300	1120	1776	2301	2730	145400	1151	1824	2362	2803	149500	1182	1872	2424	2875
137300	1090	1730	2241	2659	141400	1121	1777	2302	2732	145500	1152	1825	2364	2804	149600	1183	1873	2425	2877
137400	1091	1731	2242	2661	141500	1122	1778	2304	2733	145600	1153	1826	2365	2806	149700	1183	1874	2427	2879
137500	1092	1732	2244	2663	141600	1123	1780	2305	2735	145700	1153	1827	2367	2808	149800	1184	1875	2428	2880
137600	1093	1733	2245	2664	141700	1123	1781	2307	2737	145800	1154	1829	2368	2810	149900	1185	1876	2430	2882
137700	1093	1734	2247	2666	141800	1124	1782	2308	2739	145900	1155	1830	2370	2811	150000	1186	1878	2431	2884
137800	1094	1735	2248	2668	141900	1125	1783	2310	2741	146000	1156	1831	2371	2813					
137900	1095	1737	2250	2670	142000	1126	1784	2311	2742	146100	1156	1832	2373	2815					

Income/ Revenu ($)	Monthly Award/Paiement mensuel ($)			
	one child/ un enfant	two children/ deux enfants	three children/ trois enfants	four children/ quatre enfants
For income over $150,000	1186 plus 0.75% of income over $150,000	1878 plus 1.17% of income over $150,000	2431 plus 1.50% of income over $150,000	2884 plus 1.77% of income over $150,000
Pour revenu dépassant 150 000$	1186 plus 0,75% du revenu dépassant 150 000$	1878 plus 1,17% du revenu dépassant 150 000$	2431 plus 1,50% du revenu dépassant 150 000$	2884 plus 1,77% du revenu dépassant 150 000$

Note: This table shows amounts of child support based on income to the nearest $100. There is a mathematical formula for calculating specific child support amounts between the $100 levels. For more information, please contact the Department of Justice.

Nota: La présente table indique le montant de la pension alimentaire pour enfants à verser d'après le revenu (aux 100 $ près). Il existe une formule mathématique pour calculer le montant exact de la pension alimentaire pour enfants dans le cas des revenus qui se situent entre les tranches de 100 $. Pour plus de renseignements, veuillez communiquer avec le ministère de la Justice.

Divorce

BRITISH COLUMBIA/COLOMBIE-BRITANNIQUE

FEDERAL CHILD SUPPORT AMOUNTS : SIMPLIFIED TABLES
MONTANTS FÉDÉRAUX DE PENSIONS ALIMENTAIRES POUR ENFANTS : TABLES SIMPLIFIÉES

1997

Income/Revenu ($)	Monthly Award/Paiement mensuel ($) No. of Children/N^bre d'enfants				Income/Revenu ($)	Monthly Award/Paiement mensuel ($) No. of Children/N^bre d'enfants				Income/Revenu ($)	Monthly Award/Paiement mensuel ($) No. of Children/N^bre d'enfants				Income/Revenu ($)	Monthly Award/Paiement mensuel ($) No. of Children/N^bre d'enfants			
	1	2	3	4		1	2	3	4		1	2	3	4		1	2	3	4
6700	0	0	0	0	12000	99	157	179	201	17300	144	257	347	394	22600	198	337	449	542
6800	0	0	0	0	12100	99	160	183	205	17400	144	258	349	398	22700	199	339	451	544
6900	2	3	3	4	12200	99	163	186	209	17500	145	259	351	401	22800	200	340	453	546
7000	5	6	7	8	12300	99	166	189	212	17600	146	261	353	405	22900	201	342	455	549
7100	7	9	10	12	12400	99	169	192	216	17700	147	262	355	409	23000	202	343	457	551
7200	10	12	14	16	12500	99	172	196	220	17800	148	264	357	412	23100	203	345	459	553
7300	12	15	17	20	12600	100	175	199	223	17900	149	265	358	416	23200	204	346	461	556
7400	15	18	21	23	12700	101	177	202	227	18000	150	267	360	420	23300	205	348	463	558
7500	18	21	24	27	12800	102	180	206	231	18100	151	268	362	423	23400	206	350	465	560
7600	20	24	28	31	12900	103	183	209	235	18200	152	270	364	427	23500	207	351	467	562
7700	23	27	31	35	13000	104	186	212	238	18300	153	271	366	431	23600	208	353	469	565
7800	26	30	34	39	13100	105	189	215	242	18400	154	273	368	434	23700	209	354	470	567
7900	28	33	38	43	13200	106	192	219	246	18500	155	274	370	438	23800	210	356	472	569
8000	31	36	41	47	13300	107	195	222	249	18600	156	276	372	442	23900	211	357	474	572
8100	33	39	45	51	13400	108	198	225	253	18700	157	277	374	446	24000	212	359	476	574
8200	36	42	48	54	13500	109	200	229	257	18800	158	279	376	449	24100	213	361	478	576
8300	39	45	52	58	13600	110	203	232	261	18900	159	280	378	453	24200	214	362	480	578
8400	41	48	55	62	13700	111	205	235	264	19000	161	282	380	457	24300	214	364	482	581
8500	44	51	59	66	13800	112	207	239	268	19100	162	283	382	460	24400	215	365	484	583
8600	47	54	62	70	13900	113	208	242	272	19200	163	285	384	464	24500	216	367	486	585
8700	49	57	66	74	14000	114	210	245	275	19300	164	286	386	467	24600	217	368	488	587
8800	52	60	69	78	14100	115	211	248	279	19400	165	288	387	469	24700	218	370	490	590
8900	54	63	72	82	14200	116	213	252	283	19500	166	290	389	471	24800	219	371	492	592
9000	57	66	76	85	14300	117	214	255	287	19600	167	291	391	473	24900	220	373	494	594
9100	60	70	79	89	14400	118	216	258	290	19700	168	293	393	476	25000	221	375	496	597
9200	62	73	83	93	14500	119	217	262	294	19800	169	294	395	478	25100	222	376	498	599
9300	65	76	86	97	14600	120	219	265	298	19900	170	296	397	480	25200	223	378	500	601
9400	68	79	90	101	14700	121	220	268	301	20000	171	297	399	483	25300	224	379	502	603
9500	70	82	93	105	14800	122	222	271	305	20100	172	299	401	485	25400	225	381	504	606
9600	73	85	97	109	14900	123	223	275	309	20200	173	300	403	487	25500	226	382	506	608
9700	75	88	100	113	15000	124	225	278	313	20300	174	302	405	489	25600	227	384	508	610
9800	78	91	104	116	15100	125	226	281	316	20400	175	303	407	492	25700	228	386	510	613
9900	81	94	107	120	15200	125	227	284	320	20500	176	305	409	494	25800	229	387	512	615
10000	83	97	111	124	15300	126	229	287	323	20600	177	306	411	496	25900	230	389	514	617
10100	86	100	114	128	15400	127	230	291	327	20700	178	308	413	498	26000	231	390	516	619
10200	89	103	117	132	15500	128	232	294	330	20800	179	309	414	501	26100	232	392	518	621
10300	91	106	121	136	15600	129	233	297	334	20900	180	311	416	503	26200	233	393	520	624
10400	94	109	124	140	15700	130	234	300	337	21000	181	312	418	505	26300	234	394	521	626
10500	96	112	128	144	15800	131	236	303	341	21100	182	314	420	508	26400	234	396	523	628
10600	97	115	131	147	15900	131	237	306	344	21200	183	315	422	510	26500	235	397	525	630
10700	97	118	135	151	16000	132	239	309	348	21300	184	317	424	512	26600	236	399	527	632
10800	97	121	138	155	16100	133	240	312	351	21400	185	318	426	514	26700	237	400	529	634
10900	97	124	142	159	16200	134	241	316	355	21500	186	320	428	517	26800	238	402	531	636
11000	97	127	145	163	16300	135	243	319	359	21600	187	321	430	519	26900	239	403	533	638
11100	97	130	149	167	16400	136	244	322	362	21700	188	323	432	521	27000	240	405	534	640
11200	98	133	152	171	16500	137	245	325	366	21800	189	325	434	524	27100	241	406	536	643
11300	98	136	156	175	16600	138	247	328	369	21900	191	326	436	526	27200	242	408	538	645
11400	98	140	159	178	16700	138	248	331	373	22000	192	328	438	528	27300	242	409	540	647
11500	98	143	162	182	16800	139	250	334	376	22100	193	329	440	530	27400	243	411	542	649
11600	98	146	166	186	16900	140	251	337	380	22200	194	331	442	533	27500	244	412	544	651
11700	98	149	169	190	17000	141	252	341	383	22300	195	332	443	535	27600	245	413	545	654
11800	98	152	173	194	17100	142	254	343	387	22400	196	334	445	537	27700	246	415	547	656
11900	98	154	176	198	17200	143	255	345	390	22500	197	335	447	540	27800	247	416	549	658

Note: This table shows amounts of child support based on income to the nearest $100. There is a mathematical formula for calculating specific child support amounts between the $100 levels. For more information, please contact the Department of Justice.

Nota: La présente table indique le montant de la pension alimentaire à verser d'après le revenu (aux 100 $ près). Il existe une formule mathématique pour calculer le montant exact de la pension alimentaire pour enfants dans le cas des revenus qui se situent entre les tranches de 100 $. Pour plus de renseignements, veuillez communiquer avec le ministère de la Justice.

Appendix D

BRITISH COLUMBIA/COLOMBIE-BRITANNIQUE

FEDERAL CHILD SUPPORT AMOUNTS : SIMPLIFIED TABLES
MONTANTS FÉDÉRAUX DE PENSIONS ALIMENTAIRES POUR ENFANTS : TABLES SIMPLIFIÉES

1997

Income/ Revenu ($)	Monthly Award/ Paiement mensuel ($) No. of Children/ N^{bre} d'enfants				Income/ Revenu ($)	Monthly Award/ Paiement mensuel ($) No. of Children/ N^{bre} d'enfants				Income/ Revenu ($)	Monthly Award/ Paiement mensuel ($) No. of Children/ N^{bre} d'enfants				Income/ Revenu ($)	Monthly Award/ Paiement mensuel ($) No. of Children/ N^{bre} d'enfants			
	1	2	3	4		1	2	3	4		1	2	3	4		1	2	3	4
27900	248	418	551	660	33200	289	483	637	761	38500	331	547	721	862	43800	375	615	808	966
28000	249	419	553	662	33300	290	484	638	762	38600	332	549	722	864	43900	376	617	810	968
28100	250	421	555	664	33400	291	485	640	764	38700	333	550	724	866	44000	376	618	811	970
28200	251	422	557	667	33500	292	486	642	766	38800	333	551	725	868	44100	377	619	813	972
28300	251	424	558	669	33600	292	487	643	768	38900	334	552	727	870	44200	378	621	815	974
28400	252	425	560	671	33700	293	489	645	770	39000	335	554	729	872	44300	379	622	816	976
28500	253	427	562	673	33800	294	490	646	772	39100	336	555	730	874	44400	380	623	818	978
28600	254	428	564	675	33900	295	491	648	774	39200	337	556	732	876	44500	381	625	820	979
28700	255	429	566	677	34000	295	492	650	776	39300	337	557	734	877	44600	381	626	821	981
28800	256	431	568	680	34100	296	493	651	777	39400	338	559	735	879	44700	382	627	823	983
28900	257	432	569	682	34200	297	495	653	779	39500	339	560	737	881	44800	383	628	825	985
29000	258	433	571	684	34300	298	496	654	781	39600	340	561	738	883	44900	384	630	826	987
29100	259	435	573	686	34400	299	497	656	783	39700	341	562	740	885	45000	385	631	828	989
29200	260	436	575	688	34500	299	498	657	785	39800	341	564	742	887	45100	386	632	830	991
29300	260	438	577	690	34600	300	499	659	787	39900	342	565	743	889	45200	386	634	831	993
29400	261	439	579	693	34700	301	501	660	789	40000	343	566	745	891	45300	387	635	833	995
29500	262	440	581	695	34800	302	502	662	791	40100	344	568	746	893	45400	388	636	835	997
29600	263	442	582	697	34900	302	503	663	792	40200	345	569	748	895	45500	389	638	836	999
29700	264	443	584	699	35000	303	504	665	794	40300	346	570	750	897	45600	390	639	838	1001
29800	264	444	585	700	35100	304	505	667	796	40400	346	571	751	899	45700	391	640	840	1003
29900	265	445	587	702	35200	305	507	668	798	40500	347	573	753	901	45800	391	641	841	1005
30000	266	446	588	704	35300	305	508	670	800	40600	348	574	755	903	45900	392	643	843	1007
30100	267	447	590	705	35400	306	509	671	802	40700	349	575	756	905	46000	393	644	845	1009
30200	267	448	591	707	35500	307	510	673	804	40800	350	577	758	907	46100	394	645	846	1011
30300	268	449	593	709	35600	308	511	674	806	40900	351	578	760	909	46200	395	647	848	1013
30400	269	451	594	711	35700	309	513	676	807	41000	351	579	761	911	46300	396	648	850	1015
30500	269	452	596	712	35800	309	514	677	809	41100	352	581	763	913	46400	396	649	851	1017
30600	270	453	597	714	35900	310	515	679	811	41200	353	582	765	915	46500	397	650	853	1019
30700	271	454	598	716	36000	311	516	681	813	41300	354	583	766	917	46600	398	652	855	1021
30800	272	455	600	717	36100	312	517	682	815	41400	355	584	768	918	46700	399	653	856	1023
30900	272	456	601	719	36200	313	519	684	817	41500	356	586	770	920	46800	400	654	858	1025
31000	273	457	603	721	36300	313	520	685	819	41600	356	587	771	922	46900	401	656	860	1027
31100	274	458	604	723	36400	314	521	687	821	41700	357	588	773	924	47000	401	657	861	1029
31200	274	459	606	724	36500	315	522	689	823	41800	358	590	775	926	47100	402	658	863	1031
31300	275	460	607	726	36600	316	524	690	825	41900	359	591	776	928	47200	403	660	865	1033
31400	276	462	609	728	36700	317	525	692	827	42000	360	592	778	930	47300	404	661	866	1035
31500	276	463	610	729	36800	317	526	693	829	42100	361	593	780	932	47400	405	662	868	1037
31600	277	464	612	731	36900	318	527	695	831	42200	361	595	781	934	47500	406	663	870	1039
31700	278	465	613	733	37000	319	529	697	833	42300	362	596	783	936	47600	406	665	871	1041
31800	279	466	615	735	37100	320	530	698	835	42400	363	597	785	938	47700	407	666	873	1042
31900	279	467	616	736	37200	321	531	700	837	42500	364	599	786	940	47800	408	667	875	1044
32000	280	468	618	738	37300	321	532	701	838	42600	365	600	788	942	47900	409	669	876	1046
32100	281	469	619	740	37400	322	534	703	840	42700	366	601	790	944	48000	410	670	878	1048
32200	282	471	621	742	37500	323	535	705	842	42800	366	603	791	946	48100	411	671	880	1050
32300	282	472	622	744	37600	324	536	706	844	42900	367	604	793	948	48200	411	672	881	1052
32400	283	473	624	745	37700	325	537	708	846	43000	368	605	795	950	48300	412	674	883	1054
32500	284	474	626	747	37800	325	539	709	848	43100	369	606	796	952	48400	413	675	885	1056
32600	285	475	627	749	37900	326	540	711	850	43200	370	608	798	954	48500	414	676	886	1058
32700	285	477	629	751	38000	327	541	713	852	43300	371	609	800	956	48600	415	678	888	1060
32800	286	478	630	753	38100	328	542	714	854	43400	371	610	801	958	48700	416	679	890	1062
32900	287	479	632	755	38200	329	544	716	856	43500	372	612	803	960	48800	416	680	891	1064
33000	288	480	634	757	38300	329	545	717	858	43600	373	613	805	962	48900	417	682	893	1066
33100	288	481	635	759	38400	330	546	719	860	43700	374	614	806	964	49000	418	683	895	1068

Note: This table shows amounts of child support based on income to the nearest $100. There is a mathematical formula for calculating specific child support amounts between the $100 levels. For more information, please contact the Department of Justice.

Nota: La présente table indique le montant de la pension alimentaire pour enfants à verser d'après le revenu (aux 100 $ près). Il existe une formule mathématique pour calculer le montant exact de la pension alimentaire pour enfants dans le cas des revenus qui se situent entre les tranches de 100 $. Pour plus de renseignements, veuillez communiquer avec le ministère de la Justice.

Divorce

BRITISH COLUMBIA/COLOMBIE-BRITANNIQUE

FEDERAL CHILD SUPPORT AMOUNTS : SIMPLIFIED TABLES
MONTANTS FÉDÉRAUX DE PENSIONS ALIMENTAIRES POUR ENFANTS : TABLES SIMPLIFIÉES

1997

Income/Revenu ($)	Monthly Award/Paiement mensuel ($) No. of Children/N^{bre} d'enfants				Income/Revenu ($)	Monthly Award/Paiement mensuel ($) No. of Children/N^{bre} d'enfants				Income/Revenu ($)	Monthly Award/Paiement mensuel ($) No. of Children/N^{bre} d'enfants				Income/Revenu ($)	Monthly Award/Paiement mensuel ($) No. of Children/N^{bre} d'enfants			
	1	2	3	4		1	2	3	4		1	2	3	4		1	2	3	4
49100	419	684	896	1070	54400	463	753	985	1174	59700	499	813	1064	1269	65000	534	867	1133	1351
49200	420	685	898	1072	54500	464	754	986	1176	59800	500	814	1065	1270	65100	535	868	1135	1353
49300	421	687	900	1074	54600	465	755	988	1178	59900	500	815	1066	1272	65200	536	869	1136	1355
49400	421	688	901	1076	54700	465	757	990	1180	60000	501	816	1067	1273	65300	536	870	1137	1356
49500	422	689	903	1078	54800	466	758	991	1182	60100	501	817	1069	1275	65400	537	871	1139	1358
49600	423	691	905	1080	54900	467	759	993	1184	60200	502	817	1070	1277	65500	538	872	1140	1359
49700	424	692	906	1082	55000	468	761	995	1186	60300	502	818	1071	1278	65600	538	873	1141	1361
49800	425	693	908	1084	55100	469	762	996	1188	60400	503	819	1073	1280	65700	539	874	1143	1362
49900	426	695	910	1086	55200	470	763	998	1190	60500	504	820	1074	1281	65800	539	875	1144	1364
50000	426	696	911	1088	55300	470	764	1000	1192	60600	504	821	1075	1283	65900	540	876	1145	1366
50100	427	697	913	1090	55400	471	766	1001	1194	60700	505	822	1076	1284	66000	541	877	1147	1367
50200	428	698	915	1092	55500	472	767	1003	1196	60800	506	823	1078	1286	66100	541	878	1148	1369
50300	429	700	916	1094	55600	473	768	1005	1198	60900	506	824	1079	1287	66200	542	879	1149	1370
50400	430	701	918	1096	55700	474	770	1006	1200	61000	507	825	1080	1289	66300	543	881	1151	1372
50500	431	702	920	1098	55800	475	771	1008	1202	61100	508	826	1082	1291	66400	543	882	1152	1374
50600	431	704	921	1100	55900	475	772	1009	1204	61200	509	827	1083	1292	66500	544	883	1153	1375
50700	432	705	923	1102	56000	476	773	1011	1205	61300	509	828	1084	1294	66600	545	884	1155	1377
50800	433	706	925	1103	56100	477	774	1012	1207	61400	510	829	1085	1295	66700	545	885	1156	1378
50900	434	707	926	1105	56200	477	775	1014	1209	61500	511	830	1087	1297	66800	546	886	1158	1380
51000	435	709	928	1107	56300	478	776	1015	1211	61600	511	831	1088	1298	66900	547	887	1159	1382
51100	436	710	930	1109	56400	479	777	1017	1212	61700	512	832	1089	1300	67000	547	888	1160	1383
51200	436	711	931	1111	56500	479	779	1018	1214	61800	513	833	1091	1301	67100	548	889	1162	1385
51300	437	713	933	1113	56600	480	780	1020	1216	61900	514	834	1092	1303	67200	549	890	1163	1387
51400	438	714	935	1115	56700	480	781	1021	1218	62000	514	835	1093	1305	67300	549	891	1164	1388
51500	439	715	936	1117	56800	481	782	1022	1219	62100	515	837	1094	1306	67400	550	892	1166	1390
51600	440	717	938	1119	56900	482	783	1024	1221	62200	516	838	1096	1308	67500	551	893	1167	1391
51700	441	718	940	1121	57000	482	784	1025	1223	62300	516	839	1097	1309	67600	551	894	1169	1393
51800	441	719	941	1123	57100	483	785	1027	1225	62400	517	840	1098	1311	67700	552	895	1170	1395
51900	442	720	943	1125	57200	484	786	1028	1226	62500	518	841	1100	1312	67800	553	896	1171	1396
52000	443	722	945	1127	57300	484	787	1030	1228	62600	519	842	1101	1314	67900	553	897	1173	1398
52100	444	723	946	1129	57400	485	788	1031	1230	62700	519	843	1102	1316	68000	554	899	1174	1399
52200	445	724	948	1131	57500	486	789	1033	1231	62800	520	844	1104	1317	68100	555	900	1175	1401
52300	445	726	950	1133	57600	486	791	1034	1233	62900	521	845	1105	1319	68200	556	901	1177	1403
52400	446	727	951	1135	57700	487	792	1035	1235	63000	521	846	1106	1320	68300	556	902	1178	1404
52500	447	728	953	1137	57800	487	793	1037	1237	63100	522	848	1108	1322	68400	557	903	1180	1406
52600	448	729	955	1139	57900	488	794	1038	1238	63200	523	849	1109	1323	68500	558	904	1181	1408
52700	449	731	956	1141	58000	489	795	1040	1240	63300	523	850	1111	1325	68600	558	905	1182	1409
52800	450	732	958	1143	58100	489	796	1041	1242	63400	524	851	1112	1326	68700	559	906	1184	1411
52900	450	733	960	1145	58200	490	797	1043	1244	63500	525	852	1113	1328	68800	560	907	1185	1412
53000	451	735	961	1147	58300	491	798	1044	1245	63600	525	853	1115	1329	68900	560	908	1186	1414
53100	452	736	963	1149	58400	491	799	1046	1247	63700	526	854	1116	1331	69000	561	909	1188	1416
53200	453	737	965	1151	58500	492	800	1047	1249	63800	527	855	1117	1332	69100	562	910	1189	1417
53300	454	739	966	1153	58600	493	801	1048	1251	63900	527	856	1119	1334	69200	562	911	1191	1419
53400	455	740	968	1155	58700	493	802	1050	1252	64000	528	857	1120	1335	69300	563	912	1192	1421
53500	455	741	970	1157	58800	494	804	1051	1254	64100	529	858	1121	1337	69400	564	914	1193	1422
53600	456	742	971	1159	58900	494	805	1053	1256	64200	529	859	1123	1339	69500	564	915	1195	1424
53700	457	744	973	1161	59000	495	806	1054	1258	64300	530	860	1124	1340	69600	565	916	1196	1425
53800	458	745	975	1163	59100	496	807	1056	1259	64400	531	861	1125	1342	69700	566	917	1197	1427
53900	459	746	976	1165	59200	496	808	1057	1261	64500	531	862	1127	1343	69800	567	918	1199	1429
54000	460	748	978	1166	59300	497	809	1058	1263	64600	532	863	1128	1345	69900	567	919	1200	1430
54100	460	749	980	1168	59400	497	810	1060	1264	64700	532	864	1129	1347	70000	568	920	1202	1432
54200	461	750	981	1170	59500	498	811	1061	1266	64800	533	865	1131	1348	70100	569	921	1203	1434
54300	462	752	983	1172	59600	499	812	1062	1267	64900	534	866	1132	1350	70200	569	922	1204	1435

Note: This table shows amounts of child support based on income to the nearest $100. There is a mathematical formula for calculating specific child support amounts between the $100 levels. For more information, please contact the Department of Justice.

Nota: La présente table indique le montant de la pension alimentaire pour enfants à verser d'après le revenu (aux 100 $ près). Il existe une formule mathématique pour calculer le montant exact de la pension alimentaire pour enfants dans le cas des revenus qui se situent entre les tranches de 100 $. Pour plus de renseignements, veuillez communiquer avec le ministère de la Justice.

Appendix D

BRITISH COLUMBIA/COLOMBIE-BRITANNIQUE

1997

FEDERAL CHILD SUPPORT AMOUNTS : SIMPLIFIED TABLES
MONTANTS FÉDÉRAUX DE PENSIONS ALIMENTAIRES POUR ENFANTS : TABLES SIMPLIFIÉES

Income/ Revenu ($)	Monthly Award/ Paiement mensuel ($) No. of Children/ N^{bre} d'enfants				Income/ Revenu ($)	Monthly Award/ Paiement mensuel ($) No. of Children/ N^{bre} d'enfants				Income/ Revenu ($)	Monthly Award/ Paiement mensuel ($) No. of Children/ N^{bre} d'enfants				Income/ Revenu ($)	Monthly Award/ Paiement mensuel ($) No. of Children/ N^{bre} d'enfants			
	1	2	3	4		1	2	3	4		1	2	3	4		1	2	3	4
70300	570	923	1206	1437	75600	606	980	1278	1523	80900	643	1036	1351	1609	86200	673	1086	1416	1686
70400	571	924	1207	1438	75700	607	981	1280	1524	81000	643	1037	1353	1611	86300	673	1087	1417	1688
70500	571	925	1208	1440	75800	608	982	1281	1526	81100	644	1039	1354	1612	86400	674	1088	1418	1689
70600	572	926	1210	1442	75900	608	983	1283	1528	81200	645	1040	1355	1614	86500	675	1089	1420	1691
70700	573	927	1211	1443	76000	609	984	1284	1529	81300	645	1040	1357	1615	86600	675	1090	1421	1692
70800	573	928	1213	1445	76100	610	985	1285	1531	81400	646	1041	1358	1617	86700	676	1091	1422	1694
70900	574	930	1214	1447	76200	610	986	1287	1533	81500	646	1042	1359	1618	86800	676	1091	1423	1695
71000	575	931	1215	1448	76300	611	987	1288	1534	81600	647	1043	1360	1619	86900	677	1092	1425	1697
71100	575	932	1217	1450	76400	612	988	1289	1536	81700	647	1044	1361	1621	87000	678	1093	1426	1698
71200	576	933	1218	1451	76500	613	989	1291	1537	81800	648	1045	1362	1622	87100	678	1094	1427	1700
71300	577	934	1219	1453	76600	613	990	1292	1539	81900	648	1046	1364	1624	87200	679	1095	1429	1701
71400	578	935	1221	1455	76700	614	992	1294	1541	82000	649	1047	1365	1625	87300	680	1096	1430	1703
71500	578	936	1222	1456	76800	615	993	1295	1542	82100	649	1047	1366	1626	87400	680	1097	1431	1704
71600	579	937	1224	1458	76900	615	994	1296	1544	82200	650	1048	1367	1628	87500	681	1098	1432	1706
71700	580	938	1225	1460	77000	616	995	1298	1546	82300	650	1049	1368	1629	87600	682	1099	1434	1707
71800	580	939	1226	1461	77100	617	996	1299	1547	82400	651	1050	1369	1631	87700	682	1100	1435	1709
71900	581	940	1228	1463	77200	617	997	1300	1549	82500	651	1051	1371	1632	87800	683	1101	1436	1710
72000	582	941	1229	1464	77300	618	998	1302	1550	82600	652	1052	1372	1634	87900	684	1102	1437	1712
72100	582	942	1230	1466	77400	619	999	1303	1552	82700	652	1053	1373	1635	88000	684	1103	1439	1713
72200	583	943	1232	1468	77500	619	1000	1305	1554	82800	653	1054	1374	1636	88100	685	1104	1440	1715
72300	584	945	1233	1469	77600	620	1001	1306	1555	82900	653	1054	1375	1638	88200	685	1105	1441	1716
72400	584	946	1235	1471	77700	621	1002	1307	1557	83000	654	1055	1376	1639	88300	686	1106	1443	1718
72500	585	947	1236	1473	77800	621	1003	1309	1559	83100	654	1056	1378	1641	88400	687	1107	1444	1719
72600	586	948	1237	1474	77900	622	1004	1310	1560	83200	655	1057	1379	1642	88500	687	1108	1445	1721
72700	586	949	1239	1476	78000	623	1005	1311	1562	83300	656	1058	1380	1643	88600	688	1109	1446	1722
72800	587	950	1240	1477	78100	624	1006	1313	1563	83400	656	1059	1381	1645	88700	689	1110	1448	1724
72900	588	951	1241	1479	78200	624	1008	1314	1565	83500	657	1060	1382	1646	88800	689	1111	1449	1725
73000	589	952	1243	1481	78300	625	1009	1316	1567	83600	657	1061	1383	1648	88900	690	1112	1450	1727
73100	589	953	1244	1482	78400	626	1010	1317	1568	83700	658	1062	1385	1649	89000	691	1113	1451	1728
73200	590	954	1246	1484	78500	626	1011	1318	1570	83800	658	1062	1386	1650	89100	691	1114	1453	1730
73300	591	955	1247	1486	78600	627	1012	1320	1572	83900	659	1063	1387	1652	89200	692	1115	1454	1731
73400	591	956	1248	1487	78700	628	1013	1321	1573	84000	659	1064	1388	1653	89300	692	1116	1455	1733
73500	592	957	1250	1489	78800	628	1014	1322	1575	84100	660	1065	1389	1655	89400	693	1117	1457	1734
73600	593	958	1251	1490	78900	629	1015	1324	1576	84200	660	1066	1391	1656	89500	694	1118	1458	1736
73700	593	959	1252	1492	79000	630	1016	1325	1578	84300	661	1067	1392	1658	89600	694	1119	1459	1737
73800	594	961	1254	1494	79100	630	1017	1327	1580	84400	661	1068	1393	1659	89700	695	1120	1460	1739
73900	595	962	1255	1495	79200	631	1018	1328	1581	84500	662	1069	1394	1661	89800	696	1121	1462	1740
74000	595	963	1256	1497	79300	632	1019	1329	1583	84600	662	1070	1395	1662	89900	696	1122	1463	1742
74100	596	964	1258	1499	79400	632	1020	1331	1585	84700	663	1071	1397	1664	90000	697	1123	1464	1743
74200	597	965	1259	1500	79500	633	1021	1332	1586	84800	664	1072	1398	1665	90100	698	1124	1465	1745
74300	597	966	1261	1502	79600	634	1022	1333	1588	84900	664	1073	1399	1667	90200	698	1125	1467	1746
74400	598	967	1262	1503	79700	635	1024	1335	1589	85000	665	1074	1401	1668	90300	699	1126	1468	1748
74500	599	968	1263	1505	79800	635	1025	1336	1591	85100	666	1075	1402	1670	90400	699	1127	1469	1749
74600	600	969	1265	1507	79900	636	1026	1338	1593	85200	666	1076	1403	1671	90500	700	1128	1471	1751
74700	600	970	1266	1508	80000	637	1027	1339	1594	85300	667	1077	1404	1673	90600	701	1129	1472	1752
74800	601	971	1267	1510	80100	637	1028	1340	1596	85400	668	1078	1406	1674	90700	701	1130	1473	1754
74900	602	972	1269	1512	80200	638	1029	1342	1598	85500	668	1079	1407	1676	90800	702	1131	1474	1755
75000	602	973	1270	1513	80300	639	1030	1343	1599	85600	669	1080	1408	1677	90900	703	1132	1476	1757
75100	603	974	1272	1515	80400	639	1031	1344	1601	85700	669	1081	1409	1679	91000	703	1133	1477	1758
75200	604	975	1273	1516	80500	640	1032	1346	1602	85800	670	1082	1411	1680	91100	704	1134	1478	1760
75300	604	977	1274	1518	80600	641	1033	1347	1604	85900	671	1083	1412	1682	91200	705	1135	1480	1761
75400	605	978	1276	1520	80700	641	1034	1349	1606	86000	671	1084	1413	1683	91300	705	1136	1481	1763
75500	606	979	1277	1521	80800	642	1035	1350	1607	86100	672	1085	1415	1685	91400	706	1137	1482	1764

Note: This table shows amounts of child support based on income to the nearest $100. There is a mathematical formula for calculating specific child support amounts between the $100 levels. For more information, please contact the Department of Justice.

Nota: La présente table indique le montant de la pension alimentaire pour enfants à verser d'après le revenu (aux 100 $ près). Il existe une formule mathématique pour calculer le montant exact de la pension alimentaire pour enfants dans le cas des revenus qui se situent entre les tranches de 100 $. Pour plus de renseignements, veuillez communiquer avec le ministère de la Justice.

Divorce

BRITISH COLUMBIA/COLOMBIE-BRITANNIQUE

FEDERAL CHILD SUPPORT AMOUNTS : SIMPLIFIED TABLES 1997
MONTANTS FÉDÉRAUX DE PENSIONS ALIMENTAIRES POUR ENFANTS : TABLES SIMPLIFIÉES

Income/ Revenu ($)	Monthly Award/ Paiement mensuel ($) No. of Children/ N^{bre} d'enfants				Income/ Revenu ($)	Monthly Award/ Paiement mensuel ($) No. of Children/ N^{bre} d'enfants				Income/ Revenu ($)	Monthly Award/ Paiement mensuel ($) No. of Children/ N^{bre} d'enfants				Income/ Revenu ($)	Monthly Award/ Paiement mensuel ($) No. of Children/ N^{bre} d'enfants			
	1	2	3	4		1	2	3	4		1	2	3	4		1	2	3	4
91500	706	1138	1483	1766	96800	740	1191	1551	1846	102100	774	1243	1618	1925	107400	808	1295	1686	2005
91600	707	1139	1485	1767	96900	741	1191	1552	1847	102200	775	1244	1620	1927	107500	808	1296	1687	2007
91700	708	1140	1486	1769	97000	741	1192	1553	1849	102300	775	1245	1621	1928	107600	809	1297	1688	2008
91800	708	1141	1487	1770	97100	742	1193	1555	1850	102400	776	1246	1622	1930	107700	810	1298	1690	2010
91900	709	1142	1488	1772	97200	743	1194	1556	1852	102500	776	1247	1623	1931	107800	810	1299	1691	2011
92000	710	1143	1490	1773	97300	743	1195	1557	1853	102600	777	1248	1625	1933	107900	811	1300	1692	2013
92100	710	1144	1491	1775	97400	744	1196	1558	1855	102700	778	1249	1626	1934	108000	811	1301	1693	2014
92200	711	1145	1492	1776	97500	745	1197	1560	1856	102800	778	1250	1627	1936	108100	812	1302	1695	2016
92300	712	1146	1494	1778	97600	745	1198	1561	1858	102900	779	1251	1628	1937	108200	813	1303	1696	2017
92400	712	1147	1495	1779	97700	746	1199	1562	1859	103000	780	1252	1630	1939	108300	813	1304	1697	2019
92500	713	1148	1496	1781	97800	747	1200	1564	1861	103100	780	1253	1631	1940	108400	814	1305	1698	2020
92600	713	1149	1497	1782	97900	747	1201	1565	1862	103200	781	1254	1632	1942	108500	815	1306	1700	2022
92700	714	1150	1499	1784	98000	748	1202	1566	1864	103300	782	1255	1634	1943	108600	815	1307	1701	2023
92800	715	1151	1500	1785	98100	748	1203	1567	1865	103400	782	1256	1635	1945	108700	816	1308	1702	2025
92900	715	1152	1501	1787	98200	749	1204	1569	1867	103500	783	1257	1636	1946	108800	817	1309	1704	2026
93000	716	1153	1502	1788	98300	750	1205	1570	1868	103600	783	1258	1637	1948	108900	817	1310	1705	2028
93100	717	1154	1504	1790	98400	750	1206	1571	1870	103700	784	1259	1639	1949	109000	818	1311	1706	2029
93200	717	1155	1505	1791	98500	751	1207	1572	1871	103800	785	1260	1640	1951	109100	818	1312	1707	2031
93300	718	1156	1506	1793	98600	752	1208	1574	1873	103900	785	1261	1641	1952	109200	819	1313	1709	2032
93400	719	1157	1508	1794	98700	752	1209	1575	1874	104000	786	1262	1642	1954	109300	820	1314	1710	2034
93500	719	1158	1509	1796	98800	753	1210	1576	1876	104100	787	1263	1644	1955	109400	820	1315	1711	2035
93600	720	1159	1510	1797	98900	754	1211	1578	1877	104200	787	1264	1645	1957	109500	821	1316	1712	2037
93700	720	1160	1511	1799	99000	754	1212	1579	1879	104300	788	1265	1646	1958	109600	822	1317	1714	2038
93800	721	1161	1513	1800	99100	755	1213	1580	1880	104400	789	1266	1648	1960	109700	822	1318	1715	2040
93900	722	1162	1514	1802	99200	755	1214	1581	1882	104500	789	1267	1649	1961	109800	823	1319	1716	2041
94000	722	1163	1515	1803	99300	756	1215	1583	1883	104600	790	1268	1650	1963	109900	824	1320	1718	2043
94100	723	1164	1516	1805	99400	757	1216	1584	1885	104700	790	1269	1651	1964	110000	824	1321	1719	2044
94200	724	1165	1518	1806	99500	757	1217	1585	1886	104800	791	1270	1653	1966	110100	825	1322	1720	2046
94300	724	1166	1519	1808	99600	758	1218	1586	1888	104900	792	1271	1654	1967	110200	825	1323	1721	2047
94400	725	1167	1520	1809	99700	759	1219	1588	1889	105000	792	1272	1655	1969	110300	826	1324	1723	2049
94500	726	1168	1522	1811	99800	759	1220	1589	1891	105100	793	1273	1656	1970	110400	827	1325	1724	2050
94600	726	1169	1523	1812	99900	760	1221	1590	1892	105200	794	1274	1658	1972	110500	827	1326	1725	2052
94700	727	1170	1524	1814	100000	761	1222	1592	1894	105300	794	1275	1659	1973	110600	828	1327	1726	2053
94800	727	1171	1525	1815	100100	761	1223	1593	1895	105400	795	1276	1660	1975	110700	829	1328	1728	2055
94900	728	1172	1527	1817	100200	762	1224	1594	1897	105500	796	1277	1662	1976	110800	829	1329	1729	2056
95000	729	1173	1528	1818	100300	762	1225	1595	1898	105600	796	1278	1663	1978	110900	830	1330	1730	2058
95100	729	1174	1529	1820	100400	763	1226	1597	1900	105700	797	1279	1664	1979	111000	831	1331	1732	2059
95200	730	1175	1530	1821	100500	764	1227	1598	1901	105800	797	1280	1665	1981	111100	831	1332	1733	2061
95300	731	1176	1532	1823	100600	764	1228	1599	1903	105900	798	1281	1667	1982	111200	832	1333	1734	2062
95400	731	1177	1533	1825	100700	765	1229	1600	1904	106000	799	1282	1668	1984	111300	832	1334	1735	2064
95500	732	1178	1534	1826	100800	766	1230	1602	1906	106100	799	1283	1669	1985	111400	833	1335	1737	2065
95600	733	1179	1536	1828	100900	766	1231	1603	1907	106200	800	1284	1670	1987	111500	834	1336	1738	2067
95700	733	1180	1537	1829	101000	767	1232	1604	1909	106300	801	1285	1672	1988	111600	834	1337	1739	2068
95800	734	1181	1538	1831	101100	768	1233	1606	1910	106400	801	1286	1673	1990	111700	835	1338	1740	2070
95900	734	1182	1539	1832	101200	768	1234	1607	1912	106500	802	1287	1674	1992	111800	836	1339	1742	2071
96000	735	1183	1541	1834	101300	769	1235	1608	1913	106600	803	1288	1676	1993	111900	836	1340	1743	2073
96100	736	1184	1542	1835	101400	769	1236	1609	1915	106700	803	1289	1677	1995	112000	837	1341	1744	2074
96200	736	1185	1543	1837	101500	770	1237	1611	1916	106800	804	1290	1678	1996	112100	838	1342	1746	2076
96300	737	1186	1544	1838	101600	771	1238	1612	1918	106900	804	1291	1679	1998	112200	838	1343	1747	2077
96400	738	1187	1546	1840	101700	771	1239	1613	1919	107000	805	1292	1681	1999	112300	839	1344	1748	2079
96500	738	1188	1547	1841	101800	772	1240	1614	1921	107100	806	1292	1682	2001	112400	839	1345	1749	2080
96600	739	1189	1548	1843	101900	773	1241	1616	1922	107200	806	1293	1683	2002	112500	840	1346	1751	2082
96700	740	1190	1550	1844	102000	773	1242	1617	1924	107300	807	1294	1684	2004	112600	841	1347	1752	2083

Note: This table shows amounts of child support based on income to the nearest $100. There is a mathematical formula for calculating specific child support amounts between the $100 levels. For more information, please contact the Department of Justice.

Nota: La présente table indique le montant de la pension alimentaire pour enfants à verser d'après le revenu (aux 100 $ près). Il existe une formule mathématique pour calculer le montant exact de la pension alimentaire pour enfants dans le cas des revenus qui se situent entre les tranches de 100 $. Pour plus de renseignements, veuillez communiquer avec le ministère de la Justice.

Appendix D

BRITISH COLUMBIA/COLOMBIE-BRITANNIQUE

FEDERAL CHILD SUPPORT AMOUNTS : SIMPLIFIED TABLES 1997
MONTANTS FÉDÉRAUX DE PENSIONS ALIMENTAIRES POUR ENFANTS : TABLES SIMPLIFIÉES

Income/ Revenu ($)	Monthly Award/ Paiement mensuel ($) No. of Children/ N^bre d'enfants				Income/ Revenu ($)	Monthly Award/ Paiement mensuel ($) No. of Children/ N^bre d'enfants				Income/ Revenu ($)	Monthly Award/ Paiement mensuel ($) No. of Children/ N^bre d'enfants				Income/ Revenu ($)	Monthly Award/ Paiement mensuel ($) No. of Children/ N^bre d'enfants			
	1	2	3	4		1	2	3	4		1	2	3	4		1	2	3	4
112700	841	1348	1753	2085	118000	875	1400	1821	2165	123300	909	1453	1888	2244	128600	943	1505	1956	2324
112800	842	1349	1754	2086	118100	876	1401	1822	2166	123400	909	1454	1889	2246	128700	943	1506	1957	2326
112900	843	1350	1756	2088	118200	876	1402	1823	2168	123500	910	1455	1891	2247	128800	944	1507	1958	2327
113000	843	1351	1757	2089	118300	877	1403	1824	2169	123600	911	1456	1892	2249	128900	944	1508	1959	2329
113100	844	1352	1758	2091	118400	878	1404	1826	2171	123700	911	1457	1893	2250	129000	945	1509	1961	2330
113200	845	1353	1760	2092	118500	878	1405	1827	2172	123800	912	1458	1895	2252	129100	946	1510	1962	2332
113300	845	1354	1761	2094	118600	879	1406	1828	2174	123900	913	1459	1896	2253	129200	946	1511	1963	2333
113400	846	1355	1762	2095	118700	880	1407	1830	2175	124000	913	1460	1897	2255	129300	947	1512	1965	2335
113500	846	1356	1763	2097	118800	880	1408	1831	2177	124100	914	1461	1898	2256	129400	948	1513	1966	2336
113600	847	1357	1765	2098	118900	881	1409	1832	2178	124200	915	1462	1900	2258	129500	948	1514	1967	2338
113700	848	1358	1766	2100	119000	881	1410	1833	2180	124300	915	1463	1901	2259	129600	949	1515	1968	2339
113800	848	1359	1767	2101	119100	882	1411	1835	2181	124400	916	1464	1902	2261	129700	950	1516	1970	2341
113900	849	1360	1768	2103	119200	883	1412	1836	2183	124500	916	1465	1903	2262	129800	950	1517	1971	2342
114000	850	1361	1770	2104	119300	883	1413	1837	2184	124600	917	1466	1905	2264	129900	951	1518	1972	2344
114100	850	1362	1771	2106	119400	884	1414	1838	2186	124700	918	1467	1906	2265	130000	951	1519	1973	2345
114200	851	1363	1772	2107	119500	885	1415	1840	2187	124800	918	1468	1907	2267	130100	952	1520	1975	2347
114300	852	1364	1774	2109	119600	885	1416	1841	2189	124900	919	1469	1909	2268	130200	953	1521	1976	2348
114400	852	1365	1775	2110	119700	886	1417	1842	2190	125000	920	1470	1910	2270	130300	953	1522	1977	2350
114500	853	1366	1776	2112	119800	887	1418	1844	2192	125100	920	1471	1911	2271	130400	954	1523	1979	2351
114600	853	1367	1777	2113	119900	887	1419	1845	2193	125200	921	1472	1912	2273	130500	955	1524	1980	2353
114700	854	1368	1779	2115	120000	888	1420	1846	2195	125300	922	1473	1914	2274	130600	955	1525	1981	2354
114800	855	1369	1780	2116	120100	888	1421	1847	2196	125400	922	1474	1915	2276	130700	956	1526	1982	2356
114900	855	1370	1781	2118	120200	889	1422	1849	2198	125500	923	1475	1916	2277	130800	957	1527	1984	2357
115000	856	1371	1782	2119	120300	890	1423	1850	2199	125600	923	1476	1917	2279	130900	957	1528	1985	2359
115100	857	1372	1784	2121	120400	890	1424	1851	2201	125700	924	1477	1919	2280	131000	958	1529	1986	2360
115200	857	1373	1785	2122	120500	891	1425	1853	2202	125800	925	1478	1920	2282	131100	958	1530	1987	2362
115300	858	1374	1786	2124	120600	892	1426	1854	2204	125900	925	1479	1921	2283	131200	959	1531	1989	2363
115400	859	1375	1788	2125	120700	892	1427	1855	2205	126000	926	1480	1923	2285	131300	960	1532	1990	2365
115500	859	1376	1789	2127	120800	893	1428	1856	2207	126100	927	1481	1924	2286	131400	960	1533	1991	2366
115600	860	1377	1790	2128	120900	894	1429	1858	2208	126200	927	1482	1925	2288	131500	961	1534	1993	2368
115700	860	1378	1791	2130	121000	894	1430	1859	2210	126300	928	1483	1926	2289	131600	962	1535	1994	2369
115800	861	1379	1793	2131	121100	895	1431	1860	2211	126400	929	1484	1928	2291	131700	962	1536	1995	2371
115900	862	1380	1794	2133	121200	895	1432	1861	2213	126500	929	1485	1929	2292	131800	963	1537	1996	2372
116000	862	1381	1795	2134	121300	896	1433	1863	2214	126600	930	1486	1930	2294	131900	964	1538	1998	2374
116100	863	1382	1796	2136	121400	897	1434	1864	2216	126700	930	1487	1931	2295	132000	964	1539	1999	2375
116200	864	1383	1798	2137	121500	897	1435	1865	2217	126800	931	1488	1933	2297	132100	965	1540	2000	2377
116300	864	1384	1799	2139	121600	898	1436	1867	2219	126900	932	1489	1934	2298	132200	965	1541	2001	2378
116400	865	1385	1800	2140	121700	899	1437	1868	2220	127000	932	1490	1935	2300	132300	966	1542	2003	2380
116500	866	1386	1802	2142	121800	899	1438	1869	2222	127100	933	1491	1937	2301	132400	967	1543	2004	2381
116600	866	1387	1803	2143	121900	900	1439	1870	2223	127200	934	1492	1938	2303	132500	967	1544	2005	2383
116700	867	1388	1804	2145	122000	901	1440	1872	2225	127300	934	1493	1939	2304	132600	968	1545	2007	2384
116800	867	1389	1805	2146	122100	901	1441	1873	2226	127400	935	1493	1940	2306	132700	969	1546	2008	2386
116900	868	1390	1807	2148	122200	902	1442	1874	2228	127500	936	1494	1942	2307	132800	969	1547	2009	2387
117000	869	1391	1808	2149	122300	902	1443	1875	2229	127600	936	1495	1943	2309	132900	970	1548	2010	2389
117100	869	1392	1809	2151	122400	903	1444	1877	2231	127700	937	1496	1944	2310	133000	971	1549	2012	2390
117200	870	1392	1810	2152	122500	904	1445	1878	2232	127800	937	1497	1945	2312	133100	971	1550	2013	2392
117300	871	1393	1812	2154	122600	904	1446	1879	2234	127900	938	1498	1947	2313	133200	972	1551	2014	2393
117400	871	1394	1813	2155	122700	905	1447	1881	2235	128000	939	1499	1948	2315	133300	972	1552	2015	2395
117500	872	1395	1814	2157	122800	906	1448	1882	2237	128100	939	1500	1949	2316	133400	973	1553	2017	2396
117600	873	1396	1816	2159	122900	906	1449	1883	2238	128200	940	1501	1951	2318	133500	974	1554	2018	2398
117700	873	1397	1817	2160	123000	907	1450	1884	2240	128300	941	1502	1952	2319	133600	974	1555	2019	2399
117800	874	1398	1818	2162	123100	908	1451	1886	2241	128400	941	1503	1953	2321	133700	975	1556	2021	2401
117900	874	1399	1819	2163	123200	908	1452	1887	2243	128500	942	1504	1954	2322	133800	976	1557	2022	2402

Note: This table shows amounts of child support based on income to the nearest $100. There is a mathematical formula for calculating specific child support amounts between the $100 levels. For more information, please contact the Department of Justice.

Nota: La présente table indique le montant de la pension alimentaire pour enfants à verser d'après le revenu (aux 100 $ près). Il existe une formule mathématique pour calculer le montant exact de la pension alimentaire pour enfants dans le cas des revenus qui se situent entre les tranches de 100 $. Pour plus de renseignements, veuillez communiquer avec le ministère de la Justice.

Divorce

BRITISH COLUMBIA/COLOMBIE-BRITANNIQUE

FEDERAL CHILD SUPPORT AMOUNTS : SIMPLIFIED TABLES 1997
MONTANTS FÉDÉRAUX DE PENSIONS ALIMENTAIRES POUR ENFANTS : TABLES SIMPLIFIÉES

Income/Revenu ($)	Monthly Award/Paiement mensuel ($) No. of Children/N^{bre} d'enfants				Income/Revenu ($)	Monthly Award/Paiement mensuel ($) No. of Children/N^{bre} d'enfants				Income/Revenu ($)	Monthly Award/Paiement mensuel ($) No. of Children/N^{bre} d'enfants				Income/Revenu ($)	Monthly Award/Paiement mensuel ($) No. of Children/N^{bre} d'enfants			
	1	2	3	4		1	2	3	4		1	2	3	4		1	2	3	4
133900	976	1558	2023	2404	138000	1002	1598	2075	2465	142100	1028	1639	2127	2527	146200	1055	1680	2180	2589
134000	977	1559	2024	2405	138100	1003	1599	2077	2467	142200	1029	1640	2129	2529	146300	1055	1681	2181	2590
134100	978	1560	2026	2407	138200	1004	1600	2078	2468	142300	1030	1641	2130	2530	146400	1056	1682	2182	2592
134200	978	1561	2027	2408	138300	1004	1601	2079	2470	142400	1030	1642	2131	2532	146500	1057	1683	2183	2593
134300	979	1562	2028	2410	138400	1005	1602	2080	2471	142500	1031	1643	2133	2533	146600	1057	1684	2185	2595
134400	979	1563	2029	2411	138500	1006	1603	2082	2473	142600	1032	1644	2134	2535	146700	1058	1685	2186	2596
134500	980	1564	2031	2413	138600	1006	1604	2083	2474	142700	1032	1645	2135	2536	146800	1058	1686	2187	2598
134600	981	1565	2032	2414	138700	1007	1605	2084	2476	142800	1033	1646	2136	2538	146900	1059	1687	2189	2599
134700	981	1566	2033	2416	138800	1007	1606	2085	2477	142900	1034	1647	2138	2539	147000	1060	1688	2190	2601
134800	982	1567	2035	2417	138900	1008	1607	2087	2479	143000	1034	1648	2139	2541	147100	1060	1689	2191	2602
134900	983	1568	2036	2419	139000	1009	1608	2088	2480	143100	1035	1649	2140	2542	147200	1061	1690	2192	2604
135000	983	1569	2037	2420	139100	1009	1609	2089	2482	143200	1035	1650	2141	2544	147300	1062	1691	2194	2605
135100	984	1570	2038	2422	139200	1010	1610	2091	2483	143300	1036	1651	2143	2545	147400	1062	1692	2195	2607
135200	985	1571	2040	2423	139300	1011	1611	2092	2485	143400	1037	1652	2144	2547	147500	1063	1693	2196	2608
135300	985	1572	2041	2425	139400	1011	1612	2093	2486	143500	1037	1653	2145	2548	147600	1064	1693	2197	2610
135400	986	1573	2042	2426	139500	1012	1613	2094	2488	143600	1038	1654	2147	2550	147700	1064	1694	2199	2611
135500	986	1574	2043	2428	139600	1013	1614	2096	2489	143700	1039	1655	2148	2551	147800	1065	1695	2200	2613
135600	987	1575	2045	2429	139700	1013	1615	2097	2491	143800	1039	1656	2149	2553	147900	1065	1696	2201	2614
135700	988	1576	2046	2431	139800	1014	1616	2098	2493	143900	1040	1657	2150	2554	148000	1066	1697	2203	2616
135800	988	1577	2047	2432	139900	1014	1617	2099	2494	144000	1041	1658	2152	2556	148100	1067	1698	2204	2617
135900	989	1578	2049	2434	140000	1015	1618	2101	2496	144100	1041	1659	2153	2557	148200	1067	1699	2205	2619
136000	990	1579	2050	2435	140100	1016	1619	2102	2497	144200	1042	1660	2154	2559	148300	1068	1700	2206	2620
136100	990	1580	2051	2437	140200	1016	1620	2103	2499	144300	1042	1661	2155	2560	148400	1069	1701	2208	2622
136200	991	1581	2052	2438	140300	1017	1621	2105	2500	144400	1043	1662	2157	2562	148500	1069	1702	2209	2623
136300	992	1582	2054	2440	140400	1018	1622	2106	2502	144500	1044	1663	2158	2563	148600	1070	1703	2210	2625
136400	992	1583	2055	2441	140500	1018	1623	2107	2503	144600	1044	1664	2159	2565	148700	1071	1704	2211	2626
136500	993	1584	2056	2443	140600	1019	1624	2108	2505	144700	1045	1665	2161	2566	148800	1071	1705	2213	2628
136600	993	1585	2057	2444	140700	1020	1625	2110	2506	144800	1046	1666	2162	2568	148900	1072	1706	2214	2629
136700	994	1586	2059	2446	140800	1020	1626	2111	2508	144900	1046	1667	2163	2569	149000	1072	1707	2215	2631
136800	995	1587	2060	2447	140900	1021	1627	2112	2509	145000	1047	1668	2164	2571	149100	1073	1708	2217	2632
136900	995	1588	2061	2449	141000	1021	1628	2113	2511	145100	1048	1669	2166	2572	149200	1074	1709	2218	2634
137000	996	1589	2063	2450	141100	1022	1629	2115	2512	145200	1048	1670	2167	2574	149300	1074	1710	2219	2635
137100	997	1590	2064	2452	141200	1023	1630	2116	2514	145300	1049	1671	2168	2575	149400	1075	1711	2220	2637
137200	997	1591	2065	2453	141300	1023	1631	2117	2515	145400	1049	1672	2169	2577	149500	1076	1712	2222	2638
137300	998	1592	2066	2455	141400	1024	1632	2119	2517	145500	1050	1673	2171	2578	149600	1076	1713	2223	2640
137400	999	1593	2068	2456	141500	1025	1633	2120	2518	145600	1051	1674	2172	2580	149700	1077	1714	2224	2641
137500	999	1593	2069	2458	141600	1025	1634	2121	2520	145700	1051	1675	2173	2581	149800	1078	1715	2226	2643
137600	1000	1594	2070	2459	141700	1026	1635	2122	2521	145800	1052	1676	2175	2583	149900	1078	1716	2227	2644
137700	1000	1595	2071	2461	141800	1027	1636	2124	2523	145900	1053	1677	2176	2584	150000	1079	1717	2228	2646
137800	1001	1596	2073	2462	141900	1027	1637	2125	2524	146000	1053	1678	2177	2586					
137900	1002	1597	2074	2464	142000	1028	1638	2126	2526	146100	1054	1679	2178	2587					

Income/Revenu ($)	Monthly Award/Paiement mensuel ($)			
	one child/un enfant	two children/deux enfants	three children/trois enfants	four children/quatre enfants
For income over $150,000	**1079** plus 0.64% of income over $150,000	**1717** plus 0.99% of income over $150,000	**2228** plus 1.27% of income over $150,000	**2646** plus 1.50% of income over $150,000
Pour revenu dépassant 150 000$	**1079** plus 0,64% du revenu dépassant 150 000$	**1717** plus 0,99% du revenu dépassant 150 000$	**2228** plus 1,27% du revenu dépassant 150 000$	**2646** plus 1,50% du revenu dépassant 150 000$

Note: This table shows amounts of child support based on income to the nearest $100. There is a mathematical formula for calculating specific child support amounts between the $100 levels. For more information, please contact the Department of Justice.

Nota: La présente table indique le montant de la pension alimentaire pour enfants à verser d'après le revenu (aux 100 $ près). Il existe une formule mathématique pour calculer le montant exact de la pension alimentaire pour enfants dans le cas des revenus qui se situent entre les tranches de 100 $. Pour plus de renseignements, veuillez communiquer avec le ministère de la Justice.

Appendix D

MANITOBA

FEDERAL CHILD SUPPORT AMOUNTS : SIMPLIFIED TABLES
MONTANTS FÉDÉRAUX DE PENSIONS ALIMENTAIRES POUR ENFANTS : TABLES SIMPLIFIÉES

1997

Income/ Revenu ($)	Monthly Award/ Paiement mensuel ($) No. of Children/ N^{bre} d'enfants				Income/ Revenu ($)	Monthly Award/ Paiement mensuel ($) No. of Children/ N^{bre} d'enfants				Income/ Revenu ($)	Monthly Award/ Paiement mensuel ($) No. of Children/ N^{bre} d'enfants				Income/ Revenu ($)	Monthly Award/ Paiement mensuel ($) No. of Children/ N^{bre} d'enfants			
	1	2	3	4		1	2	3	4		1	2	3	4		1	2	3	4
6700	0	0	0	0	12000	102	188	210	232	17300	128	237	330	401	22600	178	313	420	509
6800	4	4	4	4	12100	102	190	213	235	17400	129	238	331	404	22700	179	314	422	511
6900	9	9	10	11	12200	103	193	215	238	17500	130	240	332	408	22800	180	316	424	513
7000	14	15	16	17	12300	103	195	218	241	17600	131	241	334	411	22900	181	317	426	515
7100	19	20	22	23	12400	104	197	221	245	17700	132	242	335	414	23000	182	319	428	518
7200	24	25	27	29	12500	104	199	224	248	17800	133	244	337	415	23100	183	320	430	520
7300	29	31	33	36	12600	104	199	226	251	17900	134	245	338	417	23200	184	322	432	522
7400	34	36	39	42	12700	105	199	229	254	18000	135	247	339	419	23300	185	323	434	524
7500	39	42	45	48	12800	105	200	232	257	18100	135	248	341	421	23400	186	325	436	527
7600	44	47	51	54	12900	105	200	235	261	18200	136	249	342	422	23500	187	326	438	529
7700	49	53	57	61	13000	106	200	238	264	18300	137	251	344	424	23600	188	328	440	531
7800	54	58	62	67	13100	106	200	240	267	18400	138	252	345	426	23700	189	329	442	533
7900	59	63	68	73	13200	107	201	243	270	18500	139	253	347	428	23800	190	331	443	536
8000	63	69	74	79	13300	107	201	246	273	18600	140	255	348	429	23900	191	332	445	538
8100	67	72	78	84	13400	107	201	249	277	18700	141	256	349	431	24000	192	334	447	540
8200	69	75	82	88	13500	108	201	252	280	18800	142	258	351	433	24100	193	335	449	542
8300	72	79	85	92	13600	108	202	254	283	18900	142	259	352	435	24200	194	337	451	545
8400	75	82	89	96	13700	108	202	257	286	19000	143	260	354	437	24300	195	339	453	547
8500	77	85	92	100	13800	109	202	260	289	19100	144	262	356	438	24400	196	340	455	549
8600	80	88	96	103	13900	109	202	263	293	19200	145	263	357	440	24500	197	342	457	551
8700	83	91	99	107	14000	109	203	265	296	19300	146	265	359	442	24600	198	343	459	554
8800	86	94	103	111	14100	110	204	268	299	19400	147	266	361	444	24700	199	345	461	556
8900	88	97	106	115	14200	110	205	271	302	19500	148	267	363	446	24800	200	346	463	558
9000	91	100	110	119	14300	111	206	274	305	19600	149	269	365	447	24900	201	348	465	560
9100	91	103	113	123	14400	111	207	277	308	19700	150	270	366	449	25000	202	349	467	563
9200	92	107	117	127	14500	111	208	279	312	19800	151	272	368	451	25100	203	351	469	565
9300	92	110	120	131	14600	112	209	282	315	19900	152	273	370	453	25200	205	352	470	567
9400	92	113	124	135	14700	112	210	285	318	20000	153	274	372	455	25300	206	354	472	569
9500	93	116	127	139	14800	112	211	288	321	20100	154	276	374	457	25400	207	355	474	572
9600	93	119	131	143	14900	113	212	290	324	20200	154	277	376	458	25500	208	357	476	574
9700	94	122	135	147	15000	113	213	293	328	20300	155	279	377	460	25600	209	358	478	576
9800	94	125	138	151	15100	114	214	296	331	20400	156	280	379	462	25700	210	360	480	578
9900	94	128	142	155	15200	114	215	299	334	20500	157	282	381	464	25800	211	361	482	581
10000	95	131	145	159	15300	114	216	301	337	20600	158	283	383	466	25900	212	363	484	583
10100	95	135	149	163	15400	115	217	303	340	20700	159	284	385	468	26000	213	364	486	585
10200	95	138	152	167	15500	115	218	304	344	20800	160	286	386	469	26100	214	366	488	587
10300	96	141	156	171	15600	115	219	305	347	20900	161	287	388	471	26200	215	367	489	589
10400	96	144	159	175	15700	116	220	307	350	21000	162	289	390	473	26300	216	369	491	591
10500	96	147	163	178	15800	116	221	308	353	21100	163	290	392	475	26400	216	370	493	593
10600	97	150	166	182	15900	117	222	310	356	21200	164	292	394	477	26500	217	371	495	596
10700	97	153	170	186	16000	117	223	311	360	21300	165	293	396	479	26600	218	373	496	598
10800	98	156	173	190	16100	118	224	313	363	21400	166	294	397	482	26700	219	374	498	600
10900	98	160	177	194	16200	119	225	314	366	21500	167	296	399	484	26800	220	376	500	602
11000	98	163	180	198	16300	120	226	315	369	21600	168	297	401	486	26900	221	377	502	604
11100	99	166	184	202	16400	120	227	317	372	21700	169	299	403	488	27000	222	379	504	606
11200	99	168	187	205	16500	121	228	318	376	21800	170	300	405	491	27100	223	380	505	608
11300	99	171	190	209	16600	122	229	320	379	21900	171	302	407	493	27200	224	381	507	610
11400	100	173	193	212	16700	123	230	321	382	22000	172	303	409	495	27300	225	383	509	612
11500	100	176	196	215	16800	124	231	322	385	22100	173	305	411	497	27400	226	384	511	614
11600	101	178	199	219	16900	125	232	324	388	22200	174	306	413	500	27500	227	386	513	616
11700	101	181	201	222	17000	126	233	325	392	22300	175	308	415	502	27600	228	387	514	619
11800	101	183	204	225	17100	127	234	327	395	22400	176	310	417	504	27700	229	389	516	621
11900	102	185	207	229	17200	127	236	328	398	22500	177	311	418	506	27800	230	390	518	623

Note: This table shows amounts of child support based on income to the nearest $100. There is a mathematical formula for calculating specific child support amounts between the $100 levels. For more information, please contact the Department of Justice.

Nota: La présente table indique le montant de la pension alimentaire pour enfants à verser d'après le revenu (aux 100 $ près). Il existe une formule mathématique pour calculer le montant exact de la pension alimentaire pour enfants dans le cas des revenus qui se situent entre les tranches de 100 $. Pour plus de renseignements, veuillez communiquer avec le ministère de la Justice.

Divorce

MANITOBA

FEDERAL CHILD SUPPORT AMOUNTS : SIMPLIFIED TABLES
MONTANTS FÉDÉRAUX DE PENSIONS ALIMENTAIRES POUR ENFANTS : TABLES SIMPLIFIÉES

1997

Income/Revenu ($)	Monthly Award/Paiement mensuel ($) No. of Children/N^{bre} d'enfants				Income/Revenu ($)	Monthly Award/Paiement mensuel ($) No. of Children/N^{bre} d'enfants				Income/Revenu ($)	Monthly Award/Paiement mensuel ($) No. of Children/N^{bre} d'enfants				Income/Revenu ($)	Monthly Award/Paiement mensuel ($) No. of Children/N^{bre} d'enfants				Income/Revenu ($)	Monthly Award/Paiement mensuel ($) No. of Children/N^{bre} d'enfants			
	1	2	3	4		1	2	3	4		1	2	3	4		1	2	3	4		1	2	3	4
27900	231	391	520	625	33200	273	455	600	719	38500	316	518	679	812	43800	357	585	765	912					
28000	232	393	522	627	33300	274	456	602	721	38600	317	519	681	814	43900	358	586	766	914					
28100	233	394	523	629	33400	275	457	603	723	38700	317	520	683	815	44000	359	587	768	915					
28200	234	396	525	631	33500	275	458	605	724	38800	318	522	684	817	44100	360	589	770	917					
28300	235	397	527	633	33600	276	459	606	726	38900	319	523	686	819	44200	360	590	771	919					
28400	236	399	529	636	33700	277	461	607	728	39000	320	524	687	821	44300	361	591	773	921					
28500	237	400	531	638	33800	278	462	609	729	39100	321	525	689	823	44400	362	593	774	923					
28600	238	401	533	640	33900	278	463	610	731	39200	321	527	690	825	44500	363	594	776	925					
28700	239	403	534	642	34000	279	464	612	733	39300	322	528	692	826	44600	364	595	778	927					
28800	240	404	536	644	34100	280	465	613	735	39400	323	529	694	828	44700	364	596	779	929					
28900	241	406	538	646	34200	281	466	615	736	39500	324	530	695	830	44800	365	598	781	931					
29000	242	407	540	648	34300	281	467	616	738	39600	325	532	697	832	44900	366	599	782	933					
29100	243	409	542	650	34400	282	468	618	740	39700	326	533	698	834	45000	367	600	784	934					
29200	243	410	543	653	34500	283	470	619	741	39800	326	534	700	836	45100	367	601	786	936					
29300	244	412	545	655	34600	284	471	621	743	39900	327	535	701	837	45200	368	603	787	938					
29400	245	413	547	657	34700	284	472	622	745	40000	328	537	703	839	45300	369	604	789	940					
29500	246	414	549	659	34800	285	473	623	747	40100	329	538	705	841	45400	370	605	790	942					
29600	247	416	551	661	34900	286	474	625	748	40200	330	539	706	843	45500	371	606	792	944					
29700	248	417	552	663	35000	287	475	626	750	40300	330	541	708	845	45600	371	608	794	946					
29800	249	418	554	664	35100	287	476	628	752	40400	331	542	710	847	45700	372	609	795	948					
29900	250	419	555	666	35200	288	478	629	753	40500	332	543	711	849	45800	373	610	797	950					
30000	250	420	556	668	35300	289	479	631	755	40600	333	544	713	851	45900	374	611	798	952					
30100	251	421	558	669	35400	290	480	632	757	40700	333	546	715	853	46000	374	613	800	953					
30200	252	422	559	671	35500	291	481	634	759	40800	334	547	716	854	46100	375	614	802	955					
30300	253	424	560	672	35600	291	482	635	760	40900	335	548	718	856	46200	376	615	803	957					
30400	253	425	562	674	35700	292	483	637	762	41000	336	549	719	858	46300	377	617	805	959					
30500	254	426	563	675	35800	293	484	638	764	41100	336	551	721	860	46400	377	618	807	961					
30600	255	427	564	677	35900	294	486	640	765	41200	337	552	723	862	46500	378	619	808	963					
30700	255	428	566	678	36000	295	487	641	767	41300	338	553	724	864	46600	379	620	810	965					
30800	256	429	567	680	36100	296	488	643	769	41400	339	555	726	866	46700	380	622	811	967					
30900	257	430	568	682	36200	296	489	644	771	41500	340	556	728	868	46800	381	623	813	968					
31000	257	431	570	683	36300	297	490	646	773	41600	340	557	729	870	46900	381	624	815	970					
31100	258	432	571	685	36400	298	492	647	774	41700	341	558	731	872	47000	382	625	816	972					
31200	259	433	572	686	36500	299	493	649	776	41800	342	560	732	874	47100	383	627	818	974					
31300	259	434	574	688	36600	300	494	650	778	41900	343	561	734	875	47200	384	628	819	976					
31400	260	435	575	689	36700	301	495	652	780	42000	343	562	736	877	47300	384	629	821	978					
31500	261	436	576	691	36800	302	497	653	781	42100	344	563	737	879	47400	385	630	823	980					
31600	261	437	577	692	36900	302	498	655	783	42200	345	565	739	881	47500	386	632	824	982					
31700	262	438	579	694	37000	303	499	656	785	42300	346	566	741	883	47600	387	633	826	983					
31800	263	439	580	696	37100	304	500	658	787	42400	347	567	742	885	47700	388	634	827	985					
31900	263	440	581	697	37200	305	502	659	789	42500	347	568	744	887	47800	388	636	829	987					
32000	264	441	583	699	37300	306	503	661	790	42600	348	570	745	889	47900	389	637	831	989					
32100	265	442	584	700	37400	307	504	662	792	42700	349	571	747	891	48000	390	638	832	991					
32200	266	443	586	702	37500	307	505	664	794	42800	350	572	749	893	48100	391	639	834	993					
32300	266	445	587	704	37600	308	507	665	796	42900	350	574	750	894	48200	391	641	835	995					
32400	267	446	589	705	37700	309	508	667	798	43000	351	575	752	896	48300	392	642	837	997					
32500	268	447	590	707	37800	310	509	668	799	43100	352	576	754	898	48400	393	643	839	998					
32600	269	448	591	709	37900	311	510	670	801	43200	353	577	755	900	48500	394	644	840	1000					
32700	269	449	593	711	38000	312	512	672	803	43300	354	579	757	902	48600	395	646	842	1002					
32800	270	450	594	712	38100	313	513	673	805	43400	354	580	758	904	48700	395	647	843	1004					
32900	271	451	596	714	38200	313	514	675	806	43500	355	581	760	906	48800	396	648	845	1006					
33000	272	453	597	716	38300	314	515	676	808	43600	356	582	762	908	48900	397	649	847	1008					
33100	272	454	599	717	38400	315	517	678	810	43700	357	584	763	910	49000	398	651	848	1010					

Note: This table shows amounts of child support based on income to the nearest $100. There is a mathematical formula for calculating specific child support amounts between the $100 levels. For more information, please contact the Department of Justice.

Nota: La présente table indique le montant de la pension alimentaire pour enfants à verser d'après le revenu (aux 100 $ près). Il existe une formule mathématique pour calculer le montant exact de la pension alimentaire pour enfants dans le cas des revenus qui se situent entre les tranches de 100 $. Pour plus de renseignements, veuillez communiquer avec le ministère de la Justice.

Appendix D

MANITOBA
1997

FEDERAL CHILD SUPPORT AMOUNTS : SIMPLIFIED TABLES
MONTANTS FÉDÉRAUX DE PENSIONS ALIMENTAIRES POUR ENFANTS : TABLES SIMPLIFIÉES

Income/ Revenu ($)	Monthly Award/ Paiement mensuel ($) No. of Children/ N^{bre} d'enfants				Income/ Revenu ($)	Monthly Award/ Paiement mensuel ($) No. of Children/ N^{bre} d'enfants				Income/ Revenu ($)	Monthly Award/ Paiement mensuel ($) No. of Children/ N^{bre} d'enfants				Income/ Revenu ($)	Monthly Award/ Paiement mensuel ($) No. of Children/ N^{bre} d'enfants				Income/ Revenu ($)	Monthly Award/ Paiement mensuel ($) No. of Children/ N^{bre} d'enfants			
	1	2	3	4		1	2	3	4		1	2	3	4		1	2	3	4		1	2	3	4
49100	398	652	850	1012	54400	439	718	935	1111	59700	480	781	1019	1210	65000	517	838	1096	1300					
49200	399	653	851	1014	54500	440	719	936	1113	59800	481	782	1020	1212	65100	517	839	1097	1302					
49300	400	655	853	1015	54600	441	720	938	1115	59900	481	783	1022	1213	65200	518	840	1098	1303					
49400	401	656	855	1017	54700	442	721	940	1117	60000	482	784	1023	1215	65300	518	841	1100	1305					
49500	401	657	856	1019	54800	442	723	941	1119	60100	483	786	1025	1217	65400	519	842	1101	1307					
49600	402	658	858	1021	54900	443	724	943	1121	60200	484	787	1026	1219	65500	520	843	1103	1308					
49700	403	660	859	1023	55000	444	725	944	1122	60300	484	788	1028	1220	65600	520	845	1104	1310					
49800	404	661	861	1025	55100	445	726	946	1124	60400	485	789	1029	1222	65700	521	846	1105	1312					
49900	405	662	863	1027	55200	446	727	948	1126	60500	486	790	1031	1224	65800	522	847	1107	1313					
50000	405	663	864	1029	55300	446	729	949	1128	60600	486	791	1032	1226	65900	522	848	1108	1315					
50100	406	665	866	1030	55400	447	730	951	1130	60700	487	792	1034	1227	66000	523	849	1109	1317					
50200	407	666	867	1032	55500	448	731	952	1132	60800	488	793	1035	1229	66100	524	850	1111	1318					
50300	408	667	869	1034	55600	449	732	954	1134	60900	489	794	1037	1231	66200	524	851	1112	1320					
50400	408	668	871	1036	55700	449	733	956	1136	61000	489	795	1038	1232	66300	525	852	1113	1322					
50500	409	670	872	1038	55800	450	735	957	1138	61100	490	797	1040	1234	66400	525	853	1115	1323					
50600	410	671	874	1040	55900	451	736	959	1139	61200	491	798	1041	1236	66500	526	854	1116	1325					
50700	411	672	875	1042	56000	452	737	960	1141	61300	491	799	1043	1238	66600	527	855	1117	1326					
50800	412	673	877	1044	56100	453	738	962	1143	61400	492	800	1044	1239	66700	527	856	1119	1328					
50900	412	675	879	1045	56200	453	740	964	1145	61500	493	801	1046	1241	66800	528	857	1120	1330					
51000	413	676	880	1047	56300	454	741	965	1147	61600	494	802	1047	1243	66900	529	858	1121	1331					
51100	414	677	882	1049	56400	455	742	967	1149	61700	494	803	1048	1245	67000	529	859	1123	1333					
51200	415	679	883	1051	56500	456	743	968	1151	61800	495	804	1050	1246	67100	530	860	1124	1335					
51300	415	680	885	1053	56600	456	744	970	1153	61900	496	805	1051	1248	67200	531	861	1125	1337					
51400	416	681	887	1055	56700	457	746	972	1154	62000	496	806	1053	1250	67300	532	862	1127	1338					
51500	417	682	888	1057	56800	458	747	973	1156	62100	497	808	1054	1251	67400	532	863	1128	1340					
51600	418	684	890	1059	56900	459	748	975	1158	62200	498	809	1056	1253	67500	533	864	1130	1342					
51700	419	685	891	1060	57000	460	749	976	1160	62300	498	810	1057	1255	67600	534	866	1131	1343					
51800	419	686	893	1062	57100	460	750	978	1162	62400	499	811	1059	1257	67700	534	867	1132	1345					
51900	420	687	895	1064	57200	461	752	980	1164	62500	500	812	1060	1258	67800	535	868	1134	1347					
52000	421	689	896	1066	57300	462	753	981	1166	62600	501	813	1062	1260	67900	536	869	1135	1348					
52100	422	690	898	1068	57400	463	754	983	1168	62700	501	814	1063	1262	68000	536	870	1137	1350					
52200	422	691	899	1070	57500	463	755	984	1169	62800	502	815	1065	1264	68100	537	871	1138	1352					
52300	423	692	901	1072	57600	464	756	986	1171	62900	503	816	1066	1265	68200	538	872	1139	1353					
52400	424	694	903	1074	57700	465	758	988	1173	63000	503	817	1068	1267	68300	538	873	1141	1355					
52500	425	695	904	1076	57800	466	759	989	1175	63100	504	819	1069	1269	68400	539	874	1142	1357					
52600	425	696	906	1077	57900	466	760	991	1177	63200	505	820	1071	1270	68500	540	875	1143	1358					
52700	426	697	907	1079	58000	467	761	992	1179	63300	506	821	1072	1272	68600	541	876	1145	1360					
52800	427	699	909	1081	58100	468	762	994	1181	63400	506	822	1074	1274	68700	541	877	1146	1362					
52900	428	700	911	1083	58200	469	764	996	1183	63500	507	823	1075	1276	68800	542	878	1148	1363					
53000	429	701	912	1085	58300	470	765	997	1185	63600	508	824	1076	1277	68900	543	879	1149	1365					
53100	429	702	914	1087	58400	470	766	999	1186	63700	508	825	1078	1279	69000	543	881	1150	1367					
53200	430	703	916	1089	58500	471	767	1000	1188	63800	509	826	1079	1280	69100	544	882	1152	1368					
53300	431	705	917	1091	58600	472	768	1002	1190	63900	509	827	1080	1282	69200	545	883	1153	1370					
53400	432	706	919	1092	58700	473	770	1004	1192	64000	510	828	1082	1284	69300	545	884	1154	1372					
53500	432	707	920	1094	58800	473	771	1005	1194	64100	511	829	1083	1285	69400	546	885	1156	1373					
53600	433	708	922	1096	58900	474	772	1007	1196	64200	511	830	1085	1287	69500	547	886	1157	1375					
53700	434	709	924	1098	59000	475	773	1008	1198	64300	512	831	1086	1289	69600	547	887	1159	1377					
53800	435	711	925	1100	59100	476	774	1010	1200	64400	513	832	1087	1290	69700	548	888	1160	1378					
53900	436	712	927	1102	59200	476	776	1012	1201	64500	513	833	1089	1292	69800	549	889	1161	1380					
54000	436	713	928	1104	59300	477	777	1013	1203	64600	514	834	1090	1294	69900	549	890	1163	1382					
54100	437	714	930	1106	59400	478	778	1015	1205	64700	515	835	1092	1295	70000	550	891	1164	1384					
54200	438	715	932	1107	59500	479	779	1016	1207	64800	515	836	1093	1297	70100	551	892	1165	1385					
54300	439	717	933	1109	59600	479	780	1018	1208	64900	516	837	1094	1299	70200	552	893	1167	1387					

Note: This table shows amounts of child support based on income to the nearest $100. There is a mathematical formula for calculating specific child support amounts between the $100 levels. For more information, please contact the Department of Justice.

Nota: La présente table indique le montant de la pension alimentaire pour enfants à verser d'après le revenu (aux 100 $ près). Il existe une formule mathématique pour calculer le montant exact de la pension alimentaire pour enfants dans le cas des revenus qui se situent entre les tranches de 100 $. Pour plus de renseignements, veuillez communiquer avec le ministère de la Justice.

Divorce

Manitoba

Federal Child Support Amounts : Simplified Tables
Montants fédéraux de pensions alimentaires pour enfants : Tables simplifiées

1997

Income/ Revenu ($)	Monthly Award/ Paiement mensuel ($) No. of Children/ N^{bre} d'enfants				Income/ Revenu ($)	Monthly Award/ Paiement mensuel ($) No. of Children/ N^{bre} d'enfants				Income/ Revenu ($)	Monthly Award/ Paiement mensuel ($) No. of Children/ N^{bre} d'enfants				Income/ Revenu ($)	Monthly Award/ Paiement mensuel ($) No. of Children/ N^{bre} d'enfants			
	1	2	3	4		1	2	3	4		1	2	3	4		1	2	3	4
70300	552	894	1168	1389	75600	589	951	1241	1478	80900	625	1008	1314	1565	86200	662	1065	1387	1651
70400	553	896	1170	1390	75700	589	952	1243	1479	81000	626	1009	1316	1566	86300	662	1066	1389	1653
70500	554	897	1171	1392	75800	590	953	1244	1481	81100	627	1010	1317	1568	86400	663	1067	1390	1654
70600	554	898	1172	1394	75900	591	954	1245	1483	81200	627	1011	1318	1570	86500	664	1068	1391	1656
70700	555	899	1174	1395	76000	591	956	1247	1484	81300	628	1012	1320	1571	86600	665	1069	1393	1658
70800	556	900	1175	1397	76100	592	957	1248	1486	81400	629	1013	1321	1573	86700	665	1070	1394	1659
70900	556	901	1176	1399	76200	593	958	1249	1488	81500	629	1014	1323	1575	86800	666	1071	1396	1661
71000	557	902	1178	1400	76300	594	959	1251	1489	81600	630	1016	1324	1576	86900	667	1072	1397	1662
71100	558	903	1179	1402	76400	594	960	1252	1491	81700	631	1017	1325	1578	87000	667	1073	1398	1664
71200	558	904	1181	1404	76500	595	961	1254	1493	81800	631	1018	1327	1579	87100	668	1074	1400	1666
71300	559	905	1182	1405	76600	596	962	1255	1494	81900	632	1019	1328	1581	87200	669	1076	1401	1667
71400	560	906	1183	1407	76700	596	963	1256	1496	82000	633	1020	1329	1583	87300	669	1077	1402	1669
71500	560	907	1185	1409	76800	597	964	1258	1498	82100	634	1021	1331	1584	87400	670	1078	1404	1671
71600	561	908	1186	1410	76900	598	965	1259	1499	82200	634	1022	1332	1586	87500	671	1079	1405	1672
71700	562	909	1187	1412	77000	598	966	1261	1501	82300	635	1023	1334	1588	87600	671	1080	1407	1674
71800	563	911	1189	1414	77100	599	967	1262	1503	82400	636	1024	1335	1589	87700	672	1081	1408	1676
71900	563	912	1190	1415	77200	600	968	1263	1504	82500	636	1025	1336	1591	87800	673	1082	1409	1677
72000	564	913	1192	1417	77300	600	969	1265	1506	82600	637	1026	1338	1592	87900	673	1083	1411	1679
72100	565	914	1193	1419	77400	601	971	1266	1508	82700	638	1027	1339	1594	88000	674	1084	1412	1681
72200	565	915	1194	1420	77500	602	972	1267	1509	82800	638	1028	1340	1596	88100	675	1085	1413	1682
72300	566	916	1196	1422	77600	603	973	1269	1511	82900	639	1029	1342	1597	88200	676	1086	1415	1684
72400	567	917	1197	1424	77700	603	974	1270	1513	83000	640	1031	1343	1599	88300	676	1087	1416	1685
72500	567	918	1199	1425	77800	604	975	1272	1514	83100	640	1032	1345	1601	88400	677	1088	1418	1687
72600	568	919	1200	1427	77900	605	976	1273	1516	83200	641	1033	1346	1602	88500	678	1089	1419	1689
72700	569	920	1201	1429	78000	605	977	1274	1518	83300	642	1034	1347	1604	88600	678	1091	1420	1690
72800	569	921	1203	1431	78100	606	978	1276	1519	83400	642	1035	1349	1605	88700	679	1092	1422	1692
72900	570	922	1204	1432	78200	607	979	1277	1521	83500	643	1036	1350	1607	88800	680	1093	1423	1693
73000	571	923	1205	1434	78300	607	980	1278	1522	83600	644	1037	1351	1609	88900	680	1094	1424	1695
73100	572	924	1207	1436	78400	608	981	1280	1524	83700	645	1038	1353	1610	89000	681	1095	1426	1697
73200	572	926	1208	1437	78500	609	982	1281	1526	83800	645	1039	1354	1612	89100	682	1096	1427	1698
73300	573	927	1210	1439	78600	609	983	1283	1527	83900	646	1040	1356	1614	89200	682	1097	1429	1700
73400	574	928	1211	1441	78700	610	984	1284	1529	84000	647	1041	1357	1615	89300	683	1098	1430	1702
73500	574	929	1212	1442	78800	611	986	1285	1531	84100	647	1042	1358	1617	89400	684	1099	1431	1703
73600	575	930	1214	1444	78900	611	987	1287	1532	84200	648	1043	1360	1619	89500	684	1100	1433	1705
73700	576	931	1215	1446	79000	612	988	1288	1534	84300	649	1044	1361	1620	89600	685	1101	1434	1706
73800	576	932	1216	1447	79100	613	989	1289	1535	84400	649	1046	1362	1622	89700	686	1102	1435	1708
73900	577	933	1218	1449	79200	614	990	1291	1537	84500	650	1047	1364	1623	89800	687	1103	1437	1710
74000	578	934	1219	1451	79300	614	991	1292	1539	84600	651	1048	1365	1625	89900	687	1104	1438	1711
74100	578	935	1221	1452	79400	615	992	1294	1540	84700	651	1049	1367	1627	90000	688	1106	1440	1713
74200	579	936	1222	1454	79500	616	993	1295	1542	84800	652	1050	1368	1628	90100	689	1107	1441	1715
74300	580	937	1223	1456	79600	616	994	1296	1544	84900	653	1051	1369	1630	90200	689	1108	1442	1716
74400	580	938	1225	1457	79700	617	995	1298	1545	85000	653	1052	1371	1632	90300	690	1109	1444	1718
74500	581	939	1226	1459	79800	618	996	1299	1547	85100	654	1053	1372	1633	90400	691	1110	1445	1719
74600	582	941	1227	1461	79900	618	997	1300	1549	85200	655	1054	1373	1635	90500	691	1111	1447	1721
74700	583	942	1229	1462	80000	619	998	1302	1550	85300	656	1055	1375	1636	90600	692	1112	1448	1723
74800	583	943	1230	1464	80100	620	999	1303	1552	85400	656	1056	1376	1638	90700	693	1113	1449	1724
74900	584	944	1232	1466	80200	620	1001	1305	1553	85500	657	1057	1378	1640	90800	693	1114	1451	1726
75000	585	945	1233	1467	80300	621	1002	1306	1555	85600	658	1058	1379	1641	90900	694	1115	1452	1728
75100	585	946	1234	1469	80400	622	1003	1307	1557	85700	658	1059	1380	1643	91000	695	1116	1453	1729
75200	586	947	1236	1471	80500	622	1004	1309	1558	85800	659	1061	1382	1645	91100	696	1117	1455	1731
75300	587	948	1237	1472	80600	623	1005	1310	1560	85900	660	1062	1383	1646	91200	696	1118	1456	1733
75400	587	949	1238	1474	80700	624	1006	1311	1562	86000	660	1063	1385	1648	91300	697	1119	1458	1734
75500	588	950	1240	1476	80800	625	1007	1313	1563	86100	661	1064	1386	1649	91400	698	1121	1459	1736

Note: This table shows amounts of child support based on income to the nearest $100. There is a mathematical formula for calculating specific child support amounts between the $100 levels. For more information, please contact the Department of Justice.

Nota: La présente table indique le montant de la pension alimentaire pour enfants à verser d'après le revenu (aux 100 $ près). Il existe une formule mathématique pour calculer le montant exact de la pension alimentaire pour enfants dans le cas des revenus qui se situent entre les tranches de 100 $. Pour plus de renseignements, veuillez communiquer avec le ministère de la Justice.

Appendix D

MANITOBA
1997

FEDERAL CHILD SUPPORT AMOUNTS : SIMPLIFIED TABLES
MONTANTS FÉDÉRAUX DE PENSIONS ALIMENTAIRES POUR ENFANTS : TABLES SIMPLIFIÉES

Income/ Revenu ($)	Monthly Award/ Paiement mensuel ($) No. of Children/ N^{bre} d'enfants				Income/ Revenu ($)	Monthly Award/ Paiement mensuel ($) No. of Children/ N^{bre} d'enfants				Income/ Revenu ($)	Monthly Award/ Paiement mensuel ($) No. of Children/ N^{bre} d'enfants				Income/ Revenu ($)	Monthly Award/ Paiement mensuel ($) No. of Children/ N^{bre} d'enfants			
	1	2	3	4		1	2	3	4		1	2	3	4		1	2	3	4
91500	698	1122	1460	1737	*96800*	735	1178	1533	1824	*102100*	771	1235	1606	1910	*107400*	808	1292	1679	1996
91600	699	1123	1462	1739	*96900*	735	1179	1535	1825	*102200*	772	1236	1608	1912	*107500*	808	1293	1681	1998
91700	700	1124	1463	1741	*97000*	736	1181	1536	1827	*102300*	773	1237	1609	1913	*107600*	809	1294	1682	2000
91800	700	1125	1464	1742	*97100*	737	1182	1537	1829	*102400*	773	1238	1610	1915	*107700*	810	1295	1683	2001
91900	701	1126	1466	1744	*97200*	738	1183	1539	1830	*102500*	774	1239	1612	1917	*107800*	811	1296	1685	2003
92000	702	1127	1467	1746	*97300*	738	1184	1540	1832	*102600*	775	1241	1613	1918	*107900*	811	1297	1686	2004
92100	702	1128	1469	1747	*97400*	739	1185	1542	1833	*102700*	775	1242	1615	1920	*108000*	812	1298	1688	2006
92200	703	1129	1470	1749	*97500*	740	1186	1543	1835	*102800*	776	1243	1616	1921	*108100*	813	1300	1689	2008
92300	704	1130	1471	1750	*97600*	740	1187	1544	1837	*102900*	777	1244	1617	1923	*108200*	813	1301	1690	2009
92400	704	1131	1473	1752	*97700*	741	1188	1546	1838	*103000*	777	1245	1619	1925	*108300*	814	1302	1692	2011
92500	705	1132	1474	1754	*97800*	742	1189	1547	1840	*103100*	778	1246	1620	1926	*108400*	815	1303	1693	2013
92600	706	1133	1475	1755	*97900*	742	1190	1548	1842	*103200*	779	1247	1621	1928	*108500*	815	1304	1695	2014
92700	707	1134	1477	1757	*98000*	743	1191	1550	1843	*103300*	780	1248	1623	1930	*108600*	816	1305	1696	2016
92800	707	1136	1478	1759	*98100*	744	1192	1551	1845	*103400*	780	1249	1624	1931	*108700*	817	1306	1697	2017
92900	708	1137	1480	1760	*98200*	744	1193	1553	1846	*103500*	781	1250	1626	1933	*108800*	817	1307	1699	2019
93000	709	1138	1481	1762	*98300*	745	1194	1554	1848	*103600*	782	1251	1627	1934	*108900*	818	1308	1700	2021
93100	709	1139	1482	1763	*98400*	746	1196	1555	1850	*103700*	782	1252	1628	1936	*109000*	819	1309	1701	2022
93200	710	1140	1484	1765	*98500*	746	1197	1557	1851	*103800*	783	1253	1630	1938	*109100*	820	1310	1703	2024
93300	711	1141	1485	1767	*98600*	747	1198	1558	1853	*103900*	784	1254	1631	1939	*109200*	820	1311	1704	2026
93400	711	1142	1486	1768	*98700*	748	1199	1559	1855	*104000*	784	1256	1633	1941	*109300*	821	1312	1706	2027
93500	712	1143	1488	1770	*98800*	749	1200	1561	1856	*104100*	785	1257	1634	1943	*109400*	822	1313	1707	2029
93600	713	1144	1489	1772	*98900*	749	1201	1562	1858	*104200*	786	1258	1635	1944	*109500*	822	1315	1708	2030
93700	713	1145	1491	1773	*99000*	750	1202	1564	1860	*104300*	786	1259	1637	1946	*109600*	823	1316	1710	2032
93800	714	1146	1492	1775	*99100*	751	1203	1565	1861	*104400*	787	1260	1638	1947	*109700*	824	1317	1711	2034
93900	715	1147	1493	1776	*99200*	751	1204	1566	1863	*104500*	788	1261	1639	1949	*109800*	824	1318	1712	2035
94000	715	1148	1495	1778	*99300*	752	1205	1568	1864	*104600*	789	1262	1641	1951	*109900*	825	1319	1714	2037
94100	716	1149	1496	1780	*99400*	753	1206	1569	1866	*104700*	789	1263	1642	1952	*110000*	826	1320	1715	2039
94200	717	1151	1497	1781	*99500*	753	1207	1571	1868	*104800*	790	1264	1644	1954	*110100*	826	1321	1717	2040
94300	718	1152	1499	1783	*99600*	754	1208	1572	1869	*104900*	791	1265	1645	1956	*110200*	827	1322	1718	2042
94400	718	1153	1500	1785	*99700*	755	1209	1573	1871	*105000*	791	1266	1646	1957	*110300*	828	1323	1719	2044
94500	719	1154	1502	1786	*99800*	755	1211	1575	1873	*105100*	792	1267	1648	1959	*110400*	828	1324	1721	2045
94600	720	1155	1503	1788	*99900*	756	1212	1576	1874	*105200*	793	1268	1649	1960	*110500*	829	1325	1722	2047
94700	720	1156	1504	1789	*100000*	757	1213	1577	1876	*105300*	793	1269	1650	1962	*110600*	830	1326	1723	2048
94800	721	1157	1506	1791	*100100*	758	1214	1579	1877	*105400*	794	1271	1652	1964	*110700*	831	1327	1725	2050
94900	722	1158	1507	1793	*100200*	758	1215	1580	1879	*105500*	795	1272	1653	1965	*110800*	831	1328	1726	2052
95000	722	1159	1509	1794	*100300*	759	1216	1582	1881	*105600*	795	1273	1655	1967	*110900*	832	1330	1728	2053
95100	723	1160	1510	1796	*100400*	760	1217	1583	1882	*105700*	796	1274	1656	1969	*111000*	833	1331	1729	2055
95200	724	1161	1511	1798	*100500*	760	1218	1584	1884	*105800*	797	1275	1657	1970	*111100*	833	1332	1730	2057
95300	724	1162	1513	1799	*100600*	761	1219	1586	1886	*105900*	797	1276	1659	1972	*111200*	834	1333	1732	2058
95400	725	1163	1514	1801	*100700*	762	1220	1587	1887	*106000*	798	1277	1660	1973	*111300*	835	1334	1733	2060
95500	726	1164	1515	1803	*100800*	762	1221	1588	1889	*106100*	799	1278	1661	1975	*111400*	835	1335	1734	2061
95600	727	1166	1517	1804	*100900*	763	1222	1590	1890	*106200*	800	1279	1663	1977	*111500*	836	1336	1736	2063
95700	727	1167	1518	1806	*101000*	764	1223	1591	1892	*106300*	800	1280	1664	1978	*111600*	837	1337	1737	2065
95800	728	1168	1520	1807	*101100*	764	1224	1593	1894	*106400*	801	1281	1666	1980	*111700*	837	1338	1739	2066
95900	729	1169	1521	1809	*101200*	765	1226	1594	1895	*106500*	802	1282	1667	1982	*111800*	838	1339	1740	2068
96000	729	1170	1522	1811	*101300*	766	1227	1595	1897	*106600*	802	1283	1668	1983	*111900*	839	1340	1741	2070
96100	730	1171	1524	1812	*101400*	766	1228	1597	1899	*106700*	803	1284	1670	1985	*112000*	839	1341	1743	2071
96200	731	1172	1525	1814	*101500*	767	1229	1598	1900	*106800*	804	1286	1671	1987	*112100*	840	1342	1744	2073
96300	731	1173	1526	1816	*101600*	768	1230	1599	1902	*106900*	804	1287	1672	1988	*112200*	841	1343	1745	2074
96400	732	1174	1528	1817	*101700*	769	1231	1601	1903	*107000*	805	1288	1674	1990	*112300*	842	1345	1747	2076
96500	733	1175	1529	1819	*101800*	769	1232	1602	1905	*107100*	806	1289	1675	1991	*112400*	842	1346	1748	2078
96600	733	1176	1531	1820	*101900*	770	1233	1604	1907	*107200*	806	1290	1677	1993	*112500*	843	1347	1750	2079
96700	734	1177	1532	1822	*102000*	771	1234	1605	1908	*107300*	807	1291	1678	1995	*112600*	844	1348	1751	2081

Note: This table shows amounts of child support based on income to the nearest $100. There is a mathematical formula for calculating specific child support amounts between the $100 levels. For more information, please contact the Department of Justice.

Nota: La présente table indique le montant de la pension alimentaire pour enfants à verser d'après le revenu (aux 100 $ près). Il existe une formule mathématique pour calculer le montant exact de la pension alimentaire pour enfants dans le cas des revenus qui se situent entre les tranches de 100 $. Pour plus de renseignements, veuillez communiquer avec le ministère de la Justice.

Divorce

MANITOBA
1997

FEDERAL CHILD SUPPORT AMOUNTS : SIMPLIFIED TABLES
MONTANTS FÉDÉRAUX DE PENSIONS ALIMENTAIRES POUR ENFANTS : TABLES SIMPLIFIÉES

Income/ Revenu ($)	Monthly Award/ Paiement mensuel ($) No. of Children/ N^{bre} d'enfants				Income/ Revenu ($)	Monthly Award/ Paiement mensuel ($) No. of Children/ N^{bre} d'enfants				Income/ Revenu ($)	Monthly Award/ Paiement mensuel ($) No. of Children/ N^{bre} d'enfants				Income/ Revenu ($)	Monthly Award/ Paiement mensuel ($) No. of Children/ N^{bre} d'enfants			
	1	2	3	4		1	2	3	4		1	2	3	4		1	2	3	4
112700	844	1349	1752	2083	118000	881	1406	1825	2169	123300	917	1462	1898	2255	128600	954	1519	1971	2341
112800	845	1350	1754	2084	118100	882	1407	1827	2171	123400	918	1463	1900	2257	128700	955	1520	1973	2343
112900	846	1351	1755	2086	118200	882	1408	1828	2172	123500	919	1465	1901	2258	128800	955	1521	1974	2345
113000	846	1352	1757	2087	118300	883	1409	1830	2174	123600	919	1466	1903	2260	128900	956	1522	1976	2346
113100	847	1353	1758	2089	118400	884	1410	1831	2175	123700	920	1467	1904	2262	129000	957	1523	1977	2348
113200	848	1354	1759	2091	118500	884	1411	1832	2177	123800	921	1468	1905	2263	129100	957	1525	1978	2350
113300	848	1355	1761	2092	118600	885	1412	1834	2179	123900	921	1469	1907	2265	129200	958	1526	1980	2351
113400	849	1356	1762	2094	118700	886	1413	1835	2180	124000	922	1470	1908	2267	129300	959	1527	1981	2353
113500	850	1357	1763	2096	118800	886	1414	1836	2182	124100	923	1471	1909	2268	129400	959	1528	1982	2355
113600	851	1358	1765	2097	118900	887	1415	1838	2184	124200	924	1472	1911	2270	129500	960	1529	1984	2356
113700	851	1360	1766	2099	119000	888	1416	1839	2185	124300	924	1473	1912	2271	129600	961	1530	1985	2358
113800	852	1361	1768	2100	119100	888	1417	1841	2187	124400	925	1474	1914	2273	129700	961	1531	1987	2359
113900	853	1362	1769	2102	119200	889	1418	1842	2188	124500	926	1475	1915	2275	129800	962	1532	1988	2361
114000	853	1363	1770	2104	119300	890	1420	1843	2190	124600	926	1476	1916	2276	129900	963	1533	1989	2363
114100	854	1364	1772	2105	119400	890	1421	1845	2192	124700	927	1477	1918	2278	130000	963	1534	1991	2364
114200	855	1365	1773	2107	119500	891	1422	1846	2193	124800	928	1478	1919	2280	130100	964	1535	1992	2366
114300	855	1366	1774	2109	119600	892	1423	1847	2195	124900	928	1480	1920	2281	130200	965	1536	1993	2368
114400	856	1367	1776	2110	119700	893	1424	1849	2197	125000	929	1481	1922	2283	130300	966	1537	1995	2369
114500	857	1368	1777	2112	119800	893	1425	1850	2198	125100	930	1482	1923	2284	130400	966	1538	1996	2371
114600	857	1369	1779	2114	119900	894	1426	1852	2200	125200	930	1483	1925	2286	130500	967	1540	1998	2372
114700	858	1370	1780	2115	120000	895	1427	1853	2201	125300	931	1484	1926	2288	130600	968	1541	1999	2374
114800	859	1371	1781	2117	120100	895	1428	1854	2203	125400	932	1485	1927	2289	130700	968	1542	2000	2376
114900	859	1372	1783	2118	120200	896	1429	1856	2205	125500	932	1486	1929	2291	130800	969	1543	2002	2377
115000	860	1373	1784	2120	120300	897	1430	1857	2206	125600	933	1487	1930	2293	130900	970	1544	2003	2379
115100	861	1375	1785	2122	120400	897	1431	1858	2208	125700	934	1488	1931	2294	131000	970	1545	2005	2381
115200	862	1376	1787	2123	120500	898	1432	1860	2210	125800	935	1489	1933	2296	131100	971	1546	2006	2382
115300	862	1377	1788	2125	120600	899	1433	1861	2211	125900	935	1490	1934	2298	131200	972	1547	2007	2384
115400	863	1378	1790	2127	120700	899	1435	1863	2213	126000	936	1491	1936	2299	131300	972	1548	2009	2385
115500	864	1379	1791	2128	120800	900	1436	1864	2214	126100	937	1492	1937	2301	131400	973	1549	2010	2387
115600	864	1380	1792	2130	120900	901	1437	1865	2216	126200	937	1493	1938	2302	131500	974	1550	2011	2389
115700	865	1381	1794	2131	121000	901	1438	1867	2218	126300	938	1495	1940	2304	131600	975	1551	2013	2390
115800	866	1382	1795	2133	121100	902	1439	1868	2219	126400	939	1496	1941	2306	131700	975	1552	2014	2392
115900	866	1383	1796	2135	121200	903	1440	1869	2221	126500	939	1497	1943	2307	131800	976	1553	2016	2394
116000	867	1384	1798	2136	121300	904	1441	1871	2223	126600	940	1498	1944	2309	131900	977	1555	2017	2395
116100	868	1385	1799	2138	121400	904	1442	1872	2224	126700	941	1499	1945	2311	132000	977	1556	2018	2397
116200	868	1386	1801	2140	121500	905	1443	1874	2226	126800	941	1500	1947	2312	132100	978	1557	2020	2398
116300	869	1387	1802	2141	121600	906	1444	1875	2228	126900	942	1501	1948	2314	132200	979	1558	2021	2400
116400	870	1388	1803	2143	121700	906	1445	1876	2229	127000	943	1502	1949	2315	132300	979	1559	2022	2402
116500	870	1390	1805	2144	121800	907	1446	1878	2231	127100	944	1503	1951	2317	132400	980	1560	2024	2403
116600	871	1391	1806	2146	121900	908	1447	1879	2232	127200	944	1504	1952	2319	132500	981	1561	2025	2405
116700	872	1392	1807	2148	122000	908	1448	1881	2234	127300	945	1505	1954	2320	132600	981	1562	2027	2407
116800	873	1393	1809	2149	122100	909	1450	1882	2236	127400	946	1506	1955	2322	132700	982	1563	2028	2408
116900	873	1394	1810	2151	122200	910	1451	1883	2237	127500	946	1507	1956	2324	132800	983	1564	2029	2410
117000	874	1395	1812	2153	122300	910	1452	1885	2239	127600	947	1508	1958	2325	132900	983	1565	2031	2411
117100	875	1396	1813	2154	122400	911	1453	1886	2241	127700	948	1510	1959	2327	133000	984	1566	2032	2413
117200	875	1397	1814	2156	122500	912	1454	1887	2242	127800	948	1511	1960	2328	133100	985	1567	2033	2415
117300	876	1398	1816	2157	122600	913	1455	1889	2244	127900	949	1512	1962	2330	133200	986	1568	2035	2416
117400	877	1399	1817	2159	122700	913	1456	1890	2245	128000	950	1513	1963	2332	133300	986	1570	2036	2418
117500	877	1400	1819	2161	122800	914	1457	1892	2247	128100	950	1514	1965	2333	133400	987	1571	2038	2420
117600	878	1401	1820	2162	122900	915	1458	1893	2249	128200	951	1515	1966	2335	133500	988	1572	2039	2421
117700	879	1402	1821	2164	123000	915	1459	1894	2250	128300	952	1516	1967	2337	133600	988	1573	2040	2423
117800	879	1403	1823	2166	123100	916	1460	1896	2252	128400	952	1517	1969	2338	133700	989	1574	2042	2425
117900	880	1405	1824	2167	123200	917	1461	1897	2254	128500	953	1518	1970	2340	133800	990	1575	2043	2426

Note: This table shows amounts of child support based on income to the nearest $100. There is a mathematical formula for calculating specific child support amounts between the $100 levels. For more information, please contact the Department of Justice.

Nota: La présente table indique le montant de la pension alimentaire pour enfants à verser d'après le revenu (aux 100 $ près). Il existe une formule mathématique pour calculer le montant exact de la pension alimentaire pour enfants dans le cas des revenus qui se situent entre les tranches de 100 $. Pour plus de renseignements, veuillez communiquer avec le ministère de la Justice.

Appendix D

MANITOBA

1997

FEDERAL CHILD SUPPORT AMOUNTS : SIMPLIFIED TABLES
MONTANTS FÉDÉRAUX DE PENSIONS ALIMENTAIRES POUR ENFANTS : TABLES SIMPLIFIÉES

Income/ Revenu ($)	Monthly Award/ Paiement mensuel ($) No. of Children/ N^bre d'enfants				Income/ Revenu ($)	Monthly Award/ Paiement mensuel ($) No. of Children/ N^bre d'enfants				Income/ Revenu ($)	Monthly Award/ Paiement mensuel ($) No. of Children/ N^bre d'enfants				Income/ Revenu ($)	Monthly Award/ Paiement mensuel ($) No. of Children/ N^bre d'enfants			
	1	2	3	4		1	2	3	4		1	2	3	4		1	2	3	4
133900	990	1576	2044	2428	*138000*	1019	1620	2101	2495	*142100*	1047	1664	2157	2561	*146200*	1075	1708	2214	2628
134000	991	1577	2046	2429	*138100*	1019	1621	2102	2496	*142200*	1048	1665	2159	2563	*146300*	1076	1709	2215	2630
134100	992	1578	2047	2431	*138200*	1020	1622	2104	2498	*142300*	1048	1666	2160	2565	*146400*	1076	1710	2217	2631
134200	992	1579	2049	2433	*138300*	1021	1623	2105	2499	*142400*	1049	1667	2162	2566	*146500*	1077	1711	2218	2633
134300	993	1580	2050	2434	*138400*	1021	1624	2106	2501	*142500*	1050	1668	2163	2568	*146600*	1078	1712	2219	2635
134400	994	1581	2051	2436	*138500*	1022	1625	2108	2503	*142600*	1050	1669	2164	2569	*146700*	1079	1713	2221	2636
134500	994	1582	2053	2438	*138600*	1023	1626	2109	2504	*142700*	1051	1670	2166	2571	*146800*	1079	1714	2222	2638
134600	995	1583	2054	2439	*138700*	1023	1627	2111	2506	*142800*	1052	1671	2167	2573	*146900*	1080	1715	2224	2639
134700	996	1585	2055	2441	*138800*	1024	1628	2112	2508	*142900*	1052	1672	2168	2574	*147000*	1081	1716	2225	2641
134800	997	1586	2057	2442	*138900*	1025	1630	2113	2509	*143000*	1053	1673	2170	2576	*147100*	1081	1717	2226	2643
134900	997	1587	2058	2444	*139000*	1025	1631	2115	2511	*143100*	1054	1675	2171	2578	*147200*	1082	1718	2228	2644
135000	998	1588	2060	2446	*139100*	1026	1632	2116	2512	*143200*	1054	1676	2173	2579	*147300*	1083	1720	2229	2646
135100	999	1589	2061	2447	*139200*	1027	1633	2117	2514	*143300*	1055	1677	2174	2581	*147400*	1083	1721	2230	2648
135200	999	1590	2062	2449	*139300*	1028	1634	2119	2516	*143400*	1056	1678	2175	2582	*147500*	1084	1722	2232	2649
135300	1000	1591	2064	2451	*139400*	1028	1635	2120	2517	*143500*	1056	1679	2177	2584	*147600*	1085	1723	2233	2651
135400	1001	1592	2065	2452	*139500*	1029	1636	2122	2519	*143600*	1057	1680	2178	2586	*147700*	1085	1724	2235	2652
135500	1001	1593	2067	2454	*139600*	1030	1637	2123	2521	*143700*	1058	1681	2179	2587	*147800*	1086	1725	2236	2654
135600	1002	1594	2068	2455	*139700*	1030	1638	2124	2522	*143800*	1058	1682	2181	2589	*147900*	1087	1726	2237	2656
135700	1003	1595	2069	2457	*139800*	1031	1639	2126	2524	*143900*	1059	1683	2182	2591	*148000*	1087	1727	2239	2657
135800	1003	1596	2071	2459	*139900*	1032	1640	2127	2525	*144000*	1060	1684	2184	2592	*148100*	1088	1728	2240	2659
135900	1004	1597	2072	2460	*140000*	1032	1641	2129	2527	*144100*	1061	1685	2185	2594	*148200*	1089	1729	2241	2661
136000	1005	1598	2073	2462	*140100*	1033	1642	2130	2529	*144200*	1061	1686	2186	2595	*148300*	1090	1730	2243	2662
136100	1006	1600	2075	2464	*140200*	1034	1643	2131	2530	*144300*	1062	1687	2188	2597	*148400*	1090	1731	2244	2664
136200	1006	1601	2076	2465	*140300*	1034	1645	2133	2532	*144400*	1063	1688	2189	2599	*148500*	1091	1732	2246	2666
136300	1007	1602	2078	2467	*140400*	1035	1646	2134	2534	*144500*	1063	1690	2191	2600	*148600*	1092	1734	2247	2667
136400	1008	1603	2079	2468	*140500*	1036	1647	2135	2535	*144600*	1064	1691	2192	2602	*148700*	1092	1735	2248	2669
136500	1008	1604	2080	2470	*140600*	1037	1648	2137	2537	*144700*	1065	1692	2193	2604	*148800*	1093	1736	2250	2670
136600	1009	1605	2082	2472	*140700*	1037	1649	2138	2539	*144800*	1065	1693	2195	2605	*148900*	1094	1737	2251	2672
136700	1010	1606	2083	2473	*140800*	1038	1650	2140	2540	*144900*	1066	1694	2196	2607	*149000*	1094	1738	2253	2674
136800	1010	1607	2084	2475	*140900*	1039	1651	2141	2542	*145000*	1067	1695	2197	2609	*149100*	1095	1739	2254	2675
136900	1011	1608	2086	2477	*141000*	1039	1652	2142	2543	*145100*	1068	1696	2199	2610	*149200*	1096	1740	2255	2677
137000	1012	1609	2087	2478	*141100*	1040	1653	2144	2545	*145200*	1068	1697	2200	2612	*149300*	1096	1741	2257	2679
137100	1012	1610	2089	2480	*141200*	1041	1654	2145	2547	*145300*	1069	1698	2202	2613	*149400*	1097	1742	2258	2680
137200	1013	1611	2090	2482	*141300*	1041	1655	2146	2548	*145400*	1070	1699	2203	2615	*149500*	1098	1743	2259	2682
137300	1014	1612	2091	2483	*141400*	1042	1656	2148	2550	*145500*	1070	1700	2204	2617	*149600*	1099	1744	2261	2683
137400	1014	1613	2093	2485	*141500*	1043	1657	2149	2552	*145600*	1071	1701	2206	2618	*149700*	1099	1745	2262	2685
137500	1015	1615	2094	2486	*141600*	1043	1658	2151	2553	*145700*	1072	1702	2207	2620	*149800*	1100	1746	2264	2687
137600	1016	1616	2095	2488	*141700*	1044	1660	2152	2555	*145800*	1072	1703	2208	2622	*149900*	1101	1747	2265	2688
137700	1017	1617	2097	2490	*141800*	1045	1661	2153	2556	*145900*	1073	1705	2210	2623	*150000*	1101	1749	2266	2690
137800	1017	1618	2098	2491	*141900*	1045	1662	2155	2558	*146000*	1074	1706	2211	2625					
137900	1018	1619	2100	2493	*142000*	1046	1663	2156	2560	*146100*	1074	1707	2213	2626					

Income/ Revenu ($)	Monthly Award/Paiement mensuel ($)			
	one child/ un enfant	two children/ deux enfants	three children/ trois enfants	four children/ quatre enfants
For income over $150,000	**1101** plus 0.69% of income over $150,000	**1749** plus 1.07% of income over $150,000	**2266** plus 1.38% of income over $150,000	**2690** plus 1.63% of income over $150,000
Pour revenu dépassant 150 000$	**1101** plus 0,69% du revenu dépassant 150 000$	**1749** plus 1,07% du revenu dépassant 150 000$	**2266** plus 1,38% du revenu dépassant 150 000$	**2690** plus 1,63% du revenu dépassant 150 000$

Note: This table shows amounts of child support based on income to the nearest $100. There is a mathematical formula for calculating specific child support amounts between the $100 levels. For more information, please contact the Department of Justice.

Nota: La présente table indique le montant de la pension alimentaire pour enfants à verser d'après le revenu (aux 100 $ près). Il existe une formule mathématique pour calculer le montant exact de la pension alimentaire pour enfants dans le cas des revenus qui se situent entre les tranches de 100 $. Pour plus de renseignements, veuillez communiquer avec le ministère de la Justice.

Divorce

NEW BRUNSWICK/NOUVEAU-BRUNSWICK

FEDERAL CHILD SUPPORT AMOUNTS : SIMPLIFIED TABLES
MONTANTS FÉDÉRAUX DE PENSIONS ALIMENTAIRES POUR ENFANTS : TABLES SIMPLIFIÉES

1997

Income/Revenu ($)	Monthly Award/Paiement mensuel ($) No. of Children/N^{bre} d'enfants				Income/Revenu ($)	Monthly Award/Paiement mensuel ($) No. of Children/N^{bre} d'enfants				Income/Revenu ($)	Monthly Award/Paiement mensuel ($) No. of Children/N^{bre} d'enfants				Income/Revenu ($)	Monthly Award/Paiement mensuel ($) No. of Children/N^{bre} d'enfants			
	1	2	3	4		1	2	3	4		1	2	3	4		1	2	3	4
6700	0	0	0	0	12000	94	144	166	188	17300	140	253	331	375	22600	189	330	442	534
6800	0	0	0	0	12100	94	147	169	191	17400	141	254	334	379	22700	190	331	444	537
6900	0	0	0	0	12200	94	149	172	195	17500	142	256	338	382	22800	191	333	446	539
7000	0	1	2	3	12300	94	152	175	199	17600	143	257	341	386	22900	192	334	448	541
7100	2	4	5	7	12400	94	155	178	202	17700	143	258	344	390	23000	193	336	450	543
7200	5	7	9	11	12500	95	158	182	206	17800	144	260	347	393	23100	194	337	452	545
7300	7	10	12	14	12600	96	160	185	209	17900	145	261	350	397	23200	195	339	454	548
7400	10	13	15	18	12700	97	163	188	213	18000	146	263	353	400	23300	196	340	455	550
7500	12	15	19	22	12800	98	166	191	216	18100	147	264	356	404	23400	197	342	457	552
7600	15	18	22	25	12900	98	168	194	220	18200	148	266	359	407	23500	198	343	459	554
7700	17	21	25	29	13000	99	171	197	223	18300	149	267	362	411	23600	199	344	461	556
7800	20	24	28	33	13100	100	174	200	227	18400	150	269	364	414	23700	200	346	463	559
7900	22	27	32	37	13200	101	176	203	230	18500	151	270	366	418	23800	201	347	465	561
8000	24	30	35	40	13300	102	179	207	234	18600	152	272	367	421	23900	202	349	467	563
8100	27	33	38	44	13400	103	182	210	237	18700	153	273	369	425	24000	202	350	469	565
8200	29	35	42	48	13500	104	185	213	241	18800	154	275	371	428	24100	203	352	470	568
8300	32	38	45	51	13600	105	187	216	245	18900	155	276	373	432	24200	204	353	472	570
8400	34	41	48	55	13700	106	190	219	248	19000	156	277	375	436	24300	205	355	474	572
8500	37	44	51	59	13800	107	193	222	252	19100	157	279	377	439	24400	206	356	476	574
8600	39	47	55	63	13900	108	195	225	255	19200	157	280	379	443	24500	207	358	478	576
8700	42	50	58	66	14000	109	198	228	259	19300	158	282	381	446	24600	208	359	480	579
8800	44	53	61	70	14100	110	201	232	262	19400	159	283	382	450	24700	209	360	482	581
8900	47	56	65	74	14200	111	203	235	266	19500	160	285	384	453	24800	210	362	484	583
9000	49	58	68	77	14300	112	206	238	269	19600	161	286	386	457	24900	211	363	485	585
9100	51	61	71	81	14400	113	209	241	273	19700	162	288	388	460	25000	212	365	487	587
9200	54	64	74	85	14500	113	212	244	276	19800	163	289	390	464	25100	213	366	489	590
9300	56	67	78	88	14600	114	213	247	280	19900	164	291	392	467	25200	214	368	491	592
9400	59	70	81	92	14700	115	215	250	283	20000	165	292	394	471	25300	215	369	493	594
9500	61	73	84	96	14800	116	216	253	287	20100	166	293	395	474	25400	216	371	495	596
9600	64	76	88	100	14900	117	218	256	291	20200	167	295	397	478	25500	217	372	497	599
9700	66	79	91	103	15000	118	219	260	294	20300	168	296	399	481	25600	217	374	499	601
9800	69	81	94	107	15100	119	221	263	298	20400	169	298	401	485	25700	218	375	500	603
9900	71	84	97	111	15200	120	222	266	301	20500	170	299	403	488	25800	219	377	502	605
10000	73	87	101	114	15300	121	224	269	305	20600	171	301	405	490	25900	220	378	504	607
10100	76	90	104	118	15400	122	225	272	308	20700	172	302	407	492	26000	221	379	506	609
10200	78	93	107	122	15500	123	226	275	312	20800	172	304	409	494	26100	222	381	508	612
10300	81	96	111	125	15600	124	228	278	315	20900	173	305	410	497	26200	223	382	509	614
10400	83	99	114	129	15700	125	229	281	319	21000	174	307	412	499	26300	224	383	511	616
10500	86	101	117	133	15800	126	231	285	322	21100	175	308	414	501	26400	225	385	513	618
10600	88	104	120	137	15900	127	232	288	326	21200	176	309	416	503	26500	225	386	515	620
10700	91	107	124	140	16000	128	234	291	329	21300	177	311	418	506	26600	226	387	516	622
10800	93	110	127	144	16100	128	235	294	333	21400	178	312	420	508	26700	227	389	518	624
10900	94	113	130	148	16200	129	237	297	336	21500	179	314	422	510	26800	228	390	520	626
11000	94	116	134	151	16300	130	238	300	340	21600	180	315	424	512	26900	229	391	522	628
11100	94	119	137	155	16400	131	240	303	344	21700	181	317	425	514	27000	230	393	523	630
11200	94	122	140	159	16500	132	241	306	347	21800	182	318	427	517	27100	231	394	525	632
11300	94	124	143	163	16600	133	242	309	351	21900	183	320	429	519	27200	232	396	527	634
11400	94	127	147	166	16700	134	244	313	354	22000	184	321	431	521	27300	232	397	528	636
11500	94	130	150	170	16800	135	245	316	358	22100	185	323	433	523	27400	233	398	530	638
11600	94	133	153	174	16900	136	247	319	361	22200	186	324	435	525	27500	234	400	532	640
11700	94	136	157	177	17000	137	248	322	365	22300	187	326	437	528	27600	235	401	534	642
11800	94	139	160	181	17100	138	250	325	368	22400	187	327	439	530	27700	236	402	535	644
11900	94	141	163	184	17200	139	251	328	372	22500	188	328	440	532	27800	237	404	537	646

Note: This table shows amounts of child support based on income to the nearest $100. There is a mathematical formula for calculating specific child support amounts between the $100 levels. For more information, please contact the Department of Justice.

Nota: La présente table indique le montant de la pension alimentaire pour enfants à verser d'après le revenu (aux 100 $ près). Il existe une formule mathématique pour calculer le montant exact de la pension alimentaire pour enfants dans le cas des revenus qui se situent entre les tranches de 100 $. Pour plus de renseignements, veuillez communiquer avec le ministère de la Justice.

Appendix D

NEW BRUNSWICK/NOUVEAU-BRUNSWICK
1997

FEDERAL CHILD SUPPORT AMOUNTS : SIMPLIFIED TABLES
MONTANTS FÉDÉRAUX DE PENSIONS ALIMENTAIRES POUR ENFANTS : TABLES SIMPLIFIÉES

Income/Revenu ($)	Monthly Award/Paiement mensuel ($) No. of Children/N^{bre} d'enfants				Income/Revenu ($)	Monthly Award/Paiement mensuel ($) No. of Children/N^{bre} d'enfants				Income/Revenu ($)	Monthly Award/Paiement mensuel ($) No. of Children/N^{bre} d'enfants				Income/Revenu ($)	Monthly Award/Paiement mensuel ($) No. of Children/N^{bre} d'enfants			
	1	2	3	4		1	2	3	4		1	2	3	4		1	2	3	4
27900	238	405	539	648	33200	277	466	617	741	38500	316	527	696	834	43800	357	591	779	932
28000	238	406	541	650	33300	278	467	619	743	38600	317	528	698	836	43900	358	593	780	934
28100	239	408	542	653	33400	278	468	620	745	38700	318	530	699	838	44000	359	594	782	935
28200	240	409	544	655	33500	279	469	622	746	38800	318	531	701	840	44100	360	595	783	937
28300	241	410	546	657	33600	280	471	623	748	38900	319	532	702	841	44200	361	596	785	939
28400	242	412	548	659	33700	281	472	625	750	39000	320	533	704	843	44300	361	598	786	941
28500	243	413	549	661	33800	281	473	626	752	39100	321	534	705	845	44400	362	599	788	943
28600	244	414	551	663	33900	282	474	628	753	39200	322	535	707	847	44500	363	600	790	945
28700	245	416	553	665	34000	283	475	629	755	39300	322	537	708	849	44600	364	601	791	947
28800	245	417	554	667	34100	283	476	631	757	39400	323	538	710	850	44700	365	602	793	948
28900	246	418	556	669	34200	284	477	632	758	39500	324	539	711	852	44800	365	604	794	950
29000	247	420	558	671	34300	285	479	633	760	39600	325	540	713	854	44900	366	605	796	952
29100	248	421	560	673	34400	286	480	635	762	39700	325	541	714	856	45000	367	606	797	954
29200	249	423	561	675	34500	286	481	636	764	39800	326	543	716	857	45100	368	607	799	956
29300	250	424	563	677	34600	287	482	638	765	39900	327	544	717	859	45200	368	609	801	958
29400	251	425	565	679	34700	288	483	639	767	40000	328	545	719	861	45300	369	610	802	960
29500	251	427	567	681	34800	289	484	641	769	40100	328	546	720	863	45400	370	611	804	961
29600	252	428	568	683	34900	289	485	642	770	40200	329	547	722	865	45500	371	612	805	963
29700	253	429	570	685	35000	290	486	644	772	40300	330	549	724	867	45600	372	613	807	965
29800	254	430	571	686	35100	291	488	645	774	40400	331	550	725	869	45700	372	615	808	967
29900	254	431	572	688	35200	291	489	647	776	40500	332	551	727	870	45800	373	616	810	969
30000	255	432	574	689	35300	292	490	648	777	40600	332	552	728	872	45900	374	617	812	971
30100	256	433	575	691	35400	293	491	649	779	40700	333	554	730	874	46000	375	618	813	973
30200	256	434	576	693	35500	294	492	651	781	40800	334	555	731	876	46100	376	620	815	974
30300	257	435	578	694	35600	294	493	652	783	40900	335	556	733	878	46200	376	621	816	976
30400	258	436	579	696	35700	295	494	654	784	41000	335	557	735	880	46300	377	622	818	978
30500	258	437	580	697	35800	296	495	655	786	41100	336	558	736	882	46400	378	623	819	980
30600	259	438	581	699	35900	297	497	657	788	41200	337	560	738	883	46500	379	624	821	982
30700	260	439	583	700	36000	297	498	658	789	41300	338	561	739	885	46600	379	626	823	984
30800	260	440	584	702	36100	298	499	660	791	41400	339	562	741	887	46700	380	627	824	986
30900	261	441	585	703	36200	299	500	661	793	41500	339	563	742	889	46800	381	628	826	987
31000	262	442	587	705	36300	300	501	663	795	41600	340	565	744	891	46900	382	629	827	989
31100	262	443	588	707	36400	300	503	664	797	41700	341	566	746	893	47000	383	631	829	991
31200	263	444	589	708	36500	301	504	666	798	41800	342	567	747	895	47100	383	632	830	993
31300	264	445	591	710	36600	302	505	667	800	41900	343	568	749	896	47200	384	633	832	995
31400	264	446	592	711	36700	303	506	669	802	42000	343	569	750	898	47300	385	634	834	997
31500	265	447	593	713	36800	303	507	670	804	42100	344	571	752	900	47400	386	635	835	999
31600	266	448	595	714	36900	304	508	672	806	42200	345	572	753	902	47500	387	637	837	1000
31700	266	449	596	716	37000	305	510	673	807	42300	346	573	755	904	47600	387	638	838	1002
31800	267	450	597	717	37100	306	511	675	809	42400	346	574	757	906	47700	388	639	840	1004
31900	267	451	599	719	37200	306	512	676	811	42500	347	576	758	908	47800	389	640	841	1006
32000	268	452	600	721	37300	307	513	678	813	42600	348	577	760	909	47900	390	642	843	1008
32100	269	454	601	722	37400	308	514	679	815	42700	349	578	761	911	48000	390	643	845	1010
32200	270	455	603	724	37500	309	515	681	816	42800	350	579	763	913	48100	391	644	846	1012
32300	270	456	604	726	37600	309	517	682	818	42900	350	580	764	915	48200	392	645	848	1013
32400	271	457	606	727	37700	310	518	684	820	43000	351	582	766	917	48300	393	646	849	1015
32500	272	458	607	729	37800	311	519	685	822	43100	352	583	768	919	48400	394	648	851	1017
32600	273	459	609	731	37900	312	520	687	823	43200	353	584	769	921	48500	394	649	852	1019
32700	273	460	610	733	38000	312	521	688	825	43300	354	585	771	922	48600	395	650	854	1021
32800	274	462	612	734	38100	313	523	690	827	43400	354	587	772	924	48700	396	651	856	1023
32900	275	463	613	736	38200	314	524	692	829	43500	355	588	774	926	48800	397	653	857	1025
33000	275	464	614	738	38300	315	525	693	831	43600	356	589	775	928	48900	398	654	859	1026
33100	276	465	616	740	38400	315	526	695	832	43700	357	590	777	930	49000	398	655	860	1028

Note: This table shows amounts of child support based on income to the nearest $100. There is a mathematical formula for calculating specific child support amounts between the $100 levels. For more information, please contact the Department of Justice.

Nota: La présente table indique le montant de la pension alimentaire pour enfants à verser d'après le revenu (aux 100 $ près). Il existe une formule mathématique pour calculer le montant exact de la pension alimentaire pour enfants dans le cas des revenus qui se situent entre les tranches de 100 $. Pour plus de renseignements, veuillez communiquer avec le ministère de la Justice.

Divorce

NEW BRUNSWICK/NOUVEAU-BRUNSWICK

FEDERAL CHILD SUPPORT AMOUNTS : SIMPLIFIED TABLES
MONTANTS FÉDÉRAUX DE PENSIONS ALIMENTAIRES POUR ENFANTS : TABLES SIMPLIFIÉES

1997

Income/Revenu ($)	Monthly Award/Paiement mensuel ($) No. of Children/N^{bre} d'enfants				Income/Revenu ($)	Monthly Award/Paiement mensuel ($) No. of Children/N^{bre} d'enfants				Income/Revenu ($)	Monthly Award/Paiement mensuel ($) No. of Children/N^{bre} d'enfants				Income/Revenu ($)	Monthly Award/Paiement mensuel ($) No. of Children/N^{bre} d'enfants			
	1	2	3	4		1	2	3	4		1	2	3	4		1	2	3	4
49100	399	656	862	1030	54400	441	721	945	1129	59700	482	785	1028	1226	65000	519	843	1102	1315
49200	400	657	863	1032	54500	442	722	947	1130	59800	483	786	1029	1228	65100	520	844	1104	1316
49300	401	659	865	1034	54600	442	723	948	1132	59900	483	787	1031	1230	65200	520	845	1105	1318
49400	401	660	867	1036	54700	443	725	950	1134	60000	484	789	1032	1231	65300	521	846	1106	1319
49500	402	661	868	1038	54800	444	726	951	1136	60100	485	790	1033	1233	65400	521	847	1108	1321
49600	403	662	870	1039	54900	445	727	953	1138	60200	486	791	1035	1235	65500	522	848	1109	1323
49700	404	664	871	1041	55000	445	728	955	1140	60300	486	792	1036	1236	65600	523	849	1110	1324
49800	405	665	873	1043	55100	446	730	956	1142	60400	487	793	1038	1238	65700	523	850	1112	1326
49900	405	666	874	1045	55200	447	731	958	1143	60500	488	794	1039	1240	65800	524	851	1113	1327
50000	406	667	876	1047	55300	448	732	959	1145	60600	488	795	1041	1241	65900	525	852	1115	1329
50100	407	668	878	1049	55400	449	733	961	1147	60700	489	796	1042	1243	66000	525	853	1116	1331
50200	408	670	879	1051	55500	449	734	962	1149	60800	490	797	1043	1245	66100	526	854	1117	1332
50300	409	671	881	1052	55600	450	736	964	1151	60900	491	799	1045	1246	66200	527	855	1119	1334
50400	409	672	882	1054	55700	451	737	966	1153	61000	491	800	1046	1248	66300	527	857	1120	1335
50500	410	673	884	1056	55800	452	738	967	1155	61100	492	801	1048	1250	66400	528	858	1121	1337
50600	411	675	885	1058	55900	453	739	969	1156	61200	493	802	1049	1252	66500	529	859	1123	1339
50700	412	676	887	1060	56000	453	741	970	1158	61300	493	803	1051	1253	66600	529	860	1124	1340
50800	412	677	889	1062	56100	454	742	972	1160	61400	494	804	1052	1255	66700	530	861	1125	1342
50900	413	678	890	1064	56200	455	743	973	1162	61500	495	805	1053	1257	66800	531	862	1127	1344
51000	414	679	892	1065	56300	456	744	975	1164	61600	496	806	1055	1258	66900	531	863	1128	1345
51100	415	681	893	1067	56400	456	745	977	1166	61700	496	807	1056	1260	67000	532	864	1130	1347
51200	416	682	895	1069	56500	457	747	978	1168	61800	497	809	1058	1262	67100	533	865	1131	1349
51300	416	683	896	1071	56600	458	748	980	1169	61900	498	810	1059	1263	67200	533	866	1132	1350
51400	417	684	898	1073	56700	459	749	981	1171	62000	499	811	1061	1265	67300	534	867	1134	1352
51500	418	686	900	1075	56800	460	750	983	1173	62100	499	812	1062	1267	67400	535	868	1135	1353
51600	419	687	901	1077	56900	460	752	984	1175	62200	500	813	1064	1268	67500	535	869	1137	1355
51700	420	688	903	1078	57000	461	753	986	1177	62300	501	814	1065	1270	67600	536	870	1138	1357
51800	420	689	904	1080	57100	462	754	988	1179	62400	501	815	1066	1272	67700	537	872	1139	1358
51900	421	690	906	1082	57200	463	755	989	1181	62500	502	816	1068	1274	67800	538	873	1141	1360
52000	422	692	907	1084	57300	464	756	991	1182	62600	503	817	1069	1275	67900	538	874	1142	1362
52100	423	693	909	1086	57400	464	758	992	1184	62700	504	819	1071	1277	68000	539	875	1143	1363
52200	423	694	911	1088	57500	465	759	994	1186	62800	504	820	1072	1279	68100	540	876	1145	1365
52300	424	695	912	1090	57600	466	760	995	1188	62900	505	821	1074	1280	68200	540	877	1146	1367
52400	425	697	914	1091	57700	467	761	997	1190	63000	506	822	1075	1282	68300	541	878	1148	1368
52500	426	698	915	1093	57800	467	763	999	1192	63100	506	823	1076	1284	68400	542	879	1149	1370
52600	427	699	917	1095	57900	468	764	1000	1194	63200	507	824	1078	1285	68500	542	880	1150	1372
52700	427	700	918	1097	58000	469	765	1002	1195	63300	508	825	1079	1287	68600	543	881	1152	1373
52800	428	701	920	1099	58100	470	766	1003	1197	63400	509	826	1081	1289	68700	544	882	1153	1375
52900	429	703	922	1101	58200	471	767	1005	1199	63500	509	827	1082	1290	68800	545	883	1155	1376
53000	430	704	923	1103	58300	471	769	1006	1201	63600	510	829	1083	1292	68900	545	885	1156	1378
53100	431	705	925	1104	58400	472	770	1008	1203	63700	510	830	1085	1294	69000	546	886	1157	1380
53200	431	706	926	1106	58500	473	771	1010	1205	63800	511	831	1086	1295	69100	547	887	1159	1381
53300	432	708	928	1108	58600	474	772	1011	1207	63900	512	832	1087	1297	69200	547	888	1160	1383
53400	433	709	929	1110	58700	475	774	1013	1208	64000	512	833	1089	1298	69300	548	889	1162	1385
53500	434	710	931	1112	58800	475	775	1014	1210	64100	513	834	1090	1300	69400	549	890	1163	1386
53600	434	711	933	1114	58900	476	776	1016	1212	64200	514	835	1092	1302	69500	549	891	1164	1388
53700	435	712	934	1116	59000	477	777	1017	1214	64300	514	836	1093	1303	69600	550	892	1166	1390
53800	436	714	936	1117	59100	478	778	1019	1216	64400	515	837	1094	1305	69700	551	893	1167	1391
53900	437	715	937	1119	59200	478	780	1021	1218	64500	516	838	1096	1306	69800	552	894	1169	1393
54000	438	716	939	1121	59300	479	781	1022	1219	64600	516	839	1097	1308	69900	552	895	1170	1395
54100	438	717	940	1123	59400	480	782	1023	1221	64700	517	840	1098	1310	70000	553	896	1171	1396
54200	439	719	942	1125	59500	481	783	1025	1223	64800	518	841	1100	1311	70100	554	898	1173	1398
54300	440	720	944	1127	59600	481	784	1026	1224	64900	518	842	1101	1313	70200	554	899	1174	1400

Note: This table shows amounts of child support based on income to the nearest $100. There is a mathematical formula for calculating specific child support amounts between the $100 levels. For more information, please contact the Department of Justice.

Nota: La présente table indique le montant de la pension alimentaire pour enfants à verser d'après le revenu (aux 100 $ près). Il existe une formule mathématique pour calculer le montant exact de la pension alimentaire pour enfants dans le cas des revenus qui se situent entre les tranches de 100 $. Pour plus de renseignements, veuillez communiquer avec le ministère de la Justice.

Appendix D

NEW BRUNSWICK/NOUVEAU-BRUNSWICK

1997

FEDERAL CHILD SUPPORT AMOUNTS : SIMPLIFIED TABLES
MONTANTS FÉDÉRAUX DE PENSIONS ALIMENTAIRES POUR ENFANTS : TABLES SIMPLIFIÉES

Income/ Revenu ($)	Monthly Award/ Paiement mensuel ($) No. of Children/ N^{bre} d'enfants				Income/ Revenu ($)	Monthly Award/ Paiement mensuel ($) No. of Children/ N^{bre} d'enfants				Income/ Revenu ($)	Monthly Award/ Paiement mensuel ($) No. of Children/ N^{bre} d'enfants				Income/ Revenu ($)	Monthly Award/ Paiement mensuel ($) No. of Children/ N^{bre} d'enfants			
	1	2	3	4		1	2	3	4		1	2	3	4		1	2	3	4
70300	555	900	1176	1401	75600	592	957	1249	1488	80900	629	1015	1323	1576	86200	666	1072	1397	1663
70400	556	901	1177	1403	75700	593	958	1251	1490	81000	629	1016	1324	1577	86300	666	1073	1398	1664
70500	556	902	1178	1404	75800	593	959	1252	1492	81100	630	1017	1326	1579	86400	667	1074	1400	1666
70600	557	903	1180	1406	75900	594	960	1253	1493	81200	631	1018	1327	1580	86500	668	1075	1401	1668
70700	558	904	1181	1408	76000	595	961	1255	1495	81300	632	1019	1329	1582	86600	668	1076	1402	1669
70800	558	905	1182	1409	76100	595	963	1256	1497	81400	632	1020	1330	1584	86700	669	1077	1404	1671
70900	559	906	1184	1411	76200	596	964	1258	1498	81500	633	1021	1331	1585	86800	670	1078	1405	1673
71000	560	907	1185	1413	76300	597	965	1259	1500	81600	634	1022	1333	1587	86900	671	1079	1407	1674
71100	561	908	1187	1414	76400	597	966	1260	1502	81700	634	1023	1334	1589	87000	671	1081	1408	1676
71200	561	909	1188	1416	76500	598	967	1262	1503	81800	635	1024	1336	1590	87100	672	1082	1409	1678
71300	562	911	1189	1418	76600	599	968	1263	1505	81900	636	1025	1337	1592	87200	673	1083	1411	1679
71400	563	912	1191	1419	76700	600	969	1265	1506	82000	636	1026	1338	1594	87300	673	1084	1412	1681
71500	563	913	1192	1421	76800	600	970	1266	1508	82100	637	1027	1340	1595	87400	674	1085	1414	1683
71600	564	914	1194	1423	76900	601	971	1267	1510	82200	638	1029	1341	1597	87500	675	1086	1415	1684
71700	565	915	1195	1424	77000	602	972	1269	1511	82300	639	1030	1343	1599	87600	675	1087	1416	1686
71800	565	916	1196	1426	77100	602	973	1270	1513	82400	639	1031	1344	1600	87700	676	1088	1418	1687
71900	566	917	1198	1427	77200	603	974	1272	1515	82500	640	1032	1345	1602	87800	677	1089	1419	1689
72000	567	918	1199	1429	77300	604	976	1273	1516	82600	641	1033	1347	1604	87900	677	1090	1421	1691
72100	568	919	1201	1431	77400	604	977	1274	1518	82700	641	1034	1348	1605	88000	678	1091	1422	1692
72200	568	920	1202	1432	77500	605	978	1276	1520	82800	642	1035	1350	1607	88100	679	1092	1423	1694
72300	569	921	1203	1434	77600	606	979	1277	1521	82900	643	1036	1351	1608	88200	680	1094	1425	1696
72400	570	922	1205	1436	77700	606	980	1279	1523	83000	643	1037	1352	1610	88300	680	1095	1426	1697
72500	570	924	1206	1437	77800	607	981	1280	1525	83100	644	1038	1354	1612	88400	681	1096	1428	1699
72600	571	925	1208	1439	77900	608	982	1281	1526	83200	645	1039	1355	1613	88500	682	1097	1429	1701
72700	572	926	1209	1441	78000	609	983	1283	1528	83300	645	1040	1356	1615	88600	682	1098	1430	1702
72800	572	927	1210	1442	78100	609	984	1284	1529	83400	646	1042	1358	1617	88700	683	1099	1432	1704
72900	573	928	1212	1444	78200	610	985	1285	1531	83500	647	1043	1359	1618	88800	684	1100	1433	1706
73000	574	929	1213	1446	78300	611	986	1287	1533	83600	648	1044	1361	1620	88900	684	1101	1434	1707
73100	574	930	1214	1447	78400	611	987	1288	1534	83700	648	1045	1362	1622	89000	685	1102	1436	1709
73200	575	931	1216	1449	78500	612	989	1290	1536	83800	649	1046	1363	1623	89100	686	1103	1437	1710
73300	576	932	1217	1451	78600	613	990	1291	1538	83900	650	1047	1365	1625	89200	687	1104	1439	1712
73400	577	933	1219	1452	78700	613	991	1292	1539	84000	650	1048	1366	1627	89300	687	1105	1440	1714
73500	577	934	1220	1454	78800	614	992	1294	1541	84100	651	1049	1368	1628	89400	688	1107	1441	1715
73600	578	935	1221	1455	78900	615	993	1295	1543	84200	652	1050	1369	1630	89500	689	1108	1443	1717
73700	579	937	1223	1457	79000	616	994	1297	1544	84300	652	1051	1370	1632	89600	689	1109	1444	1719
73800	579	938	1224	1459	79100	616	995	1298	1546	84400	653	1052	1372	1633	89700	690	1110	1446	1720
73900	580	939	1226	1460	79200	617	996	1299	1548	84500	654	1053	1373	1635	89800	691	1111	1447	1722
74000	581	940	1227	1462	79300	618	997	1301	1549	84600	655	1055	1375	1636	89900	691	1112	1448	1724
74100	581	941	1228	1464	79400	618	998	1302	1551	84700	655	1056	1376	1638	90000	692	1113	1450	1725
74200	582	942	1230	1465	79500	619	999	1304	1553	84800	656	1057	1377	1640	90100	693	1114	1451	1727
74300	583	943	1231	1467	79600	620	1000	1305	1554	84900	657	1058	1379	1641	90200	694	1115	1453	1729
74400	584	944	1233	1469	79700	620	1002	1306	1556	85000	657	1059	1380	1643	90300	694	1116	1454	1730
74500	584	945	1234	1470	79800	621	1003	1308	1557	85100	658	1060	1382	1645	90400	695	1117	1455	1732
74600	585	946	1235	1472	79900	622	1004	1309	1559	85200	659	1061	1383	1646	90500	696	1118	1457	1734
74700	586	947	1237	1474	80000	623	1005	1311	1561	85300	659	1062	1384	1648	90600	696	1120	1458	1735
74800	586	948	1238	1475	80100	623	1006	1312	1562	85400	660	1063	1386	1650	90700	697	1121	1460	1737
74900	587	950	1240	1477	80200	624	1007	1313	1564	85500	661	1064	1387	1651	90800	698	1122	1461	1738
75000	588	951	1241	1478	80300	625	1008	1315	1566	85600	661	1065	1389	1653	90900	698	1123	1462	1740
75100	588	952	1242	1480	80400	625	1009	1316	1567	85700	662	1066	1390	1655	91000	699	1124	1464	1742
75200	589	953	1244	1482	80500	626	1010	1318	1569	85800	663	1068	1391	1656	91100	700	1125	1465	1743
75300	590	954	1245	1483	80600	627	1011	1319	1571	85900	664	1069	1393	1658	91200	700	1126	1466	1745
75400	590	955	1247	1485	80700	627	1012	1320	1572	86000	664	1070	1394	1659	91300	701	1127	1468	1747
75500	591	956	1248	1487	80800	628	1013	1322	1574	86100	665	1071	1395	1661	91400	702	1128	1469	1748

Note: This table shows amounts of child support based on income to the nearest $100. There is a mathematical formula for calculating specific child support amounts between the $100 levels. For more information, please contact the Department of Justice.

Nota: La présente table indique le montant de la pension alimentaire pour enfants à verser d'après le revenu (aux 100 $ près). Il existe une formule mathématique pour calculer le montant exact de la pension alimentaire pour enfants dans le cas des revenus qui se situent entre les tranches de 100 $. Pour plus de renseignements, veuillez communiquer avec le ministère de la Justice.

Divorce

NEW BRUNSWICK/NOUVEAU-BRUNSWICK

FEDERAL CHILD SUPPORT AMOUNTS : SIMPLIFIED TABLES
MONTANTS FÉDÉRAUX DE PENSIONS ALIMENTAIRES POUR ENFANTS : TABLES SIMPLIFIÉES

1997

Income/ Revenu ($)	Monthly Award/ Paiement mensuel ($) No. of Children/ N^bre d'enfants				Income/ Revenu ($)	Monthly Award/ Paiement mensuel ($) No. of Children/ N^bre d'enfants				Income/ Revenu ($)	Monthly Award/ Paiement mensuel ($) No. of Children/ N^bre d'enfants				Income/ Revenu ($)	Monthly Award/ Paiement mensuel ($) No. of Children/ N^bre d'enfants			
	1	2	3	4		1	2	3	4		1	2	3	4		1	2	3	4
91500	703	1129	1471	1750	96800	737	1184	1542	1834	102100	773	1240	1613	1919	107400	809	1295	1685	2003
91600	703	1130	1472	1752	96900	738	1185	1543	1836	102200	774	1241	1615	1920	107500	809	1296	1686	2005
91700	704	1131	1473	1753	97000	738	1186	1544	1837	102300	774	1242	1616	1922	107600	810	1298	1688	2007
91800	705	1133	1475	1755	97100	739	1187	1546	1839	102400	775	1243	1617	1924	107700	811	1299	1689	2008
91900	705	1134	1476	1757	97200	740	1188	1547	1841	102500	776	1244	1619	1925	107800	811	1300	1690	2010
92000	706	1135	1478	1758	97300	740	1189	1548	1842	102600	776	1245	1620	1927	107900	812	1301	1692	2011
92100	707	1136	1479	1760	97400	741	1190	1550	1844	102700	777	1246	1621	1928	108000	813	1302	1693	2013
92200	707	1137	1480	1761	97500	742	1191	1551	1845	102800	777	1247	1623	1930	108100	813	1303	1694	2015
92300	708	1138	1482	1763	97600	742	1192	1552	1847	102900	778	1248	1624	1932	108200	814	1304	1696	2016
92400	709	1139	1483	1765	97700	743	1193	1554	1849	103000	779	1249	1625	1933	108300	815	1305	1697	2018
92500	710	1140	1485	1766	97800	744	1195	1555	1850	103100	780	1250	1627	1935	108400	815	1306	1698	2019
92600	710	1141	1486	1768	97900	744	1196	1556	1852	103200	780	1251	1628	1936	108500	816	1307	1700	2021
92700	711	1142	1487	1770	98000	745	1197	1558	1853	103300	781	1252	1629	1938	108600	817	1308	1701	2023
92800	712	1143	1489	1771	98100	746	1198	1559	1855	103400	782	1253	1631	1940	108700	817	1309	1702	2024
92900	712	1144	1490	1773	98200	747	1199	1561	1857	103500	782	1254	1632	1941	108800	818	1310	1704	2026
93000	713	1146	1492	1775	98300	747	1200	1562	1858	103600	783	1255	1633	1943	108900	819	1311	1705	2027
93100	714	1147	1493	1776	98400	748	1201	1563	1860	103700	784	1257	1635	1944	109000	819	1312	1706	2029
93200	714	1148	1494	1778	98500	749	1202	1565	1861	103800	784	1258	1636	1946	109100	820	1313	1708	2031
93300	715	1149	1496	1779	98600	749	1203	1566	1863	103900	785	1259	1638	1948	109200	821	1314	1709	2032
93400	716	1150	1497	1781	98700	750	1204	1567	1865	104000	786	1260	1639	1949	109300	821	1315	1710	2034
93500	716	1151	1498	1782	98800	751	1205	1569	1866	104100	786	1261	1640	1951	109400	822	1316	1712	2035
93600	717	1152	1499	1784	98900	751	1206	1570	1868	104200	787	1262	1642	1952	109500	823	1317	1713	2037
93700	717	1153	1501	1786	99000	752	1207	1571	1869	104300	788	1263	1643	1954	109600	824	1319	1715	2039
93800	718	1154	1502	1787	99100	753	1208	1573	1871	104400	788	1264	1644	1956	109700	824	1320	1716	2040
93900	719	1155	1503	1789	99200	753	1209	1574	1872	104500	789	1265	1646	1957	109800	825	1321	1717	2042
94000	719	1156	1505	1790	99300	754	1210	1575	1874	104600	790	1266	1647	1959	109900	826	1322	1719	2043
94100	720	1157	1506	1792	99400	755	1211	1577	1876	104700	790	1267	1648	1960	110000	826	1323	1720	2045
94200	721	1158	1507	1793	99500	755	1212	1578	1877	104800	791	1268	1650	1962	110100	827	1324	1721	2047
94300	721	1159	1509	1795	99600	756	1213	1579	1879	104900	792	1269	1651	1963	110200	828	1325	1723	2048
94400	722	1160	1510	1797	99700	757	1214	1581	1880	105000	792	1270	1652	1965	110300	828	1326	1724	2050
94500	722	1161	1511	1798	99800	757	1216	1582	1882	105100	793	1271	1654	1967	110400	829	1327	1725	2051
94600	723	1162	1513	1800	99900	758	1217	1583	1884	105200	794	1272	1655	1968	110500	830	1328	1727	2053
94700	724	1163	1514	1801	100000	759	1218	1585	1885	105300	794	1273	1656	1970	110600	830	1329	1728	2055
94800	724	1164	1515	1803	100100	759	1219	1586	1887	105400	795	1274	1658	1971	110700	831	1330	1729	2056
94900	725	1165	1516	1804	100200	760	1220	1588	1888	105500	796	1275	1659	1973	110800	832	1331	1731	2058
95000	726	1166	1518	1806	100300	761	1221	1589	1890	105600	796	1276	1660	1975	110900	832	1332	1732	2059
95100	726	1167	1519	1807	100400	761	1222	1590	1892	105700	797	1278	1662	1976	111000	833	1333	1733	2061
95200	727	1168	1520	1809	100500	762	1223	1592	1893	105800	798	1279	1663	1978	111100	834	1334	1735	2063
95300	727	1169	1522	1811	100600	763	1224	1593	1895	105900	799	1280	1665	1979	111200	834	1335	1736	2064
95400	728	1170	1523	1812	100700	763	1225	1594	1896	106000	799	1281	1666	1981	111300	835	1336	1737	2066
95500	729	1171	1524	1814	100800	764	1226	1596	1898	106100	800	1282	1667	1983	111400	836	1337	1739	2067
95600	729	1172	1526	1815	100900	765	1227	1597	1900	106200	801	1283	1669	1984	111500	836	1338	1740	2069
95700	730	1173	1527	1817	101000	765	1228	1598	1901	106300	801	1284	1670	1986	111600	837	1340	1742	2070
95800	731	1174	1528	1818	101100	766	1229	1600	1903	106400	802	1285	1671	1987	111700	838	1341	1743	2072
95900	731	1175	1530	1820	101200	767	1230	1601	1904	106500	803	1286	1673	1989	111800	838	1342	1744	2074
96000	732	1176	1531	1821	101300	767	1231	1602	1906	106600	803	1287	1674	1991	111900	839	1343	1746	2075
96100	732	1177	1532	1823	101400	768	1232	1604	1908	106700	804	1288	1675	1992	112000	840	1344	1747	2077
96200	733	1178	1534	1825	101500	769	1233	1605	1909	106800	805	1289	1677	1994	112100	840	1345	1748	2078
96300	734	1179	1535	1826	101600	769	1234	1606	1911	106900	805	1290	1678	1995	112200	841	1346	1750	2080
96400	734	1180	1536	1828	101700	770	1236	1608	1912	107000	806	1291	1679	1997	112300	842	1347	1751	2082
96500	735	1181	1538	1829	101800	771	1237	1609	1914	107100	807	1292	1681	1999	112400	842	1348	1752	2083
96600	736	1182	1539	1831	101900	772	1238	1611	1916	107200	807	1293	1682	2000	112500	843	1349	1754	2085
96700	736	1183	1540	1833	102000	772	1239	1612	1917	107300	808	1294	1683	2002	112600	844	1350	1755	2086

Note: This table shows amounts of child support based on income to the nearest $100. There is a mathematical formula for calculating specific child support amounts between the $100 levels. For more information, please contact the Department of Justice.

Nota: La présente table indique le montant de la pension alimentaire pour enfants à verser d'après le revenu (aux 100 $ près). Il existe une formule mathématique pour calculer le montant exact de la pension alimentaire pour enfants dans le cas des revenus qui se situent entre les tranches de 100 $. Pour plus de renseignements, veuillez communiquer avec le ministère de la Justice.

Appendix D

NEW BRUNSWICK/NOUVEAU-BRUNSWICK
1997

FEDERAL CHILD SUPPORT AMOUNTS : SIMPLIFIED TABLES
MONTANTS FÉDÉRAUX DE PENSIONS ALIMENTAIRES POUR ENFANTS : TABLES SIMPLIFIÉES

Income/ Revenu ($)	Monthly Award/ Paiement mensuel ($) No. of Children/ N^{bre} d'enfants				Income/ Revenu ($)	Monthly Award/ Paiement mensuel ($) No. of Children/ N^{bre} d'enfants				Income/ Revenu ($)	Monthly Award/ Paiement mensuel ($) No. of Children/ N^{bre} d'enfants				Income/ Revenu ($)	Monthly Award/ Paiement mensuel ($) No. of Children/ N^{bre} d'enfants			
	1	2	3	4		1	2	3	4		1	2	3	4		1	2	3	4
112700	844	1351	1756	2088	118000	880	1407	1828	2173	123300	916	1462	1900	2257	128600	952	1518	1971	2342
112800	845	1352	1758	2090	118100	881	1408	1829	2174	123400	917	1464	1901	2259	128700	953	1519	1973	2343
112900	846	1353	1759	2091	118200	882	1409	1831	2176	123500	917	1465	1902	2260	128800	953	1520	1974	2345
113000	846	1354	1760	2093	118300	882	1410	1832	2177	123600	918	1466	1904	2262	128900	954	1521	1975	2347
113100	847	1355	1762	2094	118400	883	1411	1833	2179	123700	919	1467	1905	2264	129000	955	1522	1977	2348
113200	848	1356	1763	2096	118500	884	1412	1835	2181	123800	919	1468	1906	2265	129100	955	1523	1978	2350
113300	849	1357	1765	2098	118600	884	1413	1836	2182	123900	920	1469	1908	2267	129200	956	1524	1979	2351
113400	849	1358	1766	2099	118700	885	1414	1837	2184	124000	921	1470	1909	2268	129300	957	1526	1981	2353
113500	850	1360	1767	2101	118800	886	1415	1839	2185	124100	921	1471	1910	2270	129400	957	1527	1982	2355
113600	851	1361	1769	2102	118900	886	1416	1840	2187	124200	922	1472	1912	2272	129500	958	1528	1983	2356
113700	851	1362	1770	2104	119000	887	1417	1842	2189	124300	923	1473	1913	2273	129600	959	1529	1985	2358
113800	852	1363	1771	2106	119100	888	1418	1843	2190	124400	923	1474	1914	2275	129700	959	1530	1986	2359
113900	853	1364	1773	2107	119200	888	1419	1844	2192	124500	924	1475	1916	2276	129800	960	1531	1987	2361
114000	853	1365	1774	2109	119300	889	1420	1846	2193	124600	925	1476	1917	2278	129900	961	1532	1989	2363
114100	854	1366	1775	2110	119400	890	1421	1847	2195	124700	926	1477	1919	2280	130000	961	1533	1990	2364
114200	855	1367	1777	2112	119500	890	1423	1848	2197	124800	926	1478	1920	2281	130100	962	1534	1991	2366
114300	855	1368	1778	2114	119600	891	1424	1850	2198	124900	927	1479	1921	2283	130200	963	1535	1993	2367
114400	856	1369	1779	2115	119700	892	1425	1851	2200	125000	928	1480	1923	2284	130300	963	1536	1994	2369
114500	857	1370	1781	2117	119800	892	1426	1852	2201	125100	928	1481	1924	2286	130400	964	1537	1996	2371
114600	857	1371	1782	2118	119900	893	1427	1854	2203	125200	929	1482	1925	2288	130500	965	1538	1997	2372
114700	858	1372	1783	2120	120000	894	1428	1855	2205	125300	930	1483	1927	2289	130600	965	1539	1998	2374
114800	859	1373	1785	2122	120100	894	1429	1856	2206	125400	930	1485	1928	2291	130700	966	1540	2000	2375
114900	859	1374	1786	2123	120200	895	1430	1858	2208	125500	931	1486	1929	2292	130800	967	1541	2001	2377
115000	860	1375	1787	2125	120300	896	1431	1859	2209	125600	932	1487	1931	2294	130900	967	1542	2002	2379
115100	861	1376	1789	2126	120400	896	1432	1860	2211	125700	932	1488	1932	2296	131000	968	1543	2004	2380
115200	861	1377	1790	2128	120500	897	1433	1862	2213	125800	933	1489	1933	2297	131100	969	1544	2005	2382
115300	862	1378	1792	2130	120600	898	1434	1863	2214	125900	934	1490	1935	2299	131200	969	1545	2006	2383
115400	863	1379	1793	2131	120700	898	1435	1864	2216	126000	934	1491	1936	2300	131300	970	1547	2008	2385
115500	863	1381	1794	2133	120800	899	1436	1866	2217	126100	935	1492	1937	2302	131400	971	1548	2009	2387
115600	864	1382	1796	2134	120900	900	1437	1867	2219	126200	936	1493	1939	2304	131500	971	1549	2010	2388
115700	865	1383	1797	2136	121000	901	1438	1869	2221	126300	936	1494	1940	2305	131600	972	1550	2012	2390
115800	865	1384	1798	2138	121100	901	1439	1870	2222	126400	937	1495	1941	2307	131700	973	1551	2013	2391
115900	866	1385	1800	2139	121200	902	1440	1871	2224	126500	938	1496	1943	2308	131800	973	1552	2014	2393
116000	867	1386	1801	2141	121300	903	1441	1873	2225	126600	938	1497	1944	2310	131900	974	1553	2016	2395
116100	867	1387	1802	2142	121400	903	1443	1874	2227	126700	939	1498	1946	2312	132000	975	1554	2017	2396
116200	868	1388	1804	2144	121500	904	1444	1875	2229	126800	940	1499	1947	2313	132100	976	1555	2018	2398
116300	869	1389	1805	2146	121600	905	1445	1877	2230	126900	940	1500	1948	2315	132200	976	1556	2020	2399
116400	869	1390	1806	2147	121700	905	1446	1878	2232	127000	941	1501	1950	2316	132300	977	1557	2021	2401
116500	870	1391	1808	2149	121800	906	1447	1879	2233	127100	942	1502	1951	2318	132400	978	1558	2023	2403
116600	871	1392	1809	2150	121900	907	1448	1881	2235	127200	942	1503	1952	2320	132500	978	1559	2024	2404
116700	871	1393	1810	2152	122000	907	1449	1882	2237	127300	943	1505	1954	2321	132600	979	1560	2025	2406
116800	872	1394	1812	2153	122100	908	1450	1883	2238	127400	944	1506	1955	2323	132700	980	1561	2027	2407
116900	873	1395	1813	2155	122200	909	1451	1885	2240	127500	944	1507	1956	2324	132800	980	1562	2028	2409
117000	874	1396	1815	2157	122300	909	1452	1886	2241	127600	945	1508	1958	2326	132900	981	1563	2029	2411
117100	874	1397	1816	2158	122400	910	1453	1887	2243	127700	946	1509	1959	2328	133000	982	1564	2031	2412
117200	875	1398	1817	2160	122500	911	1454	1889	2244	127800	946	1510	1960	2329	133100	982	1565	2032	2414
117300	876	1399	1819	2161	122600	911	1455	1890	2246	127900	947	1511	1962	2331	133200	983	1567	2033	2415
117400	876	1400	1820	2163	122700	912	1456	1892	2248	128000	948	1512	1963	2332	133300	984	1568	2035	2417
117500	877	1402	1821	2165	122800	913	1457	1893	2249	128100	948	1513	1964	2334	133400	984	1569	2036	2419
117600	878	1403	1823	2166	122900	913	1458	1894	2251	128200	949	1514	1966	2336	133500	985	1570	2037	2420
117700	878	1404	1824	2168	123000	914	1459	1896	2252	128300	950	1515	1967	2337	133600	986	1571	2039	2422
117800	879	1405	1825	2169	123100	915	1460	1897	2254	128400	951	1516	1969	2339	133700	986	1572	2040	2423
117900	880	1406	1827	2171	123200	915	1461	1898	2256	128500	951	1517	1970	2340	133800	987	1573	2041	2425

Note: This table shows amounts of child support based on income to the nearest $100. There is a mathematical formula for calculating specific child support amounts between the $100 levels. For more information, please contact the Department of Justice.

Nota: La présente table indique le montant de la pension alimentaire pour enfants à verser d'après le revenu (aux 100 $ près). Il existe une formule mathématique pour calculer le montant exact de la pension alimentaire pour enfants dans le cas des revenus qui se situent entre les tranches de 100 $. Pour plus de renseignements, veuillez communiquer avec le ministère de la Justice.

Divorce

NEW BRUNSWICK/NOUVEAU-BRUNSWICK

FEDERAL CHILD SUPPORT AMOUNTS : SIMPLIFIED TABLES
MONTANTS FÉDÉRAUX DE PENSIONS ALIMENTAIRES POUR ENFANTS : TABLES SIMPLIFIÉES

1997

Income/Revenu ($)	Monthly Award/Paiement mensuel ($) No. of Children/N^bre d'enfants				Income/Revenu ($)	Monthly Award/Paiement mensuel ($) No. of Children/N^bre d'enfants				Income/Revenu ($)	Monthly Award/Paiement mensuel ($) No. of Children/N^bre d'enfants				Income/Revenu ($)	Monthly Award/Paiement mensuel ($) No. of Children/N^bre d'enfants				Income/Revenu ($)	Monthly Award/Paiement mensuel ($) No. of Children/N^bre d'enfants			
	1	2	3	4		1	2	3	4		1	2	3	4		1	2	3	4		1	2	3	4
133900	988	1574	2043	2427	138000	1015	1617	2098	2492	142100	1043	1660	2154	2557	146200	1071	1703	2209	2623					
134000	988	1575	2044	2428	138100	1016	1618	2100	2494	142200	1044	1661	2155	2559	146300	1071	1704	2210	2624					
134100	989	1576	2046	2430	138200	1017	1619	2101	2495	142300	1044	1662	2156	2561	146400	1072	1705	2212	2626					
134200	990	1577	2047	2431	138300	1017	1620	2102	2497	142400	1045	1663	2158	2562	146500	1073	1706	2213	2628					
134300	990	1578	2048	2433	138400	1018	1621	2104	2498	142500	1046	1664	2159	2564	146600	1073	1707	2214	2629					
134400	991	1579	2050	2434	138500	1019	1622	2105	2500	142600	1046	1665	2160	2565	146700	1074	1708	2216	2631					
134500	992	1580	2051	2436	138600	1019	1623	2106	2502	142700	1047	1666	2162	2567	146800	1075	1709	2217	2632					
134600	992	1581	2052	2438	138700	1020	1624	2108	2503	142800	1048	1667	2163	2569	146900	1075	1710	2218	2634					
134700	993	1582	2054	2439	138800	1021	1625	2109	2505	142900	1048	1668	2164	2570	147000	1076	1712	2220	2636					
134800	994	1583	2055	2441	138900	1021	1626	2110	2506	143000	1049	1669	2166	2572	147100	1077	1713	2221	2637					
134900	994	1584	2056	2442	139000	1022	1627	2112	2508	143100	1050	1671	2167	2573	147200	1077	1714	2222	2639					
135000	995	1585	2058	2444	139100	1023	1628	2113	2510	143200	1050	1672	2168	2575	147300	1078	1715	2224	2640					
135100	996	1586	2059	2446	139200	1023	1630	2114	2511	143300	1051	1673	2170	2577	147400	1079	1716	2225	2642					
135200	996	1588	2060	2447	139300	1024	1631	2116	2513	143400	1052	1674	2171	2578	147500	1080	1717	2227	2644					
135300	997	1589	2062	2449	139400	1025	1632	2117	2514	143500	1053	1675	2173	2580	147600	1080	1718	2228	2645					
135400	998	1590	2063	2450	139500	1025	1633	2118	2516	143600	1053	1676	2174	2581	147700	1081	1719	2229	2647					
135500	998	1591	2064	2452	139600	1026	1634	2120	2518	143700	1054	1677	2175	2583	147800	1082	1720	2231	2648					
135600	999	1592	2066	2454	139700	1027	1635	2121	2519	143800	1055	1678	2177	2585	147900	1082	1721	2232	2650					
135700	1000	1593	2067	2455	139800	1028	1636	2123	2521	143900	1055	1679	2178	2586	148000	1083	1722	2233	2652					
135800	1000	1594	2068	2457	139900	1028	1637	2124	2522	144000	1056	1680	2179	2588	148100	1084	1723	2235	2653					
135900	1001	1595	2070	2458	140000	1029	1638	2125	2524	144100	1057	1681	2181	2589	148200	1084	1724	2236	2655					
136000	1002	1596	2071	2460	140100	1030	1639	2127	2526	144200	1057	1682	2182	2591	148300	1085	1725	2237	2656					
136100	1003	1597	2073	2462	140200	1030	1640	2128	2527	144300	1058	1683	2183	2593	148400	1086	1726	2239	2658					
136200	1003	1598	2074	2463	140300	1031	1641	2129	2529	144400	1059	1684	2185	2594	148500	1086	1727	2240	2660					
136300	1004	1599	2075	2465	140400	1032	1642	2131	2530	144500	1059	1685	2186	2596	148600	1087	1728	2241	2661					
136400	1005	1600	2077	2466	140500	1032	1643	2132	2532	144600	1060	1686	2187	2597	148700	1088	1729	2243	2663					
136500	1005	1601	2078	2468	140600	1033	1644	2133	2533	144700	1061	1687	2189	2599	148800	1088	1730	2244	2664					
136600	1006	1602	2079	2470	140700	1034	1645	2135	2535	144800	1061	1688	2190	2601	148900	1089	1731	2245	2666					
136700	1007	1603	2081	2471	140800	1034	1646	2136	2537	144900	1062	1689	2191	2602	149000	1090	1733	2247	2668					
136800	1007	1604	2082	2473	140900	1035	1647	2137	2538	145000	1063	1690	2193	2604	149100	1090	1734	2248	2669					
136900	1008	1605	2083	2474	141000	1036	1648	2139	2540	145100	1063	1692	2194	2605	149200	1091	1735	2250	2671					
137000	1009	1606	2085	2476	141100	1036	1650	2140	2541	145200	1064	1693	2195	2607	149300	1092	1736	2251	2672					
137100	1009	1607	2086	2478	141200	1037	1651	2141	2543	145300	1065	1694	2197	2609	149400	1092	1737	2252	2674					
137200	1010	1609	2087	2479	141300	1038	1652	2143	2545	145400	1065	1695	2198	2610	149500	1093	1738	2254	2676					
137300	1011	1610	2089	2481	141400	1038	1653	2144	2546	145500	1066	1696	2200	2612	149600	1094	1739	2255	2677					
137400	1011	1611	2090	2482	141500	1039	1654	2145	2548	145600	1067	1697	2201	2613	149700	1094	1740	2256	2679					
137500	1012	1612	2091	2484	141600	1040	1655	2147	2549	145700	1067	1698	2202	2615	149800	1095	1741	2258	2680					
137600	1013	1613	2093	2486	141700	1040	1656	2148	2551	145800	1068	1699	2204	2617	149900	1096	1742	2259	2682					
137700	1013	1614	2094	2487	141800	1041	1657	2150	2553	145900	1069	1700	2205	2618	150000	1096	1743	2260	2684					
137800	1014	1615	2096	2489	141900	1042	1658	2151	2554	146000	1069	1701	2206	2620										
137900	1015	1616	2097	2490	142000	1042	1659	2152	2556	146100	1070	1702	2208	2621										

Income/Revenu ($)	Monthly Award/Paiement mensuel ($)			
	one child/un enfant	two children/deux enfants	three children/trois enfants	four children/quatre enfants
For income over $150,000	1096 plus 0.68% of income over $150,000	1743 plus 1.05% of income over $150,000	2260 plus 1.35% of income over $150,000	2684 plus 1.60% of income over $150,000
Pour revenu dépassant 150 000$	1096 plus 0,68% du revenu dépassant 150 000$	1743 plus 1,05% du revenu dépassant 150 000$	2260 plus 1,35% du revenu dépassant 150 000$	2684 plus 1,60% du revenu dépassant 150 000$

Note: This table shows amounts of child support based on income to the nearest $100. There is a mathematical formula for calculating specific child support amounts between the $100 levels. For more information, please contact the Department of Justice.

Nota: La présente table indique le montant de la pension alimentaire pour enfants à verser d'après le revenu (aux 100 $ près). Il existe une formule mathématique pour calculer le montant exact de la pension alimentaire pour enfants dans le cas des revenus qui se situent entre les tranches de 100 $. Pour plus de renseignements, veuillez communiquer avec le ministère de la Justice.

Appendix D

NEWFOUNDLAND/TERRE-NEUVE

1997

FEDERAL CHILD SUPPORT AMOUNTS : SIMPLIFIED TABLES
MONTANTS FÉDÉRAUX DE PENSIONS ALIMENTAIRES POUR ENFANTS : TABLES SIMPLIFIÉES

Income/ Revenu ($)	Monthly Award/ Paiement mensuel ($) No. of Children/ N^{bre} d'enfants				Income/ Revenu ($)	Monthly Award/ Paiement mensuel ($) No. of Children/ N^{bre} d'enfants				Income/ Revenu ($)	Monthly Award/ Paiement mensuel ($) No. of Children/ N^{bre} d'enfants				Income/ Revenu ($)	Monthly Award/ Paiement mensuel ($) No. of Children/ N^{bre} d'enfants			
	1	2	3	4		1	2	3	4		1	2	3	4		1	2	3	4
6700	0	0	0	0	12000	92	141	162	184	17300	137	249	324	368	22600	186	326	438	529
6800	0	0	0	0	12100	92	143	166	188	17400	138	251	327	372	22700	187	327	439	531
6900	0	0	0	0	12200	92	146	169	191	17500	139	252	330	375	22800	188	329	441	533
7000	0	1	2	3	12300	92	148	172	195	17600	140	254	333	379	22900	189	330	443	536
7100	2	4	5	7	12400	92	151	175	198	17700	141	255	337	382	23000	190	331	445	538
7200	5	6	8	10	12500	93	154	178	202	17800	142	257	340	386	23100	191	333	447	540
7300	7	9	12	14	12600	93	156	181	205	17900	142	258	343	389	23200	192	334	449	542
7400	9	12	15	18	12700	94	159	184	209	18000	143	260	346	393	23300	192	336	450	544
7500	12	15	18	21	12800	95	162	187	212	18100	144	261	349	396	23400	193	337	452	547
7600	14	18	21	25	12900	96	164	190	216	18200	145	262	352	400	23500	194	339	454	549
7700	16	20	25	29	13000	97	167	193	219	18300	146	264	355	403	23600	195	340	456	551
7800	19	23	28	32	13100	98	170	196	223	18400	147	265	358	407	23700	196	342	458	553
7900	21	26	31	36	13200	99	172	199	226	18500	148	267	361	410	23800	197	343	460	555
8000	24	29	34	39	13300	100	175	202	230	18600	149	268	363	413	23900	198	344	462	557
8100	26	32	37	43	13400	101	177	205	233	18700	150	270	365	417	24000	199	346	463	560
8200	28	34	41	47	13500	102	180	208	236	18800	151	271	367	420	24100	200	347	465	562
8300	31	37	44	50	13600	103	183	211	240	18900	152	272	369	424	24200	201	349	467	564
8400	33	40	47	54	13700	104	185	214	243	19000	153	274	371	427	24300	202	350	469	566
8500	36	43	50	58	13800	105	188	217	247	19100	154	275	373	431	24400	203	352	471	568
8600	38	46	53	61	13900	105	191	220	250	19200	155	277	375	434	24500	204	353	473	571
8700	40	49	57	65	14000	106	193	224	254	19300	155	278	376	438	24600	205	355	475	573
8800	43	51	60	69	14100	107	196	227	257	19400	156	280	378	441	24700	205	356	476	575
8900	45	54	63	72	14200	108	199	230	261	19500	157	281	380	445	24800	206	357	478	577
9000	47	57	66	76	14300	109	201	233	264	19600	158	283	382	448	24900	207	359	480	579
9100	50	60	70	79	14400	110	204	236	268	19700	159	284	384	452	25000	208	360	482	582
9200	52	63	73	83	14500	111	206	239	271	19800	160	285	386	455	25100	209	362	484	584
9300	55	65	76	87	14600	112	209	242	275	19900	161	287	388	459	25200	210	363	486	586
9400	57	68	79	90	14700	113	212	245	278	20000	162	288	389	462	25300	211	365	488	588
9500	59	71	82	94	14800	114	213	248	282	20100	163	290	391	465	25400	212	366	489	590
9600	62	74	86	98	14900	115	215	251	285	20200	164	291	393	469	25500	213	367	491	592
9700	64	77	89	101	15000	116	216	254	289	20300	165	293	395	472	25600	214	369	493	595
9800	67	79	92	105	15100	117	218	257	292	20400	166	294	397	476	25700	215	370	495	597
9900	69	82	95	109	15200	118	219	260	295	20500	167	296	399	479	25800	216	372	497	599
10000	71	85	99	112	15300	118	221	263	299	20600	167	297	401	483	25900	217	373	499	601
10100	74	88	102	116	15400	119	222	266	302	20700	168	298	402	486	26000	217	375	500	603
10200	76	91	105	119	15500	120	224	269	306	20800	169	300	404	490	26100	218	376	502	605
10300	78	93	108	123	15600	121	225	272	309	20900	170	301	406	492	26200	219	377	504	607
10400	81	96	111	127	15700	122	226	275	313	21000	171	303	408	494	26300	220	379	505	609
10500	83	99	115	130	15800	123	228	279	316	21100	172	304	410	496	26400	221	380	507	611
10600	86	102	118	134	15900	124	229	282	320	21200	173	306	412	498	26500	222	381	509	613
10700	88	105	121	138	16000	125	231	285	323	21300	174	307	413	501	26600	223	383	511	615
10800	90	107	124	141	16100	126	232	288	327	21400	175	308	415	503	26700	223	384	512	617
10900	92	110	128	145	16200	127	234	291	330	21500	176	310	417	505	26800	224	385	514	619
11000	92	113	131	149	16300	128	235	294	334	21600	177	311	419	507	26900	225	387	516	621
11100	92	116	134	152	16400	129	236	297	337	21700	178	313	421	509	27000	226	388	517	623
11200	92	119	137	156	16500	130	238	300	341	21800	179	314	423	512	27100	227	389	519	626
11300	92	121	140	159	16600	130	239	303	344	21900	180	316	425	514	27200	228	391	521	628
11400	92	124	144	163	16700	131	241	306	348	22000	180	317	426	516	27300	229	392	523	630
11500	92	127	147	167	16800	132	242	309	351	22100	181	319	428	518	27400	229	393	524	632
11600	92	130	150	170	16900	133	244	312	354	22200	182	320	430	520	27500	230	395	526	634
11700	92	133	153	174	17000	134	245	315	358	22300	183	321	432	522	27600	231	396	528	636
11800	92	135	156	177	17100	135	247	318	361	22400	184	323	434	525	27700	232	397	529	638
11900	92	138	159	181	17200	136	248	321	365	22500	185	324	436	527	27800	233	399	531	640

Note: This table shows amounts of child support based on income to the nearest $100. There is a mathematical formula for calculating specific child support amounts between the $100 levels. For more information, please contact the Department of Justice.

Nota: La présente table indique le montant de pensions alimentaires pour enfants à verser d'après le revenu (aux 100 $ près). Il existe une formule mathématique pour calculer le montant exact de la pension alimentaire pour enfants dans le cas des revenus qui se situent entre les tranches de 100 $. Pour plus de renseignements, veuillez communiquer avec le ministère de la Justice.

Divorce

NEWFOUNDLAND/TERRE-NEUVE

FEDERAL CHILD SUPPORT AMOUNTS : SIMPLIFIED TABLES
MONTANTS FÉDÉRAUX DE PENSIONS ALIMENTAIRES POUR ENFANTS : TABLES SIMPLIFIÉES

1997

Income/Revenu ($)	Monthly Award/Paiement mensuel ($) No. of Children/N^{bre} d'enfants				Income/Revenu ($)	Monthly Award/Paiement mensuel ($) No. of Children/N^{bre} d'enfants				Income/Revenu ($)	Monthly Award/Paiement mensuel ($) No. of Children/N^{bre} d'enfants				Income/Revenu ($)	Monthly Award/Paiement mensuel ($) No. of Children/N^{bre} d'enfants			
	1	2	3	4		1	2	3	4		1	2	3	4		1	2	3	4
27900	234	400	533	642	33200	272	460	610	733	38500	311	519	687	823	43800	351	582	767	919
28000	235	401	535	644	33300	273	461	611	734	38600	311	521	688	825	43900	352	583	769	920
28100	235	403	536	646	33400	274	462	613	736	38700	312	522	690	827	44000	352	585	770	922
28200	236	404	538	648	33500	274	463	614	738	38800	313	523	691	829	44100	353	586	772	924
28300	237	405	540	650	33600	275	464	615	739	38900	313	524	693	830	44200	354	587	773	926
28400	238	407	541	652	33700	276	465	617	741	39000	314	525	694	832	44300	355	588	775	928
28500	239	408	543	654	33800	276	466	618	743	39100	315	526	695	834	44400	355	589	776	929
28600	240	409	545	656	33900	277	467	620	744	39200	316	528	697	836	44500	356	591	778	931
28700	241	411	547	658	34000	278	469	621	746	39300	316	529	698	837	44600	357	592	779	933
28800	241	412	548	660	34100	279	470	623	748	39400	317	530	700	839	44700	358	593	781	935
28900	242	413	550	662	34200	279	471	624	749	39500	318	531	701	841	44800	359	594	783	937
29000	243	415	552	664	34300	280	472	625	751	39600	319	532	703	843	44900	359	595	784	939
29100	244	416	553	666	34400	281	473	627	753	39700	319	533	704	844	45000	360	596	786	940
29200	245	417	555	668	34500	281	474	628	754	39800	320	534	706	846	45100	361	598	787	942
29300	246	419	557	670	34600	282	475	630	756	39900	321	536	707	848	45200	362	599	789	944
29400	247	420	559	672	34700	283	476	631	758	40000	322	537	709	850	45300	362	600	790	946
29500	247	421	560	674	34800	283	477	633	759	40100	322	538	710	851	45400	363	601	792	948
29600	248	423	562	676	34900	284	479	634	761	40200	323	539	712	853	45500	364	602	793	949
29700	249	424	563	678	35000	285	480	635	763	40300	324	540	713	855	45600	365	604	795	951
29800	249	425	565	679	35100	286	481	637	764	40400	325	542	715	857	45700	365	605	796	953
29900	250	426	566	681	35200	286	482	638	766	40500	325	543	717	859	45800	366	606	798	955
30000	251	427	567	682	35300	287	483	640	768	40600	326	544	718	861	45900	367	607	799	957
30100	251	428	568	684	35400	288	484	641	770	40700	327	545	720	862	46000	368	608	801	959
30200	252	429	570	685	35500	288	485	642	771	40800	328	546	721	864	46100	368	610	803	960
30300	253	430	571	687	35600	289	486	644	773	40900	329	548	723	866	46200	369	611	804	962
30400	253	431	572	688	35700	290	487	645	775	41000	329	549	724	868	46300	370	612	806	964
30500	254	431	574	690	35800	291	488	647	776	41100	330	550	726	870	46400	371	613	807	966
30600	255	432	575	691	35900	291	490	648	778	41200	331	551	727	871	46500	372	614	809	968
30700	255	433	576	693	36000	292	491	650	780	41300	332	552	729	873	46600	372	616	810	969
30800	256	434	577	694	36100	293	492	651	781	41400	332	553	730	875	46700	373	617	812	971
30900	257	435	579	696	36200	294	493	653	783	41500	333	555	732	877	46800	374	618	813	973
31000	257	436	580	697	36300	294	494	654	785	41600	334	556	733	879	46900	375	619	815	975
31100	258	437	581	699	36400	295	495	656	787	41700	335	557	735	880	47000	375	620	816	977
31200	258	438	582	700	36500	296	496	657	788	41800	335	558	736	882	47100	376	622	818	978
31300	259	439	584	702	36600	296	498	659	790	41900	336	559	738	884	47200	377	623	819	980
31400	260	440	585	703	36700	297	499	660	792	42000	337	561	740	886	47300	378	624	821	982
31500	260	441	586	705	36800	298	500	661	794	42100	338	562	741	888	47400	378	625	822	984
31600	261	442	588	706	36900	299	501	663	795	42200	339	563	743	890	47500	379	626	824	986
31700	262	443	589	708	37000	299	502	664	797	42300	339	564	744	891	47600	380	628	826	988
31800	262	444	590	709	37100	300	503	666	799	42400	340	565	746	893	47700	381	629	827	989
31900	263	445	591	711	37200	301	505	667	801	42500	341	567	747	895	47800	382	630	829	991
32000	264	446	593	712	37300	302	506	669	802	42600	342	568	749	897	47900	382	631	830	993
32100	264	448	594	714	37400	302	507	670	804	42700	342	569	750	899	48000	383	632	832	995
32200	265	449	596	716	37500	303	508	672	806	42800	343	570	752	900	48100	384	633	833	997
32300	266	450	597	717	37600	304	509	673	808	42900	344	571	753	902	48200	385	635	835	998
32400	266	451	598	719	37700	305	510	675	809	43000	345	573	755	904	48300	385	636	836	1000
32500	267	452	600	721	37800	305	511	676	811	43100	345	574	756	906	48400	386	637	838	1002
32600	268	453	601	723	37900	306	513	678	813	43200	346	575	758	908	48500	387	638	839	1004
32700	269	454	603	724	38000	307	514	679	815	43300	347	576	760	910	48600	388	639	841	1006
32800	269	455	604	726	38100	308	515	681	816	43400	348	577	761	911	48700	388	641	842	1008
32900	270	456	606	728	38200	308	516	682	818	43500	349	579	763	913	48800	389	642	844	1009
33000	271	458	607	729	38300	309	517	684	820	43600	349	580	764	915	48900	390	643	846	1011
33100	271	459	608	731	38400	310	518	685	822	43700	350	581	766	917	49000	391	644	847	1013

Note: This table shows amounts of child support based on income to the nearest $100. There is a mathematical formula for calculating specific child support amounts between the $100 levels. For more information, please contact the Department of Justice.

Nota: La présente table indique le montant de pensions alimentaires pour enfants à verser d'après le revenu (aux 100 $ près). Il existe une formule mathématique pour calculer le montant exact de la pension alimentaire pour enfants dans le cas des revenus qui se situent entre les tranches de 100 $. Pour plus de renseignements, veuillez communiquer avec le ministère de la Justice.

Appendix D

NEWFOUNDLAND/TERRE-NEUVE

1997

FEDERAL CHILD SUPPORT AMOUNTS : SIMPLIFIED TABLES
MONTANTS FÉDÉRAUX DE PENSIONS ALIMENTAIRES POUR ENFANTS : TABLES SIMPLIFIÉES

Income/ Revenu ($)	Monthly Award/ Paiement mensuel ($) No. of Children/ N^{bre} d'enfants				Income/ Revenu ($)	Monthly Award/ Paiement mensuel ($) No. of Children/ N^{bre} d'enfants				Income/ Revenu ($)	Monthly Award/ Paiement mensuel ($) No. of Children/ N^{bre} d'enfants				Income/ Revenu ($)	Monthly Award/ Paiement mensuel ($) No. of Children/ N^{bre} d'enfants			
	1	2	3	4		1	2	3	4		1	2	3	4		1	2	3	4
49100	392	645	849	1015	54400	432	709	930	1111	59700	471	769	1008	1204	65000	504	823	1077	1286
49200	392	647	850	1017	54500	433	710	931	1113	59800	471	770	1010	1206	65100	505	824	1079	1287
49300	393	648	852	1018	54600	434	711	933	1115	59900	472	771	1011	1207	65200	505	824	1080	1289
49400	394	649	853	1020	54700	435	712	935	1116	60000	472	772	1012	1209	65300	506	825	1081	1290
49500	395	650	855	1022	54800	435	714	936	1118	60100	473	773	1014	1210	65400	506	826	1082	1292
49600	395	651	856	1024	54900	436	715	938	1120	60200	474	774	1015	1212	65500	507	827	1084	1293
49700	396	653	858	1026	55000	437	716	939	1122	60300	474	775	1016	1213	65600	508	828	1085	1295
49800	397	654	859	1027	55100	438	717	941	1124	60400	475	776	1017	1215	65700	508	829	1086	1296
49900	398	655	861	1029	55200	438	718	942	1125	60500	475	777	1019	1216	65800	509	830	1087	1298
50000	398	656	862	1031	55300	439	719	944	1127	60600	476	778	1020	1218	65900	509	831	1089	1299
50100	399	657	864	1033	55400	440	721	945	1129	60700	477	779	1021	1219	66000	510	832	1090	1301
50200	400	659	865	1035	55500	441	722	947	1131	60800	477	780	1023	1221	66100	511	833	1091	1302
50300	401	660	867	1037	55600	441	723	948	1133	60900	478	781	1024	1222	66200	511	834	1092	1304
50400	401	661	869	1038	55700	442	724	950	1135	61000	478	782	1025	1224	66300	512	835	1094	1305
50500	402	662	870	1040	55800	443	725	951	1136	61100	479	783	1026	1226	66400	512	836	1095	1307
50600	403	663	872	1042	55900	444	727	953	1138	61200	480	784	1028	1227	66500	513	837	1096	1308
50700	404	665	873	1044	56000	444	728	955	1140	61300	480	785	1029	1229	66600	514	838	1097	1310
50800	405	666	875	1046	56100	445	729	956	1142	61400	481	786	1030	1230	66700	514	839	1099	1311
50900	405	667	876	1047	56200	446	730	958	1144	61500	482	787	1032	1232	66800	515	840	1100	1313
51000	406	668	878	1049	56300	447	731	959	1145	61600	482	788	1033	1233	66900	516	841	1101	1314
51100	407	669	879	1051	56400	448	733	961	1147	61700	483	789	1034	1235	67000	516	842	1103	1316
51200	408	671	881	1053	56500	448	734	962	1149	61800	484	790	1036	1237	67100	517	843	1104	1317
51300	408	672	882	1055	56600	449	735	964	1151	61900	484	792	1037	1238	67200	518	844	1105	1319
51400	409	673	884	1057	56700	450	736	965	1153	62000	485	793	1039	1240	67300	518	845	1107	1320
51500	410	674	885	1058	56800	451	737	967	1155	62100	486	794	1040	1241	67400	519	846	1108	1322
51600	411	675	887	1060	56900	451	739	968	1156	62200	487	795	1041	1243	67500	520	847	1109	1324
51700	411	676	889	1062	57000	452	740	970	1158	62300	487	796	1043	1244	67600	520	848	1110	1325
51800	412	678	890	1064	57100	453	741	971	1160	62400	488	797	1044	1246	67700	521	849	1112	1327
51900	413	679	892	1066	57200	454	742	973	1162	62500	489	798	1045	1248	67800	521	850	1113	1328
52000	414	680	893	1067	57300	454	743	974	1164	62600	489	799	1047	1249	67900	522	851	1114	1330
52100	415	681	895	1069	57400	455	745	976	1165	62700	490	800	1048	1251	68000	523	852	1116	1331
52200	415	682	896	1071	57500	456	746	978	1167	62800	491	801	1049	1252	68100	523	853	1117	1333
52300	416	684	898	1073	57600	457	747	979	1169	62900	491	802	1051	1254	68200	524	854	1118	1334
52400	417	685	899	1075	57700	457	748	981	1171	63000	492	803	1052	1256	68300	525	855	1119	1336
52500	418	686	901	1076	57800	458	749	982	1173	63100	493	804	1053	1257	68400	525	856	1121	1337
52600	418	687	902	1078	57900	459	750	983	1174	63200	493	805	1055	1259	68500	526	857	1122	1339
52700	419	688	904	1080	58000	460	751	985	1176	63300	494	806	1056	1260	68600	527	858	1123	1340
52800	420	690	905	1082	58100	460	753	986	1178	63400	495	807	1057	1262	68700	527	859	1125	1342
52900	421	691	907	1084	58200	461	754	988	1179	63500	495	808	1058	1263	68800	528	860	1126	1343
53000	421	692	908	1086	58300	462	755	989	1181	63600	496	809	1060	1265	68900	529	861	1127	1345
53100	422	693	910	1087	58400	462	756	991	1183	63700	496	810	1061	1266	69000	529	862	1129	1346
53200	423	694	912	1089	58500	463	757	992	1184	63800	497	811	1062	1268	69100	530	863	1130	1348
53300	424	696	913	1091	58600	464	758	994	1186	63900	498	812	1064	1269	69200	531	864	1131	1350
53400	425	697	915	1093	58700	464	759	995	1188	64000	498	813	1065	1271	69300	531	865	1132	1351
53500	425	698	916	1095	58800	465	760	996	1190	64100	499	814	1066	1272	69400	532	866	1134	1353
53600	426	699	918	1096	58900	466	761	998	1191	64200	499	815	1067	1274	69500	532	867	1135	1354
53700	427	700	919	1098	59000	466	762	999	1193	64300	500	816	1069	1275	69600	533	868	1136	1356
53800	428	702	921	1100	59100	467	764	1001	1195	64400	501	817	1070	1277	69700	534	869	1138	1357
53900	428	703	922	1102	59200	468	765	1002	1196	64500	501	818	1071	1278	69800	534	870	1139	1359
54000	429	704	924	1104	59300	468	766	1003	1198	64600	502	819	1072	1280	69900	535	871	1140	1360
54100	430	705	925	1106	59400	469	767	1005	1199	64700	502	820	1074	1281	70000	536	872	1142	1362
54200	431	706	927	1107	59500	469	767	1006	1201	64800	503	821	1075	1283	70100	536	873	1143	1363
54300	431	708	928	1109	59600	470	768	1007	1202	64900	504	822	1076	1284	70200	537	874	1144	1365

Note: This table shows amounts of child support based on income to the nearest $100. There is a mathematical formula for calculating specific child support amounts between the $100 levels. For more information, please contact the Department of Justice.

Nota: La présente table indique le montant de pensions alimentaires pour enfants à verser d'après le revenu (aux 100 $ près). Il existe une formule mathématique pour calculer le montant exact de la pension alimentaire pour enfants dans le cas des revenus qui se situent entre les tranches de 100 $. Pour plus de renseignements, veuillez communiquer avec le ministère de la Justice.

Divorce

NEWFOUNDLAND/TERRE-NEUVE

FEDERAL CHILD SUPPORT AMOUNTS : SIMPLIFIED TABLES
MONTANTS FÉDÉRAUX DE PENSIONS ALIMENTAIRES POUR ENFANTS : TABLES SIMPLIFIÉES

1997

Income/Revenu ($)	Monthly Award/Paiement mensuel ($) No. of Children/N^{bre} d'enfants				Income/Revenu ($)	Monthly Award/Paiement mensuel ($) No. of Children/N^{bre} d'enfants				Income/Revenu ($)	Monthly Award/Paiement mensuel ($) No. of Children/N^{bre} d'enfants				Income/Revenu ($)	Monthly Award/Paiement mensuel ($) No. of Children/N^{bre} d'enfants			
	1	2	3	4		1	2	3	4		1	2	3	4		1	2	3	4
70300	538	875	1145	1366	75600	572	929	1214	1448	80900	606	982	1283	1529	86200	641	1036	1352	1610
70400	538	876	1147	1368	75700	573	930	1215	1449	81000	607	983	1284	1530	86300	641	1037	1353	1612
70500	539	877	1148	1369	75800	573	931	1217	1451	81100	608	984	1285	1532	86400	642	1038	1354	1613
70600	540	878	1149	1371	75900	574	932	1218	1452	81200	608	985	1287	1533	86500	643	1039	1355	1615
70700	540	879	1151	1373	76000	575	933	1219	1454	81300	609	986	1288	1535	86600	643	1040	1357	1616
70800	541	880	1152	1374	76100	575	934	1221	1455	81400	610	987	1289	1536	86700	644	1041	1358	1618
70900	542	881	1153	1376	76200	576	935	1222	1457	81500	610	988	1291	1538	86800	645	1042	1359	1619
71000	542	882	1154	1377	76300	577	936	1223	1458	81600	611	989	1292	1540	86900	645	1043	1361	1621
71100	543	883	1156	1379	76400	577	937	1224	1460	81700	612	990	1293	1541	87000	646	1044	1362	1622
71200	543	884	1157	1380	76500	578	938	1226	1461	81800	612	991	1294	1543	87100	647	1045	1363	1624
71300	544	885	1158	1382	76600	578	939	1227	1463	81900	613	992	1296	1544	87200	647	1046	1364	1625
71400	545	886	1160	1383	76700	579	940	1228	1464	82000	614	993	1297	1546	87300	648	1047	1366	1627
71500	545	887	1161	1385	76800	580	941	1230	1466	82100	614	994	1298	1547	87400	649	1048	1367	1628
71600	546	888	1162	1386	76900	580	942	1231	1468	82200	615	995	1300	1549	87500	649	1049	1368	1630
71700	547	889	1164	1388	77000	581	943	1232	1469	82300	615	996	1301	1550	87600	650	1050	1370	1631
71800	547	890	1165	1389	77100	582	944	1234	1471	82400	616	997	1302	1552	87700	650	1051	1371	1633
71900	548	891	1166	1391	77200	582	945	1235	1472	82500	617	998	1304	1553	87800	651	1052	1372	1635
72000	549	892	1167	1392	77300	583	946	1236	1474	82600	617	999	1305	1555	87900	652	1053	1374	1636
72100	549	893	1169	1394	77400	584	947	1237	1475	82700	618	1000	1306	1556	88000	652	1054	1375	1638
72200	550	894	1170	1396	77500	584	948	1239	1477	82800	619	1001	1307	1558	88100	653	1055	1376	1639
72300	551	895	1171	1397	77600	585	949	1240	1478	82900	619	1002	1309	1559	88200	654	1056	1377	1641
72400	551	896	1173	1399	77700	586	950	1241	1480	83000	620	1003	1310	1561	88300	654	1057	1379	1642
72500	552	897	1174	1400	77800	586	951	1243	1481	83100	621	1004	1311	1563	88400	655	1058	1380	1644
72600	553	898	1175	1402	77900	587	952	1244	1483	83200	621	1005	1313	1564	88500	656	1059	1381	1645
72700	553	899	1177	1403	78000	588	953	1245	1484	83300	622	1006	1314	1566	88600	656	1060	1383	1647
72800	554	901	1178	1405	78100	588	954	1247	1486	83400	623	1007	1315	1567	88700	657	1061	1384	1648
72900	555	902	1179	1406	78200	589	955	1248	1487	83500	623	1008	1317	1569	88800	658	1062	1385	1650
73000	555	903	1180	1408	78300	590	956	1249	1489	83600	624	1009	1318	1570	88900	658	1063	1387	1651
73100	556	904	1182	1409	78400	590	957	1250	1491	83700	625	1010	1319	1572	89000	659	1064	1388	1653
73200	556	905	1183	1411	78500	591	958	1252	1492	83800	625	1011	1320	1573	89100	660	1065	1389	1654
73300	557	906	1184	1412	78600	591	959	1253	1494	83900	626	1012	1322	1575	89200	660	1066	1390	1656
73400	558	907	1186	1414	78700	592	960	1254	1495	84000	626	1013	1323	1576	89300	661	1067	1392	1658
73500	558	908	1187	1415	78800	593	961	1256	1497	84100	627	1014	1324	1578	89400	661	1068	1393	1659
73600	559	909	1188	1417	78900	593	962	1257	1498	84200	628	1015	1326	1579	89500	662	1069	1394	1661
73700	560	910	1189	1418	79000	594	963	1258	1500	84300	628	1016	1327	1581	89600	663	1070	1396	1662
73800	560	911	1191	1420	79100	595	964	1259	1501	84400	629	1017	1328	1582	89700	663	1071	1397	1664
73900	561	912	1192	1422	79200	595	965	1261	1503	84500	630	1018	1329	1584	89800	664	1072	1398	1665
74000	562	913	1193	1423	79300	596	966	1262	1504	84600	630	1019	1331	1585	89900	665	1073	1399	1667
74100	562	914	1195	1425	79400	597	967	1263	1506	84700	631	1020	1332	1587	90000	665	1074	1401	1668
74200	563	915	1196	1426	79500	597	968	1265	1507	84800	632	1022	1333	1589	90100	666	1075	1402	1670
74300	564	916	1197	1428	79600	598	969	1266	1509	84900	632	1023	1335	1590	90200	667	1076	1403	1671
74400	564	917	1199	1429	79700	599	970	1267	1510	85000	633	1024	1336	1592	90300	667	1077	1405	1673
74500	565	918	1200	1431	79800	599	971	1269	1512	85100	634	1025	1337	1593	90400	668	1078	1406	1674
74600	566	919	1201	1432	79900	600	972	1270	1513	85200	634	1026	1339	1595	90500	669	1079	1407	1676
74700	566	920	1202	1434	80000	601	973	1271	1515	85300	635	1027	1340	1596	90600	669	1080	1409	1677
74800	567	921	1204	1435	80100	601	974	1272	1517	85400	636	1028	1341	1598	90700	670	1081	1410	1679
74900	567	922	1205	1437	80200	602	975	1274	1518	85500	636	1029	1342	1599	90800	671	1082	1411	1680
75000	568	923	1206	1438	80300	602	976	1275	1520	85600	637	1030	1344	1601	90900	671	1083	1412	1682
75100	569	924	1208	1440	80400	603	977	1276	1521	85700	637	1031	1345	1602	91000	672	1084	1414	1684
75200	569	925	1209	1441	80500	604	978	1278	1523	85800	638	1032	1346	1604	91100	672	1085	1415	1685
75300	570	926	1210	1443	80600	604	979	1279	1524	85900	639	1033	1348	1605	91200	673	1086	1416	1687
75400	571	927	1212	1445	80700	605	980	1280	1526	86000	639	1034	1349	1607	91300	674	1087	1418	1688
75500	571	928	1213	1446	80800	606	981	1282	1527	86100	640	1035	1350	1608	91400	674	1088	1419	1690

Note: This table shows amounts of child support based on income to the nearest $100. There is a mathematical formula for calculating specific child support amounts between the $100 levels. For more information, please contact the Department of Justice.

Nota: La présente table indique le montant de pensions alimentaires pour enfants à verser d'après le revenu (aux 100 $ près). Il existe une formule mathématique pour calculer le montant exact de la pension alimentaire pour enfants dans le cas des revenus qui se situent entre les tranches de 100 $. Pour plus de renseignements, veuillez communiquer avec le ministère de la Justice.

Appendix D

NEWFOUNDLAND/TERRE-NEUVE

FEDERAL CHILD SUPPORT AMOUNTS : SIMPLIFIED TABLES
MONTANTS FÉDÉRAUX DE PENSIONS ALIMENTAIRES POUR ENFANTS : TABLES SIMPLIFIÉES

1997

Income/ Revenu ($)	Monthly Award/ Paiement mensuel ($) No. of Children/ N^{bre} d'enfants				Income/ Revenu ($)	Monthly Award/ Paiement mensuel ($) No. of Children/ N^{bre} d'enfants				Income/ Revenu ($)	Monthly Award/ Paiement mensuel ($) No. of Children/ N^{bre} d'enfants				Income/ Revenu ($)	Monthly Award/ Paiement mensuel ($) No. of Children/ N^{bre} d'enfants			
	1	2	3	4		1	2	3	4		1	2	3	4		1	2	3	4
91500	675	1089	1420	1691	96800	709	1142	1489	1772	102100	744	1196	1558	1854	107400	778	1249	1626	1935
91600	676	1090	1422	1693	96900	710	1144	1490	1774	102200	744	1197	1559	1855	107500	779	1250	1628	1936
91700	676	1091	1423	1694	97000	711	1145	1492	1775	102300	745	1198	1560	1857	107600	779	1251	1629	1938
91800	677	1092	1424	1696	97100	711	1146	1493	1777	102400	746	1199	1562	1858	107700	780	1252	1630	1939
91900	678	1093	1425	1697	97200	712	1147	1494	1779	102500	746	1200	1563	1860	107800	781	1253	1632	1941
92000	678	1094	1427	1699	97300	713	1148	1495	1780	102600	747	1201	1564	1861	107900	781	1254	1633	1942
92100	679	1095	1428	1700	97400	713	1149	1497	1782	102700	748	1202	1565	1863	108000	782	1255	1634	1944
92200	680	1096	1429	1702	97500	714	1150	1498	1783	102800	748	1203	1567	1864	108100	783	1256	1635	1946
92300	680	1097	1431	1703	97600	715	1151	1499	1785	102900	749	1204	1568	1866	108200	783	1257	1637	1947
92400	681	1098	1432	1705	97700	715	1152	1501	1786	103000	750	1205	1569	1867	108300	784	1258	1638	1949
92500	682	1099	1433	1707	97800	716	1153	1502	1788	103100	750	1206	1571	1869	108400	785	1259	1639	1950
92600	682	1100	1434	1708	97900	717	1154	1503	1789	103200	751	1207	1572	1870	108500	785	1260	1641	1952
92700	683	1101	1436	1710	98000	717	1155	1505	1791	103300	752	1208	1573	1872	108600	786	1261	1642	1953
92800	684	1102	1437	1711	98100	718	1156	1506	1792	103400	752	1209	1575	1874	108700	787	1262	1643	1955
92900	684	1103	1438	1713	98200	719	1157	1507	1794	103500	753	1210	1576	1875	108800	787	1263	1645	1956
93000	685	1104	1440	1714	98300	719	1158	1508	1795	103600	754	1211	1577	1877	108900	788	1264	1646	1958
93100	685	1105	1441	1716	98400	720	1159	1510	1797	103700	754	1212	1578	1878	109000	789	1266	1647	1959
93200	686	1106	1442	1717	98500	720	1160	1511	1798	103800	755	1213	1580	1880	109100	789	1267	1648	1961
93300	687	1107	1444	1719	98600	721	1161	1512	1800	103900	755	1214	1581	1881	109200	790	1268	1650	1962
93400	687	1108	1445	1720	98700	722	1162	1514	1802	104000	756	1215	1582	1883	109300	790	1269	1651	1964
93500	688	1109	1446	1722	98800	722	1163	1515	1803	104100	757	1216	1584	1884	109400	791	1270	1652	1965
93600	689	1110	1447	1723	98900	723	1164	1516	1805	104200	757	1217	1585	1886	109500	792	1271	1654	1967
93700	689	1111	1449	1725	99000	724	1165	1517	1806	104300	758	1218	1586	1887	109600	792	1272	1655	1969
93800	690	1112	1450	1726	99100	724	1166	1519	1808	104400	759	1219	1587	1889	109700	793	1273	1656	1970
93900	691	1113	1451	1728	99200	725	1167	1520	1809	104500	759	1220	1589	1890	109800	794	1274	1657	1972
94000	691	1114	1453	1730	99300	726	1168	1521	1811	104600	760	1221	1590	1892	109900	794	1275	1659	1973
94100	692	1115	1454	1731	99400	726	1169	1523	1812	104700	761	1222	1591	1893	110000	795	1276	1660	1975
94200	693	1116	1455	1733	99500	727	1170	1524	1814	104800	761	1223	1593	1895	110100	796	1277	1661	1976
94300	693	1117	1457	1734	99600	728	1171	1525	1815	104900	762	1224	1594	1896	110200	796	1278	1663	1978
94400	694	1118	1458	1736	99700	728	1172	1527	1817	105000	763	1225	1595	1898	110300	797	1279	1664	1979
94500	695	1119	1459	1737	99800	729	1173	1528	1818	105100	763	1226	1597	1900	110400	798	1280	1665	1981
94600	695	1120	1460	1739	99900	730	1174	1529	1820	105200	764	1227	1598	1901	110500	798	1281	1667	1982
94700	696	1121	1462	1740	100000	730	1175	1530	1821	105300	765	1228	1599	1903	110600	799	1282	1668	1984
94800	696	1122	1463	1742	100100	731	1176	1532	1823	105400	765	1229	1600	1904	110700	800	1283	1669	1985
94900	697	1123	1464	1743	100200	731	1177	1533	1824	105500	766	1230	1602	1906	110800	800	1284	1670	1987
95000	698	1124	1466	1745	100300	732	1178	1534	1826	105600	766	1231	1603	1907	110900	801	1285	1672	1988
95100	698	1125	1467	1746	100400	733	1179	1536	1828	105700	767	1232	1604	1909	111000	801	1286	1673	1990
95200	699	1126	1468	1748	100500	733	1180	1537	1829	105800	768	1233	1606	1910	111100	802	1287	1674	1991
95300	700	1127	1470	1749	100600	734	1181	1538	1831	105900	768	1234	1607	1912	111200	803	1288	1676	1993
95400	700	1128	1471	1751	100700	735	1182	1540	1832	106000	769	1235	1608	1913	111300	803	1289	1677	1995
95500	701	1129	1472	1752	100800	735	1183	1541	1834	106100	770	1236	1610	1915	111400	804	1290	1678	1996
95600	702	1130	1473	1754	100900	736	1184	1542	1835	106200	770	1237	1611	1916	111500	805	1291	1680	1998
95700	702	1131	1475	1756	101000	737	1185	1543	1837	106300	771	1238	1612	1918	111600	805	1292	1681	1999
95800	703	1132	1476	1757	101100	737	1186	1545	1838	106400	772	1239	1613	1919	111700	806	1293	1682	2001
95900	704	1133	1477	1759	101200	738	1187	1546	1840	106500	772	1240	1615	1921	111800	807	1294	1683	2002
96000	704	1134	1479	1760	101300	739	1188	1547	1841	106600	773	1241	1616	1923	111900	807	1295	1685	2004
96100	705	1135	1480	1762	101400	739	1189	1549	1843	106700	774	1242	1617	1924	112000	808	1296	1686	2005
96200	706	1136	1481	1763	101500	740	1190	1550	1844	106800	774	1243	1619	1926	112100	809	1297	1687	2007
96300	706	1137	1483	1765	101600	741	1191	1551	1846	106900	775	1244	1620	1927	112200	809	1298	1689	2008
96400	707	1138	1484	1766	101700	741	1192	1552	1847	107000	776	1245	1621	1929	112300	810	1299	1690	2010
96500	707	1139	1485	1768	101800	742	1193	1554	1849	107100	776	1246	1622	1930	112400	811	1300	1691	2011
96600	708	1140	1486	1769	101900	742	1194	1555	1851	107200	777	1247	1624	1932	112500	811	1301	1692	2013
96700	709	1141	1488	1771	102000	743	1195	1556	1852	107300	777	1248	1625	1933	112600	812	1302	1694	2014

Note: This table shows amounts of child support based on income to the nearest $100. There is a mathematical formula for calculating specific child support amounts between the $100 levels. For more information, please contact the Department of Justice.

Nota: La présente table indique le montant de pensions alimentaires pour enfants à verser d'après le revenu (aux 100 $ près). Il existe une formule mathématique pour calculer le montant exact de la pension alimentaire pour enfants dans le cas des revenus qui se situent entre les tranches de 100 $. Pour plus de renseignements, veuillez communiquer avec le ministère de la Justice.

Divorce

NEWFOUNDLAND/TERRE-NEUVE

FEDERAL CHILD SUPPORT AMOUNTS : SIMPLIFIED TABLES
MONTANTS FÉDÉRAUX DE PENSIONS ALIMENTAIRES POUR ENFANTS : TABLES SIMPLIFIÉES

1997

Income/ Revenu ($)	Monthly Award/ Paiement mensuel ($) No. of Children/ N^bre d'enfants				Income/ Revenu ($)	Monthly Award/ Paiement mensuel ($) No. of Children/ N^bre d'enfants				Income/ Revenu ($)	Monthly Award/ Paiement mensuel ($) No. of Children/ N^bre d'enfants				Income/ Revenu ($)	Monthly Award/ Paiement mensuel ($) No. of Children/ N^bre d'enfants			
	1	2	3	4		1	2	3	4		1	2	3	4		1	2	3	4
112700	812	1303	1695	2016	118000	847	1356	1764	2097	123300	881	1410	1832	2178	128600	916	1463	1901	2260
112800	813	1304	1696	2018	118100	847	1357	1765	2099	123400	882	1411	1834	2180	128700	916	1464	1902	2261
112900	814	1305	1698	2019	118200	848	1358	1766	2100	123500	882	1412	1835	2181	128800	917	1465	1904	2263
113000	814	1306	1699	2021	118300	849	1359	1768	2102	123600	883	1413	1836	2183	128900	917	1466	1905	2264
113100	815	1307	1700	2022	118400	849	1360	1769	2103	123700	884	1414	1838	2185	129000	918	1467	1906	2266
113200	816	1308	1702	2024	118500	850	1361	1770	2105	123800	884	1415	1839	2186	129100	919	1468	1908	2267
113300	816	1309	1703	2025	118600	851	1362	1772	2106	123900	885	1416	1840	2188	129200	919	1469	1909	2269
113400	817	1310	1704	2027	118700	851	1363	1773	2108	124000	886	1417	1842	2189	129300	920	1470	1910	2270
113500	818	1311	1705	2028	118800	852	1364	1774	2109	124100	886	1418	1843	2191	129400	921	1471	1912	2272
113600	818	1312	1707	2030	118900	853	1365	1775	2111	124200	887	1419	1844	2192	129500	921	1472	1913	2273
113700	819	1313	1708	2031	119000	853	1366	1777	2113	124300	888	1420	1845	2194	129600	922	1473	1914	2275
113800	820	1314	1709	2033	119100	854	1367	1778	2114	124400	888	1421	1847	2195	129700	923	1474	1915	2276
113900	820	1315	1711	2034	119200	855	1368	1779	2116	124500	889	1422	1848	2197	129800	923	1475	1917	2278
114000	821	1316	1712	2036	119300	855	1369	1781	2117	124600	890	1423	1849	2198	129900	924	1476	1918	2280
114100	822	1317	1713	2037	119400	856	1370	1782	2119	124700	890	1424	1851	2200	130000	925	1477	1919	2281
114200	822	1318	1715	2039	119500	857	1371	1783	2120	124800	891	1425	1852	2201	130100	925	1478	1921	2283
114300	823	1319	1716	2041	119600	857	1372	1785	2122	124900	892	1426	1853	2203	130200	926	1479	1922	2284
114400	824	1320	1717	2042	119700	858	1373	1786	2123	125000	892	1427	1855	2204	130300	927	1480	1923	2286
114500	824	1321	1718	2044	119800	859	1374	1787	2125	125100	893	1428	1856	2206	130400	927	1481	1925	2287
114600	825	1322	1720	2045	119900	859	1375	1788	2126	125200	894	1429	1857	2208	130500	928	1482	1926	2289
114700	825	1323	1721	2047	120000	860	1376	1790	2128	125300	894	1430	1858	2209	130600	929	1483	1927	2290
114800	826	1324	1722	2048	120100	860	1377	1791	2129	125400	895	1431	1860	2211	130700	929	1484	1928	2292
114900	827	1325	1724	2050	120200	861	1378	1792	2131	125500	895	1432	1861	2212	130800	930	1485	1930	2293
115000	827	1326	1725	2051	120300	862	1379	1794	2132	125600	896	1433	1862	2214	130900	930	1486	1931	2295
115100	828	1327	1726	2053	120400	862	1380	1795	2134	125700	897	1434	1864	2215	131000	931	1487	1932	2296
115200	829	1328	1727	2054	120500	863	1381	1796	2136	125800	897	1435	1865	2217	131100	932	1488	1934	2298
115300	829	1329	1729	2056	120600	864	1382	1797	2137	125900	898	1436	1866	2218	131200	932	1489	1935	2299
115400	830	1330	1730	2057	120700	864	1383	1799	2139	126000	899	1437	1867	2220	131300	933	1490	1936	2301
115500	831	1331	1731	2059	120800	865	1384	1800	2140	126100	899	1438	1869	2221	131400	934	1491	1937	2302
115600	831	1332	1733	2060	120900	866	1385	1801	2142	126200	900	1439	1870	2223	131500	934	1492	1939	2304
115700	832	1333	1734	2062	121000	866	1386	1803	2143	126300	901	1440	1871	2224	131600	935	1493	1940	2306
115800	833	1334	1735	2063	121100	867	1388	1804	2145	126400	901	1441	1873	2226	131700	936	1494	1941	2307
115900	833	1335	1737	2065	121200	868	1389	1805	2146	126500	902	1442	1874	2227	131800	936	1495	1943	2309
116000	834	1336	1738	2067	121300	868	1390	1807	2148	126600	903	1443	1875	2229	131900	937	1496	1944	2310
116100	835	1337	1739	2068	121400	869	1391	1808	2149	126700	903	1444	1877	2230	132000	938	1497	1945	2312
116200	835	1338	1740	2070	121500	870	1392	1809	2151	126800	904	1445	1878	2232	132100	938	1498	1947	2313
116300	836	1339	1742	2071	121600	870	1393	1810	2152	126900	905	1446	1879	2234	132200	939	1499	1948	2315
116400	836	1340	1743	2073	121700	871	1394	1812	2154	127000	905	1447	1880	2235	132300	940	1500	1949	2316
116500	837	1341	1744	2074	121800	871	1395	1813	2155	127100	906	1448	1882	2237	132400	940	1501	1950	2318
116600	838	1342	1746	2076	121900	872	1396	1814	2157	127200	906	1449	1883	2238	132500	941	1502	1952	2319
116700	838	1343	1747	2077	122000	873	1397	1816	2158	127300	907	1450	1884	2240	132600	941	1503	1953	2321
116800	839	1344	1748	2079	122100	873	1398	1817	2160	127400	908	1451	1886	2241	132700	942	1504	1954	2322
116900	840	1345	1750	2080	122200	874	1399	1818	2162	127500	908	1452	1887	2243	132800	943	1505	1956	2324
117000	840	1346	1751	2082	122300	875	1400	1820	2163	127600	909	1453	1888	2244	132900	943	1506	1957	2325
117100	841	1347	1752	2083	122400	875	1401	1821	2165	127700	910	1454	1890	2246	133000	944	1507	1958	2327
117200	842	1348	1753	2085	122500	876	1402	1822	2166	127800	910	1455	1891	2247	133100	945	1509	1960	2329
117300	842	1349	1755	2086	122600	877	1403	1823	2168	127900	911	1456	1892	2249	133200	945	1510	1961	2330
117400	843	1350	1756	2088	122700	877	1404	1825	2169	128000	912	1457	1893	2252	133300	946	1511	1962	2332
117500	844	1351	1757	2090	122800	878	1405	1826	2171	128100	912	1458	1895	2252	133400	947	1512	1963	2333
117600	844	1352	1759	2091	122900	879	1406	1827	2172	128200	913	1459	1896	2253	133500	947	1513	1965	2335
117700	845	1353	1760	2093	123000	879	1407	1829	2174	128300	914	1460	1897	2255	133600	948	1514	1966	2336
117800	846	1354	1761	2094	123100	880	1408	1830	2175	128400	914	1461	1899	2257	133700	949	1515	1967	2338
117900	846	1355	1762	2096	123200	881	1409	1831	2177	128500	915	1462	1900	2258	133800	949	1516	1969	2339

Note: This table shows amounts of child support based on income to the nearest $100. There is a mathematical formula for calculating specific child support amounts between the $100 levels. For more information, please contact the Department of Justice.

Nota: La présente table indique le montant de pensions alimentaires pour enfants à verser d'après le revenu (aux 100 $ près). Il existe une formule mathématique pour calculer le montant exact de la pension alimentaire pour enfants dans le cas des revenus qui se situent entre les tranches de 100 $. Pour plus de renseignements, veuillez communiquer avec le ministère de la Justice.

Appendix D

NEWFOUNDLAND/TERRE-NEUVE

FEDERAL CHILD SUPPORT AMOUNTS : SIMPLIFIED TABLES
MONTANTS FÉDÉRAUX DE PENSIONS ALIMENTAIRES POUR ENFANTS : TABLES SIMPLIFIÉES

1997

Income/ Revenu ($)	Monthly Award/ Paiement mensuel ($) No. of Children/ N^{bre} d'enfants				Income/ Revenu ($)	Monthly Award/ Paiement mensuel ($) No. of Children/ N^{bre} d'enfants				Income/ Revenu ($)	Monthly Award/ Paiement mensuel ($) No. of Children/ N^{bre} d'enfants				Income/ Revenu ($)	Monthly Award/ Paiement mensuel ($) No. of Children/ N^{bre} d'enfants			
	1	2	3	4		1	2	3	4		1	2	3	4		1	2	3	4
133900	950	1517	1970	2341	138000	976	1558	2023	2404	142100	1003	1599	2076	2466	146200	1030	1641	2129	2529
134000	951	1518	1971	2342	138100	977	1559	2024	2405	142200	1004	1600	2077	2468	146300	1030	1642	2131	2531
134100	951	1519	1972	2344	138200	978	1560	2026	2407	142300	1004	1601	2079	2469	146400	1031	1643	2132	2532
134200	952	1520	1974	2345	138300	978	1561	2027	2408	142400	1005	1602	2080	2471	146500	1032	1644	2133	2534
134300	953	1521	1975	2347	138400	979	1562	2028	2410	142500	1006	1603	2081	2473	146600	1032	1645	2135	2535
134400	953	1522	1976	2348	138500	980	1563	2030	2411	142600	1006	1604	2083	2474	146700	1033	1646	2136	2537
134500	954	1523	1978	2350	138600	980	1564	2031	2413	142700	1007	1605	2084	2476	146800	1034	1647	2137	2538
134600	954	1524	1979	2352	138700	981	1565	2032	2414	142800	1008	1606	2085	2477	146900	1034	1648	2138	2540
134700	955	1525	1980	2353	138800	982	1566	2033	2416	142900	1008	1607	2087	2479	147000	1035	1649	2140	2542
134800	956	1526	1982	2355	138900	982	1567	2035	2417	143000	1009	1608	2088	2480	147100	1035	1650	2141	2543
134900	956	1527	1983	2356	139000	983	1568	2036	2419	143100	1010	1609	2089	2482	147200	1036	1651	2142	2545
135000	957	1528	1984	2358	139100	984	1569	2037	2420	143200	1010	1610	2090	2483	147300	1037	1652	2144	2546
135100	958	1529	1985	2359	139200	984	1570	2039	2422	143300	1011	1611	2092	2485	147400	1037	1653	2145	2548
135200	958	1530	1987	2361	139300	985	1571	2040	2424	143400	1011	1612	2093	2486	147500	1038	1654	2146	2549
135300	959	1531	1988	2362	139400	986	1572	2041	2425	143500	1012	1613	2094	2488	147600	1039	1655	2147	2551
135400	960	1532	1989	2364	139500	986	1573	2042	2427	143600	1013	1614	2096	2489	147700	1039	1656	2149	2552
135500	960	1533	1991	2365	139600	987	1574	2044	2428	143700	1013	1615	2097	2491	147800	1040	1657	2150	2554
135600	961	1534	1992	2367	139700	988	1575	2045	2430	143800	1014	1616	2098	2492	147900	1041	1658	2151	2555
135700	962	1535	1993	2368	139800	988	1576	2046	2431	143900	1015	1617	2100	2494	148000	1041	1659	2153	2557
135800	962	1536	1995	2370	139900	989	1577	2048	2433	144000	1015	1618	2101	2496	148100	1042	1660	2154	2558
135900	963	1537	1996	2371	140000	989	1578	2049	2434	144100	1016	1619	2102	2497	148200	1043	1661	2155	2560
136000	964	1538	1997	2373	140100	990	1579	2050	2436	144200	1017	1620	2103	2499	148300	1043	1662	2157	2561
136100	964	1539	1998	2375	140200	991	1580	2052	2437	144300	1017	1621	2105	2500	148400	1044	1663	2158	2563
136200	965	1540	2000	2376	140300	991	1581	2053	2439	144400	1018	1622	2106	2502	148500	1045	1664	2159	2564
136300	965	1541	2001	2378	140400	992	1582	2054	2440	144500	1019	1623	2107	2503	148600	1045	1665	2160	2566
136400	966	1542	2002	2379	140500	993	1583	2055	2442	144600	1019	1624	2109	2505	148700	1046	1666	2162	2568
136500	967	1543	2004	2381	140600	993	1584	2057	2443	144700	1020	1625	2110	2506	148800	1046	1667	2163	2569
136600	967	1544	2005	2382	140700	994	1585	2058	2445	144800	1021	1626	2111	2508	148900	1047	1668	2164	2571
136700	968	1545	2006	2384	140800	995	1586	2059	2447	144900	1021	1627	2112	2509	149000	1048	1669	2166	2572
136800	969	1546	2007	2385	140900	995	1587	2061	2448	145000	1022	1628	2114	2511	149100	1048	1670	2167	2574
136900	969	1547	2009	2387	141000	996	1588	2062	2450	145100	1023	1629	2115	2512	149200	1049	1671	2168	2575
137000	970	1548	2010	2388	141100	997	1589	2063	2451	145200	1023	1631	2116	2514	149300	1050	1672	2170	2577
137100	971	1549	2011	2390	141200	997	1590	2065	2453	145300	1024	1632	2118	2515	149400	1050	1673	2171	2578
137200	971	1550	2013	2391	141300	998	1591	2066	2454	145400	1024	1633	2119	2517	149500	1051	1674	2172	2580
137300	972	1551	2014	2393	141400	999	1592	2067	2456	145500	1025	1634	2120	2519	149600	1052	1675	2173	2581
137400	973	1552	2015	2394	141500	999	1593	2068	2457	145600	1026	1635	2122	2520	149700	1052	1676	2175	2583
137500	973	1553	2017	2396	141600	1000	1594	2070	2459	145700	1026	1636	2123	2522	149800	1053	1677	2176	2584
137600	974	1554	2018	2397	141700	1000	1595	2071	2460	145800	1027	1637	2124	2523	149900	1054	1678	2177	2586
137700	975	1555	2019	2399	141800	1001	1596	2072	2462	145900	1028	1638	2125	2525	150000	1054	1679	2179	2587
137800	975	1556	2020	2401	141900	1002	1597	2074	2463	146000	1028	1639	2127	2526					
137900	976	1557	2022	2402	142000	1002	1598	2075	2465	146100	1029	1640	2128	2528					

Income/ Revenu ($)	Monthly Award/Paiement mensuel ($)			
	one child/ un enfant	two children/ deux enfants	three children/ trois enfants	four children/ quatre enfants
For income over $150,000	1054 plus 0.65% of income over $150,000	1679 plus 1.01% of income over $150,000	2179 plus 1.30% of income over $150,000	2587 plus 1.53% of income over $150,000
Pour revenu dépassant 150 000$	1054 plus 0,65% du revenu dépassant 150 000$	1679 plus 1,01% du revenu dépassant 150 000$	2179 plus 1,30% du revenu dépassant 150 000$	2587 plus 1,53% du revenu dépassant 150 000$

Note: This table shows amounts of child support based on income to the nearest $100. There is a mathematical formula for calculating specific child support amounts between the $100 levels. For more information, please contact the Department of Justice.

Nota: La présente table indique le montant de pensions alimentaires pour enfants à verser d'après le revenu (aux 100 $ près). Il existe une formule mathématique pour calculer le montant exact de la pension alimentaire pour enfants dans le cas des revenus qui se situent entre les tranches de 100 $. Pour plus de renseignements, veuillez communiquer avec le ministère de la Justice.

Divorce

NOVA SCOTIA/NOUVELLE-ÉCOSSE

FEDERAL CHILD SUPPORT AMOUNTS : SIMPLIFIED TABLES
MONTANTS FÉDÉRAUX DE PENSIONS ALIMENTAIRES POUR ENFANTS : TABLES SIMPLIFIÉES

1997

Income/Revenu ($)	Monthly Award/Paiement mensuel ($) No. of Children/N^{bre} d'enfants				Income/Revenu ($)	Monthly Award/Paiement mensuel ($) No. of Children/N^{bre} d'enfants				Income/Revenu ($)	Monthly Award/Paiement mensuel ($) No. of Children/N^{bre} d'enfants				Income/Revenu ($)	Monthly Award/Paiement mensuel ($) No. of Children/N^{bre} d'enfants			
	1	2	3	4		1	2	3	4		1	2	3	4		1	2	3	4
6700	0	0	0	0	12000	111	173	195	217	17300	136	252	345	399	22600	185	323	432	522
6800	0	0	0	0	12100	111	176	198	220	17400	136	253	346	402	22700	187	324	434	524
6900	0	0	0	1	12200	111	178	201	224	17500	137	254	347	405	22800	188	326	436	527
7000	2	3	4	5	12300	111	181	204	228	17600	138	255	349	408	22900	189	327	438	529
7100	5	7	8	10	12400	111	184	208	231	17700	138	256	350	411	23000	190	329	440	532
7200	9	11	13	15	12500	112	187	211	235	17800	139	257	352	415	23100	191	331	443	534
7300	12	14	17	19	12600	112	190	214	238	17900	140	257	353	418	23200	192	332	445	536
7400	15	18	21	24	12700	113	192	217	242	18000	141	258	354	421	23300	193	334	447	539
7500	19	22	25	28	12800	114	195	220	246	18100	142	259	356	424	23400	194	336	449	541
7600	22	26	29	33	12900	114	198	224	249	18200	143	260	357	427	23500	195	337	451	543
7700	25	29	33	37	13000	115	201	227	253	18300	144	261	358	430	23600	197	339	453	546
7800	29	33	37	42	13100	115	203	230	257	18400	145	262	360	434	23700	198	341	455	548
7900	32	37	42	46	13200	116	206	233	260	18500	145	263	361	437	23800	199	342	457	551
8000	35	40	46	51	13300	117	209	236	264	18600	146	264	362	440	23900	200	344	459	553
8100	38	44	50	56	13400	117	212	240	267	18700	147	265	364	443	24000	201	345	461	555
8200	42	48	54	60	13500	118	213	243	271	18800	148	266	365	446	24100	202	347	463	558
8300	45	52	58	65	13600	119	214	246	275	18900	149	268	366	448	24200	203	349	465	560
8400	48	55	62	69	13700	119	215	249	278	19000	150	269	368	450	24300	204	350	467	562
8500	52	59	66	74	13800	120	216	252	282	19100	151	271	369	451	24400	206	352	469	565
8600	55	63	71	78	13900	120	218	256	285	19200	152	272	371	453	24500	207	354	471	567
8700	58	66	75	83	14000	121	219	259	289	19300	152	273	372	455	24600	208	355	473	570
8800	62	70	79	87	14100	122	220	262	293	19400	153	275	373	457	24700	209	357	475	572
8900	65	74	83	92	14200	122	221	265	296	19500	154	276	375	458	24800	210	358	477	574
9000	68	78	87	97	14300	123	222	268	300	19600	155	277	376	460	24900	211	360	479	577
9100	72	81	91	101	14400	123	224	271	303	19700	156	279	377	462	25000	212	362	481	579
9200	75	85	95	106	14500	124	225	275	307	19800	157	280	379	464	25100	213	363	483	581
9300	78	89	100	110	14600	125	226	278	311	19900	158	281	380	465	25200	215	365	485	584
9400	81	93	104	115	14700	125	227	281	314	20000	159	283	382	467	25300	216	367	487	586
9500	85	96	108	119	14800	126	228	284	318	20100	160	284	384	469	25400	217	368	489	588
9600	88	100	112	124	14900	127	229	287	321	20200	160	286	386	470	25500	218	370	491	591
9700	91	104	116	128	15000	127	231	291	325	20300	161	287	387	472	25600	219	371	493	593
9800	95	107	120	133	15100	128	232	293	328	20400	162	288	389	474	25700	220	373	495	596
9900	98	111	124	138	15200	128	233	296	331	20500	163	290	391	476	25800	221	375	498	598
10000	101	115	128	142	15300	128	233	299	335	20600	164	291	393	477	25900	222	376	500	600
10100	103	117	131	146	15400	129	234	302	338	20700	165	292	394	479	26000	224	378	501	603
10200	106	120	135	149	15500	129	235	305	341	20800	166	294	396	481	26100	225	379	503	605
10300	108	123	138	153	15600	130	236	307	344	20900	167	295	398	482	26200	226	381	505	607
10400	110	126	142	157	15700	130	237	310	347	21000	167	296	400	484	26300	227	382	507	609
10500	110	129	145	161	15800	130	238	313	351	21100	169	298	402	487	26400	228	384	509	611
10600	110	132	148	164	15900	131	239	316	354	21200	170	300	404	489	26500	229	386	511	614
10700	110	135	152	168	16000	131	240	318	357	21300	171	301	406	491	26600	230	387	513	616
10800	110	138	155	172	16100	131	241	321	360	21400	172	303	408	494	26700	231	389	515	618
10900	110	141	158	176	16200	132	242	324	363	21500	173	305	410	496	26800	232	390	517	620
11000	110	144	162	180	16300	132	243	327	367	21600	174	306	412	498	26900	233	392	519	622
11100	111	147	165	183	16400	133	244	330	370	21700	175	308	414	501	27000	234	393	520	625
11200	111	150	168	187	16500	133	245	332	373	21800	176	310	416	503	27100	235	395	522	627
11300	111	153	172	191	16600	133	245	335	376	21900	178	311	418	506	27200	236	396	524	629
11400	111	156	175	195	16700	134	246	337	379	22000	179	313	420	508	27300	237	398	526	631
11500	111	159	179	198	16800	134	247	338	383	22100	180	314	422	510	27400	238	399	528	633
11600	111	162	182	202	16900	134	248	339	386	22200	181	316	424	513	27500	238	401	530	636
11700	111	165	185	206	17000	135	249	341	389	22300	182	318	426	515	27600	239	402	532	638
11800	111	167	188	210	17100	135	250	342	392	22400	183	319	428	517	27700	240	404	534	640
11900	111	170	192	213	17200	136	251	343	395	22500	184	321	430	520	27800	241	405	536	642

Note: This table shows amounts of child support based on income to the nearest $100. There is a mathematical formula for calculating specific child support amounts between the $100 levels. For more information, please contact the Department of Justice.

Nota: La présente table indique le montant de la pension alimentaire pour enfants à verser d'après le revenu (aux 100 $ près). Il existe une formule mathématique pour calculer le montant exact de la pension alimentaire pour enfants dans le cas des revenus qui se situent entre les tranches de 100 $. Pour plus de renseignements, veuillez communiquer avec le ministère de la Justice.

Appendix D

NOVA SCOTIA/NOUVELLE-ÉCOSSE

FEDERAL CHILD SUPPORT AMOUNTS : SIMPLIFIED TABLES
MONTANTS FÉDÉRAUX DE PENSIONS ALIMENTAIRES POUR ENFANTS : TABLES SIMPLIFIÉES

1997

Income/Revenu ($)	Monthly Award/Paiement mensuel ($) No. of Children/N^{bre} d'enfants				Income/Revenu ($)	Monthly Award/Paiement mensuel ($) No. of Children/N^{bre} d'enfants				Income/Revenu ($)	Monthly Award/Paiement mensuel ($) No. of Children/N^{bre} d'enfants				Income/Revenu ($)	Monthly Award/Paiement mensuel ($) No. of Children/N^{bre} d'enfants			
	1	2	3	4		1	2	3	4		1	2	3	4		1	2	3	4
27900	242	407	538	644	33200	282	473	625	746	38500	322	536	706	846	43800	365	602	791	946
28000	243	408	539	647	33300	283	474	627	748	38600	323	537	708	848	43900	366	603	793	948
28100	244	410	541	649	33400	284	475	628	750	38700	324	538	710	850	44000	366	604	794	950
28200	245	411	543	651	33500	284	477	630	752	38800	325	539	711	852	44100	367	605	796	952
28300	245	413	545	653	33600	285	478	632	754	38900	326	541	713	853	44200	368	607	798	954
28400	246	414	547	655	33700	286	479	633	756	39000	326	542	714	855	44300	369	608	799	956
28500	247	416	549	658	33800	287	480	635	757	39100	327	543	716	857	44400	370	609	801	958
28600	248	418	551	660	33900	287	481	636	759	39200	328	544	717	859	44500	370	610	802	959
28700	249	419	553	662	34000	288	482	638	761	39300	329	545	719	861	44600	371	612	804	961
28800	250	421	555	664	34100	289	483	639	763	39400	329	547	720	863	44700	372	613	806	963
28900	251	422	556	666	34200	290	485	641	765	39500	330	548	722	864	44800	373	614	807	965
29000	252	424	558	669	34300	290	486	642	767	39600	331	549	724	866	44900	374	615	809	967
29100	253	425	560	671	34400	291	487	644	769	39700	332	550	725	868	45000	374	617	810	969
29200	253	427	562	673	34500	292	488	645	771	39800	333	552	727	870	45100	375	618	812	971
29300	254	428	564	675	34600	293	489	647	773	39900	333	553	728	872	45200	376	619	814	973
29400	255	430	566	678	34700	293	490	648	774	40000	334	554	730	874	45300	377	620	815	975
29500	256	431	568	680	34800	294	492	650	776	40100	335	555	731	876	45400	378	622	817	977
29600	257	433	570	682	34900	295	493	651	778	40200	336	556	733	878	45500	378	623	818	978
29700	258	434	571	684	35000	296	494	653	780	40300	337	558	735	879	45600	379	624	820	980
29800	258	435	573	685	35100	296	495	654	782	40400	337	559	736	881	45700	380	625	822	982
29900	259	436	574	687	35200	297	496	656	784	40500	338	560	738	883	45800	381	627	823	984
30000	260	438	576	689	35300	298	497	657	786	40600	339	561	739	885	45900	382	628	825	986
30100	260	439	577	691	35400	299	499	659	788	40700	340	563	741	887	46000	382	629	827	988
30200	261	440	579	692	35500	299	500	660	790	40800	341	564	743	889	46100	383	630	828	990
30300	262	441	580	694	35600	300	501	662	791	40900	341	565	744	891	46200	384	632	830	992
30400	262	442	582	696	35700	301	502	663	793	41000	342	567	746	893	46300	385	633	831	994
30500	263	443	583	697	35800	302	503	665	795	41100	343	568	748	895	46400	386	634	833	996
30600	264	444	585	699	35900	302	504	666	797	41200	344	569	749	897	46500	387	635	835	998
30700	264	445	586	701	36000	303	506	668	799	41300	345	570	751	898	46600	387	637	836	999
30800	265	446	588	703	36100	304	507	669	801	41400	345	572	752	900	46700	388	638	838	1001
30900	266	447	589	704	36200	305	508	671	803	41500	346	573	754	902	46800	389	639	839	1003
31000	266	449	591	706	36300	305	509	672	805	41600	347	574	756	904	46900	390	640	841	1005
31100	267	450	592	708	36400	306	510	674	807	41700	348	575	757	906	47000	391	642	843	1007
31200	268	451	594	710	36500	307	512	675	809	41800	349	577	759	908	47100	391	643	844	1009
31300	268	452	595	711	36600	308	513	677	811	41900	349	578	760	910	47200	392	645	846	1011
31400	269	453	597	713	36700	308	514	679	813	42000	350	579	762	912	47300	393	645	847	1013
31500	270	454	598	715	36800	309	515	680	815	42100	351	580	764	914	47400	394	647	849	1015
31600	270	455	600	716	36900	310	516	682	817	42200	352	582	765	916	47500	395	648	851	1017
31700	271	456	601	718	37000	311	518	683	819	42300	353	583	767	918	47600	395	649	852	1018
31800	272	457	603	720	37100	312	519	685	820	42400	353	584	769	919	47700	396	650	854	1020
31900	272	458	604	722	37200	312	520	686	822	42500	354	585	770	921	47800	397	652	856	1022
32000	273	459	606	723	37300	313	521	688	824	42600	355	587	772	923	47900	398	653	857	1024
32100	274	460	607	725	37400	314	523	689	826	42700	356	588	773	925	48000	399	654	859	1026
32200	275	461	609	727	37500	315	524	691	828	42800	357	589	775	927	48100	399	655	860	1028
32300	275	463	611	729	37600	315	525	693	830	42900	358	590	777	929	48200	400	657	862	1030
32400	276	464	612	731	37700	316	526	694	831	43000	358	592	778	931	48300	401	658	864	1032
32500	277	465	614	733	37800	317	527	696	833	43100	359	593	780	933	48400	402	659	865	1034
32600	278	466	615	735	37900	318	529	697	835	43200	360	594	781	935	48500	403	660	867	1036
32700	278	467	617	737	38000	319	530	699	837	43300	361	595	783	937	48600	403	662	868	1037
32800	279	468	619	738	38100	319	531	700	839	43400	362	597	785	938	48700	404	663	870	1039
32900	280	470	620	740	38200	320	532	702	841	43500	362	598	786	940	48800	405	664	872	1041
33000	281	471	622	742	38300	321	533	703	842	43600	363	599	788	942	48900	406	666	873	1043
33100	281	472	624	744	38400	322	535	705	844	43700	364	600	789	944	49000	407	667	875	1045

Note: This table shows amounts of child support based on income to the nearest $100. There is a mathematical formula for calculating specific child support amounts between the $100 levels. For more information, please contact the Department of Justice.

Nota: La présente table indique le montant de la pension alimentaire pour enfants à verser d'après le revenu (aux 100 $ près). Il existe une formule mathématique pour calculer le montant exact de la pension alimentaire pour enfants dans le cas des revenus qui se situent entre les tranches de 100 $. Pour plus de renseignements, veuillez communiquer avec le ministère de la Justice.

Divorce

NOVA SCOTIA/NOUVELLE-ÉCOSSE

FEDERAL CHILD SUPPORT AMOUNTS : SIMPLIFIED TABLES 1997
MONTANTS FÉDÉRAUX DE PENSIONS ALIMENTAIRES POUR ENFANTS : TABLES SIMPLIFIÉES

Income/ Revenu ($)	Monthly Award/ Paiement mensuel ($) No. of Children/ N^{bre} d'enfants				Income/ Revenu ($)	Monthly Award/ Paiement mensuel ($) No. of Children/ N^{bre} d'enfants				Income/ Revenu ($)	Monthly Award/ Paiement mensuel ($) No. of Children/ N^{bre} d'enfants				Income/ Revenu ($)	Monthly Award/ Paiement mensuel ($) No. of Children/ N^{bre} d'enfants			
	1	2	3	4		1	2	3	4		1	2	3	4		1	2	3	4
49100	407	668	876	1047	54400	450	734	962	1148	59700	493	800	1047	1248	65000	531	860	1124	1339
49200	408	669	878	1049	54500	451	736	963	1150	59800	493	801	1048	1250	65100	531	861	1125	1341
49300	409	671	880	1051	54600	452	737	965	1152	59900	494	803	1050	1252	65200	532	862	1126	1343
49400	410	672	881	1053	54700	453	738	967	1154	60000	495	804	1051	1253	65300	533	863	1128	1344
49500	411	673	883	1055	54800	453	739	968	1156	60100	495	805	1052	1255	65400	533	864	1129	1346
49600	411	674	885	1057	54900	454	741	970	1157	60200	496	806	1054	1257	65500	534	865	1131	1347
49700	412	676	886	1058	55000	455	742	972	1159	60300	497	807	1055	1258	65600	535	866	1132	1349
49800	413	677	888	1060	55100	456	743	973	1161	60400	498	808	1057	1260	65700	535	867	1133	1351
49900	414	678	889	1062	55200	457	744	975	1163	60500	498	809	1058	1262	65800	536	869	1135	1352
50000	415	679	891	1064	55300	457	746	976	1165	60600	499	811	1060	1264	65900	537	870	1136	1354
50100	416	681	893	1066	55400	458	747	978	1167	60700	500	812	1061	1265	66000	537	871	1138	1356
50200	416	682	894	1068	55500	459	748	980	1169	60800	501	813	1063	1267	66100	538	872	1139	1357
50300	417	683	896	1070	55600	460	749	981	1171	60900	501	814	1064	1269	66200	539	873	1140	1359
50400	418	684	897	1072	55700	461	751	983	1173	61000	502	815	1066	1271	66300	539	874	1142	1361
50500	419	686	899	1074	55800	461	752	984	1175	61100	503	816	1067	1272	66400	540	875	1143	1362
50600	420	687	901	1076	55900	462	753	986	1177	61200	504	818	1069	1274	66500	541	876	1144	1364
50700	420	688	902	1077	56000	463	754	988	1178	61300	504	819	1070	1276	66600	541	877	1146	1366
50800	421	689	904	1079	56100	464	756	989	1180	61400	505	820	1072	1278	66700	542	878	1147	1367
50900	422	691	905	1081	56200	465	757	991	1182	61500	506	821	1073	1279	66800	543	879	1149	1369
51000	423	692	907	1083	56300	465	758	992	1184	61600	507	822	1075	1281	66900	543	881	1150	1371
51100	424	693	909	1085	56400	466	760	994	1186	61700	507	823	1076	1283	67000	544	882	1152	1373
51200	424	694	910	1087	56500	467	761	996	1188	61800	508	824	1078	1285	67100	545	883	1153	1374
51300	425	696	912	1089	56600	468	762	997	1190	61900	509	826	1079	1286	67200	546	884	1155	1376
51400	426	697	914	1091	56700	469	763	999	1192	62000	509	827	1081	1288	67300	546	885	1156	1378
51500	427	698	915	1093	56800	469	765	1001	1194	62100	510	828	1082	1290	67400	547	886	1157	1379
51600	428	699	917	1095	56900	470	766	1002	1196	62200	511	829	1083	1292	67500	548	887	1159	1381
51700	428	701	918	1097	57000	471	767	1004	1197	62300	512	830	1085	1293	67600	548	888	1160	1383
51800	429	702	920	1098	57100	472	768	1005	1199	62400	512	831	1086	1295	67700	549	889	1162	1384
51900	430	703	922	1100	57200	473	770	1007	1201	62500	513	832	1088	1297	67800	550	891	1163	1386
52000	431	704	923	1102	57300	474	771	1009	1203	62600	514	834	1089	1299	67900	551	892	1165	1388
52100	432	706	925	1104	57400	474	772	1010	1205	62700	515	835	1091	1300	68000	551	893	1166	1390
52200	432	707	926	1106	57500	475	773	1012	1207	62800	515	836	1092	1302	68100	552	894	1167	1391
52300	433	708	928	1108	57600	476	775	1013	1209	62900	516	837	1094	1304	68200	553	895	1169	1393
52400	434	709	930	1110	57700	477	776	1015	1211	63000	517	838	1095	1306	68300	553	896	1170	1395
52500	435	711	931	1112	57800	478	777	1017	1213	63100	518	839	1097	1307	68400	554	897	1172	1396
52600	436	712	933	1114	57900	478	778	1018	1215	63200	518	841	1098	1309	68500	555	898	1173	1398
52700	436	713	934	1116	58000	479	780	1020	1217	63300	519	842	1100	1311	68600	556	899	1175	1400
52800	437	714	936	1117	58100	480	781	1021	1218	63400	520	843	1101	1313	68700	556	901	1176	1401
52900	438	716	938	1119	58200	481	782	1023	1220	63500	521	844	1103	1314	68800	557	902	1178	1403
53000	439	717	939	1121	58300	482	783	1025	1222	63600	521	845	1104	1316	68900	558	903	1179	1405
53100	440	718	941	1123	58400	482	785	1026	1224	63700	522	846	1105	1318	69000	558	904	1180	1407
53200	440	719	943	1125	58500	483	786	1028	1226	63800	523	847	1107	1319	69100	559	905	1182	1408
53300	441	721	944	1127	58600	484	787	1030	1228	63900	523	848	1108	1321	69200	560	906	1183	1410
53400	442	722	946	1129	58700	485	788	1031	1230	64000	524	849	1110	1323	69300	561	907	1185	1412
53500	443	723	947	1131	58800	486	790	1033	1232	64100	525	850	1111	1324	69400	561	908	1186	1413
53600	444	724	949	1133	58900	486	791	1034	1234	64200	525	851	1112	1326	69500	562	910	1188	1415
53700	445	726	951	1135	59000	487	792	1036	1236	64300	526	852	1114	1328	69600	563	911	1189	1417
53800	445	727	952	1137	59100	488	793	1038	1237	64400	527	854	1115	1329	69700	563	912	1190	1418
53900	446	728	954	1138	59200	489	795	1039	1239	64500	527	855	1117	1331	69800	564	913	1192	1420
54000	447	729	955	1140	59300	490	796	1041	1241	64600	528	856	1118	1333	69900	565	914	1193	1422
54100	448	731	957	1142	59400	490	797	1042	1243	64700	529	857	1119	1334	70000	566	915	1195	1424
54200	449	732	959	1144	59500	491	798	1044	1245	64800	529	858	1121	1336	70100	566	916	1196	1425
54300	449	733	960	1146	59600	492	799	1045	1246	64900	530	859	1122	1338	70200	567	917	1198	1427

Note: This table shows amounts of child support based on income to the nearest $100. There is a mathematical formula for calculating specific child support amounts between the $100 levels. For more information, please contact the Department of Justice.

Nota: La présente table indique le montant de la pension alimentaire pour enfants à verser d'après le revenu (aux 100 $ près). Il existe une formule mathématique pour calculer le montant exact de la pension alimentaire pour enfants dans le cas des revenus qui se situent entre les tranches de 100 $. Pour plus de renseignements, veuillez communiquer avec le ministère de la Justice.

Appendix D

NOVA SCOTIA/NOUVELLE-ÉCOSSE

FEDERAL CHILD SUPPORT AMOUNTS : SIMPLIFIED TABLES
MONTANTS FÉDÉRAUX DE PENSIONS ALIMENTAIRES POUR ENFANTS : TABLES SIMPLIFIÉES

1997

Income/Revenu ($)	Monthly Award/Paiement mensuel ($) No. of Children/N^{bre} d'enfants				Income/Revenu ($)	Monthly Award/Paiement mensuel ($) No. of Children/N^{bre} d'enfants				Income/Revenu ($)	Monthly Award/Paiement mensuel ($) No. of Children/N^{bre} d'enfants				Income/Revenu ($)	Monthly Award/Paiement mensuel ($) No. of Children/N^{bre} d'enfants			
	1	2	3	4		1	2	3	4		1	2	3	4		1	2	3	4
70300	568	918	1199	1429	75600	606	978	1275	1519	80900	643	1035	1350	1607	86200	679	1092	1423	1693
70400	569	920	1200	1430	75700	607	979	1277	1520	81000	643	1037	1351	1609	86300	679	1093	1424	1695
70500	569	921	1202	1432	75800	607	980	1278	1522	81100	644	1038	1352	1610	86400	680	1094	1425	1697
70600	570	922	1203	1434	75900	608	981	1279	1524	81200	644	1039	1354	1612	86500	681	1095	1427	1698
70700	571	923	1205	1435	76000	609	982	1281	1525	81300	645	1040	1355	1613	86600	681	1096	1428	1700
70800	571	924	1206	1437	76100	609	983	1282	1527	81400	646	1041	1356	1615	86700	682	1097	1430	1702
70900	572	925	1208	1439	76200	610	984	1284	1529	81500	646	1042	1358	1617	86800	683	1098	1431	1703
71000	573	926	1209	1440	76300	611	986	1285	1530	81600	647	1043	1359	1618	86900	683	1100	1432	1705
71100	574	927	1211	1442	76400	612	987	1287	1532	81700	648	1044	1361	1620	87000	684	1101	1434	1706
71200	574	929	1212	1444	76500	612	988	1288	1534	81800	648	1045	1362	1621	87100	685	1102	1435	1708
71300	575	930	1213	1446	76600	613	989	1290	1536	81900	649	1046	1363	1623	87200	685	1103	1437	1710
71400	576	931	1215	1447	76700	614	990	1291	1537	82000	650	1047	1365	1625	87300	686	1104	1438	1711
71500	576	932	1216	1449	76800	614	991	1292	1539	82100	650	1048	1366	1626	87400	687	1105	1439	1713
71600	577	933	1218	1451	76900	615	992	1294	1541	82200	651	1049	1367	1628	87500	688	1106	1441	1715
71700	578	934	1219	1452	77000	616	993	1295	1542	82300	651	1050	1369	1629	87600	688	1107	1442	1716
71800	579	935	1221	1454	77100	617	994	1297	1544	82400	652	1051	1370	1631	87700	689	1108	1444	1718
71900	579	936	1222	1456	77200	617	996	1298	1546	82500	653	1052	1371	1633	87800	690	1109	1445	1720
72000	580	937	1223	1457	77300	618	997	1300	1547	82600	654	1053	1373	1634	87900	690	1110	1446	1721
72100	581	939	1225	1459	77400	619	998	1301	1549	82700	654	1054	1374	1636	88000	691	1111	1448	1723
72200	581	940	1226	1461	77500	620	999	1302	1551	82800	655	1055	1375	1637	88100	692	1112	1449	1725
72300	582	941	1228	1463	77600	620	1000	1304	1553	82900	656	1056	1377	1639	88200	692	1114	1450	1726
72400	583	942	1229	1464	77700	621	1001	1305	1554	83000	656	1057	1378	1641	88300	693	1115	1452	1728
72500	584	943	1231	1466	77800	622	1002	1307	1556	83100	657	1058	1380	1642	88400	694	1116	1453	1729
72600	584	944	1232	1468	77900	622	1003	1308	1558	83200	658	1060	1381	1644	88500	694	1117	1455	1731
72700	585	945	1234	1469	78000	623	1005	1310	1559	83300	658	1061	1382	1646	88600	695	1118	1456	1733
72800	586	946	1235	1471	78100	624	1006	1311	1561	83400	659	1062	1384	1647	88700	696	1119	1457	1734
72900	586	948	1236	1473	78200	625	1007	1313	1563	83500	660	1063	1385	1649	88800	697	1120	1459	1736
73000	587	949	1238	1474	78300	625	1008	1314	1564	83600	660	1064	1387	1651	88900	697	1121	1460	1738
73100	588	950	1239	1476	78400	626	1009	1315	1566	83700	661	1065	1388	1652	89000	698	1122	1462	1739
73200	589	951	1241	1478	78500	627	1010	1317	1568	83800	662	1066	1389	1654	89100	699	1123	1463	1741
73300	589	952	1242	1480	78600	627	1011	1318	1570	83900	663	1067	1391	1656	89200	699	1124	1464	1743
73400	590	953	1244	1481	78700	628	1012	1320	1571	84000	663	1068	1392	1657	89300	700	1125	1466	1744
73500	591	954	1245	1483	78800	629	1013	1321	1573	84100	664	1069	1394	1659	89400	701	1127	1467	1746
73600	592	955	1246	1485	78900	630	1015	1323	1575	84200	665	1070	1395	1660	89500	701	1128	1469	1748
73700	592	956	1248	1486	79000	630	1016	1324	1576	84300	665	1071	1396	1662	89600	702	1129	1470	1749
73800	593	958	1249	1488	79100	631	1017	1325	1578	84400	666	1073	1398	1664	89700	703	1130	1471	1751
73900	594	959	1251	1490	79200	632	1018	1327	1580	84500	667	1074	1399	1665	89800	704	1131	1473	1752
74000	594	960	1252	1491	79300	632	1019	1328	1581	84600	667	1075	1400	1667	89900	704	1132	1474	1754
74100	595	961	1254	1493	79400	633	1020	1330	1583	84700	668	1076	1402	1669	90000	705	1133	1476	1756
74200	596	962	1255	1495	79500	634	1021	1331	1585	84800	669	1077	1403	1670	90100	706	1134	1477	1757
74300	597	963	1257	1497	79600	634	1022	1332	1586	84900	669	1078	1405	1672	90200	706	1135	1478	1759
74400	597	964	1258	1498	79700	635	1023	1334	1588	85000	670	1079	1406	1674	90300	707	1136	1480	1761
74500	598	965	1259	1500	79800	636	1024	1335	1589	85100	671	1080	1407	1675	90400	708	1137	1481	1762
74600	599	967	1261	1502	79900	636	1025	1336	1591	85200	672	1081	1409	1677	90500	708	1138	1482	1764
74700	599	968	1262	1503	80000	637	1026	1338	1593	85300	672	1082	1410	1679	90600	709	1140	1484	1766
74800	600	969	1264	1505	80100	638	1027	1339	1594	85400	673	1083	1412	1680	90700	710	1141	1485	1767
74900	601	970	1265	1507	80200	638	1028	1340	1596	85500	674	1084	1413	1682	90800	710	1142	1487	1769
75000	602	971	1267	1508	80300	639	1029	1342	1597	85600	674	1085	1414	1683	90900	711	1143	1488	1770
75100	602	972	1268	1510	80400	639	1030	1343	1599	85700	675	1087	1416	1685	91000	712	1144	1489	1772
75200	603	973	1269	1512	80500	640	1031	1344	1601	85800	676	1088	1417	1687	91100	713	1145	1491	1774
75300	604	974	1271	1513	80600	641	1032	1346	1602	85900	676	1089	1419	1688	91200	713	1146	1492	1775
75400	604	975	1272	1515	80700	641	1033	1347	1604	86000	677	1090	1420	1690	91300	714	1147	1494	1777
75500	605	977	1274	1517	80800	642	1034	1348	1605	86100	678	1091	1421	1692	91400	715	1148	1495	1779

Note: This table shows amounts of child support based on income to the nearest $100. There is a mathematical formula for calculating specific child support amounts between the $100 levels. For more information, please contact the Department of Justice.

Nota: La présente table indique le montant de la pension alimentaire pour enfants à verser d'après le revenu (aux 100 $ près). Il existe une formule mathématique pour calculer le montant exact de la pension alimentaire pour enfants dans le cas des revenus qui se situent entre les tranches de 100 $. Pour plus de renseignements, veuillez communiquer avec le ministère de la Justice.

Divorce

NOVA SCOTIA/NOUVELLE-ÉCOSSE

FEDERAL CHILD SUPPORT AMOUNTS : SIMPLIFIED TABLES
MONTANTS FÉDÉRAUX DE PENSIONS ALIMENTAIRES POUR ENFANTS : TABLES SIMPLIFIÉES

1997

Income/Revenu ($)	Monthly Award/Paiement mensuel ($) No. of Children/N^bre d'enfants				Income/Revenu ($)	Monthly Award/Paiement mensuel ($) No. of Children/N^bre d'enfants				Income/Revenu ($)	Monthly Award/Paiement mensuel ($) No. of Children/N^bre d'enfants				Income/Revenu ($)	Monthly Award/Paiement mensuel ($) No. of Children/N^bre d'enfants			
	1	2	3	4		1	2	3	4		1	2	3	4		1	2	3	4
91500	715	1149	1496	1780	96800	752	1207	1570	1867	102100	789	1264	1644	1954	107400	826	1321	1717	2041
91600	716	1150	1498	1782	96900	753	1208	1571	1869	102200	790	1265	1645	1956	107500	826	1322	1719	2043
91700	717	1151	1499	1784	97000	754	1209	1573	1871	102300	790	1266	1646	1958	107600	827	1323	1720	2045
91800	717	1152	1501	1785	97100	754	1210	1574	1872	102400	791	1267	1648	1959	107700	828	1324	1721	2046
91900	718	1154	1502	1787	97200	755	1211	1576	1874	102500	792	1268	1649	1961	107800	829	1325	1723	2048
92000	719	1155	1503	1789	97300	756	1212	1577	1876	102600	792	1269	1651	1963	107900	829	1326	1724	2050
92100	719	1156	1505	1790	97400	756	1213	1578	1877	102700	793	1270	1652	1964	108000	830	1328	1726	2051
92200	720	1157	1506	1792	97500	757	1214	1580	1879	102800	794	1271	1653	1966	108100	831	1329	1727	2053
92300	721	1158	1507	1793	97600	758	1215	1581	1881	102900	795	1272	1655	1968	108200	831	1330	1728	2055
92400	722	1159	1509	1795	97700	758	1216	1582	1882	103000	795	1274	1656	1969	108300	832	1331	1730	2056
92500	722	1160	1510	1797	97800	759	1217	1584	1884	103100	796	1275	1658	1971	108400	833	1332	1731	2058
92600	723	1161	1512	1798	97900	760	1218	1585	1885	103200	797	1276	1659	1972	108500	833	1333	1733	2059
92700	724	1162	1513	1800	98000	760	1219	1587	1887	103300	797	1277	1660	1974	108600	834	1334	1734	2061
92800	724	1163	1514	1802	98100	761	1221	1588	1889	103400	798	1278	1662	1976	108700	835	1335	1735	2063
92900	725	1164	1516	1803	98200	762	1222	1589	1890	103500	799	1279	1663	1977	108800	836	1336	1737	2064
93000	726	1165	1517	1805	98300	763	1223	1591	1892	103600	799	1280	1664	1979	108900	836	1337	1738	2066
93100	726	1167	1519	1807	98400	763	1224	1592	1894	103700	800	1281	1666	1981	109000	837	1338	1739	2068
93200	727	1168	1520	1808	98500	764	1225	1594	1895	103800	801	1282	1667	1982	109100	838	1339	1741	2069
93300	728	1169	1521	1810	98600	765	1226	1595	1897	103900	801	1283	1669	1984	109200	838	1341	1742	2071
93400	729	1170	1523	1812	98700	765	1227	1596	1899	104000	802	1284	1670	1986	109300	839	1342	1744	2073
93500	729	1171	1524	1813	98800	766	1228	1598	1900	104100	803	1285	1671	1987	109400	840	1343	1745	2074
93600	730	1172	1526	1815	98900	767	1229	1599	1902	104200	804	1286	1673	1989	109500	840	1344	1746	2076
93700	731	1173	1527	1816	99000	767	1230	1601	1903	104300	804	1288	1674	1991	109600	841	1345	1748	2078
93800	731	1174	1528	1818	99100	768	1231	1602	1905	104400	805	1289	1676	1992	109700	842	1346	1749	2079
93900	732	1175	1530	1820	99200	769	1232	1603	1907	104500	806	1290	1677	1994	109800	842	1347	1751	2081
94000	733	1176	1531	1821	99300	770	1234	1605	1908	104600	806	1291	1678	1995	109900	843	1348	1752	2082
94100	733	1177	1532	1823	99400	770	1235	1606	1910	104700	807	1292	1680	1997	110000	844	1349	1753	2084
94200	734	1178	1534	1825	99500	771	1236	1607	1912	104800	808	1293	1681	1999	110100	845	1350	1755	2086
94300	735	1179	1535	1826	99600	772	1237	1609	1913	104900	808	1294	1683	2000	110200	845	1351	1756	2087
94400	735	1181	1537	1828	99700	772	1238	1610	1915	105000	809	1295	1684	2002	110300	846	1352	1758	2089
94500	736	1182	1538	1830	99800	773	1239	1612	1917	105100	810	1296	1685	2004	110400	847	1353	1759	2091
94600	737	1183	1539	1831	99900	774	1240	1613	1918	105200	811	1297	1687	2005	110500	847	1355	1760	2092
94700	738	1184	1541	1833	100000	774	1241	1614	1920	105300	811	1298	1688	2007	110600	848	1356	1762	2094
94800	738	1185	1542	1835	100100	775	1242	1616	1922	105400	812	1299	1689	2009	110700	849	1357	1763	2096
94900	739	1186	1544	1836	100200	776	1243	1617	1923	105500	813	1301	1691	2010	110800	849	1358	1764	2097
95000	740	1187	1545	1838	100300	776	1244	1619	1925	105600	813	1302	1692	2012	110900	850	1359	1766	2099
95100	740	1188	1546	1839	100400	777	1245	1620	1926	105700	814	1303	1694	2014	111000	851	1360	1767	2101
95200	741	1189	1548	1841	100500	778	1246	1621	1928	105800	815	1304	1695	2015	111100	851	1361	1769	2102
95300	742	1190	1549	1843	100600	779	1248	1623	1930	105900	815	1305	1696	2017	111200	852	1362	1770	2104
95400	742	1191	1551	1844	100700	779	1249	1624	1931	106000	816	1306	1698	2018	111300	853	1363	1771	2105
95500	743	1192	1552	1846	100800	780	1250	1626	1933	106100	817	1307	1699	2020	111400	854	1364	1773	2107
95600	744	1194	1553	1848	100900	781	1251	1627	1935	106200	817	1308	1701	2022	111500	854	1365	1774	2109
95700	745	1195	1555	1849	101000	781	1252	1628	1936	106300	818	1309	1702	2023	111600	855	1366	1776	2110
95800	745	1196	1556	1851	101100	782	1253	1630	1938	106400	819	1310	1703	2025	111700	856	1368	1777	2112
95900	746	1197	1557	1853	101200	783	1254	1631	1940	106500	820	1311	1705	2027	111800	856	1369	1778	2114
96000	747	1198	1559	1854	101300	783	1255	1633	1941	106600	820	1312	1706	2028	111900	857	1370	1780	2115
96100	747	1199	1560	1856	101400	784	1256	1634	1943	106700	821	1313	1708	2030	112000	858	1371	1781	2117
96200	748	1200	1562	1858	101500	785	1257	1635	1945	106800	822	1315	1709	2032	112100	858	1372	1783	2119
96300	749	1201	1563	1859	101600	785	1258	1637	1946	106900	822	1316	1710	2033	112200	859	1373	1784	2120
96400	749	1202	1564	1861	101700	786	1259	1638	1948	107000	823	1317	1712	2035	112300	860	1374	1785	2122
96500	750	1203	1566	1862	101800	787	1261	1639	1949	107100	824	1318	1713	2037	112400	861	1375	1787	2124
96600	751	1204	1567	1864	101900	788	1262	1641	1951	107200	824	1319	1714	2038	112500	861	1376	1788	2125
96700	751	1205	1569	1866	102000	788	1263	1642	1953	107300	825	1320	1716	2040	112600	862	1377	1790	2127

Note: This table shows amounts of child support based on income to the nearest $100. There is a mathematical formula for calculating specific child support amounts between the $100 levels. For more information, please contact the Department of Justice.

Nota: La présente table indique le montant de la pension alimentaire pour enfants à verser d'après le revenu (aux 100 $ près). Il existe une formule mathématique pour calculer le montant exact de la pension alimentaire pour enfants dans le cas des revenus qui se situent entre les tranches de 100 $. Pour plus de renseignements, veuillez communiquer avec le ministère de la Justice.

Appendix D

NOVA SCOTIA/NOUVELLE-ÉCOSSE

FEDERAL CHILD SUPPORT AMOUNTS : SIMPLIFIED TABLES 1997
MONTANTS FÉDÉRAUX DE PENSIONS ALIMENTAIRES POUR ENFANTS : TABLES SIMPLIFIÉES

Income/ Revenu ($)	Monthly Award/ Paiement mensuel ($) No. of Children/ N^{bre} d'enfants				Income/ Revenu ($)	Monthly Award/ Paiement mensuel ($) No. of Children/ N^{bre} d'enfants				Income/ Revenu ($)	Monthly Award/ Paiement mensuel ($) No. of Children/ N^{bre} d'enfants				Income/ Revenu ($)	Monthly Award/ Paiement mensuel ($) No. of Children/ N^{bre} d'enfants			
	1	2	3	4		1	2	3	4		1	2	3	4		1	2	3	4
112700	863	1378	1791	2128	118000	899	1436	1865	2215	123300	939	1495	1941	2305	128600	977	1555	2017	2395
112800	863	1379	1792	2130	118100	900	1437	1866	2217	123400	939	1497	1942	2307	128700	978	1556	2019	2397
112900	864	1380	1794	2132	118200	901	1438	1867	2219	123500	940	1498	1944	2309	128800	978	1557	2020	2399
113000	865	1382	1795	2133	118300	902	1439	1869	2220	123600	941	1499	1945	2310	128900	979	1558	2021	2400
113100	865	1383	1796	2135	118400	902	1440	1870	2222	123700	942	1500	1947	2312	129000	980	1559	2023	2402
113200	866	1384	1798	2137	118500	903	1441	1871	2224	123800	942	1501	1948	2314	129100	980	1560	2024	2404
113300	867	1385	1799	2138	118600	904	1442	1873	2225	123900	943	1502	1950	2316	129200	981	1561	2026	2406
113400	867	1386	1801	2140	118700	904	1443	1874	2227	124000	944	1503	1951	2317	129300	982	1563	2027	2407
113500	868	1387	1802	2142	118800	905	1444	1876	2229	124100	945	1504	1952	2319	129400	983	1564	2029	2409
113600	869	1388	1803	2143	118900	906	1445	1877	2230	124200	945	1506	1954	2321	129500	983	1565	2030	2411
113700	870	1389	1805	2145	119000	906	1446	1878	2232	124300	946	1507	1955	2322	129600	984	1566	2031	2412
113800	870	1390	1806	2147	119100	907	1447	1880	2234	124400	947	1508	1957	2324	129700	985	1567	2033	2414
113900	871	1391	1808	2148	119200	908	1449	1881	2235	124500	947	1509	1958	2326	129800	985	1568	2034	2416
114000	872	1392	1809	2150	119300	908	1450	1883	2237	124600	948	1510	1960	2327	129900	986	1569	2036	2417
114100	872	1393	1810	2151	119400	909	1451	1884	2238	124700	949	1511	1961	2329	130000	987	1570	2037	2419
114200	873	1395	1812	2153	119500	910	1452	1885	2240	124800	950	1512	1963	2331	130100	988	1572	2039	2421
114300	874	1396	1813	2155	119600	911	1453	1887	2242	124900	950	1513	1964	2333	130200	988	1573	2040	2423
114400	874	1397	1815	2156	119700	911	1454	1888	2243	125000	951	1515	1965	2334	130300	989	1574	2042	2424
114500	875	1398	1816	2158	119800	912	1455	1890	2245	125100	952	1516	1967	2336	130400	990	1575	2043	2426
114600	876	1399	1817	2160	119900	913	1456	1891	2247	125200	952	1517	1968	2338	130500	990	1576	2044	2428
114700	877	1400	1819	2161	120000	913	1457	1892	2248	125300	953	1518	1970	2339	130600	991	1577	2046	2429
114800	877	1401	1820	2163	120100	914	1458	1894	2250	125400	954	1519	1971	2341	130700	992	1578	2047	2431
114900	878	1402	1821	2165	120200	915	1459	1895	2252	125500	955	1520	1973	2343	130800	993	1579	2049	2433
115000	879	1403	1823	2166	120300	915	1460	1896	2253	125600	955	1521	1974	2344	130900	993	1580	2050	2434
115100	879	1404	1824	2168	120400	916	1462	1898	2255	125700	956	1522	1975	2346	131000	994	1582	2052	2436
115200	880	1405	1826	2170	120500	917	1463	1899	2257	125800	957	1523	1977	2348	131100	995	1583	2053	2438
115300	881	1406	1827	2171	120600	918	1464	1901	2258	125900	957	1525	1978	2350	131200	995	1584	2054	2440
115400	881	1408	1828	2173	120700	918	1465	1902	2260	126000	958	1526	1980	2351	131300	996	1585	2056	2441
115500	882	1409	1830	2174	120800	919	1466	1904	2262	126100	959	1527	1981	2353	131400	997	1586	2057	2443
115600	883	1410	1831	2176	120900	920	1467	1905	2263	126200	960	1528	1983	2355	131500	998	1587	2059	2445
115700	883	1411	1833	2178	121000	921	1468	1907	2265	126300	960	1529	1984	2356	131600	998	1588	2060	2446
115800	884	1412	1834	2179	121100	921	1470	1908	2267	126400	961	1530	1985	2358	131700	999	1589	2062	2448
115900	885	1413	1835	2181	121200	922	1471	1910	2269	126500	962	1531	1987	2360	131800	1000	1591	2063	2450
116000	886	1414	1837	2183	121300	923	1472	1911	2270	126600	962	1532	1988	2361	131900	1001	1592	2065	2451
116100	886	1415	1838	2184	121400	924	1473	1913	2272	126700	963	1534	1990	2363	132000	1001	1593	2066	2453
116200	887	1416	1840	2186	121500	925	1474	1914	2274	126800	964	1535	1991	2365	132100	1002	1594	2067	2455
116300	888	1417	1841	2188	121600	925	1475	1916	2276	126900	965	1536	1993	2367	132200	1003	1595	2069	2457
116400	888	1418	1842	2189	121700	926	1477	1917	2277	127000	965	1537	1994	2368	132300	1003	1596	2070	2458
116500	889	1419	1844	2191	121800	927	1478	1919	2279	127100	966	1538	1996	2370	132400	1004	1597	2072	2460
116600	890	1420	1845	2192	121900	928	1479	1920	2281	127200	967	1539	1997	2372	132500	1005	1598	2073	2462
116700	890	1422	1846	2194	122000	928	1480	1921	2283	127300	967	1540	1998	2373	132600	1006	1599	2075	2463
116800	891	1423	1848	2196	122100	929	1481	1923	2284	127400	968	1541	2000	2375	132700	1006	1601	2076	2465
116900	892	1424	1849	2197	122200	930	1482	1924	2286	127500	969	1542	2001	2377	132800	1007	1602	2077	2467
117000	892	1425	1851	2199	122300	931	1484	1926	2288	127600	970	1544	2003	2378	132900	1008	1603	2079	2468
117100	893	1426	1852	2201	122400	932	1485	1927	2290	127700	970	1545	2004	2380	133000	1008	1604	2080	2470
117200	894	1427	1853	2202	122500	932	1486	1929	2291	127800	971	1546	2006	2382	133100	1009	1605	2082	2472
117300	895	1428	1855	2204	122600	933	1487	1930	2293	127900	972	1547	2007	2383	133200	1010	1606	2083	2473
117400	895	1429	1856	2206	122700	934	1488	1932	2295	128000	973	1548	2008	2385	133300	1011	1607	2085	2475
117500	896	1430	1858	2207	122800	935	1489	1933	2297	128100	973	1549	2010	2387	133400	1011	1608	2086	2477
117600	897	1431	1859	2209	122900	935	1491	1935	2298	128200	974	1550	2011	2389	133500	1012	1610	2087	2479
117700	897	1432	1860	2211	123000	936	1492	1936	2300	128300	975	1551	2013	2390	133600	1013	1611	2089	2480
117800	898	1433	1862	2212	123100	937	1493	1938	2302	128400	975	1553	2014	2392	133700	1013	1612	2090	2482
117900	899	1435	1863	2214	123200	938	1494	1939	2303	128500	976	1554	2016	2394	133800	1014	1613	2092	2484

Note: This table shows amounts of child support based on income to the nearest $100. There is a mathematical formula for calculating specific child support amounts between the $100 levels. For more information, please contact the Department of Justice.

Nota: La présente table indique le montant de la pension alimentaire pour enfants à verser d'après le revenu (aux 100 $ près). Il existe une formule mathématique pour calculer le montant exact de la pension alimentaire pour enfants dans le cas des revenus qui se situent entre les tranches de 100 $. Pour plus de renseignements, veuillez communiquer avec le ministère de la Justice.

Divorce

NOVA SCOTIA/NOUVELLE-ÉCOSSE

FEDERAL CHILD SUPPORT AMOUNTS : SIMPLIFIED TABLES 1997
MONTANTS FÉDÉRAUX DE PENSIONS ALIMENTAIRES POUR ENFANTS : TABLES SIMPLIFIÉES

Income/ Revenu ($)	Monthly Award/ Paiement mensuel ($) No. of Children/ N^{bre} d'enfants				Income/ Revenu ($)	Monthly Award/ Paiement mensuel ($) No. of Children/ N^{bre} d'enfants				Income/ Revenu ($)	Monthly Award/ Paiement mensuel ($) No. of Children/ N^{bre} d'enfants				Income/ Revenu ($)	Monthly Award/ Paiement mensuel ($) No. of Children/ N^{bre} d'enfants			
	1	2	3	4		1	2	3	4		1	2	3	4		1	2	3	4
133900	1015	1614	2093	2485	138000	1044	1660	2152	2555	142100	1074	1706	2211	2625	146200	1103	1751	2270	2694
134000	1016	1615	2095	2487	138100	1045	1661	2154	2557	142200	1075	1707	2212	2626	146300	1104	1753	2271	2696
134100	1016	1616	2096	2489	138200	1046	1662	2155	2558	142300	1075	1708	2214	2628	146400	1105	1754	2273	2698
134200	1017	1617	2098	2490	138300	1046	1663	2156	2560	142400	1076	1709	2215	2630	146500	1105	1755	2274	2699
134300	1018	1618	2099	2492	138400	1047	1664	2158	2562	142500	1077	1710	2217	2631	146600	1106	1756	2276	2701
134400	1018	1620	2100	2494	138500	1048	1665	2159	2563	142600	1077	1711	2218	2633	146700	1107	1757	2277	2703
134500	1019	1621	2102	2496	138600	1049	1666	2161	2565	142700	1078	1712	2220	2635	146800	1108	1758	2279	2704
134600	1020	1622	2103	2497	138700	1049	1668	2162	2567	142800	1079	1713	2221	2636	146900	1108	1759	2280	2706
134700	1021	1623	2105	2499	138800	1050	1669	2164	2569	142900	1080	1715	2223	2638	147000	1109	1760	2281	2708
134800	1021	1624	2106	2501	138900	1051	1670	2165	2570	143000	1080	1716	2224	2640	147100	1110	1761	2283	2709
134900	1022	1625	2108	2502	139000	1052	1671	2166	2572	143100	1081	1717	2225	2642	147200	1110	1763	2284	2711
135000	1023	1626	2109	2504	139100	1052	1672	2168	2574	143200	1082	1718	2227	2643	147300	1111	1764	2286	2713
135100	1024	1627	2110	2506	139200	1053	1673	2169	2575	143300	1082	1719	2228	2645	147400	1112	1765	2287	2715
135200	1024	1628	2112	2507	139300	1054	1674	2171	2577	143400	1083	1720	2230	2647	147500	1113	1766	2289	2716
135300	1025	1630	2113	2509	139400	1054	1675	2172	2579	143500	1084	1721	2231	2648	147600	1113	1767	2290	2718
135400	1026	1631	2115	2511	139500	1055	1677	2174	2580	143600	1085	1722	2233	2650	147700	1114	1768	2291	2720
135500	1026	1632	2116	2513	139600	1056	1678	2175	2582	143700	1085	1723	2234	2652	147800	1115	1769	2293	2721
135600	1027	1633	2118	2514	139700	1057	1679	2177	2584	143800	1086	1725	2235	2653	147900	1115	1770	2294	2723
135700	1028	1634	2119	2516	139800	1057	1680	2178	2586	143900	1087	1726	2237	2655	148000	1116	1772	2296	2725
135800	1029	1635	2121	2518	139900	1058	1681	2179	2587	144000	1087	1727	2238	2657	148100	1117	1773	2297	2726
135900	1029	1636	2122	2519	140000	1059	1682	2181	2589	144100	1088	1728	2240	2659	148200	1118	1774	2299	2728
136000	1030	1637	2123	2521	140100	1059	1683	2182	2591	144200	1089	1729	2241	2660	148300	1118	1775	2300	2730
136100	1031	1639	2125	2523	140200	1060	1684	2184	2592	144300	1090	1730	2243	2662	148400	1119	1776	2302	2732
136200	1031	1640	2126	2524	140300	1061	1685	2185	2594	144400	1090	1731	2244	2664	148500	1120	1777	2303	2733
136300	1032	1641	2128	2526	140400	1062	1687	2187	2596	144500	1091	1732	2246	2665	148600	1120	1778	2304	2735
136400	1033	1642	2129	2528	140500	1062	1688	2188	2597	144600	1092	1734	2247	2667	148700	1121	1779	2306	2737
136500	1034	1643	2131	2530	140600	1063	1689	2189	2599	144700	1092	1735	2248	2669	148800	1122	1780	2307	2738
136600	1034	1644	2132	2531	140700	1064	1690	2191	2601	144800	1093	1736	2250	2670	148900	1123	1782	2309	2740
136700	1035	1645	2133	2533	140800	1064	1691	2192	2603	144900	1094	1737	2251	2672	149000	1123	1783	2310	2742
136800	1036	1646	2135	2535	140900	1065	1692	2194	2604	145000	1095	1738	2253	2674	149100	1124	1784	2312	2743
136900	1036	1647	2136	2536	141000	1066	1693	2195	2606	145100	1095	1739	2254	2676	149200	1125	1785	2313	2745
137000	1037	1649	2138	2538	141100	1067	1694	2197	2608	145200	1096	1740	2256	2677	149300	1126	1786	2314	2747
137100	1038	1650	2139	2540	141200	1067	1696	2198	2609	145300	1097	1741	2257	2679	149400	1126	1787	2316	2749
137200	1039	1651	2141	2541	141300	1068	1697	2200	2611	145400	1097	1742	2258	2681	149500	1127	1788	2317	2750
137300	1039	1652	2142	2543	141400	1069	1698	2201	2613	145500	1098	1744	2260	2682	149600	1128	1789	2319	2752
137400	1040	1653	2144	2545	141500	1069	1699	2202	2614	145600	1099	1745	2261	2684	149700	1128	1791	2320	2754
137500	1041	1654	2145	2546	141600	1070	1700	2204	2616	145700	1100	1746	2263	2686	149800	1129	1792	2322	2755
137600	1041	1655	2146	2548	141700	1071	1701	2205	2618	145800	1100	1747	2264	2687	149900	1130	1793	2323	2757
137700	1042	1656	2148	2550	141800	1072	1702	2207	2619	145900	1101	1748	2266	2689	150000	1131	1794	2325	2759
137800	1043	1658	2149	2552	141900	1072	1703	2208	2621	146000	1102	1749	2267	2691					
137900	1044	1659	2151	2553	142000	1073	1704	2210	2623	146100	1103	1750	2268	2692					

Income/ Revenu ($)	Monthly Award/Paiement mensuel ($)			
	one child/ un enfant	two children/ deux enfants	three children/ trois enfants	four children/ quatre enfants
For income over $150,000	1131 plus 0.72% of income over $150,000	1794 plus 1.12% of income over $150,000	2325 plus 1.44% of income over $150,000	2759 plus 1.70% of income over $150,000
Pour revenu dépassant 150 000$	1131 plus 0,72% du revenu dépassant 150 000$	1794 plus 1,12% du revenu dépassant 150 000$	2325 plus 1,44% du revenu dépassant 150 000$	2759 plus 1,70% du revenu dépassant 150 000$

Note: This table shows amounts of child support based on income to the nearest $100. There is a mathematical formula for calculating specific child support amounts between the $100 levels. For more information, please contact the Department of Justice.

Nota: La présente table indique le montant de la pension alimentaire pour enfants à verser d'après le revenu (aux 100 $ près). Il existe une formule mathématique pour calculer le montant exact de la pension alimentaire pour enfants dans le cas des revenus qui se situent entre les tranches de 100 $. Pour plus de renseignements, veuillez communiquer avec le ministère de la Justice.

Appendix D

ONTARIO

FEDERAL CHILD SUPPORT AMOUNTS : SIMPLIFIED TABLES
MONTANTS FÉDÉRAUX DE PENSIONS ALIMENTAIRES POUR ENFANTS : TABLES SIMPLIFIÉES

1997

Income/ Revenu ($)	Monthly Award/ Paiement mensuel ($) No. of Children/ N^{bre} d'enfants				Income/ Revenu ($)	Monthly Award/ Paiement mensuel ($) No. of Children/ N^{bre} d'enfants				Income/ Revenu ($)	Monthly Award/ Paiement mensuel ($) No. of Children/ N^{bre} d'enfants				Income/ Revenu ($)	Monthly Award/ Paiement mensuel ($) No. of Children/ N^{bre} d'enfants			
	1	2	3	4		1	2	3	4		1	2	3	4		1	2	3	4
6700	0	0	0	0	12000	96	176	198	220	17300	136	252	344	412	22600	199	317	434	529
6800	4	4	4	4	12100	97	179	202	224	17400	136	253	346	416	22700	200	318	435	531
6900	9	9	10	11	12200	98	182	205	228	17500	137	254	348	419	22800	201	320	437	533
7000	14	15	16	17	12300	99	185	208	231	17600	138	255	349	423	22900	202	321	439	535
7100	19	20	22	23	12400	100	188	211	235	17700	138	257	351	427	23000	203	322	440	537
7200	24	25	27	29	12500	100	190	214	238	17800	139	258	353	430	23100	204	323	442	539
7300	29	31	33	36	12600	101	193	218	242	17900	140	259	354	433	23200	205	325	444	541
7400	34	36	39	42	12700	102	195	221	246	18000	140	260	356	435	23300	206	326	445	543
7500	39	42	45	48	12800	103	196	224	249	18100	141	262	358	437	23400	207	328	447	545
7600	44	47	51	54	12900	104	197	227	253	18200	142	263	360	439	23500	208	330	449	547
7700	49	53	57	61	13000	105	198	230	256	18300	142	264	361	441	23600	209	332	450	549
7800	54	58	62	67	13100	106	200	234	260	18400	143	265	363	443	23700	210	334	452	551
7900	58	63	68	73	13200	106	201	237	264	18500	144	266	365	445	23800	211	336	454	553
8000	62	67	72	78	13300	107	202	240	267	18600	144	268	366	447	23900	212	338	455	556
8100	62	71	76	82	13400	108	203	243	271	18700	145	269	368	449	24000	213	340	457	558
8200	63	74	80	86	13500	109	205	246	275	18800	146	270	370	451	24100	213	342	459	560
8300	64	78	84	91	13600	110	206	250	278	18900	147	271	371	453	24200	214	344	461	562
8400	65	81	88	95	13700	111	207	253	282	19000	148	273	373	455	24300	215	346	462	564
8500	66	85	92	100	13800	112	208	256	285	19100	149	274	375	457	24400	216	348	464	566
8600	67	89	96	104	13900	112	210	259	289	19200	151	275	376	459	24500	217	350	466	568
8700	68	92	100	109	14000	113	211	262	293	19300	152	276	378	461	24600	218	352	467	570
8800	69	96	104	113	14100	114	212	266	296	19400	154	278	380	463	24700	219	354	469	572
8900	69	99	108	117	14200	115	213	269	300	19500	155	279	381	465	24800	220	356	471	574
9000	70	102	112	121	14300	115	215	272	304	19600	157	280	383	467	24900	221	358	472	576
9100	71	104	114	124	14400	116	216	275	307	19700	158	281	385	469	25000	222	360	474	578
9200	72	106	116	126	14500	117	217	278	311	19800	160	283	386	472	25100	223	362	476	580
9300	73	107	118	129	14600	117	218	282	314	19900	161	284	388	474	25200	224	364	477	582
9400	74	109	120	131	14700	118	219	285	318	20000	163	285	390	476	25300	225	366	479	584
9500	75	111	122	134	14800	119	221	288	322	20100	164	286	392	478	25400	226	368	481	586
9600	75	112	124	136	14900	119	222	291	325	20200	166	287	393	480	25500	227	370	482	588
9700	76	114	126	139	15000	120	223	294	329	20300	167	289	395	482	25600	228	372	484	590
9800	77	115	128	141	15100	121	224	298	333	20400	169	290	397	484	25700	229	374	486	592
9900	78	117	130	144	15200	121	226	301	336	20500	170	291	398	486	25800	230	375	487	594
10000	79	119	132	146	15300	122	227	304	340	20600	172	292	400	488	25900	231	377	489	596
10100	80	121	135	149	15400	123	228	307	343	20700	173	294	402	490	26000	232	379	491	598
10200	81	124	138	153	15500	123	229	310	347	20800	175	295	403	492	26100	232	381	492	600
10300	81	127	142	156	15600	124	231	314	351	20900	176	296	405	494	26200	233	383	494	602
10400	82	130	145	160	15700	125	232	317	354	21000	178	297	407	496	26300	234	385	495	604
10500	83	133	148	164	15800	126	233	319	358	21100	179	299	408	498	26400	235	387	497	606
10600	84	136	152	168	15900	126	234	321	361	21200	181	300	410	500	26500	236	389	498	608
10700	85	138	155	172	16000	127	236	323	365	21300	182	301	412	502	26600	237	390	500	610
10800	86	141	158	175	16100	128	237	324	369	21400	184	302	413	504	26700	238	392	502	612
10900	87	144	162	179	16200	128	238	326	372	21500	185	304	415	506	26800	239	394	503	613
11000	87	147	165	183	16300	129	239	328	376	21600	187	305	417	508	26900	239	396	505	615
11100	88	150	168	187	16400	130	241	329	380	21700	188	306	418	510	27000	240	398	506	617
11200	89	153	172	190	16500	130	242	331	383	21800	189	307	420	512	27100	241	400	508	619
11300	90	156	175	194	16600	131	243	333	387	21900	191	309	422	515	27200	242	402	509	621
11400	91	159	179	198	16700	132	244	334	390	22000	192	310	424	517	27300	243	403	511	623
11500	92	162	182	202	16800	132	245	336	394	22100	194	311	425	519	27400	244	405	512	625
11600	93	165	185	206	16900	133	247	338	398	22200	195	312	427	521	27500	245	407	514	627
11700	93	168	189	209	17000	134	248	339	401	22300	196	313	429	523	27600	246	409	516	629
11800	94	171	192	213	17100	134	249	341	405	22400	197	315	430	525	27700	246	411	518	630
11900	95	174	195	217	17200	135	250	343	409	22500	198	316	432	527	27800	247	413	521	632

Note: This table shows amounts of child support based on income to the nearest $100. There is a mathematical formula for calculating specific child support amounts between the $100 levels. For more information, please contact the Department of Justice.

Nota: La présente table indique le montant de la pension alimentaire pour enfants à verser d'après le revenu (aux 100 $ près). Il existe une formule mathématique pour calculer le montant exact de la pension alimentaire pour enfants dans le cas des revenus qui se situent entre les tranches de 100 $. Pour plus de renseignements, veuillez communiquer avec le ministère de la Justice.

Divorce

ONTARIO

FEDERAL CHILD SUPPORT AMOUNTS : SIMPLIFIED TABLES
MONTANTS FÉDÉRAUX DE PENSIONS ALIMENTAIRES POUR ENFANTS : TABLES SIMPLIFIÉES

1997

Income/Revenu ($)	Monthly Award/Paiement mensuel ($) No. of Children/N^{bre} d'enfants				Income/Revenu ($)	Monthly Award/Paiement mensuel ($) No. of Children/N^{bre} d'enfants				Income/Revenu ($)	Monthly Award/Paiement mensuel ($) No. of Children/N^{bre} d'enfants				Income/Revenu ($)	Monthly Award/Paiement mensuel ($) No. of Children/N^{bre} d'enfants			
	1	2	3	4		1	2	3	4		1	2	3	4		1	2	3	4
27900	248	415	523	634	33200	291	483	637	738	38500	333	551	723	864	43800	377	619	813	971
28000	249	416	525	636	33300	291	484	639	741	38600	334	552	725	866	43900	378	621	814	973
28100	250	418	527	638	33400	292	486	640	743	38700	335	553	727	868	44000	379	622	816	975
28200	251	420	529	640	33500	293	487	642	746	38800	336	554	728	870	44100	380	623	818	977
28300	252	422	532	642	33600	294	488	643	748	38900	337	556	730	872	44200	381	624	819	979
28400	253	424	534	644	33700	295	489	645	751	39000	337	557	732	874	44300	382	626	821	981
28500	254	426	536	646	33800	296	491	647	753	39100	338	558	733	876	44400	382	627	823	983
28600	254	428	538	647	33900	296	492	648	756	39200	339	559	735	878	44500	383	628	824	985
28700	255	429	540	649	34000	297	493	650	758	39300	340	561	737	880	44600	384	630	826	987
28800	256	430	543	651	34100	298	494	651	761	39400	341	562	738	882	44700	385	631	828	989
28900	257	432	545	653	34200	299	496	653	763	39500	341	563	740	884	44800	386	632	829	991
29000	258	433	547	655	34300	300	497	655	766	39600	342	564	742	886	44900	387	634	831	993
29100	259	434	549	657	34400	301	498	656	768	39700	343	566	743	888	45000	387	635	833	995
29200	260	436	551	659	34500	301	499	658	771	39800	344	567	745	890	45100	388	636	834	997
29300	261	437	554	661	34600	302	501	659	773	39900	345	568	747	892	45200	389	637	836	999
29400	261	439	556	662	34700	303	502	661	776	40000	345	570	748	894	45300	390	639	838	1001
29500	262	440	558	664	34800	304	503	663	778	40100	346	571	750	896	45400	391	640	840	1003
29600	263	441	560	666	34900	304	504	664	781	40200	347	572	752	898	45500	392	641	841	1005
29700	264	442	562	668	35000	305	506	666	783	40300	348	573	753	900	45600	392	643	843	1007
29800	265	443	564	669	35100	306	507	667	786	40400	349	575	755	902	45700	393	644	845	1009
29900	265	444	566	670	35200	307	508	669	788	40500	350	576	757	904	45800	394	645	846	1011
30000	266	446	568	672	35300	308	509	671	791	40600	350	577	759	906	45900	395	647	848	1013
30100	267	447	570	673	35400	308	511	672	793	40700	351	579	760	908	46000	396	648	850	1015
30200	267	448	572	674	35500	309	512	674	796	40800	352	580	762	910	46100	397	649	851	1017
30300	268	449	575	675	35600	310	513	675	798	40900	353	581	764	912	46200	398	651	853	1019
30400	269	450	577	677	35700	311	514	677	801	41000	354	583	765	914	46300	398	652	855	1021
30500	269	451	579	678	35800	311	516	679	803	41100	355	584	767	916	46400	399	653	856	1023
30600	270	452	581	679	35900	312	517	680	806	41200	356	585	769	918	46500	400	654	858	1025
30700	271	453	583	681	36000	313	518	682	809	41300	356	587	771	920	46600	401	656	860	1027
30800	272	454	585	682	36100	314	520	683	811	41400	357	588	772	922	46700	402	657	861	1029
30900	272	455	587	684	36200	315	521	685	814	41500	358	589	774	924	46800	403	658	863	1031
31000	273	456	589	685	36300	315	522	687	816	41600	359	590	776	926	46900	403	660	865	1032
31100	274	458	591	688	36400	316	523	688	819	41700	360	592	777	928	47000	404	661	866	1034
31200	275	459	594	690	36500	317	525	690	821	41800	361	593	779	930	47100	405	662	868	1036
31300	275	460	596	692	36600	318	526	692	824	41900	361	594	781	932	47200	406	664	870	1038
31400	276	461	598	695	36700	319	527	693	827	42000	362	596	782	934	47300	407	665	871	1040
31500	277	462	600	697	36800	319	529	695	829	42100	363	597	784	936	47400	408	666	873	1042
31600	278	463	602	699	36900	320	530	697	832	42200	364	598	786	938	47500	408	668	875	1044
31700	278	465	604	702	37000	321	531	698	834	42300	365	600	787	940	47600	409	669	876	1046
31800	279	466	606	704	37100	322	533	700	837	42400	366	601	789	942	47700	410	670	878	1048
31900	280	467	608	706	37200	323	534	702	839	42500	366	602	791	944	47800	411	671	880	1050
32000	281	468	611	709	37300	324	535	703	841	42600	367	604	792	946	47900	412	673	882	1052
32100	281	469	613	711	37400	324	537	705	843	42700	368	605	794	948	48000	413	674	883	1054
32200	282	470	615	714	37500	325	538	707	845	42800	369	606	796	950	48100	413	675	885	1056
32300	283	472	617	716	37600	326	539	708	847	42900	370	607	798	952	48200	414	677	887	1058
32400	284	473	620	718	37700	327	540	710	849	43000	371	609	799	954	48300	415	678	888	1060
32500	285	474	622	721	37800	328	542	712	851	43100	371	610	801	956	48400	416	679	890	1062
32600	286	476	624	723	37900	328	543	713	853	43200	372	611	803	958	48500	417	681	892	1064
32700	286	477	627	726	38000	329	544	715	855	43300	373	613	804	960	48600	418	682	893	1066
32800	287	478	629	728	38100	330	546	717	857	43400	374	614	806	962	48700	419	683	895	1068
32900	288	479	631	731	38200	331	547	718	859	43500	375	615	808	964	48800	419	685	897	1070
33000	289	481	633	733	38300	332	548	720	861	43600	376	617	809	966	48900	420	686	898	1072
33100	290	482	635	736	38400	332	549	722	862	43700	377	618	811	969	49000	421	687	900	1074

Note: This table shows amounts of child support based on income to the nearest $100. There is a mathematical formula for calculating specific child support amounts between the $100 levels. For more information, please contact the Department of Justice.

Nota: La présente table indique le montant de la pension alimentaire pour enfants à verser d'après le revenu (aux 100 $ près). Il existe une formule mathématique pour calculer le montant exact de la pension alimentaire pour enfants dans le cas des revenus qui se situent entre les tranches de 100 $. Pour plus de renseignements, veuillez communiquer avec le ministère de la Justice.

Appendix D

ONTARIO

FEDERAL CHILD SUPPORT AMOUNTS : SIMPLIFIED TABLES
MONTANTS FÉDÉRAUX DE PENSIONS ALIMENTAIRES POUR ENFANTS : TABLES SIMPLIFIÉES

1997

Income/ Revenu ($)	Monthly Award/ Paiement mensuel ($) No. of Children/ N^bre d'enfants				Income/ Revenu ($)	Monthly Award/ Paiement mensuel ($) No. of Children/ N^bre d'enfants				Income/ Revenu ($)	Monthly Award/ Paiement mensuel ($) No. of Children/ N^bre d'enfants				Income/ Revenu ($)	Monthly Award/ Paiement mensuel ($) No. of Children/ N^bre d'enfants			
	1	2	3	4		1	2	3	4		1	2	3	4		1	2	3	4
49100	422	688	902	1076	54400	464	755	988	1178	59700	505	820	1071	1277	65000	543	879	1148	1368
49200	423	690	903	1078	54500	465	756	989	1180	59800	506	821	1073	1279	65100	543	880	1150	1370
49300	424	691	905	1080	54600	465	757	991	1182	59900	506	822	1074	1281	65200	544	881	1151	1371
49400	424	692	907	1082	54700	466	758	992	1184	60000	507	823	1076	1283	65300	544	882	1152	1373
49500	425	694	908	1084	54800	467	760	994	1186	60100	508	824	1077	1284	65400	545	883	1153	1374
49600	426	695	910	1086	54900	467	761	996	1188	60200	509	825	1079	1286	65500	545	884	1154	1376
49700	427	696	912	1088	55000	468	762	997	1189	60300	509	826	1080	1288	65600	546	885	1156	1377
49800	428	698	913	1090	55100	469	763	999	1191	60400	510	828	1082	1290	65700	546	886	1157	1379
49900	429	699	915	1092	55200	470	764	1000	1193	60500	511	829	1083	1291	65800	547	886	1158	1380
50000	429	700	917	1094	55300	470	766	1002	1195	60600	511	830	1085	1293	65900	547	887	1159	1382
50100	430	702	918	1096	55400	471	767	1003	1197	60700	512	831	1086	1295	66000	548	888	1160	1383
50200	431	703	920	1098	55500	472	768	1005	1199	60800	513	832	1088	1297	66100	548	889	1162	1385
50300	432	704	922	1100	55600	472	769	1006	1200	60900	514	833	1089	1298	66200	549	890	1163	1386
50400	433	705	924	1102	55700	473	770	1008	1202	61000	514	834	1091	1300	66300	549	891	1164	1388
50500	434	707	925	1104	55800	474	771	1009	1204	61100	515	836	1092	1302	66400	550	892	1165	1389
50600	434	708	927	1106	55900	475	773	1011	1206	61200	516	837	1093	1303	66500	550	893	1166	1390
50700	435	709	929	1108	56000	475	774	1013	1208	61300	517	838	1095	1305	66600	551	894	1168	1392
50800	436	711	930	1110	56100	476	775	1014	1210	61400	517	839	1096	1307	66700	552	895	1169	1393
50900	437	712	932	1112	56200	477	776	1016	1212	61500	518	840	1098	1309	66800	552	895	1170	1395
51000	438	713	934	1114	56300	478	778	1017	1214	61600	519	841	1099	1310	66900	553	896	1171	1396
51100	439	715	935	1116	56400	479	779	1019	1215	61700	520	843	1101	1312	67000	553	897	1173	1398
51200	440	716	937	1118	56500	479	780	1021	1217	61800	520	844	1102	1314	67100	554	898	1174	1399
51300	440	717	939	1120	56600	480	781	1022	1219	61900	521	845	1104	1316	67200	554	899	1175	1401
51400	441	719	940	1122	56700	481	783	1024	1221	62000	522	846	1105	1317	67300	555	900	1176	1402
51500	442	720	942	1124	56800	482	784	1025	1223	62100	523	847	1107	1319	67400	555	901	1178	1404
51600	443	721	944	1126	56900	483	785	1027	1225	62200	523	848	1108	1321	67500	556	902	1179	1405
51700	444	722	945	1128	57000	483	786	1029	1227	62300	524	849	1110	1323	67600	556	903	1180	1407
51800	445	724	947	1130	57100	484	788	1030	1229	62400	525	851	1111	1324	67700	557	904	1181	1408
51900	445	725	949	1132	57200	485	789	1032	1231	62500	525	852	1113	1326	67800	558	905	1183	1410
52000	446	726	950	1134	57300	486	790	1033	1233	62600	526	853	1114	1328	67900	558	906	1184	1411
52100	447	728	952	1136	57400	487	791	1035	1234	62700	527	854	1116	1330	68000	559	907	1185	1413
52200	448	729	954	1138	57500	488	793	1037	1236	62800	528	855	1117	1331	68100	559	908	1186	1414
52300	449	730	955	1140	57600	488	794	1038	1238	62900	528	856	1119	1333	68200	560	909	1188	1416
52400	450	731	957	1142	57700	489	795	1040	1240	63000	529	857	1120	1335	68300	560	910	1189	1417
52500	450	733	959	1143	57800	490	796	1042	1242	63100	530	859	1121	1337	68400	561	911	1190	1419
52600	451	734	960	1145	57900	491	798	1043	1244	63200	531	860	1123	1338	68500	562	912	1192	1421
52700	452	735	962	1147	58000	492	799	1045	1246	63300	531	861	1124	1340	68600	562	913	1193	1422
52800	452	736	963	1149	58100	492	800	1046	1248	63400	532	862	1126	1342	68700	563	914	1194	1424
52900	453	737	965	1151	58200	493	801	1048	1250	63500	533	863	1127	1344	68800	564	915	1196	1425
53000	454	739	966	1153	58300	494	803	1050	1252	63600	533	864	1129	1345	68900	564	916	1197	1427
53100	455	740	968	1154	58400	495	804	1051	1253	63700	534	865	1130	1347	69000	565	917	1198	1428
53200	455	741	969	1156	58500	496	805	1053	1255	63800	535	866	1132	1348	69100	566	918	1200	1430
53300	456	742	971	1158	58600	496	806	1054	1257	63900	535	867	1133	1350	69200	566	919	1201	1432
53400	457	743	972	1160	58700	497	808	1056	1259	64000	536	868	1134	1352	69300	567	920	1202	1433
53500	457	744	974	1162	58800	498	809	1058	1261	64100	537	870	1136	1353	69400	568	921	1204	1435
53600	458	746	976	1164	58900	499	810	1059	1263	64200	537	871	1137	1355	69500	568	922	1205	1436
53700	459	747	977	1165	59000	500	811	1061	1265	64300	538	872	1138	1357	69600	569	923	1206	1438
53800	460	748	979	1167	59100	500	813	1062	1267	64400	539	873	1140	1358	69700	570	924	1208	1440
53900	460	749	980	1169	59200	501	814	1064	1269	64500	539	874	1141	1360	69800	570	925	1209	1441
54000	461	750	982	1171	59300	502	815	1065	1270	64600	540	875	1143	1362	69900	571	926	1210	1443
54100	462	751	983	1173	59400	503	816	1067	1272	64700	541	876	1144	1363	70000	572	927	1212	1444
54200	462	753	985	1175	59500	503	817	1068	1274	64800	541	877	1145	1365	70100	572	928	1213	1446
54300	463	754	986	1177	59600	504	818	1070	1276	64900	542	878	1147	1367	70200	573	929	1214	1447

Note: This table shows amounts of child support based on income to the nearest $100. There is a mathematical formula for calculating specific child support amounts between the $100 levels. For more information, please contact the Department of Justice.

Nota: La présente table indique le montant de la pension alimentaire pour enfants à verser d'après le revenu (aux 100 $ près). Il existe une formule mathématique pour calculer le montant exact de la pension alimentaire pour enfants dans le cas des revenus qui se situent entre les tranches de 100 $. Pour plus de renseignements, veuillez communiquer avec le ministère de la Justice.

Divorce

Ontario

FEDERAL CHILD SUPPORT AMOUNTS : SIMPLIFIED TABLES
MONTANTS FÉDÉRAUX DE PENSIONS ALIMENTAIRES POUR ENFANTS : TABLES SIMPLIFIÉES

1997

Income/ Revenu ($)	Monthly Award/ Paiement mensuel ($) No. of Children/ N^{bre} d'enfants				Income/ Revenu ($)	Monthly Award/ Paiement mensuel ($) No. of Children/ N^{bre} d'enfants				Income/ Revenu ($)	Monthly Award/ Paiement mensuel ($) No. of Children/ N^{bre} d'enfants				Income/ Revenu ($)	Monthly Award/ Paiement mensuel ($) No. of Children/ N^{bre} d'enfants			
	1	2	3	4		1	2	3	4		1	2	3	4		1	2	3	4
70300	574	930	1216	1449	75600	609	986	1287	1533	80900	645	1041	1358	1617	86200	680	1096	1429	1701
70400	574	931	1217	1451	75700	610	987	1288	1535	81000	645	1042	1359	1618	86300	681	1097	1430	1702
70500	575	932	1218	1452	75800	611	988	1289	1536	81100	646	1043	1360	1620	86400	682	1098	1431	1704
70600	576	934	1220	1454	75900	611	989	1291	1538	81200	647	1044	1362	1622	86500	682	1099	1433	1705
70700	576	935	1221	1455	76000	612	990	1292	1539	81300	647	1045	1363	1623	86600	683	1100	1434	1707
70800	577	936	1222	1457	76100	613	991	1293	1541	81400	648	1046	1364	1625	86700	684	1101	1435	1709
70900	578	937	1224	1459	76200	613	992	1295	1542	81500	649	1047	1366	1626	86800	684	1102	1437	1710
71000	578	938	1225	1460	76300	614	993	1296	1544	81600	649	1048	1367	1628	86900	685	1103	1438	1712
71100	579	939	1226	1462	76400	615	994	1297	1546	81700	650	1049	1368	1630	87000	686	1104	1439	1713
71200	580	940	1228	1463	76500	615	995	1299	1547	81800	651	1050	1370	1631	87100	686	1105	1441	1715
71300	581	941	1229	1465	76600	616	996	1300	1549	81900	651	1051	1371	1633	87200	687	1106	1442	1717
71400	581	942	1230	1466	76700	617	997	1301	1550	82000	652	1052	1372	1634	87300	688	1107	1443	1718
71500	582	943	1232	1468	76800	617	998	1303	1552	82100	653	1053	1374	1636	87400	688	1109	1445	1720
71600	583	944	1233	1470	76900	618	999	1304	1554	82200	654	1054	1375	1637	87500	689	1110	1446	1721
71700	583	945	1234	1471	77000	619	1000	1305	1555	82300	654	1055	1376	1639	87600	690	1111	1447	1723
71800	584	946	1236	1473	77100	619	1001	1307	1557	82400	655	1056	1378	1641	87700	690	1112	1449	1724
71900	585	947	1237	1474	77200	620	1002	1308	1558	82500	656	1057	1379	1642	87800	691	1113	1450	1726
72000	585	948	1238	1476	77300	621	1003	1309	1560	82600	656	1059	1380	1644	87900	692	1114	1451	1728
72100	586	949	1240	1478	77400	621	1004	1311	1561	82700	657	1060	1382	1645	88000	692	1115	1453	1729
72200	587	950	1241	1479	77500	622	1005	1312	1563	82800	658	1061	1383	1647	88100	693	1116	1454	1731
72300	587	951	1242	1481	77600	623	1006	1313	1565	82900	658	1062	1384	1649	88200	694	1117	1455	1732
72400	588	952	1244	1482	77700	623	1007	1315	1566	83000	659	1063	1386	1650	88300	694	1118	1457	1734
72500	589	953	1245	1484	77800	624	1009	1316	1568	83100	660	1064	1387	1652	88400	695	1119	1458	1736
72600	589	954	1246	1485	77900	625	1010	1317	1569	83200	660	1065	1388	1653	88500	696	1120	1459	1737
72700	590	955	1248	1487	78000	625	1011	1319	1571	83300	661	1066	1390	1655	88600	696	1121	1461	1739
72800	591	956	1249	1489	78100	626	1012	1320	1573	83400	662	1067	1391	1656	88700	697	1122	1462	1740
72900	591	957	1250	1490	78200	627	1013	1321	1574	83500	662	1068	1392	1658	88800	698	1123	1463	1742
73000	592	959	1252	1492	78300	627	1014	1323	1576	83600	663	1069	1394	1660	88900	698	1124	1465	1743
73100	593	960	1253	1493	78400	628	1015	1324	1577	83700	664	1070	1395	1661	89000	699	1125	1466	1745
73200	593	961	1255	1495	78500	629	1016	1325	1579	83800	664	1071	1396	1663	89100	700	1126	1467	1747
73300	594	962	1256	1497	78600	629	1017	1327	1580	83900	665	1072	1398	1664	89200	700	1127	1469	1748
73400	595	963	1257	1498	78700	630	1018	1328	1582	84000	666	1073	1399	1666	89300	701	1128	1470	1750
73500	595	964	1259	1500	78800	631	1019	1330	1584	84100	666	1074	1400	1668	89400	702	1129	1471	1751
73600	596	965	1260	1501	78900	631	1020	1331	1585	84200	667	1075	1402	1669	89500	702	1130	1473	1753
73700	597	966	1261	1503	79000	632	1021	1332	1587	84300	668	1076	1403	1671	89600	703	1131	1474	1755
73800	597	967	1263	1504	79100	633	1022	1334	1588	84400	668	1077	1405	1672	89700	704	1132	1476	1756
73900	598	968	1264	1506	79200	633	1023	1335	1590	84500	669	1078	1406	1674	89800	704	1134	1477	1758
74000	599	969	1265	1508	79300	634	1024	1336	1592	84600	670	1079	1407	1675	89900	705	1135	1478	1759
74100	599	970	1267	1509	79400	635	1025	1338	1593	84700	670	1080	1409	1677	90000	706	1136	1480	1761
74200	600	971	1268	1511	79500	635	1026	1339	1595	84800	671	1081	1410	1679	90100	706	1137	1481	1762
74300	601	972	1269	1512	79600	636	1027	1340	1596	84900	672	1082	1411	1680	90200	707	1138	1482	1764
74400	601	973	1271	1514	79700	637	1028	1342	1598	85000	672	1084	1413	1682	90300	708	1139	1484	1766
74500	602	974	1272	1516	79800	637	1029	1343	1599	85100	673	1085	1414	1683	90400	708	1140	1485	1767
74600	603	975	1273	1517	79900	638	1030	1344	1601	85200	674	1086	1415	1685	90500	709	1141	1486	1769
74700	603	976	1275	1519	80000	639	1031	1346	1603	85300	674	1087	1417	1687	90600	710	1142	1488	1770
74800	604	977	1276	1520	80100	639	1032	1347	1604	85400	675	1088	1418	1688	90700	710	1143	1489	1772
74900	605	978	1277	1522	80200	640	1034	1348	1606	85500	676	1089	1419	1690	90800	711	1144	1490	1774
75000	605	979	1279	1523	80300	641	1035	1350	1607	85600	676	1090	1421	1691	90900	712	1145	1492	1775
75100	606	980	1280	1525	80400	641	1036	1351	1609	85700	677	1091	1422	1693	91000	712	1146	1493	1777
75200	607	981	1281	1527	80500	642	1037	1352	1611	85800	678	1092	1423	1694	91100	713	1147	1494	1778
75300	607	982	1283	1528	80600	643	1038	1354	1612	85900	678	1093	1425	1696	91200	714	1148	1496	1780
75400	608	984	1284	1530	80700	643	1039	1355	1614	86000	679	1094	1426	1698	91300	714	1149	1497	1781
75500	609	985	1285	1531	80800	644	1040	1356	1615	86100	680	1095	1427	1699	91400	715	1150	1498	1783

Note: This table shows amounts of child support based on income to the nearest $100. There is a mathematical formula for calculating specific child support amounts between the $100 levels. For more information, please contact the Department of Justice.

Nota: La présente table indique le montant de la pension alimentaire pour enfants à verser d'après le revenu (aux 100 $ près). Il existe une formule mathématique pour calculer le montant exact de la pension alimentaire pour enfants dans le cas des revenus qui se situent entre les tranches de 100 $. Pour plus de renseignements, veuillez communiquer avec le ministère de la Justice.

Appendix D

ONTARIO

FEDERAL CHILD SUPPORT AMOUNTS : SIMPLIFIED TABLES
MONTANTS FÉDÉRAUX DE PENSIONS ALIMENTAIRES POUR ENFANTS : TABLES SIMPLIFIÉES

1997

Income/ Revenu ($)	Monthly Award/ Paiement mensuel ($) No. of Children/ N^{bre} d'enfants				Income/ Revenu ($)	Monthly Award/ Paiement mensuel ($) No. of Children/ N^{bre} d'enfants				Income/ Revenu ($)	Monthly Award/ Paiement mensuel ($) No. of Children/ N^{bre} d'enfants				Income/ Revenu ($)	Monthly Award/ Paiement mensuel ($) No. of Children/ N^{bre} d'enfants			
	1	2	3	4		1	2	3	4		1	2	3	4		1	2	3	4
112700	858	1372	1784	2120	118000	893	1427	1855	2204	123300	929	1483	1926	2288	128600	964	1538	1997	2372
112800	858	1373	1785	2122	118100	894	1428	1856	2206	123400	929	1484	1927	2290	128700	965	1539	1998	2373
112900	859	1374	1786	2123	118200	895	1429	1857	2207	123500	930	1485	1928	2291	128800	966	1540	1999	2375
113000	860	1375	1788	2125	118300	895	1430	1859	2209	123600	931	1486	1930	2293	128900	966	1541	2001	2377
113100	860	1376	1789	2127	118400	896	1431	1860	2210	123700	931	1487	1931	2294	129000	967	1542	2002	2378
113200	861	1377	1790	2128	118500	897	1433	1861	2212	123800	932	1488	1932	2296	129100	968	1543	2003	2380
113300	862	1378	1792	2130	118600	897	1434	1863	2214	123900	933	1489	1934	2298	129200	968	1544	2005	2381
113400	862	1379	1793	2131	118700	898	1435	1864	2215	124000	933	1490	1935	2299	129300	969	1545	2006	2383
113500	863	1380	1794	2133	118800	899	1436	1865	2217	124100	934	1491	1936	2301	129400	970	1546	2007	2385
113600	864	1381	1796	2134	118900	899	1437	1867	2218	124200	935	1492	1938	2302	129500	970	1547	2009	2386
113700	864	1383	1797	2136	119000	900	1438	1868	2220	124300	935	1493	1939	2304	129600	971	1548	2010	2388
113800	865	1384	1798	2138	119100	901	1439	1869	2222	124400	936	1494	1940	2305	129700	972	1549	2011	2389
113900	866	1385	1800	2139	119200	901	1440	1871	2223	124500	937	1495	1942	2307	129800	972	1550	2013	2391
114000	866	1386	1801	2141	119300	902	1441	1872	2225	124600	937	1496	1943	2309	129900	973	1551	2014	2392
114100	867	1387	1802	2142	119400	903	1442	1873	2226	124700	938	1497	1944	2310	130000	974	1552	2015	2394
114200	868	1388	1804	2144	119500	903	1443	1875	2228	124800	939	1498	1946	2312	130100	974	1553	2017	2396
114300	868	1389	1805	2146	119600	904	1444	1876	2229	124900	939	1499	1947	2313	130200	975	1554	2018	2397
114400	869	1390	1806	2147	119700	905	1445	1877	2231	125000	940	1500	1948	2315	130300	976	1555	2019	2399
114500	870	1391	1808	2149	119800	905	1446	1879	2233	125100	941	1501	1950	2316	130400	976	1556	2021	2400
114600	870	1392	1809	2150	119900	906	1447	1880	2234	125200	941	1502	1951	2318	130500	977	1558	2022	2402
114700	871	1393	1810	2152	120000	907	1448	1881	2236	125300	942	1503	1952	2320	130600	978	1559	2023	2404
114800	872	1394	1812	2153	120100	907	1449	1883	2237	125400	943	1504	1954	2321	130700	978	1560	2025	2405
114900	872	1395	1813	2155	120200	908	1450	1884	2239	125500	943	1505	1955	2323	130800	979	1561	2026	2407
115000	873	1396	1814	2157	120300	909	1451	1885	2241	125600	944	1506	1956	2324	130900	980	1562	2027	2408
115100	874	1397	1816	2158	120400	909	1452	1887	2242	125700	945	1508	1958	2326	131000	980	1563	2029	2410
115200	874	1398	1817	2160	120500	910	1453	1888	2244	125800	945	1509	1959	2328	131100	981	1564	2030	2411
115300	875	1399	1818	2161	120600	911	1454	1889	2245	125900	946	1510	1960	2329	131200	982	1565	2031	2413
115400	876	1400	1820	2163	120700	911	1455	1891	2247	126000	947	1511	1962	2331	131300	982	1566	2033	2415
115500	877	1401	1821	2165	120800	912	1456	1892	2248	126100	947	1512	1963	2332	131400	983	1567	2034	2416
115600	877	1402	1822	2166	120900	913	1458	1893	2250	126200	948	1513	1964	2334	131500	984	1568	2035	2418
115700	878	1403	1824	2168	121000	913	1459	1895	2252	126300	949	1514	1966	2335	131600	984	1569	2037	2419
115800	879	1404	1825	2169	121100	914	1460	1896	2253	126400	950	1515	1967	2337	131700	985	1570	2038	2421
115900	879	1405	1826	2171	121200	915	1461	1897	2255	126500	950	1516	1968	2339	131800	986	1571	2039	2423
116000	880	1406	1828	2172	121300	915	1462	1899	2256	126600	951	1517	1970	2340	131900	986	1572	2041	2424
116100	881	1408	1829	2174	121400	916	1463	1900	2258	126700	952	1518	1971	2342	132000	987	1573	2042	2426
116200	881	1409	1830	2176	121500	917	1464	1901	2260	126800	952	1519	1972	2343	132100	988	1574	2043	2427
116300	882	1410	1832	2177	121600	917	1465	1903	2261	126900	953	1520	1974	2345	132200	988	1575	2045	2429
116400	883	1411	1833	2179	121700	918	1466	1904	2263	127000	954	1521	1975	2347	132300	989	1576	2046	2430
116500	883	1412	1834	2180	121800	919	1467	1905	2264	127100	954	1522	1976	2348	132400	990	1577	2047	2432
116600	884	1413	1836	2182	121900	919	1468	1907	2266	127200	955	1523	1978	2350	132500	990	1578	2049	2434
116700	885	1414	1837	2184	122000	920	1469	1908	2267	127300	956	1524	1979	2351	132600	991	1579	2050	2435
116800	885	1415	1838	2185	122100	921	1470	1909	2269	127400	956	1525	1980	2353	132700	992	1580	2051	2437
116900	886	1416	1840	2187	122200	921	1471	1911	2271	127500	957	1526	1982	2354	132800	992	1581	2053	2438
117000	887	1417	1841	2188	122300	922	1472	1912	2272	127600	958	1527	1983	2356	132900	993	1583	2054	2440
117100	887	1418	1842	2190	122400	923	1473	1913	2274	127700	958	1528	1984	2358	133000	994	1584	2055	2442
117200	888	1419	1844	2191	122500	923	1474	1915	2275	127800	959	1529	1986	2359	133100	994	1585	2057	2443
117300	889	1420	1845	2193	122600	924	1475	1916	2277	127900	960	1530	1987	2361	133200	995	1586	2058	2445
117400	889	1421	1847	2195	122700	925	1476	1917	2279	128000	960	1531	1988	2362	133300	996	1587	2059	2446
117500	890	1422	1848	2196	122800	925	1477	1919	2280	128100	961	1533	1990	2364	133400	996	1588	2061	2448
117600	891	1423	1849	2198	122900	926	1478	1920	2282	128200	962	1534	1991	2366	133500	997	1589	2062	2449
117700	891	1424	1851	2199	123000	927	1479	1922	2283	128300	962	1535	1993	2367	133600	998	1590	2063	2451
117800	892	1425	1852	2201	123100	927	1480	1923	2285	128400	963	1536	1994	2369	133700	998	1591	2065	2453
117900	893	1426	1853	2203	123200	928	1481	1924	2286	128500	964	1537	1995	2370	133800	999	1592	2066	2454

Note: This table shows amounts of child support based on income to the nearest $100. There is a mathematical formula for calculating specific child support amounts between the $100 levels. For more information, please contact the Department of Justice.

Nota: La présente table indique le montant de la pension alimentaire pour enfants à verser d'après le revenu (aux 100 $ près). Il existe une formule mathématique pour calculer le montant exact de la pension alimentaire pour enfants dans le cas des revenus qui se situent entre les tranches de 100 $. Pour plus de renseignements, veuillez communiquer avec le ministère de la Justice.

Divorce

Ontario

Federal Child Support Amounts : Simplified Tables
Montants Fédéraux de Pensions Alimentaires Pour Enfants : Tables Simplifiées

1997

Income/Revenu ($)	Monthly Award/Paiement mensuel ($) No. of Children/N^bre d'enfants				Income/Revenu ($)	Monthly Award/Paiement mensuel ($) No. of Children/N^bre d'enfants				Income/Revenu ($)	Monthly Award/Paiement mensuel ($) No. of Children/N^bre d'enfants				Income/Revenu ($)	Monthly Award/Paiement mensuel ($) No. of Children/N^bre d'enfants				Income/Revenu ($)	Monthly Award/Paiement mensuel ($) No. of Children/N^bre d'enfants			
	1	2	3	4		1	2	3	4		1	2	3	4		1	2	3	4		1	2	3	4
133900	1000	1593	2068	2456	138000	1027	1636	2122	2521	142100	1055	1678	2177	2586	146200	1082	1721	2232	2650					
134000	1000	1594	2069	2457	138100	1028	1637	2124	2522	142200	1055	1679	2179	2587	146300	1083	1722	2234	2652					
134100	1001	1595	2070	2459	138200	1029	1638	2125	2524	142300	1056	1680	2180	2589	146400	1083	1723	2235	2654					
134200	1002	1596	2072	2461	138300	1029	1639	2126	2525	142400	1057	1681	2181	2590	146500	1084	1724	2236	2655					
134300	1002	1597	2073	2462	138400	1030	1640	2128	2527	142500	1057	1683	2183	2592	146600	1085	1725	2238	2657					
134400	1003	1598	2074	2464	138500	1031	1641	2129	2529	142600	1058	1684	2184	2594	146700	1085	1726	2239	2658					
134500	1004	1599	2076	2465	138600	1031	1642	2130	2530	142700	1059	1685	2185	2595	146800	1086	1727	2240	2660					
134600	1004	1600	2077	2467	138700	1032	1643	2132	2532	142800	1059	1686	2187	2597	146900	1087	1728	2242	2662					
134700	1005	1601	2078	2468	138800	1033	1644	2133	2533	142900	1060	1687	2188	2598	147000	1087	1729	2243	2663					
134800	1006	1602	2080	2470	138900	1033	1645	2134	2535	143000	1061	1688	2189	2600	147100	1088	1730	2244	2665					
134900	1006	1603	2081	2472	139000	1034	1646	2136	2537	143100	1061	1689	2191	2601	147200	1089	1731	2246	2666					
135000	1007	1604	2082	2473	139100	1035	1647	2137	2538	143200	1062	1690	2192	2603	147300	1089	1733	2247	2668					
135100	1008	1605	2084	2475	139200	1035	1648	2138	2540	143300	1063	1691	2193	2605	147400	1090	1734	2248	2669					
135200	1008	1606	2085	2476	139300	1036	1649	2140	2541	143400	1063	1692	2195	2606	147500	1091	1735	2250	2671					
135300	1009	1608	2086	2478	139400	1037	1650	2141	2543	143500	1064	1693	2196	2608	147600	1091	1736	2251	2673					
135400	1010	1609	2088	2480	139500	1037	1651	2143	2544	143600	1065	1694	2197	2609	147700	1092	1737	2252	2674					
135500	1010	1610	2089	2481	139600	1038	1652	2144	2546	143700	1065	1695	2199	2611	147800	1093	1738	2254	2676					
135600	1011	1611	2090	2483	139700	1039	1653	2145	2548	143800	1066	1696	2200	2612	147900	1093	1739	2255	2677					
135700	1012	1612	2092	2484	139800	1039	1654	2147	2549	143900	1067	1697	2201	2614	148000	1094	1740	2256	2679					
135800	1012	1613	2093	2486	139900	1040	1655	2148	2551	144000	1067	1698	2203	2616	148100	1095	1741	2258	2681					
135900	1013	1614	2094	2487	140000	1041	1656	2149	2552	144100	1068	1699	2204	2617	148200	1095	1742	2259	2682					
136000	1014	1615	2096	2489	140100	1041	1658	2151	2554	144200	1069	1700	2205	2619	148300	1096	1743	2260	2684					
136100	1014	1616	2097	2491	140200	1042	1659	2152	2556	144300	1069	1701	2207	2620	148400	1097	1744	2262	2685					
136200	1015	1617	2098	2492	140300	1043	1660	2153	2557	144400	1070	1702	2208	2622	148500	1098	1745	2263	2687					
136300	1016	1618	2100	2494	140400	1043	1661	2155	2559	144500	1071	1703	2209	2624	148600	1098	1746	2264	2688					
136400	1016	1619	2101	2495	140500	1044	1662	2156	2560	144600	1071	1704	2211	2625	148700	1099	1747	2266	2690					
136500	1017	1620	2102	2497	140600	1045	1663	2157	2562	144700	1072	1705	2212	2627	148800	1100	1748	2267	2692					
136600	1018	1621	2104	2499	140700	1045	1664	2159	2563	144800	1073	1706	2214	2628	148900	1100	1749	2268	2693					
136700	1018	1622	2105	2500	140800	1046	1665	2160	2565	144900	1073	1708	2215	2630	149000	1101	1750	2270	2695					
136800	1019	1623	2106	2502	140900	1047	1666	2161	2567	145000	1074	1709	2216	2631	149100	1102	1751	2271	2696					
136900	1020	1624	2108	2503	141000	1047	1667	2163	2568	145100	1075	1710	2218	2633	149200	1102	1752	2272	2698					
137000	1020	1625	2109	2505	141100	1048	1668	2164	2570	145200	1075	1711	2219	2635	149300	1103	1753	2274	2700					
137100	1021	1626	2110	2506	141200	1049	1669	2165	2571	145300	1076	1712	2220	2636	149400	1104	1754	2275	2701					
137200	1022	1627	2112	2508	141300	1049	1670	2167	2573	145400	1077	1713	2222	2638	149500	1104	1755	2276	2703					
137300	1023	1628	2113	2510	141400	1050	1671	2168	2575	145500	1077	1714	2223	2639	149600	1105	1756	2278	2704					
137400	1023	1629	2114	2511	141500	1051	1672	2169	2576	145600	1078	1715	2224	2641	149700	1106	1758	2279	2706					
137500	1024	1630	2116	2513	141600	1051	1673	2171	2578	145700	1079	1716	2226	2643	149800	1106	1759	2280	2707					
137600	1025	1631	2117	2514	141700	1052	1674	2172	2579	145800	1079	1717	2227	2644	149900	1107	1760	2282	2709					
137700	1025	1633	2118	2516	141800	1053	1675	2173	2581	145900	1080	1718	2228	2646	150000	1108	1761	2283	2711					
137800	1026	1634	2120	2518	141900	1053	1676	2175	2582	146000	1081	1719	2230	2647										
137900	1027	1635	2121	2519	142000	1054	1677	2176	2584	146100	1081	1720	2231	2649										

Income/Revenu ($)	Monthly Award/Paiement mensuel ($)			
	one child/un enfant	two children/deux enfants	three children/trois enfants	four children/quatre enfants
For income over $150,000	1108 plus 0.67% of income over $150,000	1761 plus 1.04% of income over $150,000	2283 plus 1.34% of income over $150,000	2711 plus 1.58% of income over $150,000
Pour revenu dépassant 150 000$	1108 plus 0,67% du revenu dépassant 150 000$	1761 plus 1,04% du revenu dépassant 150 000$	2283 plus 1,34% du revenu dépassant 150 000$	2711 plus 1,58% du revenu dépassant 150 000$

Note: This table shows amounts of child support based on income to the nearest $100. There is a mathematical formula for calculating specific child support amounts between the $100 levels. For more information, please contact the Department of Justice.

Nota: La présente table indique le montant de la pension alimentaire pour enfants à verser d'après le revenu (aux 100 $ près). Il existe une formule mathématique pour calculer le montant exact de la pension alimentaire pour enfants dans le cas des revenus qui se situent entre les tranches de 100 $. Pour plus de renseignements, veuillez communiquer avec le ministère de la Justice.

Appendix D

PRINCE EDWARD ISLAND/ÎLE DU PRINCE-ÉDOUARD

1997

FEDERAL CHILD SUPPORT AMOUNTS : SIMPLIFIED TABLES
MONTANTS FÉDÉRAUX DE PENSIONS ALIMENTAIRES POUR ENFANTS : TABLES SIMPLIFIÉES

Income/ Revenu ($)	Monthly Award/ Paiement mensuel ($) No. of Children/ N^{bre} d'enfants				Income/ Revenu ($)	Monthly Award/ Paiement mensuel ($) No. of Children/ N^{bre} d'enfants				Income/ Revenu ($)	Monthly Award/ Paiement mensuel ($) No. of Children/ N^{bre} d'enfants				Income/ Revenu ($)	Monthly Award/ Paiement mensuel ($) No. of Children/ N^{bre} d'enfants			
	1	2	3	4		1	2	3	4		1	2	3	4		1	2	3	4
6700	0	0	0	0	12000	96	147	169	191	17300	142	256	338	382	22600	192	334	447	539
6800	0	0	0	0	12100	96	150	172	195	17400	143	257	341	385	22700	193	335	449	541
6900	0	0	0	0	12200	96	153	175	198	17500	144	259	344	389	22800	194	337	450	544
7000	0	1	2	3	12300	96	155	179	202	17600	145	260	347	393	22900	195	338	452	546
7100	3	4	6	7	12400	96	158	182	205	17700	146	261	350	396	23000	196	340	454	548
7200	5	7	9	11	12500	97	161	185	209	17800	147	263	354	400	23100	197	341	456	550
7300	8	10	12	15	12600	98	164	188	213	17900	148	264	357	403	23200	198	342	458	553
7400	10	13	16	18	12700	99	167	191	216	18000	149	266	360	407	23300	199	344	460	555
7500	13	16	19	22	12800	100	169	195	220	18100	150	267	361	410	23400	200	345	462	557
7600	15	19	22	26	12900	101	172	198	223	18200	151	269	363	414	23500	201	347	464	559
7700	18	22	26	30	13000	101	175	201	227	18300	152	270	365	418	23600	202	348	466	561
7800	20	25	29	34	13100	102	178	204	231	18400	153	272	367	421	23700	203	350	467	564
7900	23	28	32	37	13200	103	180	207	234	18500	154	273	369	425	23800	204	351	469	566
8000	25	30	36	41	13300	104	183	210	238	18600	154	275	371	428	23900	205	353	471	568
8100	28	33	39	45	13400	105	186	214	241	18700	155	276	373	432	24000	206	354	473	570
8200	30	36	42	49	13500	106	189	217	245	18800	156	278	375	436	24100	207	356	475	573
8300	33	39	46	52	13600	107	191	220	249	18900	157	279	377	439	24200	208	357	477	575
8400	35	42	49	56	13700	108	194	223	252	19000	158	281	378	443	24300	208	359	479	577
8500	38	45	52	60	13800	109	197	226	256	19100	159	282	380	446	24400	209	360	481	579
8600	40	48	56	64	13900	110	200	230	259	19200	160	284	382	450	24500	210	362	483	582
8700	43	51	59	67	14000	111	202	233	263	19300	161	285	384	454	24600	211	363	485	584
8800	45	54	63	71	14100	112	205	236	267	19400	162	287	386	457	24700	212	365	486	586
8900	48	57	66	75	14200	113	208	239	270	19500	163	288	388	461	24800	213	366	488	588
9000	50	60	69	79	14300	114	211	242	274	19600	164	289	390	464	24900	214	368	490	591
9100	53	63	73	82	14400	115	213	245	277	19700	165	291	392	468	25000	215	369	492	593
9200	55	66	76	86	14500	116	214	249	281	19800	166	292	394	472	25100	216	370	494	595
9300	58	69	79	90	14600	117	216	252	285	19900	167	294	396	475	25200	217	372	496	597
9400	60	71	83	94	14700	118	217	255	288	20000	168	295	397	479	25300	218	373	498	600
9500	63	74	86	98	14800	119	219	258	292	20100	169	297	399	482	25400	219	375	500	602
9600	65	77	89	101	14900	119	220	261	295	20200	170	298	401	485	25500	220	376	502	604
9700	68	80	93	105	15000	120	222	265	299	20300	171	300	403	488	25600	221	378	503	606
9800	70	83	96	109	15100	121	223	268	303	20400	172	301	405	490	25700	222	379	505	608
9900	73	86	99	113	15200	122	225	271	306	20500	172	303	407	492	25800	223	381	507	611
10000	75	89	103	116	15300	123	226	274	310	20600	173	304	409	494	25900	224	382	509	613
10100	78	92	106	120	15400	124	228	277	313	20700	174	306	411	497	26000	224	384	511	615
10200	80	95	109	124	15500	125	229	280	317	20800	175	307	413	499	26100	225	385	513	617
10300	83	98	113	128	15600	126	231	284	321	20900	176	309	414	501	26200	226	386	514	619
10400	85	101	116	131	15700	127	232	287	324	21000	177	310	416	503	26300	227	388	516	621
10500	88	104	119	135	15800	128	233	290	328	21100	178	312	418	506	26400	228	389	518	623
10600	91	107	123	139	15900	129	235	293	331	21200	179	313	420	508	26500	229	390	520	625
10700	93	110	126	143	16000	130	236	296	335	21300	180	314	422	510	26600	230	392	521	628
10800	95	113	129	146	16100	131	238	300	339	21400	181	316	424	512	26700	231	393	523	630
10900	95	115	133	150	16200	132	239	303	342	21500	182	317	426	515	26800	232	395	525	632
11000	96	118	136	154	16300	133	241	306	346	21600	183	319	428	517	26900	232	396	527	634
11100	96	121	140	158	16400	134	242	309	349	21700	184	320	430	519	27000	233	397	528	636
11200	96	124	143	161	16500	135	244	312	353	21800	185	322	432	521	27100	234	399	530	638
11300	96	127	146	165	16600	136	245	315	357	21900	186	323	433	523	27200	235	400	532	640
11400	96	130	150	169	16700	137	247	319	360	22000	187	325	435	526	27300	236	401	534	642
11500	96	133	153	173	16800	137	248	322	364	22100	188	326	437	528	27400	237	403	535	644
11600	96	136	156	177	16900	138	250	325	367	22200	189	328	439	530	27500	238	404	537	646
11700	96	139	160	180	17000	139	251	328	371	22300	190	329	441	532	27600	239	405	539	648
11800	96	142	163	184	17100	140	253	331	375	22400	190	331	443	535	27700	239	407	541	650
11900	96	144	166	188	17200	141	254	334	378	22500	191	332	445	537	27800	240	408	542	652

Note: This table shows amounts of child support based on income to the nearest $100. There is a mathematical formula for calculating specific child support amounts between the $100 levels. For more information, please contact the Department of Justice.

Nota: La présente table indique le montant de la pension alimentaire pour enfants à verser d'après le revenu (aux 100 $ près). Il existe une formule mathématique pour calculer le montant exact de la pension alimentaire pour enfants dans le cas des revenus qui se situent entre les tranches de 100 $. Pour plus de renseignements, veuillez communiquer avec le ministère de la Justice.

Divorce

PRINCE EDWARD ISLAND/ÎLE DU PRINCE-ÉDOUARD

FEDERAL CHILD SUPPORT AMOUNTS : SIMPLIFIED TABLES
MONTANTS FÉDÉRAUX DE PENSIONS ALIMENTAIRES POUR ENFANTS : TABLES SIMPLIFIÉES
1997

Income/Revenu ($)	Monthly Award/Paiement mensuel ($) No. of Children/N^{bre} d'enfants				Income/Revenu ($)	Monthly Award/Paiement mensuel ($) No. of Children/N^{bre} d'enfants				Income/Revenu ($)	Monthly Award/Paiement mensuel ($) No. of Children/N^{bre} d'enfants				Income/Revenu ($)	Monthly Award/Paiement mensuel ($) No. of Children/N^{bre} d'enfants			
	1	2	3	4		1	2	3	4		1	2	3	4		1	2	3	4
27900	241	410	544	654	33200	281	472	624	749	38500	321	534	705	844	43800	363	600	789	943
28000	242	411	546	657	33300	282	473	626	751	38600	322	535	706	846	43900	364	601	790	945
28100	243	412	548	659	33400	283	474	627	753	38700	323	537	708	848	44000	365	602	792	947
28200	244	414	550	661	33500	283	475	629	754	38800	324	538	709	849	44100	366	603	794	949
28300	245	415	551	663	33600	284	476	630	756	38900	324	539	711	851	44200	367	605	795	951
28400	246	416	553	665	33700	285	478	632	758	39000	325	540	712	853	44300	367	606	797	953
28500	246	418	555	667	33800	286	479	633	760	39100	326	541	714	855	44400	368	607	798	955
28600	247	419	557	669	33900	286	480	635	761	39200	327	543	715	857	44500	369	608	800	957
28700	248	420	558	671	34000	287	481	636	763	39300	328	544	717	859	44600	370	610	802	959
28800	249	422	560	673	34100	288	482	638	765	39400	328	545	718	860	44700	371	611	803	961
28900	250	423	562	675	34200	289	483	639	767	39500	329	546	720	862	44800	371	612	805	962
29000	251	425	564	677	34300	289	484	641	768	39600	330	547	722	864	44900	372	613	806	964
29100	252	426	565	679	34400	290	486	642	770	39700	331	549	723	866	45000	373	615	808	966
29200	253	427	567	681	34500	291	487	644	772	39800	331	550	725	868	45100	374	616	810	968
29300	253	429	569	683	34600	292	488	645	774	39900	332	551	726	870	45200	375	617	811	970
29400	254	430	571	686	34700	292	489	647	775	40000	333	552	728	871	45300	375	618	813	972
29500	255	431	572	688	34800	293	490	648	777	40100	334	554	729	873	45400	376	620	814	974
29600	256	433	574	690	34900	294	491	650	779	40200	335	555	731	875	45500	377	621	816	976
29700	257	434	575	691	35000	295	493	651	781	40300	335	556	733	877	45600	378	622	818	978
29800	257	435	577	693	35100	295	494	652	782	40400	336	557	734	879	45700	379	623	819	979
29900	258	436	578	694	35200	296	495	654	784	40500	337	559	736	881	45800	379	625	821	981
30000	259	437	579	696	35300	297	496	655	786	40600	338	560	737	883	45900	380	626	822	983
30100	259	438	581	698	35400	298	497	657	788	40700	339	561	739	885	46000	381	627	824	985
30200	260	439	582	699	35500	298	498	658	789	40800	339	562	741	887	46100	382	628	826	987
30300	261	440	583	701	35600	299	500	660	791	40900	340	564	742	888	46200	383	630	827	989
30400	261	441	585	702	35700	300	501	661	793	41000	341	565	744	890	46300	383	631	829	991
30500	262	442	586	704	35800	300	502	663	795	41100	342	566	745	892	46400	384	632	830	993
30600	263	443	588	706	35900	301	503	664	796	41200	343	567	747	894	46500	385	633	832	995
30700	263	444	589	707	36000	302	504	666	798	41300	343	569	749	896	46600	386	635	834	997
30800	264	445	590	709	36100	303	505	667	800	41400	344	570	750	898	46700	387	636	835	998
30900	265	446	592	710	36200	304	507	669	802	41500	345	571	752	900	46800	387	637	837	1000
31000	265	447	593	712	36300	304	508	671	804	41600	346	572	753	902	46900	388	638	839	1002
31100	266	448	594	714	36400	305	509	672	806	41700	347	574	755	904	47000	389	640	840	1004
31200	267	449	596	715	36500	306	510	674	807	41800	347	575	757	906	47100	390	641	842	1006
31300	268	451	597	717	36600	307	511	675	809	41900	348	576	758	907	47200	391	642	843	1008
31400	268	452	598	718	36700	307	513	677	811	42000	349	577	760	909	47300	392	643	845	1010
31500	269	453	600	720	36800	308	514	678	813	42100	350	579	762	911	47400	392	645	847	1012
31600	270	454	601	722	36900	309	515	680	815	42200	351	580	763	913	47500	393	646	848	1014
31700	270	455	602	723	37000	310	516	681	817	42300	351	581	765	915	47600	394	647	850	1016
31800	271	456	604	725	37100	311	517	683	818	42400	352	582	766	917	47700	395	648	851	1017
31900	272	457	605	726	37200	311	519	684	820	42500	353	584	768	919	47800	396	650	853	1019
32000	272	458	606	728	37300	312	520	686	822	42600	354	585	770	921	47900	396	651	855	1021
32100	273	459	608	730	37400	313	521	688	824	42700	355	586	771	923	48000	397	652	856	1023
32200	274	460	609	731	37500	314	522	689	826	42800	355	587	773	925	48100	398	653	858	1025
32300	274	461	611	733	37600	314	523	691	828	42900	356	589	774	926	48200	399	655	859	1027
32400	275	463	612	735	37700	315	525	692	829	43000	357	590	776	928	48300	400	656	861	1029
32500	276	464	614	737	37800	316	526	694	831	43100	358	591	778	930	48400	400	657	863	1031
32600	277	465	615	738	37900	317	527	695	833	43200	359	592	779	932	48500	401	658	864	1033
32700	277	466	617	740	38000	317	528	697	835	43300	359	594	781	934	48600	402	660	866	1034
32800	278	467	618	742	38100	318	529	698	837	43400	360	595	782	936	48700	403	661	867	1036
32900	279	468	620	744	38200	319	531	700	838	43500	361	596	784	938	48800	404	662	869	1038
33000	280	469	621	745	38300	320	532	701	840	43600	362	597	786	940	48900	404	663	871	1040
33100	280	471	623	747	38400	321	533	703	842	43700	363	598	787	942	49000	405	665	872	1042

Note: This table shows amounts of child support based on income to the nearest $100. There is a mathematical formula for calculating specific child support amounts between the $100 levels. For more information, please contact the Department of Justice.

Nota: La présente table indique le montant de la pension alimentaire pour enfants à verser d'après le revenu (aux 100 $ près). Il existe une formule mathématique pour calculer le montant exact de la pension alimentaire pour enfants dans le cas des revenus qui se situent entre les tranches de 100 $. Pour plus de renseignements, veuillez communiquer avec le ministère de la Justice.

Appendix D

PRINCE EDWARD ISLAND/ÎLE DU PRINCE-ÉDOUARD

FEDERAL CHILD SUPPORT AMOUNTS : SIMPLIFIED TABLES 1997
MONTANTS FÉDÉRAUX DE PENSIONS ALIMENTAIRES POUR ENFANTS : TABLES SIMPLIFIÉES

Income/ Revenu ($)	Monthly Award/ Paiement mensuel ($) No. of Children/ N^{bre} d'enfants				Income/ Revenu ($)	Monthly Award/ Paiement mensuel ($) No. of Children/ N^{bre} d'enfants				Income/ Revenu ($)	Monthly Award/ Paiement mensuel ($) No. of Children/ N^{bre} d'enfants				Income/ Revenu ($)	Monthly Award/ Paiement mensuel ($) No. of Children/ N^{bre} d'enfants			
	1	2	3	4		1	2	3	4		1	2	3	4		1	2	3	4
49100	406	666	874	1044	54400	448	732	959	1144	59700	491	798	1043	1244	65000	528	857	1120	1335
49200	407	667	875	1046	54500	449	733	960	1146	59800	491	799	1045	1246	65100	529	858	1121	1336
49300	408	668	877	1048	54600	450	734	962	1148	59900	492	800	1046	1248	65200	530	859	1122	1338
49400	408	670	879	1050	54700	451	736	964	1150	60000	493	801	1048	1249	65300	530	860	1124	1340
49500	409	671	880	1052	54800	452	737	965	1152	60100	494	802	1049	1251	65400	531	861	1125	1341
49600	410	672	882	1053	54900	452	738	967	1154	60200	494	803	1050	1253	65500	532	862	1127	1343
49700	411	673	883	1055	55000	453	739	968	1156	60300	495	804	1052	1254	65600	532	863	1128	1345
49800	412	675	885	1057	55100	454	741	970	1158	60400	496	806	1053	1256	65700	533	864	1129	1346
49900	412	676	887	1059	55200	455	742	972	1160	60500	496	807	1055	1258	65800	534	865	1131	1348
50000	413	677	888	1061	55300	456	743	973	1161	60600	497	808	1056	1260	65900	534	866	1132	1350
50100	414	678	890	1063	55400	456	744	975	1163	60700	498	809	1058	1261	66000	535	868	1134	1351
50200	415	680	891	1065	55500	457	746	976	1165	60800	499	810	1059	1263	66100	536	869	1135	1353
50300	416	681	893	1067	55600	458	747	978	1167	60900	499	811	1061	1265	66200	536	870	1136	1355
50400	416	682	895	1069	55700	459	748	980	1169	61000	500	812	1062	1267	66300	537	871	1138	1356
50500	417	683	896	1070	55800	460	749	981	1171	61100	501	814	1064	1268	66400	538	872	1139	1358
50600	418	685	898	1072	55900	460	751	983	1173	61200	502	815	1065	1270	66500	538	873	1141	1359
50700	419	686	899	1074	56000	461	752	984	1175	61300	502	816	1067	1272	66600	539	874	1142	1361
50800	420	687	901	1076	56100	462	753	986	1177	61400	503	817	1068	1274	66700	540	875	1143	1363
50900	420	688	903	1078	56200	463	754	988	1179	61500	504	818	1070	1275	66800	540	876	1145	1365
51000	421	690	904	1080	56300	464	756	989	1180	61600	505	819	1071	1277	66900	541	877	1146	1366
51100	422	691	906	1082	56400	464	757	991	1182	61700	505	820	1072	1279	67000	542	878	1148	1368
51200	423	692	907	1084	56500	465	758	993	1184	61800	506	822	1074	1280	67100	543	880	1149	1370
51300	424	693	909	1086	56600	466	759	994	1186	61900	507	823	1075	1282	67200	543	881	1150	1371
51400	424	695	911	1088	56700	467	761	996	1188	62000	507	824	1077	1284	67300	544	882	1152	1373
51500	425	696	912	1089	56800	468	762	997	1190	62100	508	825	1078	1286	67400	545	883	1153	1375
51600	426	697	914	1091	56900	469	763	999	1192	62200	509	826	1080	1287	67500	545	884	1155	1376
51700	427	698	916	1093	57000	469	764	1001	1194	62300	510	827	1081	1289	67600	546	885	1156	1378
51800	428	700	917	1095	57100	470	766	1002	1196	62400	510	828	1083	1291	67700	547	886	1158	1380
51900	428	701	919	1097	57200	471	767	1004	1198	62500	511	830	1084	1293	67800	548	887	1159	1381
52000	429	702	920	1099	57300	472	768	1005	1199	62600	512	831	1086	1294	67900	548	888	1160	1383
52100	430	703	922	1101	57400	473	769	1007	1201	62700	513	832	1087	1296	68000	549	890	1162	1385
52200	431	705	924	1103	57500	473	771	1009	1203	62800	513	833	1089	1298	68100	550	891	1163	1386
52300	432	706	925	1105	57600	474	772	1010	1205	62900	514	834	1090	1300	68200	550	892	1165	1388
52400	432	707	927	1107	57700	475	773	1012	1207	63000	515	835	1092	1301	68300	551	893	1166	1390
52500	433	708	928	1108	57800	476	774	1013	1209	63100	516	836	1093	1303	68400	552	894	1168	1392
52600	434	710	930	1110	57900	477	776	1015	1211	63200	516	838	1095	1305	68500	553	895	1169	1393
52700	435	711	932	1112	58000	477	777	1017	1213	63300	517	839	1096	1307	68600	553	896	1170	1395
52800	436	712	933	1114	58100	478	778	1018	1215	63400	518	840	1097	1308	68700	554	897	1172	1397
52900	436	713	935	1116	58200	479	779	1020	1216	63500	518	841	1099	1310	68800	555	898	1173	1398
53000	437	715	936	1118	58300	480	781	1021	1218	63600	519	842	1100	1312	68900	555	900	1175	1400
53100	438	716	938	1120	58400	481	782	1023	1220	63700	520	843	1102	1313	69000	556	901	1176	1402
53200	439	717	940	1122	58500	481	783	1025	1222	63800	520	844	1103	1315	69100	557	902	1178	1403
53300	440	718	941	1124	58600	482	784	1026	1224	63900	521	845	1104	1317	69200	558	903	1179	1405
53400	440	720	943	1125	58700	483	786	1028	1226	64000	522	846	1106	1318	69300	558	904	1180	1407
53500	441	721	944	1127	58800	484	787	1029	1228	64100	522	847	1107	1320	69400	559	905	1182	1408
53600	442	722	946	1129	58900	485	788	1031	1230	64200	523	848	1109	1321	69500	560	906	1183	1410
53700	443	723	948	1131	59000	485	789	1033	1232	64300	524	849	1110	1323	69600	560	907	1185	1412
53800	444	725	949	1133	59100	486	791	1034	1234	64400	524	851	1111	1325	69700	561	908	1186	1413
53900	444	726	951	1135	59200	487	792	1036	1235	64500	525	852	1113	1326	69800	562	910	1188	1415
54000	445	727	952	1137	59300	488	793	1037	1237	64600	526	853	1114	1328	69900	563	911	1189	1417
54100	446	728	954	1139	59400	488	794	1039	1239	64700	526	854	1116	1330	70000	563	912	1190	1419
54200	447	730	956	1141	59500	489	795	1040	1241	64800	527	855	1117	1331	70100	564	913	1192	1420
54300	448	731	957	1143	59600	490	796	1042	1242	64900	528	856	1118	1333	70200	565	914	1193	1422

Note: This table shows amounts of child support based on income to the nearest $100. There is a mathematical formula for calculating specific child support amounts between the $100 levels. For more information, please contact the Department of Justice.

Nota: La présente table indique le montant de la pension alimentaire pour enfants à verser d'après le revenu (aux 100 $ près). Il existe une formule mathématique pour calculer le montant exact de la pension alimentaire pour enfants dans le cas des revenus qui se situent entre les tranches de 100 $. Pour plus de renseignements, veuillez communiquer avec le ministère de la Justice.

Divorce

PRINCE EDWARD ISLAND/ÎLE DU PRINCE-ÉDOUARD

FEDERAL CHILD SUPPORT AMOUNTS : SIMPLIFIED TABLES
MONTANTS FÉDÉRAUX DE PENSIONS ALIMENTAIRES POUR ENFANTS : TABLES SIMPLIFIÉES

1997

Income/ Revenu ($)	Monthly Award/ Paiement mensuel ($) No. of Children/ N^bre d'enfants				Income/ Revenu ($)	Monthly Award/ Paiement mensuel ($) No. of Children/ N^bre d'enfants				Income/ Revenu ($)	Monthly Award/ Paiement mensuel ($) No. of Children/ N^bre d'enfants				Income/ Revenu ($)	Monthly Award/ Paiement mensuel ($) No. of Children/ N^bre d'enfants			
	1	2	3	4		1	2	3	4		1	2	3	4		1	2	3	4
70300	565	915	1195	1424	75600	603	974	1270	1513	80900	641	1033	1346	1603	86200	679	1092	1422	1692
70400	566	916	1196	1425	75700	604	975	1272	1515	81000	642	1034	1348	1604	86300	680	1093	1423	1694
70500	567	917	1198	1427	75800	605	976	1273	1516	81100	643	1035	1349	1606	86400	680	1094	1425	1695
70600	568	918	1199	1429	75900	605	977	1275	1518	81200	643	1036	1350	1608	86500	681	1095	1426	1697
70700	568	920	1200	1430	76000	606	978	1276	1520	81300	644	1037	1352	1609	86600	682	1096	1428	1699
70800	569	921	1202	1432	76100	607	980	1278	1522	81400	645	1038	1353	1611	86700	683	1097	1429	1700
70900	570	922	1203	1434	76200	608	981	1279	1523	81500	645	1040	1355	1613	86800	683	1098	1430	1702
71000	570	923	1205	1435	76300	608	982	1280	1525	81600	646	1041	1356	1614	86900	684	1100	1432	1704
71100	571	924	1206	1437	76400	609	983	1282	1527	81700	647	1042	1358	1616	87000	685	1101	1433	1706
71200	572	925	1208	1439	76500	610	984	1283	1528	81800	648	1043	1359	1618	87100	685	1102	1435	1707
71300	573	926	1209	1440	76600	610	985	1285	1530	81900	648	1044	1360	1619	87200	686	1103	1436	1709
71400	573	927	1210	1442	76700	611	986	1286	1532	82000	649	1045	1362	1621	87300	687	1104	1438	1711
71500	574	928	1212	1444	76800	612	987	1288	1533	82100	650	1046	1363	1623	87400	688	1105	1439	1712
71600	575	930	1213	1446	76900	613	988	1289	1535	82200	650	1047	1365	1625	87500	688	1106	1440	1714
71700	575	931	1215	1447	77000	613	990	1290	1537	82300	651	1048	1366	1626	87600	689	1107	1442	1716
71800	576	932	1216	1449	77100	614	991	1292	1538	82400	652	1050	1368	1628	87700	690	1108	1443	1717
71900	577	933	1218	1451	77200	615	992	1293	1540	82500	653	1051	1369	1630	87800	690	1110	1445	1719
72000	578	934	1219	1452	77300	615	993	1295	1542	82600	653	1052	1370	1631	87900	691	1111	1446	1721
72100	578	935	1220	1454	77400	616	994	1296	1543	82700	654	1053	1372	1633	88000	692	1112	1448	1722
72200	579	936	1222	1456	77500	617	995	1298	1545	82800	655	1054	1373	1635	88100	693	1113	1449	1724
72300	580	937	1223	1457	77600	618	996	1299	1547	82900	655	1055	1375	1636	88200	693	1114	1450	1726
72400	580	938	1225	1459	77700	618	997	1300	1549	83000	656	1056	1376	1638	88300	694	1115	1452	1727
72500	581	940	1226	1461	77800	619	998	1302	1550	83100	657	1057	1378	1640	88400	695	1116	1453	1729
72600	582	941	1228	1462	77900	620	1000	1303	1552	83200	658	1058	1379	1641	88500	695	1117	1455	1731
72700	583	942	1229	1464	78000	620	1001	1305	1554	83300	658	1060	1380	1643	88600	696	1118	1456	1733
72800	583	943	1230	1466	78100	621	1002	1306	1555	83400	659	1061	1382	1645	88700	697	1120	1458	1734
72900	584	944	1232	1467	78200	622	1003	1308	1557	83500	660	1062	1383	1646	88800	698	1121	1459	1736
73000	585	945	1233	1469	78300	623	1004	1309	1559	83600	660	1063	1385	1648	88900	698	1122	1460	1738
73100	585	946	1235	1471	78400	623	1005	1310	1560	83700	661	1064	1386	1650	89000	699	1123	1462	1739
73200	586	947	1236	1473	78500	624	1006	1312	1562	83800	662	1065	1388	1652	89100	700	1124	1463	1741
73300	587	948	1238	1474	78600	625	1007	1313	1564	83900	663	1066	1389	1653	89200	700	1125	1465	1743
73400	588	950	1239	1476	78700	625	1008	1315	1565	84000	663	1067	1390	1655	89300	701	1126	1466	1744
73500	588	951	1240	1478	78800	626	1010	1316	1567	84100	664	1068	1392	1657	89400	702	1127	1468	1746
73600	589	952	1242	1479	78900	627	1011	1318	1569	84200	665	1070	1393	1658	89500	703	1128	1469	1748
73700	590	953	1243	1481	79000	628	1012	1319	1570	84300	665	1071	1395	1660	89600	703	1130	1470	1749
73800	590	954	1245	1483	79100	628	1013	1320	1572	84400	666	1072	1396	1662	89700	704	1131	1472	1751
73900	591	955	1246	1484	79200	629	1014	1322	1574	84500	667	1073	1398	1663	89800	705	1132	1473	1753
74000	592	956	1248	1486	79300	630	1015	1323	1576	84600	668	1074	1399	1665	89900	705	1133	1475	1754
74100	593	957	1249	1488	79400	630	1016	1325	1577	84700	668	1075	1400	1667	90000	706	1134	1476	1756
74200	593	958	1250	1489	79500	631	1017	1326	1579	84800	669	1076	1402	1668	90100	707	1135	1478	1758
74300	594	960	1252	1491	79600	632	1018	1328	1581	84900	670	1077	1403	1670	90200	708	1136	1479	1760
74400	595	961	1253	1493	79700	633	1020	1329	1582	85000	670	1078	1405	1672	90300	708	1137	1480	1761
74500	595	962	1255	1495	79800	633	1021	1330	1584	85100	671	1080	1406	1673	90400	709	1138	1482	1763
74600	596	963	1256	1496	79900	634	1022	1332	1586	85200	672	1081	1408	1675	90500	710	1140	1483	1765
74700	597	964	1258	1498	80000	635	1023	1333	1587	85300	673	1082	1409	1677	90600	710	1141	1485	1766
74800	598	965	1259	1500	80100	635	1024	1335	1589	85400	673	1083	1410	1679	90700	711	1142	1486	1768
74900	598	966	1260	1501	80200	636	1025	1336	1591	85500	674	1084	1412	1680	90800	712	1143	1488	1770
75000	599	967	1262	1503	80300	637	1026	1338	1592	85600	675	1085	1413	1682	90900	713	1144	1489	1771
75100	600	968	1263	1505	80400	638	1027	1339	1594	85700	675	1086	1415	1684	91000	713	1145	1490	1773
75200	600	970	1265	1506	80500	638	1028	1340	1596	85800	676	1087	1416	1685	91100	714	1146	1492	1775
75300	601	971	1266	1508	80600	639	1030	1342	1597	85900	677	1088	1418	1687	91200	715	1147	1493	1776
75400	602	972	1268	1510	80700	640	1031	1343	1599	86000	678	1090	1419	1689	91300	715	1148	1495	1778
75500	603	973	1269	1511	80800	640	1032	1345	1601	86100	678	1091	1420	1690	91400	716	1150	1496	1780

Note: This table shows amounts of child support based on income to the nearest $100. There is a mathematical formula for calculating specific child support amounts between the $100 levels. For more information, please contact the Department of Justice.

Nota: La présente table indique le montant de la pension alimentaire pour enfants à verser d'après le revenu (aux 100 $ près). Il existe une formule mathématique pour calculer le montant exact de la pension alimentaire pour enfants dans le cas des revenus qui se situent entre les tranches de 100 $. Pour plus de renseignements, veuillez communiquer avec le ministère de la Justice.

Appendix D

PRINCE EDWARD ISLAND/ÎLE DU PRINCE-ÉDOUARD

1997

FEDERAL CHILD SUPPORT AMOUNTS : SIMPLIFIED TABLES
MONTANTS FÉDÉRAUX DE PENSIONS ALIMENTAIRES POUR ENFANTS : TABLES SIMPLIFIÉES

Income/ Revenu ($)	Monthly Award/ Paiement mensuel ($) No. of Children/ N^{bre} d'enfants				Income/ Revenu ($)	Monthly Award/ Paiement mensuel ($) No. of Children/ N^{bre} d'enfants				Income/ Revenu ($)	Monthly Award/ Paiement mensuel ($) No. of Children/ N^{bre} d'enfants				Income/ Revenu ($)	Monthly Award/ Paiement mensuel ($) No. of Children/ N^{bre} d'enfants			
	1	2	3	4		1	2	3	4		1	2	3	4		1	2	3	4
91500	717	1151	1498	1782	96800	752	1206	1570	1867	102100	788	1263	1643	1954	107400	825	1320	1716	2040
91600	718	1152	1499	1783	96900	753	1207	1571	1869	102200	789	1264	1644	1955	107500	826	1321	1718	2042
91700	718	1153	1500	1785	97000	753	1208	1573	1871	102300	790	1265	1646	1957	107600	826	1322	1719	2044
91800	719	1154	1502	1787	97100	754	1210	1574	1872	102400	791	1266	1647	1959	107700	827	1323	1720	2045
91900	720	1155	1503	1788	97200	755	1211	1575	1874	102500	791	1268	1649	1960	107800	828	1324	1722	2047
92000	720	1156	1505	1790	97300	755	1212	1577	1875	102600	792	1269	1650	1962	107900	829	1326	1723	2048
92100	721	1157	1506	1792	97400	756	1213	1578	1877	102700	793	1270	1651	1964	108000	829	1327	1724	2050
92200	722	1158	1508	1793	97500	757	1214	1580	1879	102800	793	1271	1653	1965	108100	830	1328	1726	2052
92300	723	1160	1509	1795	97600	757	1215	1581	1880	102900	794	1272	1654	1967	108200	831	1329	1727	2053
92400	723	1161	1510	1797	97700	758	1216	1582	1882	103000	795	1273	1655	1968	108300	831	1330	1729	2055
92500	724	1162	1512	1798	97800	759	1217	1584	1884	103100	795	1274	1657	1970	108400	832	1331	1730	2057
92600	725	1163	1513	1800	97900	759	1218	1585	1885	103200	796	1275	1658	1972	108500	833	1332	1731	2058
92700	725	1164	1515	1802	98000	760	1219	1586	1887	103300	797	1276	1660	1973	108600	833	1333	1733	2060
92800	726	1165	1516	1803	98100	761	1220	1588	1889	103400	797	1277	1661	1975	108700	834	1334	1734	2061
92900	727	1166	1517	1805	98200	762	1221	1589	1890	103500	798	1278	1662	1977	108800	835	1335	1736	2063
93000	727	1167	1519	1807	98300	762	1222	1591	1892	103600	799	1279	1664	1978	108900	835	1336	1737	2065
93100	728	1168	1520	1808	98400	763	1224	1592	1893	103700	800	1280	1665	1980	109000	836	1337	1738	2066
93200	729	1169	1521	1810	98500	764	1225	1593	1895	103800	800	1281	1667	1982	109100	837	1338	1740	2068
93300	729	1170	1523	1811	98600	764	1226	1595	1897	103900	801	1283	1668	1983	109200	837	1339	1741	2070
93400	730	1171	1524	1813	98700	765	1227	1596	1898	104000	802	1284	1669	1985	109300	838	1341	1742	2071
93500	731	1172	1525	1815	98800	766	1228	1597	1900	104100	802	1285	1671	1986	109400	839	1342	1744	2073
93600	731	1173	1527	1816	98900	766	1229	1599	1902	104200	803	1286	1672	1988	109500	840	1343	1745	2075
93700	732	1174	1528	1818	99000	767	1230	1600	1903	104300	804	1287	1673	1990	109600	840	1344	1747	2076
93800	732	1175	1529	1819	99100	768	1231	1602	1905	104400	804	1288	1675	1991	109700	841	1345	1748	2078
93900	733	1176	1531	1821	99200	768	1232	1603	1906	104500	805	1289	1676	1993	109800	842	1346	1749	2079
94000	734	1177	1532	1822	99300	769	1233	1604	1908	104600	806	1290	1678	1995	109900	842	1347	1751	2081
94100	734	1178	1533	1824	99400	770	1234	1606	1910	104700	806	1291	1679	1996	110000	843	1348	1752	2083
94200	735	1179	1535	1826	99500	771	1235	1607	1911	104800	807	1292	1680	1998	110100	844	1349	1753	2084
94300	736	1180	1536	1827	99600	771	1236	1609	1913	104900	808	1293	1682	1999	110200	844	1350	1755	2086
94400	736	1181	1537	1829	99700	772	1237	1610	1915	105000	808	1294	1683	2001	110300	845	1351	1756	2088
94500	737	1182	1539	1830	99800	773	1239	1611	1916	105100	809	1295	1684	2003	110400	846	1352	1758	2089
94600	737	1183	1540	1832	99900	773	1240	1613	1918	105200	810	1297	1686	2004	110500	846	1353	1759	2091
94700	738	1184	1541	1834	100000	774	1241	1614	1920	105300	811	1298	1687	2006	110600	847	1354	1760	2092
94800	739	1185	1543	1835	100100	775	1242	1615	1921	105400	811	1299	1689	2008	110700	848	1356	1762	2094
94900	739	1186	1544	1837	100200	775	1243	1617	1923	105500	812	1300	1690	2009	110800	849	1357	1763	2096
95000	740	1187	1545	1838	100300	776	1244	1618	1924	105600	813	1301	1691	2011	110900	849	1358	1765	2097
95100	741	1189	1547	1840	100400	777	1245	1620	1926	105700	813	1302	1693	2013	111000	850	1359	1766	2099
95200	741	1190	1548	1842	100500	777	1246	1621	1928	105800	814	1303	1694	2014	111100	851	1360	1767	2101
95300	742	1191	1549	1843	100600	778	1247	1622	1929	105900	815	1304	1695	2016	111200	851	1361	1769	2102
95400	743	1192	1551	1845	100700	779	1248	1624	1931	106000	815	1305	1697	2017	111300	852	1362	1770	2104
95500	743	1193	1552	1846	100800	779	1249	1625	1933	106100	816	1306	1698	2019	111400	853	1363	1771	2106
95600	744	1194	1553	1848	100900	780	1250	1626	1934	106200	817	1307	1700	2021	111500	853	1364	1773	2107
95700	744	1195	1555	1849	101000	781	1251	1628	1936	106300	817	1308	1701	2022	111600	854	1365	1774	2109
95800	745	1196	1556	1851	101100	782	1252	1629	1937	106400	818	1309	1702	2024	111700	855	1366	1776	2110
95900	746	1197	1557	1853	101200	782	1254	1631	1939	106500	819	1310	1704	2026	111800	855	1367	1777	2112
96000	746	1198	1559	1854	101300	783	1255	1632	1941	106600	820	1312	1705	2027	111900	856	1368	1778	2114
96100	747	1199	1560	1856	101400	784	1256	1633	1942	106700	820	1313	1707	2029	112000	857	1370	1780	2115
96200	748	1200	1562	1858	101500	784	1257	1635	1944	106800	821	1314	1708	2030	112100	857	1371	1781	2117
96300	748	1201	1563	1859	101600	785	1258	1636	1946	106900	822	1315	1709	2032	112200	858	1372	1782	2119
96400	749	1202	1564	1861	101700	786	1259	1638	1947	107000	822	1316	1711	2034	112300	859	1373	1784	2120
96500	750	1203	1566	1862	101800	786	1260	1639	1949	107100	823	1317	1712	2035	112400	860	1374	1785	2122
96600	750	1204	1567	1864	101900	787	1261	1640	1951	107200	824	1318	1713	2037	112500	860	1375	1787	2123
96700	751	1205	1568	1866	102000	788	1262	1642	1952	107300	824	1319	1715	2039	112600	861	1376	1788	2125

Note: This table shows amounts of child support based on income to the nearest $100. There is a mathematical formula for calculating specific child support amounts between the $100 levels. For more information, please contact the Department of Justice.

Nota: La présente table indique le montant de la pension alimentaire pour enfants à verser d'après le revenu (aux 100 $ près). Il existe une formule mathématique pour calculer le montant exact de la pension alimentaire pour enfants dans le cas des revenus qui se situent entre les tranches de 100 $. Pour plus de renseignements, veuillez communiquer avec le ministère de la Justice.

Divorce

PRINCE EDWARD ISLAND/ÎLE DU PRINCE-ÉDOUARD

FEDERAL CHILD SUPPORT AMOUNTS : SIMPLIFIED TABLES
MONTANTS FÉDÉRAUX DE PENSIONS ALIMENTAIRES POUR ENFANTS : TABLES SIMPLIFIÉES

1997

Income/Revenu ($)	Monthly Award/Paiement mensuel ($) No. of Children/N^{bre} d'enfants				Income/Revenu ($)	Monthly Award/Paiement mensuel ($) No. of Children/N^{bre} d'enfants				Income/Revenu ($)	Monthly Award/Paiement mensuel ($) No. of Children/N^{bre} d'enfants				Income/Revenu ($)	Monthly Award/Paiement mensuel ($) No. of Children/N^{bre} d'enfants			
	1	2	3	4		1	2	3	4		1	2	3	4		1	2	3	4
112700	862	1377	1789	2127	118000	898	1434	1863	2213	123300	935	1491	1936	2300	128600	971	1548	2009	2386
112800	862	1378	1791	2128	118100	899	1435	1864	2215	123400	935	1492	1937	2301	128700	972	1549	2010	2388
112900	863	1379	1792	2130	118200	900	1436	1865	2216	123500	936	1493	1938	2303	128800	973	1550	2012	2389
113000	864	1380	1794	2132	118300	900	1437	1867	2218	123600	937	1494	1940	2305	128900	973	1551	2013	2391
113100	864	1381	1795	2133	118400	901	1438	1868	2220	123700	938	1495	1941	2306	129000	974	1552	2014	2393
113200	865	1382	1796	2135	118500	902	1439	1869	2221	123800	938	1496	1943	2308	129100	975	1553	2016	2394
113300	866	1383	1798	2137	118600	902	1440	1871	2223	123900	939	1497	1944	2309	129200	976	1554	2017	2396
113400	866	1385	1799	2138	118700	903	1441	1872	2225	124000	940	1498	1945	2311	129300	976	1555	2019	2398
113500	867	1386	1800	2140	118800	904	1443	1874	2226	124100	940	1499	1947	2313	129400	977	1556	2020	2399
113600	868	1387	1802	2141	118900	904	1444	1875	2228	124200	941	1501	1948	2314	129500	978	1557	2021	2401
113700	869	1388	1803	2143	119000	905	1445	1876	2230	124300	942	1502	1950	2316	129600	978	1559	2023	2402
113800	869	1389	1805	2145	119100	906	1446	1878	2231	124400	942	1503	1951	2318	129700	979	1560	2024	2404
113900	870	1390	1806	2146	119200	907	1447	1879	2233	124500	943	1504	1952	2319	129800	980	1561	2025	2406
114000	871	1391	1807	2148	119300	907	1448	1880	2234	124600	944	1505	1954	2321	129900	980	1562	2027	2407
114100	871	1392	1809	2150	119400	908	1449	1882	2236	124700	944	1506	1955	2323	130000	981	1563	2028	2409
114200	872	1393	1810	2151	119500	909	1450	1883	2238	124800	945	1507	1956	2324	130100	982	1564	2030	2411
114300	873	1394	1811	2153	119600	909	1451	1885	2239	124900	946	1508	1958	2326	130200	982	1565	2031	2412
114400	873	1395	1813	2154	119700	910	1452	1886	2241	125000	947	1509	1959	2327	130300	983	1566	2032	2414
114500	874	1396	1814	2156	119800	911	1453	1887	2243	125100	947	1510	1961	2329	130400	984	1567	2034	2416
114600	875	1397	1816	2158	119900	911	1454	1889	2244	125200	948	1511	1962	2331	130500	985	1568	2035	2417
114700	875	1399	1817	2159	120000	912	1455	1890	2246	125300	949	1512	1963	2332	130600	985	1569	2036	2419
114800	876	1400	1818	2161	120100	913	1457	1892	2247	125400	949	1513	1965	2334	130700	986	1570	2038	2420
114900	877	1401	1820	2163	120200	913	1458	1893	2249	125500	950	1514	1966	2336	130800	987	1571	2039	2422
115000	878	1402	1821	2164	120300	914	1459	1894	2251	125600	951	1516	1967	2337	130900	987	1572	2041	2424
115100	878	1403	1823	2166	120400	915	1460	1896	2252	125700	951	1517	1969	2339	131000	988	1574	2042	2425
115200	879	1404	1824	2168	120500	915	1461	1897	2254	125800	952	1518	1970	2340	131100	989	1575	2043	2427
115300	880	1405	1825	2169	120600	916	1462	1898	2256	125900	953	1519	1972	2342	131200	989	1576	2045	2429
115400	880	1406	1827	2171	120700	917	1463	1900	2257	126000	953	1520	1973	2344	131300	990	1577	2046	2430
115500	881	1407	1828	2172	120800	918	1464	1901	2259	126100	954	1521	1974	2345	131400	991	1578	2048	2432
115600	882	1408	1829	2174	120900	918	1465	1903	2261	126200	955	1522	1976	2347	131500	991	1579	2049	2433
115700	882	1409	1831	2176	121000	919	1466	1904	2262	126300	956	1523	1977	2349	131600	992	1580	2050	2435
115800	883	1410	1832	2177	121100	920	1467	1905	2264	126400	956	1524	1979	2350	131700	993	1581	2052	2437
115900	884	1411	1834	2179	121200	920	1468	1907	2265	126500	957	1525	1980	2352	131800	993	1582	2053	2438
116000	884	1412	1835	2181	121300	921	1469	1908	2267	126600	958	1526	1981	2354	131900	994	1583	2054	2440
116100	885	1414	1836	2182	121400	922	1470	1909	2269	126700	958	1527	1983	2355	132000	995	1584	2056	2442
116200	886	1415	1838	2184	121500	922	1472	1911	2270	126800	959	1528	1984	2357	132100	996	1585	2057	2443
116300	886	1416	1839	2185	121600	923	1473	1912	2272	126900	960	1530	1985	2358	132200	996	1586	2059	2445
116400	887	1417	1840	2187	121700	924	1474	1914	2274	127000	960	1531	1987	2360	132300	997	1588	2060	2447
116500	888	1418	1842	2189	121800	924	1475	1915	2275	127100	961	1532	1988	2362	132400	998	1589	2061	2448
116600	889	1419	1843	2190	121900	925	1476	1916	2277	127200	962	1533	1990	2363	132500	998	1590	2063	2450
116700	889	1420	1845	2192	122000	926	1477	1918	2278	127300	962	1534	1991	2365	132600	999	1591	2064	2451
116800	890	1421	1846	2194	122100	927	1478	1919	2280	127400	963	1535	1992	2367	132700	1000	1592	2065	2453
116900	891	1422	1847	2195	122200	927	1479	1921	2282	127500	964	1536	1994	2368	132800	1000	1593	2067	2455
117000	891	1423	1849	2197	122300	928	1480	1922	2283	127600	964	1537	1995	2370	132900	1001	1594	2068	2456
117100	892	1424	1850	2199	122400	929	1481	1923	2285	127700	965	1538	1996	2371	133000	1002	1595	2070	2458
117200	893	1425	1851	2200	122500	929	1482	1925	2287	127800	966	1539	1998	2373	133100	1002	1596	2071	2460
117300	893	1426	1853	2202	122600	930	1483	1926	2288	127900	967	1540	1999	2375	133200	1003	1597	2072	2461
117400	894	1428	1854	2203	122700	931	1484	1927	2290	128000	967	1541	2001	2376	133300	1004	1598	2074	2463
117500	895	1429	1856	2205	122800	931	1485	1929	2292	128100	968	1542	2002	2378	133400	1005	1599	2075	2464
117600	895	1430	1857	2207	122900	932	1487	1930	2293	128200	969	1543	2003	2380	133500	1005	1600	2077	2466
117700	896	1431	1858	2208	123000	933	1488	1932	2295	128300	969	1545	2005	2381	133600	1006	1601	2078	2468
117800	897	1432	1860	2210	123100	933	1489	1933	2296	128400	970	1546	2006	2383	133700	1007	1603	2079	2469
117900	898	1433	1861	2212	123200	934	1490	1934	2298	128500	971	1547	2008	2385	133800	1007	1604	2081	2471

Note: This table shows amounts of child support based on income to the nearest $100. There is a mathematical formula for calculating specific child support amounts between the $100 levels. For more information, please contact the Department of Justice.

Nota: La présente table indique le montant de la pension alimentaire pour enfants à verser d'après le revenu (aux 100 $ près). Il existe une formule mathématique pour calculer le montant exact de la pension alimentaire pour enfants dans le cas des revenus qui se situent entre les tranches de 100 $. Pour plus de renseignements, veuillez communiquer avec le ministère de la Justice.

Appendix D

PRINCE EDWARD ISLAND/ÎLE DU PRINCE-ÉDOUARD

FEDERAL CHILD SUPPORT AMOUNTS : SIMPLIFIED TABLES
MONTANTS FÉDÉRAUX DE PENSIONS ALIMENTAIRES POUR ENFANTS : TABLES SIMPLIFIÉES

1997

Income/Revenu ($)	Monthly Award/Paiement mensuel ($) No. of Children/N^bre d'enfants				Income/Revenu ($)	Monthly Award/Paiement mensuel ($) No. of Children/N^bre d'enfants				Income/Revenu ($)	Monthly Award/Paiement mensuel ($) No. of Children/N^bre d'enfants				Income/Revenu ($)	Monthly Award/Paiement mensuel ($) No. of Children/N^bre d'enfants			
	1	2	3	4		1	2	3	4		1	2	3	4		1	2	3	4
133900	1008	1605	2082	2473	138000	1036	1649	2139	2540	142100	1065	1693	2195	2606	146200	1093	1737	2252	2673
134000	1009	1606	2083	2474	138100	1037	1650	2140	2541	142200	1065	1694	2197	2608	146300	1094	1738	2253	2675
134100	1009	1607	2085	2476	138200	1038	1651	2141	2543	142300	1066	1695	2198	2610	146400	1094	1739	2255	2677
134200	1010	1608	2086	2478	138300	1038	1652	2143	2544	142400	1067	1696	2199	2611	146500	1095	1740	2256	2678
134300	1011	1609	2088	2479	138400	1039	1653	2144	2546	142500	1067	1697	2201	2613	146600	1096	1741	2257	2680
134400	1011	1610	2089	2481	138500	1040	1654	2146	2548	142600	1068	1698	2202	2615	146700	1096	1742	2259	2681
134500	1012	1611	2090	2482	138600	1040	1655	2147	2549	142700	1069	1699	2204	2616	146800	1097	1743	2260	2683
134600	1013	1612	2092	2484	138700	1041	1656	2148	2551	142800	1069	1700	2205	2618	146900	1098	1744	2262	2685
134700	1013	1613	2093	2486	138800	1042	1657	2150	2553	142900	1070	1701	2206	2619	147000	1098	1745	2263	2686
134800	1014	1614	2094	2487	138900	1042	1658	2151	2554	143000	1071	1702	2208	2621	147100	1099	1746	2264	2688
134900	1015	1615	2096	2489	139000	1043	1659	2152	2556	143100	1071	1703	2209	2623	147200	1100	1747	2266	2690
135000	1016	1616	2097	2491	139100	1044	1661	2154	2557	143200	1072	1705	2210	2624	147300	1100	1749	2267	2691
135100	1016	1618	2099	2492	139200	1045	1662	2155	2559	143300	1073	1706	2212	2626	147400	1101	1750	2268	2693
135200	1017	1619	2100	2494	139300	1045	1663	2157	2561	143400	1074	1707	2213	2628	147500	1102	1751	2270	2695
135300	1018	1620	2101	2495	139400	1046	1664	2158	2562	143500	1074	1708	2215	2629	147600	1103	1752	2271	2696
135400	1018	1621	2103	2497	139500	1047	1665	2159	2564	143600	1075	1709	2216	2631	147700	1103	1753	2273	2698
135500	1019	1622	2104	2499	139600	1047	1666	2161	2566	143700	1076	1710	2217	2633	147800	1104	1754	2274	2699
135600	1020	1623	2106	2500	139700	1048	1667	2162	2567	143800	1076	1711	2219	2634	147900	1105	1755	2275	2701
135700	1020	1624	2107	2502	139800	1049	1668	2164	2569	143900	1077	1712	2220	2636	148000	1105	1756	2277	2703
135800	1021	1625	2108	2504	139900	1049	1669	2165	2571	144000	1078	1713	2221	2637	148100	1106	1757	2278	2704
135900	1022	1626	2110	2505	140000	1050	1670	2167	2572	144100	1078	1714	2223	2639	148200	1107	1758	2279	2706
136000	1022	1627	2111	2507	140100	1051	1671	2168	2574	144200	1079	1715	2224	2641	148300	1107	1759	2281	2708
136100	1023	1628	2112	2509	140200	1051	1672	2169	2575	144300	1080	1716	2226	2642	148400	1108	1760	2282	2709
136200	1024	1629	2114	2510	140300	1052	1673	2170	2577	144400	1080	1717	2227	2644	148500	1109	1761	2284	2711
136300	1025	1630	2115	2512	140400	1053	1674	2172	2579	144500	1081	1719	2228	2646	148600	1109	1763	2285	2712
136400	1025	1632	2117	2513	140500	1054	1676	2173	2580	144600	1082	1720	2230	2647	148700	1110	1764	2286	2714
136500	1026	1633	2118	2515	140600	1054	1677	2175	2582	144700	1083	1721	2231	2649	148800	1111	1765	2288	2716
136600	1027	1634	2119	2517	140700	1055	1678	2176	2584	144800	1083	1722	2233	2650	148900	1112	1766	2289	2717
136700	1027	1635	2121	2518	140800	1056	1679	2177	2585	144900	1084	1723	2234	2652	149000	1112	1767	2291	2719
136800	1028	1636	2122	2520	140900	1056	1680	2179	2587	145000	1085	1724	2235	2654	149100	1113	1768	2292	2721
136900	1029	1637	2123	2522	141000	1057	1681	2180	2588	145100	1085	1725	2237	2655	149200	1114	1769	2293	2722
137000	1029	1638	2125	2523	141100	1058	1682	2181	2590	145200	1086	1726	2238	2657	149300	1114	1770	2295	2724
137100	1030	1639	2126	2525	141200	1058	1683	2183	2592	145300	1087	1727	2239	2659	149400	1115	1771	2296	2726
137200	1031	1640	2128	2526	141300	1059	1684	2184	2593	145400	1087	1728	2241	2660	149500	1116	1772	2297	2727
137300	1031	1641	2129	2528	141400	1060	1685	2186	2595	145500	1088	1729	2242	2662	149600	1116	1773	2299	2729
137400	1032	1642	2130	2530	141500	1060	1686	2187	2597	145600	1089	1730	2244	2664	149700	1117	1774	2300	2730
137500	1033	1643	2132	2531	141600	1061	1687	2188	2598	145700	1089	1731	2245	2665	149800	1118	1775	2302	2732
137600	1034	1644	2133	2533	141700	1062	1688	2190	2600	145800	1090	1732	2246	2667	149900	1118	1776	2303	2734
137700	1034	1645	2135	2535	141800	1063	1690	2191	2602	145900	1091	1734	2248	2668	150000	**1119**	**1778**	**2304**	**2735**
137800	1035	1647	2136	2536	141900	1063	1691	2192	2603	146000	1091	1735	2249	2670					
137900	1036	1648	2137	2538	142000	1064	1692	2194	2605	146100	1092	1736	2250	2672					

Income/Revenu ($)	Monthly Award/Paiement mensuel ($)			
	one child/un enfant	two children/deux enfants	three children/trois enfants	four children/quatre enfants
For income over $150,000	1119 plus 0.69% of income over $150,000	1778 plus 1.07% of income over $150,000	2304 plus 1.38% of income over $150,000	2735 plus 1.63% of income over $150,000
Pour revenu dépassant 150 000$	1119 plus 0,69% du revenu dépassant 150 000$	1778 plus 1,07% du revenu dépassant 150 000$	2304 plus 1,38% du revenu dépassant 150 000$	2735 plus 1,63% du revenu dépassant 150 000$

Note: This table shows amounts of child support based on income to the nearest $100. There is a mathematical formula for calculating specific child support amounts between the $100 levels. For more information, please contact the Department of Justice.

Nota: La présente table indique le montant de la pension alimentaire pour enfants à verser d'après le revenu (aux 100 $ près). Il existe une formule mathématique pour calculer le montant exact de la pension alimentaire pour enfants dans le cas des revenus qui se situent entre les tranches de 100 $. Pour plus de renseignements, veuillez communiquer avec le ministère de la Justice.

Divorce

SASKATCHEWAN
1997

FEDERAL CHILD SUPPORT AMOUNTS : SIMPLIFIED TABLES
MONTANTS FÉDÉRAUX DE PENSIONS ALIMENTAIRES POUR ENFANTS : TABLES SIMPLIFIÉES

Income/ Revenu ($)	Monthly Award/ Paiement mensuel ($) No. of Children/ N^{bre} d'enfants				Income/ Revenu ($)	Monthly Award/ Paiement mensuel ($) No. of Children/ N^{bre} d'enfants				Income/ Revenu ($)	Monthly Award/ Paiement mensuel ($) No. of Children/ N^{bre} d'enfants				Income/ Revenu ($)	Monthly Award/ Paiement mensuel ($) No. of Children/ N^{bre} d'enfants			
	1	2	3	4		1	2	3	4		1	2	3	4		1	2	3	4
6700	0	0	0	0	12000	79	142	164	186	17300	129	235	322	366	22600	187	319	425	511
6800	0	0	0	0	12100	80	144	167	189	17400	130	236	325	370	22700	188	321	427	513
6900	0	0	0	1	12200	81	147	170	192	17500	131	238	326	373	22800	189	322	429	516
7000	2	3	4	5	12300	82	149	172	196	17600	133	240	328	377	22900	190	324	431	518
7100	5	7	8	10	12400	82	151	175	199	17700	134	241	330	380	23000	191	325	433	520
7200	9	11	13	15	12500	83	154	178	202	17800	135	243	331	384	23100	193	327	435	523
7300	12	14	17	19	12600	84	156	180	205	17900	136	244	333	388	23200	194	329	437	525
7400	15	18	21	24	12700	85	158	183	208	18000	137	246	334	391	23300	195	330	438	527
7500	18	21	24	27	12800	86	161	186	211	18100	138	248	336	395	23400	196	332	440	529
7600	20	24	27	31	12900	87	163	189	214	18200	139	249	338	398	23500	197	333	442	532
7700	23	27	31	35	13000	87	165	191	217	18300	140	251	339	402	23600	198	335	444	534
7800	25	30	34	39	13100	88	168	194	221	18400	142	252	341	405	23700	199	336	446	536
7900	28	33	37	42	13200	89	170	197	224	18500	143	254	343	409	23800	200	338	448	539
8000	30	35	41	46	13300	90	172	200	227	18600	144	256	345	412	23900	201	340	450	541
8100	33	38	44	50	13400	91	174	202	230	18700	145	257	347	416	24000	202	341	452	543
8200	35	41	47	53	13500	91	177	205	233	18800	146	259	349	420	24100	203	343	454	545
8300	38	44	51	57	13600	92	179	208	236	18900	147	261	351	423	24200	204	344	456	548
8400	40	47	54	61	13700	93	181	210	239	19000	148	262	353	427	24300	205	346	458	550
8500	42	50	57	65	13800	94	184	213	243	19100	149	264	355	430	24400	206	347	460	552
8600	45	53	61	68	13900	95	186	216	246	19200	150	265	357	434	24500	207	349	462	555
8700	47	56	64	72	14000	96	188	219	249	19300	152	267	359	437	24600	209	350	464	557
8800	50	59	67	76	14100	96	191	222	252	19400	153	269	361	439	24700	210	352	466	559
8900	52	61	70	79	14200	97	194	225	256	19500	154	270	363	441	24800	211	354	468	562
9000	55	64	74	83	14300	98	196	228	260	19600	155	272	365	443	24900	212	355	470	564
9100	56	67	77	87	14400	99	198	231	263	19700	156	273	367	445	25000	213	357	472	566
9200	56	70	80	91	14500	100	199	234	267	19800	157	275	369	447	25100	214	358	474	568
9300	57	73	84	94	14600	100	200	237	270	19900	158	277	371	449	25200	215	360	476	571
9400	58	76	87	98	14700	101	202	241	274	20000	159	278	373	451	25300	216	362	478	573
9500	59	79	90	102	14800	102	203	244	277	20100	160	280	376	454	25400	216	363	480	575
9600	60	82	94	106	14900	103	204	247	281	20200	162	282	378	456	25500	217	365	482	578
9700	61	85	97	109	15000	104	205	250	284	20300	163	283	380	458	25600	218	366	484	580
9800	61	87	100	113	15100	105	206	253	288	20400	164	285	382	461	25700	219	368	486	582
9900	62	90	104	117	15200	106	207	256	292	20500	165	286	384	463	25800	220	369	488	585
10000	63	93	107	120	15300	107	209	259	295	20600	166	288	385	465	25900	221	371	490	587
10100	64	96	110	124	15400	108	210	263	299	20700	167	289	387	468	26000	222	373	492	589
10200	65	98	113	127	15500	109	211	266	302	20800	168	291	389	470	26100	223	374	494	591
10300	65	101	115	130	15600	110	212	269	306	20900	169	293	391	472	26200	224	376	495	593
10400	66	103	118	134	15700	111	213	272	309	21000	170	294	393	474	26300	225	377	497	596
10500	67	106	121	137	15800	113	214	275	313	21100	171	296	395	477	26400	225	379	499	598
10600	68	108	124	140	15900	114	215	278	316	21200	172	297	397	479	26500	226	380	501	600
10700	69	111	127	144	16000	115	217	281	320	21300	173	299	399	481	26600	227	382	503	602
10800	69	113	130	147	16100	116	218	285	324	21400	174	300	401	484	26700	228	383	505	604
10900	70	115	133	150	16200	117	219	288	327	21500	175	302	403	486	26800	229	384	507	606
11000	71	118	136	154	16300	118	220	291	331	21600	177	304	405	488	26900	230	386	508	608
11100	72	120	139	157	16400	119	221	294	334	21700	178	305	407	491	27000	231	387	510	611
11200	73	123	142	160	16500	120	222	297	338	21800	179	307	409	493	27100	231	389	512	613
11300	74	125	144	163	16600	121	224	300	341	21900	180	308	411	495	27200	232	390	514	615
11400	74	128	147	167	16700	123	225	303	345	22000	181	310	413	497	27300	233	392	516	617
11500	75	130	150	170	16800	124	227	307	348	22100	182	311	415	500	27400	234	393	518	619
11600	76	133	153	173	16900	125	228	310	352	22200	183	313	417	502	27500	235	395	519	621
11700	77	135	156	177	17000	126	230	313	356	22300	184	314	419	504	27600	236	396	521	624
11800	78	138	159	180	17100	127	231	316	359	22400	185	316	421	507	27700	237	398	523	626
11900	78	140	161	183	17200	128	233	319	363	22500	186	318	423	509	27800	237	399	525	628

Note: This table shows amounts of child support based on income to the nearest $100. There is a mathematical formula for calculating specific child support amounts between the $100 levels. For more information, please contact the Department of Justice.

Nota: La présente table indique le montant de la pension alimentaire pour enfants à verser d'après le revenu (aux 100 $ près). Il existe une formule mathématique pour calculer le montant exact de la pension alimentaire pour enfants dans le cas des revenus qui se situent entre les tranches de 100 $. Pour plus de renseignements, veuillez communiquer avec le ministère de la Justice.

Appendix D

SASKATCHEWAN
1997

FEDERAL CHILD SUPPORT AMOUNTS : SIMPLIFIED TABLES
MONTANTS FÉDÉRAUX DE PENSIONS ALIMENTAIRES POUR ENFANTS : TABLES SIMPLIFIÉES

Income/ Revenu ($)	1	2	3	4	Income/ Revenu ($)	1	2	3	4	Income/ Revenu ($)	1	2	3	4	Income/ Revenu ($)	1	2	3	4
27900	238	401	527	630	33200	277	465	612	729	38500	317	526	694	829	43800	355	587	772	924
28000	239	402	529	632	33300	278	466	614	731	38600	318	527	695	831	43900	355	588	774	926
28100	240	404	531	634	33400	279	467	616	733	38700	318	529	697	833	44000	356	589	775	928
28200	241	405	532	636	33500	280	468	617	735	38800	319	530	698	835	44100	357	590	777	930
28300	242	407	534	639	33600	280	469	619	737	38900	320	531	700	837	44200	358	591	778	931
28400	243	408	536	641	33700	281	471	620	738	39000	321	532	701	839	44300	358	593	780	933
28500	243	410	538	643	33800	282	472	622	740	39100	321	533	703	840	44400	359	594	781	935
28600	244	411	540	645	33900	282	473	624	742	39200	322	534	704	842	44500	360	595	783	937
28700	245	413	542	647	34000	283	474	625	744	39300	323	536	706	844	44600	361	596	784	939
28800	246	414	544	649	34100	284	475	627	746	39400	324	537	707	846	44700	361	597	786	940
28900	247	416	545	652	34200	285	476	628	748	39500	324	538	709	848	44800	362	598	788	942
29000	248	417	547	654	34300	285	477	630	749	39600	325	539	710	850	44900	363	600	789	944
29100	249	419	549	656	34400	286	479	632	751	39700	326	540	712	852	45000	364	601	791	946
29200	249	420	551	658	34500	287	480	633	753	39800	327	542	713	854	45100	364	602	792	948
29300	250	422	553	660	34600	288	481	635	755	39900	327	543	715	856	45200	365	603	794	949
29400	251	423	555	662	34700	288	482	636	757	40000	328	544	717	858	45300	366	604	795	951
29500	252	425	557	664	34800	289	483	638	759	40100	329	545	718	860	45400	367	606	797	953
29600	253	426	558	667	34900	290	484	640	761	40200	330	546	720	862	45500	368	607	798	955
29700	253	427	560	668	35000	290	485	641	762	40300	331	548	721	863	45600	368	608	800	956
29800	254	428	561	670	35100	291	486	643	764	40400	331	549	723	865	45700	369	609	801	958
29900	255	430	563	672	35200	292	488	644	766	40500	332	550	724	867	45800	370	610	803	960
30000	255	431	564	673	35300	293	489	646	768	40600	333	551	726	869	45900	371	611	804	962
30100	256	432	566	675	35400	293	490	647	770	40700	333	552	727	870	46000	371	613	806	964
30200	257	433	567	677	35500	294	491	648	772	40800	334	553	729	872	46100	372	614	807	965
30300	257	434	569	678	35600	295	492	650	773	40900	335	554	730	874	46200	373	615	809	967
30400	258	435	570	680	35700	296	493	651	775	41000	335	555	732	876	46300	374	616	810	969
30500	259	436	571	682	35800	296	494	653	777	41100	336	557	733	877	46400	374	617	812	971
30600	259	437	573	683	35900	297	496	654	779	41200	337	558	734	879	46500	375	619	813	973
30700	260	438	574	685	36000	298	497	656	781	41300	337	559	736	881	46600	376	620	815	974
30800	261	439	576	687	36100	299	498	657	783	41400	338	560	737	883	46700	377	621	816	976
30900	261	440	577	688	36200	299	499	659	785	41500	339	561	739	884	46800	377	622	818	978
31000	262	441	579	690	36300	300	500	660	787	41600	339	562	740	886	46900	378	623	819	980
31100	263	442	580	692	36400	301	501	662	789	41700	340	563	742	888	47000	379	624	821	982
31200	263	443	582	693	36500	302	503	663	791	41800	341	564	743	889	47100	380	626	822	983
31300	264	444	583	695	36600	302	504	665	792	41900	341	565	745	891	47200	380	627	824	985
31400	265	445	585	697	36700	303	505	666	794	42000	342	567	746	893	47300	381	628	825	987
31500	265	446	586	699	36800	304	506	668	796	42100	343	568	748	895	47400	382	629	827	989
31600	266	447	587	700	36900	305	507	669	798	42200	344	569	749	896	47500	383	630	828	990
31700	267	448	589	702	37000	305	509	671	800	42300	344	570	750	898	47600	383	631	830	992
31800	267	449	590	704	37100	306	510	673	802	42400	345	571	752	900	47700	384	633	831	994
31900	268	450	592	705	37200	307	511	674	804	42500	346	572	753	902	47800	385	634	833	996
32000	269	451	593	707	37300	308	512	676	806	42600	346	573	755	903	47900	386	635	834	998
32100	269	452	595	709	37400	308	513	677	808	42700	347	574	756	905	48000	386	636	836	999
32200	270	454	597	711	37500	309	514	679	810	42800	348	575	758	907	48100	387	637	837	1001
32300	271	455	598	712	37600	310	516	680	812	42900	348	577	759	909	48200	388	639	839	1003
32400	272	456	600	714	37700	311	517	682	814	43000	349	578	761	910	48300	389	640	840	1005
32500	272	457	601	716	37800	311	518	683	815	43100	350	579	762	912	48400	389	641	842	1007
32600	273	458	603	718	37900	312	519	685	817	43200	350	580	763	914	48500	390	642	843	1008
32700	274	459	604	720	38000	313	520	686	819	43300	351	581	765	915	48600	391	643	845	1010
32800	274	460	606	722	38100	314	521	688	821	43400	352	582	766	917	48700	392	644	847	1012
32900	275	462	608	724	38200	314	523	689	823	43500	352	583	768	919	48800	392	646	848	1014
33000	276	463	609	725	38300	315	524	691	825	43600	353	584	769	921	48900	393	647	850	1015
33100	277	464	611	727	38400	316	525	692	827	43700	354	586	771	922	49000	394	648	851	1017

Note: This table shows amounts of child support based on income to the nearest $100. There is a mathematical formula for calculating specific child support amounts between the $100 levels. For more information, please contact the Department of Justice.

Nota: La présente table indique le montant de la pension alimentaire pour enfants à verser d'après le revenu (aux 100 $ près). Il existe une formule mathématique pour calculer le montant exact de la pension alimentaire pour enfants dans le cas des revenus qui se situent entre les tranches de 100 $. Pour plus de renseignements, veuillez communiquer avec le ministère de la Justice.

Divorce

SASKATCHEWAN

FEDERAL CHILD SUPPORT AMOUNTS : SIMPLIFIED TABLES
MONTANTS FÉDÉRAUX DE PENSIONS ALIMENTAIRES POUR ENFANTS : TABLES SIMPLIFIÉES

1997

Income/ Revenu ($)	Monthly Award/ Paiement mensuel ($) No. of Children/ N^{bre} d'enfants				Income/ Revenu ($)	Monthly Award/ Paiement mensuel ($) No. of Children/ N^{bre} d'enfants				Income/ Revenu ($)	Monthly Award/ Paiement mensuel ($) No. of Children/ N^{bre} d'enfants				Income/ Revenu ($)	Monthly Award/ Paiement mensuel ($) No. of Children/ N^{bre} d'enfants				Income/ Revenu ($)	Monthly Award/ Paiement mensuel ($) No. of Children/ N^{bre} d'enfants			
	1	2	3	4		1	2	3	4		1	2	3	4		1	2	3	4		1	2	3	4
49100	395	649	853	1019	54400	435	711	933	1114	59700	475	773	1012	1208	65000	510	829	1084	1293
49200	396	650	854	1021	54500	436	713	934	1116	59800	475	774	1014	1209	65100	511	830	1085	1294
49300	396	651	856	1023	54600	436	714	936	1117	59900	476	775	1015	1211	65200	511	831	1086	1296
49400	397	653	857	1024	54700	437	715	937	1119	60000	477	776	1016	1213	65300	512	832	1088	1297
49500	398	654	859	1026	54800	438	716	939	1121	60100	477	778	1018	1214	65400	512	833	1089	1299
49600	399	655	860	1028	54900	439	717	940	1123	60200	478	779	1019	1216	65500	513	834	1090	1300
49700	399	656	862	1030	55000	439	719	942	1125	60300	479	780	1020	1217	65600	514	835	1092	1302
49800	400	657	863	1032	55100	440	720	943	1126	60400	479	781	1022	1219	65700	514	836	1093	1303
49900	401	659	865	1033	55200	441	721	945	1128	60500	480	782	1023	1221	65800	515	837	1094	1305
50000	402	660	866	1035	55300	442	722	946	1130	60600	481	783	1025	1222	65900	515	838	1095	1306
50100	402	661	868	1037	55400	442	723	948	1132	60700	481	784	1026	1224	66000	516	839	1097	1308
50200	403	662	869	1039	55500	443	724	949	1134	60800	482	785	1027	1226	66100	517	840	1098	1309
50300	404	663	871	1041	55600	444	726	951	1135	60900	483	786	1029	1227	66200	517	841	1099	1311
50400	405	664	872	1042	55700	445	727	952	1137	61000	484	787	1030	1229	66300	518	842	1101	1313
50500	405	666	874	1044	55800	445	728	954	1139	61100	484	788	1031	1230	66400	519	843	1102	1314
50600	406	667	875	1046	55900	446	729	955	1141	61200	485	789	1033	1232	66500	519	844	1103	1316
50700	407	668	877	1048	56000	447	730	957	1142	61300	486	790	1034	1234	66600	520	845	1105	1317
50800	408	669	878	1049	56100	448	731	958	1144	61400	486	791	1036	1235	66700	520	846	1106	1319
50900	408	670	880	1051	56200	448	733	960	1146	61500	487	793	1037	1237	66800	521	847	1107	1320
51000	409	671	881	1053	56300	449	734	962	1148	61600	488	794	1038	1239	66900	522	848	1109	1322
51100	410	673	883	1055	56400	450	735	963	1150	61700	488	795	1040	1240	67000	522	849	1110	1324
51200	411	674	884	1057	56500	451	736	965	1151	61800	489	796	1041	1242	67100	523	850	1111	1325
51300	411	675	886	1058	56600	451	737	966	1153	61900	490	797	1042	1243	67200	524	851	1113	1327
51400	412	676	887	1060	56700	452	739	968	1155	62000	490	798	1044	1245	67300	524	852	1114	1328
51500	413	677	889	1062	56800	453	740	969	1157	62100	491	799	1045	1247	67400	525	853	1115	1330
51600	414	679	890	1064	56900	454	741	971	1159	62200	492	800	1047	1248	67500	526	854	1117	1331
51700	414	680	892	1066	57000	455	742	972	1160	62300	492	801	1048	1250	67600	526	855	1118	1333
51800	415	681	893	1067	57100	455	743	974	1162	62400	493	802	1049	1252	67700	527	856	1119	1335
51900	416	682	895	1069	57200	456	744	975	1164	62500	494	803	1051	1253	67800	528	857	1121	1336
52000	417	683	896	1071	57300	457	746	977	1166	62600	495	804	1052	1255	67900	528	858	1122	1338
52100	417	684	898	1073	57400	458	747	978	1167	62700	495	805	1053	1256	68000	529	859	1123	1339
52200	418	686	899	1074	57500	458	748	980	1169	62800	496	806	1055	1258	68100	530	860	1125	1341
52300	419	687	901	1076	57600	459	749	981	1171	62900	497	807	1056	1260	68200	530	861	1126	1342
52400	420	688	903	1078	57700	460	750	983	1173	63000	497	809	1058	1261	68300	531	862	1127	1344
52500	420	689	904	1080	57800	461	751	984	1175	63100	498	810	1059	1263	68400	532	863	1129	1346
52600	421	690	906	1082	57900	461	753	986	1176	63200	499	811	1060	1265	68500	532	864	1130	1347
52700	422	691	907	1083	58000	462	754	987	1178	63300	499	812	1062	1266	68600	533	865	1131	1349
52800	423	693	909	1085	58100	463	755	989	1180	63400	500	813	1063	1268	68700	534	866	1133	1350
52900	424	694	910	1087	58200	464	756	990	1182	63500	501	814	1064	1269	68800	534	867	1134	1352
53000	424	695	912	1089	58300	464	757	992	1184	63600	501	815	1066	1271	68900	535	869	1135	1353
53100	425	696	913	1091	58400	465	759	993	1185	63700	502	816	1067	1272	69000	536	870	1137	1355
53200	426	697	915	1092	58500	466	760	995	1187	63800	503	817	1068	1274	69100	536	871	1138	1357
53300	427	699	916	1094	58600	467	761	996	1189	63900	503	818	1070	1276	69200	537	872	1139	1358
53400	427	700	918	1096	58700	467	762	998	1191	64000	504	819	1071	1277	69300	538	873	1141	1360
53500	428	701	919	1098	58800	468	763	999	1193	64100	504	820	1072	1279	69400	538	874	1142	1361
53600	429	702	921	1100	58900	469	764	1001	1194	64200	505	821	1073	1280	69500	539	875	1143	1363
53700	430	703	922	1101	59000	470	766	1002	1196	64300	506	822	1075	1282	69600	540	876	1145	1365
53800	430	704	924	1103	59100	470	767	1004	1198	64400	506	823	1076	1283	69700	540	877	1146	1366
53900	431	706	925	1105	59200	471	768	1005	1200	64500	507	824	1077	1285	69800	541	878	1147	1368
54000	432	707	927	1107	59300	472	769	1007	1201	64600	507	825	1079	1286	69900	542	879	1149	1369
54100	433	708	928	1108	59400	473	770	1008	1203	64700	508	826	1080	1288	70000	542	880	1150	1371
54200	433	709	930	1110	59500	473	771	1009	1204	64800	509	827	1081	1289	70100	543	881	1151	1372
54300	434	710	931	1112	59600	474	772	1011	1206	64900	509	828	1083	1291	70200	544	882	1153	1374

Note: This table shows amounts of child support based on income to the nearest $100. There is a mathematical formula for calculating specific child support amounts between the $100 levels. For more information, please contact the Department of Justice.

Nota: La présente table indique le montant de la pension alimentaire pour enfants à verser d'après le revenu (aux 100 $ près). Il existe une formule mathématique pour calculer le montant exact de la pension alimentaire pour enfants dans le cas des revenus qui se situent entre les tranches de 100 $. Pour plus de renseignements, veuillez communiquer avec le ministère de la Justice.

Appendix D

SASKATCHEWAN
1997

FEDERAL CHILD SUPPORT AMOUNTS : SIMPLIFIED TABLES
MONTANTS FÉDÉRAUX DE PENSIONS ALIMENTAIRES POUR ENFANTS : TABLES SIMPLIFIÉES

Income/Revenu ($)	Monthly Award/Paiement mensuel ($) No. of Children/N^{bre} d'enfants				Income/Revenu ($)	Monthly Award/Paiement mensuel ($) No. of Children/N^{bre} d'enfants				Income/Revenu ($)	Monthly Award/Paiement mensuel ($) No. of Children/N^{bre} d'enfants				Income/Revenu ($)	Monthly Award/Paiement mensuel ($) No. of Children/N^{bre} d'enfants			
	1	2	3	4		1	2	3	4		1	2	3	4		1	2	3	4
70300	544	883	1154	1376	75600	580	938	1225	1459	80900	615	993	1295	1543	86200	651	1048	1366	1626
70400	545	884	1155	1377	75700	581	939	1226	1461	81000	616	994	1297	1544	86300	651	1049	1368	1628
70500	546	885	1157	1379	75800	581	940	1227	1462	81100	617	995	1298	1546	86400	652	1050	1369	1630
70600	546	886	1158	1380	75900	582	941	1229	1464	81200	617	996	1299	1548	86500	653	1051	1370	1631
70700	547	887	1159	1382	76000	583	942	1230	1465	81300	618	997	1301	1549	86600	653	1052	1372	1633
70800	548	888	1161	1383	76100	583	943	1231	1467	81400	619	998	1302	1551	86700	654	1053	1373	1634
70900	548	889	1162	1385	76200	584	944	1233	1469	81500	619	999	1303	1552	86800	655	1054	1374	1636
71000	549	890	1163	1387	76300	585	945	1234	1470	81600	620	1000	1305	1554	86900	655	1055	1376	1637
71100	550	891	1165	1388	76400	585	946	1235	1472	81700	621	1001	1306	1555	87000	656	1056	1377	1639
71200	550	892	1166	1390	76500	586	947	1237	1473	81800	621	1002	1307	1557	87100	657	1057	1378	1641
71300	551	893	1167	1391	76600	587	948	1238	1475	81900	622	1004	1309	1559	87200	657	1059	1380	1642
71400	552	894	1169	1393	76700	587	950	1239	1477	82000	623	1005	1310	1560	87300	658	1060	1381	1644
71500	552	896	1170	1394	76800	588	951	1241	1478	82100	623	1006	1311	1562	87400	659	1061	1382	1645
71600	553	897	1171	1396	76900	589	952	1242	1480	82200	624	1007	1313	1563	87500	659	1062	1384	1647
71700	554	898	1173	1398	77000	589	953	1243	1481	82300	625	1008	1314	1565	87600	660	1063	1385	1648
71800	554	899	1174	1399	77100	590	954	1245	1483	82400	625	1009	1315	1566	87700	661	1064	1386	1650
71900	555	900	1175	1401	77200	591	955	1246	1484	82500	626	1010	1317	1568	87800	661	1065	1388	1652
72000	556	901	1177	1402	77300	591	956	1247	1486	82600	627	1011	1318	1570	87900	662	1066	1389	1653
72100	556	902	1178	1404	77400	592	957	1249	1488	82700	627	1012	1319	1571	88000	663	1067	1390	1655
72200	557	903	1179	1406	77500	593	958	1250	1489	82800	628	1013	1321	1573	88100	663	1068	1392	1656
72300	558	904	1181	1407	77600	593	959	1251	1491	82900	629	1014	1322	1574	88200	664	1069	1393	1658
72400	559	905	1182	1409	77700	594	960	1253	1492	83000	629	1015	1323	1576	88300	665	1070	1394	1660
72500	559	906	1183	1410	77800	595	961	1254	1494	83100	630	1016	1325	1577	88400	665	1071	1396	1661
72600	560	907	1185	1412	77900	595	962	1255	1495	83200	631	1017	1326	1579	88500	666	1072	1397	1663
72700	561	908	1186	1413	78000	596	963	1257	1497	83300	631	1018	1327	1581	88600	667	1073	1398	1664
72800	561	909	1187	1415	78100	597	964	1258	1499	83400	632	1019	1329	1582	88700	667	1074	1400	1666
72900	562	910	1189	1417	78200	597	965	1259	1500	83500	633	1020	1330	1584	88800	668	1075	1401	1667
73000	563	911	1190	1418	78300	598	966	1261	1502	83600	633	1021	1331	1585	88900	669	1076	1402	1669
73100	563	912	1191	1420	78400	599	967	1262	1503	83700	634	1022	1333	1587	89000	669	1077	1404	1671
73200	564	913	1193	1421	78500	599	968	1263	1505	83800	635	1023	1334	1589	89100	670	1078	1405	1672
73300	565	914	1194	1423	78600	600	969	1265	1507	83900	635	1024	1335	1590	89200	671	1079	1406	1674
73400	565	915	1195	1424	78700	601	970	1266	1508	84000	636	1025	1337	1592	89300	671	1080	1408	1675
73500	566	916	1197	1426	78800	601	971	1267	1510	84100	637	1026	1338	1593	89400	672	1081	1409	1677
73600	567	917	1198	1428	78900	602	972	1269	1511	84200	637	1027	1339	1595	89500	673	1082	1410	1678
73700	567	918	1199	1429	79000	603	973	1270	1513	84300	638	1028	1341	1596	89600	673	1083	1412	1680
73800	568	919	1201	1431	79100	603	974	1271	1514	84400	639	1029	1342	1598	89700	674	1084	1413	1682
73900	569	920	1202	1432	79200	604	975	1273	1516	84500	639	1031	1343	1600	89800	675	1086	1414	1683
74000	569	921	1203	1434	79300	605	977	1274	1518	84600	640	1032	1345	1601	89900	675	1087	1416	1685
74100	570	923	1205	1436	79400	605	978	1275	1519	84700	641	1033	1346	1603	90000	676	1088	1417	1686
74200	571	924	1206	1437	79500	606	979	1277	1521	84800	641	1034	1347	1604	90100	677	1089	1418	1688
74300	571	925	1207	1439	79600	607	980	1278	1522	84900	642	1035	1349	1606	90200	677	1090	1420	1689
74400	572	926	1209	1440	79700	607	981	1279	1524	85000	643	1036	1350	1607	90300	678	1091	1421	1691
74500	573	927	1210	1442	79800	608	982	1281	1525	85100	643	1037	1352	1609	90400	679	1092	1422	1693
74600	573	928	1211	1443	79900	609	983	1282	1527	85200	644	1038	1353	1611	90500	679	1093	1424	1694
74700	574	929	1213	1445	80000	609	984	1283	1529	85300	645	1039	1354	1612	90600	680	1094	1425	1696
74800	575	930	1214	1447	80100	610	985	1285	1530	85400	645	1040	1356	1614	90700	681	1095	1426	1697
74900	575	931	1215	1448	80200	611	986	1286	1532	85500	646	1041	1357	1615	90800	681	1096	1428	1699
75000	576	932	1217	1450	80300	611	987	1287	1533	85600	647	1042	1358	1617	90900	682	1097	1429	1701
75100	577	933	1218	1451	80400	612	988	1289	1535	85700	647	1043	1360	1619	91000	683	1098	1430	1702
75200	577	934	1219	1453	80500	613	989	1290	1536	85800	648	1044	1361	1620	91100	683	1099	1432	1704
75300	578	935	1221	1454	80600	613	990	1291	1538	85900	649	1045	1362	1622	91200	684	1100	1433	1705
75400	579	936	1222	1456	80700	614	991	1293	1540	86000	649	1046	1364	1623	91300	685	1101	1434	1707
75500	579	937	1223	1458	80800	615	992	1294	1541	86100	650	1047	1365	1625	91400	685	1102	1436	1708

Note: This table shows amounts of child support based on income to the nearest $100. There is a mathematical formula for calculating specific child support amounts between the $100 levels. For more information, please contact the Department of Justice.

Nota: La présente table indique le montant de la pension alimentaire pour enfants à verser d'après le revenu (aux 100 $ près). Il existe une formule mathématique pour calculer le montant exact de la pension alimentaire pour enfants dans le cas des revenus qui se situent entre les tranches de 100 $. Pour plus de renseignements, veuillez communiquer avec le ministère de la Justice.

Divorce

SASKATCHEWAN
FEDERAL CHILD SUPPORT AMOUNTS : SIMPLIFIED TABLES
MONTANTS FÉDÉRAUX DE PENSIONS ALIMENTAIRES POUR ENFANTS : TABLES SIMPLIFIÉES

1997

Income/Revenu ($)	Monthly Award/ Paiement mensuel ($) No. of Children/ N^{bre} d'enfants				Income/Revenu ($)	Monthly Award/ Paiement mensuel ($) No. of Children/ N^{bre} d'enfants				Income/Revenu ($)	Monthly Award/ Paiement mensuel ($) No. of Children/ N^{bre} d'enfants				Income/Revenu ($)	Monthly Award/ Paiement mensuel ($) No. of Children/ N^{bre} d'enfants			
	1	2	3	4		1	2	3	4		1	2	3	4		1	2	3	4
91500	686	1103	1437	1710	96800	721	1158	1508	1794	102100	757	1213	1578	1877	107400	792	1268	1649	1961
91600	687	1104	1438	1712	96900	722	1159	1509	1795	102200	757	1214	1580	1879	107500	793	1269	1651	1962
91700	687	1105	1440	1713	97000	723	1160	1510	1797	102300	758	1215	1581	1880	107600	793	1270	1652	1964
91800	688	1106	1441	1715	97100	723	1161	1512	1798	102400	759	1216	1582	1882	107700	794	1271	1653	1966
91900	689	1107	1442	1716	97200	724	1162	1513	1800	102500	759	1217	1584	1884	107800	795	1272	1655	1967
92000	689	1108	1444	1718	97300	725	1163	1514	1802	102600	760	1218	1585	1885	107900	795	1273	1656	1969
92100	690	1109	1445	1719	97400	725	1164	1516	1803	102700	761	1219	1586	1887	108000	796	1274	1657	1970
92200	691	1110	1446	1721	97500	726	1165	1517	1805	102800	761	1220	1588	1888	108100	797	1276	1659	1972
92300	691	1111	1448	1723	97600	727	1167	1518	1806	102900	762	1222	1589	1890	108200	797	1277	1660	1973
92400	692	1113	1449	1724	97700	727	1168	1520	1808	103000	763	1223	1590	1891	108300	798	1278	1661	1975
92500	693	1114	1450	1726	97800	728	1169	1521	1809	103100	763	1224	1592	1893	108400	799	1279	1663	1977
92600	693	1115	1452	1727	97900	729	1170	1522	1811	103200	764	1225	1593	1895	108500	799	1280	1664	1978
92700	694	1116	1453	1729	98000	729	1171	1524	1813	103300	765	1226	1594	1896	108600	800	1281	1665	1980
92800	695	1117	1454	1731	98100	730	1172	1525	1814	103400	765	1227	1596	1898	108700	801	1282	1667	1981
92900	695	1118	1456	1732	98200	731	1173	1526	1816	103500	766	1228	1597	1899	108800	801	1283	1668	1983
93000	696	1119	1457	1734	98300	731	1174	1528	1817	103600	767	1229	1598	1901	108900	802	1284	1669	1985
93100	697	1120	1458	1735	98400	732	1175	1529	1819	103700	767	1230	1600	1902	109000	803	1285	1671	1986
93200	697	1121	1460	1737	98500	733	1176	1530	1820	103800	768	1231	1601	1904	109100	803	1286	1672	1988
93300	698	1122	1461	1738	98600	733	1177	1532	1822	103900	769	1232	1602	1906	109200	804	1287	1673	1989
93400	699	1123	1462	1740	98700	734	1178	1533	1824	104000	769	1233	1604	1907	109300	805	1288	1675	1991
93500	699	1124	1464	1742	98800	735	1179	1534	1825	104100	770	1234	1605	1909	109400	805	1289	1676	1992
93600	700	1125	1465	1743	98900	735	1180	1536	1827	104200	771	1235	1606	1910	109500	806	1290	1677	1994
93700	701	1126	1466	1745	99000	736	1181	1537	1828	104300	771	1236	1608	1912	109600	807	1291	1679	1996
93800	701	1127	1468	1746	99100	737	1182	1538	1830	104400	772	1237	1609	1914	109700	807	1292	1680	1997
93900	702	1128	1469	1748	99200	737	1183	1540	1831	104500	773	1238	1610	1915	109800	808	1293	1681	1999
94000	703	1129	1470	1749	99300	738	1184	1541	1833	104600	773	1239	1612	1917	109900	809	1294	1683	2000
94100	703	1130	1472	1751	99400	739	1185	1542	1835	104700	774	1240	1613	1918	110000	809	1295	1684	2002
94200	704	1131	1473	1753	99500	739	1186	1544	1836	104800	775	1241	1614	1920	110100	810	1296	1685	2003
94300	705	1132	1474	1754	99600	740	1187	1545	1838	104900	775	1242	1616	1921	110200	811	1297	1687	2005
94400	705	1133	1476	1756	99700	741	1188	1546	1839	105000	776	1243	1617	1923	110300	811	1298	1688	2007
94500	706	1134	1477	1757	99800	741	1189	1548	1841	105100	777	1244	1618	1925	110400	812	1299	1689	2008
94600	707	1135	1478	1759	99900	742	1190	1549	1843	105200	777	1245	1620	1926	110500	813	1300	1691	2010
94700	707	1136	1480	1760	100000	743	1191	1550	1844	105300	778	1246	1621	1928	110600	813	1301	1692	2011
94800	708	1137	1481	1762	100100	743	1192	1552	1846	105400	779	1247	1622	1929	110700	814	1303	1693	2013
94900	709	1138	1482	1764	100200	744	1194	1553	1847	105500	779	1249	1624	1931	110800	815	1304	1695	2014
95000	709	1140	1484	1765	100300	745	1195	1554	1849	105600	780	1250	1625	1932	110900	815	1305	1696	2016
95100	710	1141	1485	1767	100400	745	1196	1556	1850	105700	781	1251	1626	1934	111000	816	1306	1697	2018
95200	711	1142	1486	1768	100500	746	1197	1557	1852	105800	781	1252	1628	1936	111100	817	1307	1699	2019
95300	711	1143	1488	1770	100600	747	1198	1558	1854	105900	782	1253	1629	1937	111200	817	1308	1700	2021
95400	712	1144	1489	1772	100700	747	1199	1560	1855	106000	783	1254	1630	1939	111300	818	1309	1701	2022
95500	713	1145	1490	1773	100800	748	1200	1561	1857	106100	783	1255	1632	1940	111400	819	1310	1703	2024
95600	713	1146	1492	1775	100900	749	1201	1562	1858	106200	784	1256	1633	1942	111500	819	1311	1704	2026
95700	714	1147	1493	1776	101000	749	1202	1564	1860	106300	785	1257	1634	1943	111600	820	1312	1705	2027
95800	715	1148	1494	1778	101100	750	1203	1565	1861	106400	785	1258	1636	1945	111700	821	1313	1707	2029
95900	715	1149	1496	1779	101200	751	1204	1566	1863	106500	786	1259	1637	1947	111800	821	1314	1708	2030
96000	716	1150	1497	1781	101300	751	1205	1568	1865	106600	787	1260	1638	1948	111900	822	1315	1709	2032
96100	717	1151	1498	1783	101400	752	1206	1569	1866	106700	787	1261	1640	1950	112000	823	1316	1711	2033
96200	717	1152	1500	1784	101500	753	1207	1570	1868	106800	788	1262	1641	1951	112100	823	1317	1712	2035
96300	718	1153	1501	1786	101600	753	1208	1572	1869	106900	789	1263	1643	1953	112200	824	1318	1713	2037
96400	719	1154	1502	1787	101700	754	1209	1573	1871	107000	789	1264	1644	1955	112300	825	1319	1715	2038
96500	719	1155	1504	1789	101800	755	1210	1574	1872	107100	790	1265	1645	1956	112400	825	1320	1716	2040
96600	720	1156	1505	1790	101900	755	1211	1576	1874	107200	791	1266	1647	1958	112500	826	1321	1717	2041
96700	721	1157	1506	1792	102000	756	1212	1577	1876	107300	791	1267	1648	1959	112600	827	1322	1719	2043

Note: This table shows amounts of child support based on income to the nearest $100. There is a mathematical formula for calculating specific child support amounts between the $100 levels. For more information, please contact the Department of Justice.

Nota: La présente table indique le montant de la pension alimentaire pour enfants à verser d'après le revenu (aux 100 $ près). Il existe une formule mathématique pour calculer le montant exact de la pension alimentaire pour enfants dans le cas des revenus qui se situent entre les tranches de 100 $. Pour plus de renseignements, veuillez communiquer avec le ministère de la Justice.

Appendix D

SASKATCHEWAN

1997

FEDERAL CHILD SUPPORT AMOUNTS : SIMPLIFIED TABLES
MONTANTS FÉDÉRAUX DE PENSIONS ALIMENTAIRES POUR ENFANTS : TABLES SIMPLIFIÉES

Income/ Revenu ($)	Monthly Award/ Paiement mensuel ($) No. of Children/ N^{bre} d'enfants				Income/ Revenu ($)	Monthly Award/ Paiement mensuel ($) No. of Children/ N^{bre} d'enfants				Income/ Revenu ($)	Monthly Award/ Paiement mensuel ($) No. of Children/ N^{bre} d'enfants				Income/ Revenu ($)	Monthly Award/ Paiement mensuel ($) No. of Children/ N^{bre} d'enfants			
	1	2	3	4		1	2	3	4		1	2	3	4		1	2	3	4
112700	827	1323	1720	2044	*118000*	863	1378	1791	2128	*123300*	898	1433	1861	2212	*128600*	934	1488	1932	2295
112800	828	1324	1721	2046	*118100*	864	1379	1792	2130	*123400*	899	1434	1863	2213	*128700*	934	1489	1934	2297
112900	829	1325	1723	2048	*118200*	864	1380	1793	2131	*123500*	900	1435	1864	2215	*128800*	935	1490	1935	2298
113000	829	1326	1724	2049	*118300*	865	1381	1795	2133	*123600*	900	1436	1865	2216	*128900*	936	1491	1936	2300
113100	830	1327	1725	2051	*118400*	866	1382	1796	2134	*123700*	901	1437	1867	2218	*129000*	936	1493	1938	2302
113200	831	1328	1727	2052	*118500*	866	1383	1797	2136	*123800*	902	1439	1868	2220	*129100*	937	1494	1939	2303
113300	831	1330	1728	2054	*118600*	867	1385	1799	2138	*123900*	902	1440	1869	2221	*129200*	938	1495	1940	2305
113400	832	1331	1729	2055	*118700*	868	1386	1800	2139	*124000*	903	1441	1871	2223	*129300*	938	1496	1942	2306
113500	833	1332	1731	2057	*118800*	868	1387	1801	2141	*124100*	904	1442	1872	2224	*129400*	939	1497	1943	2308
113600	833	1333	1732	2059	*118900*	869	1388	1803	2142	*124200*	904	1443	1873	2226	*129500*	940	1498	1944	2309
113700	834	1334	1733	2060	*119000*	870	1389	1804	2144	*124300*	905	1444	1875	2227	*129600*	940	1499	1946	2311
113800	835	1335	1735	2062	*119100*	870	1390	1805	2145	*124400*	906	1445	1876	2229	*129700*	941	1500	1947	2313
113900	835	1336	1736	2063	*119200*	871	1391	1807	2147	*124500*	906	1446	1877	2231	*129800*	942	1501	1948	2314
114000	836	1337	1737	2065	*119300*	872	1392	1808	2149	*124600*	907	1447	1879	2232	*129900*	942	1502	1950	2316
114100	837	1338	1739	2067	*119400*	872	1393	1809	2150	*124700*	908	1448	1880	2234	*130000*	943	1503	1951	2317
114200	837	1339	1740	2068	*119500*	873	1394	1811	2152	*124800*	908	1449	1881	2235	*130100*	944	1504	1952	2319
114300	838	1340	1741	2070	*119600*	874	1395	1812	2153	*124900*	909	1450	1883	2237	*130200*	944	1505	1954	2321
114400	839	1341	1743	2071	*119700*	874	1396	1813	2155	*125000*	910	1451	1884	2238	*130300*	945	1506	1955	2322
114500	839	1342	1744	2073	*119800*	875	1397	1815	2156	*125100*	910	1452	1885	2240	*130400*	946	1507	1956	2324
114600	840	1343	1745	2074	*119900*	876	1398	1816	2158	*125200*	911	1453	1887	2242	*130500*	946	1508	1958	2325
114700	841	1344	1747	2076	*120000*	876	1399	1817	2160	*125300*	912	1454	1888	2243	*130600*	947	1509	1959	2327
114800	841	1345	1748	2078	*120100*	877	1400	1819	2161	*125400*	912	1455	1889	2245	*130700*	948	1510	1960	2328
114900	842	1346	1749	2079	*120200*	878	1401	1820	2163	*125500*	913	1456	1891	2246	*130800*	948	1511	1962	2330
115000	843	1347	1751	2081	*120300*	878	1402	1821	2164	*125600*	914	1457	1892	2248	*130900*	949	1512	1963	2332
115100	843	1348	1752	2082	*120400*	879	1403	1823	2166	*125700*	914	1458	1893	2250	*131000*	950	1513	1964	2333
115200	844	1349	1753	2084	*120500*	880	1404	1824	2168	*125800*	915	1459	1895	2251	*131100*	950	1514	1966	2335
115300	845	1350	1755	2085	*120600*	880	1405	1825	2169	*125900*	916	1460	1896	2253	*131200*	951	1515	1967	2336
115400	845	1351	1756	2087	*120700*	881	1406	1827	2171	*126000*	916	1461	1897	2254	*131300*	952	1516	1968	2338
115500	846	1352	1757	2089	*120800*	882	1407	1828	2172	*126100*	917	1462	1899	2256	*131400*	952	1517	1970	2339
115600	847	1353	1759	2090	*120900*	882	1408	1829	2174	*126200*	918	1463	1900	2257	*131500*	953	1518	1971	2341
115700	847	1354	1760	2092	*121000*	883	1409	1831	2175	*126300*	918	1464	1901	2259	*131600*	954	1520	1972	2343
115800	848	1355	1761	2093	*121100*	884	1410	1832	2177	*126400*	919	1466	1903	2261	*131700*	954	1521	1974	2344
115900	849	1357	1763	2095	*121200*	884	1412	1833	2179	*126500*	920	1467	1904	2262	*131800*	955	1522	1975	2346
116000	849	1358	1764	2097	*121300*	885	1413	1835	2180	*126600*	920	1468	1905	2264	*131900*	956	1523	1976	2347
116100	850	1359	1765	2098	*121400*	886	1414	1836	2182	*126700*	921	1469	1907	2265	*132000*	956	1524	1978	2349
116200	851	1360	1767	2100	*121500*	886	1415	1837	2183	*126800*	922	1470	1908	2267	*132100*	957	1525	1979	2350
116300	852	1361	1768	2101	*121600*	887	1416	1839	2185	*126900*	922	1471	1909	2268	*132200*	958	1526	1980	2352
116400	852	1362	1769	2103	*121700*	888	1417	1840	2186	*127000*	923	1472	1911	2270	*132300*	958	1527	1982	2354
116500	853	1363	1771	2104	*121800*	888	1418	1841	2188	*127100*	924	1473	1912	2272	*132400*	959	1528	1983	2355
116600	854	1364	1772	2106	*121900*	889	1419	1843	2190	*127200*	924	1474	1913	2273	*132500*	960	1529	1984	2357
116700	854	1365	1773	2108	*122000*	890	1420	1844	2191	*127300*	925	1475	1915	2275	*132600*	960	1530	1986	2358
116800	855	1366	1775	2109	*122100*	890	1421	1845	2193	*127400*	926	1476	1916	2276	*132700*	961	1531	1987	2360
116900	856	1367	1776	2111	*122200*	891	1422	1847	2194	*127500*	926	1477	1917	2278	*132800*	962	1532	1988	2362
117000	856	1368	1777	2112	*122300*	892	1423	1848	2196	*127600*	927	1478	1919	2280	*132900*	962	1533	1990	2363
117100	857	1369	1779	2114	*122400*	892	1424	1849	2197	*127700*	928	1479	1920	2281	*133000*	963	1534	1991	2365
117200	858	1370	1780	2115	*122500*	893	1425	1851	2199	*127800*	928	1480	1921	2283	*133100*	964	1535	1992	2366
117300	858	1371	1781	2117	*122600*	894	1426	1852	2201	*127900*	929	1481	1923	2284	*133200*	964	1536	1994	2368
117400	859	1372	1783	2119	*122700*	894	1427	1853	2202	*128000*	930	1482	1924	2286	*133300*	965	1537	1995	2369
117500	860	1373	1784	2120	*122800*	895	1428	1855	2204	*128100*	930	1483	1925	2287	*133400*	966	1538	1996	2371
117600	860	1374	1785	2122	*122900*	896	1429	1856	2205	*128200*	931	1484	1927	2289	*133500*	966	1539	1998	2373
117700	861	1375	1787	2123	*123000*	896	1430	1857	2207	*128300*	932	1485	1928	2291	*133600*	967	1540	1999	2374
117800	862	1376	1788	2125	*123100*	897	1431	1859	2209	*128400*	932	1486	1929	2292	*133700*	968	1541	2000	2376
117900	862	1377	1789	2126	*123200*	898	1432	1860	2210	*128500*	933	1487	1931	2294	*133800*	968	1542	2002	2377

Note: This table shows amounts of child support based on income to the nearest $100. There is a mathematical formula for calculating specific child support amounts between the $100 levels. For more information, please contact the Department of Justice.

Nota: La présente table indique le montant de la pension alimentaire pour enfants à verser d'après le revenu (aux 100 $ près). Il existe une formule mathématique pour calculer le montant exact de la pension alimentaire pour enfants dans le cas des revenus qui se situent entre les tranches de 100 $. Pour plus de renseignements, veuillez communiquer avec le ministère de la Justice.

Divorce

SASKATCHEWAN
1997

FEDERAL CHILD SUPPORT AMOUNTS : SIMPLIFIED TABLES
MONTANTS FÉDÉRAUX DE PENSIONS ALIMENTAIRES POUR ENFANTS : TABLES SIMPLIFIÉES

Income/ Revenu ($)	Monthly Award/ Paiement mensuel ($) No. of Children/ N^{bre} d'enfants				Income/ Revenu ($)	Monthly Award/ Paiement mensuel ($) No. of Children/ N^{bre} d'enfants				Income/ Revenu ($)	Monthly Award/ Paiement mensuel ($) No. of Children/ N^{bre} d'enfants				Income/ Revenu ($)	Monthly Award/ Paiement mensuel ($) No. of Children/ N^{bre} d'enfants				Income/ Revenu ($)	Monthly Award/ Paiement mensuel ($) No. of Children/ N^{bre} d'enfants			
	1	2	3	4		1	2	3	4		1	2	3	4		1	2	3	4		1	2	3	4
133900	969	1543	2003	2379	138000	996	1586	2058	2444	142100	1024	1629	2112	2508	146200	1051	1671	2167	2573
134000	970	1544	2004	2380	138100	997	1587	2059	2445	142200	1024	1630	2114	2510	146300	1052	1672	2168	2575
134100	970	1545	2006	2382	138200	998	1588	2060	2447	142300	1025	1631	2115	2511	146400	1052	1673	2170	2576
134200	971	1546	2007	2384	138300	998	1589	2062	2448	142400	1026	1632	2116	2513	146500	1053	1674	2171	2578
134300	972	1548	2008	2385	138400	999	1590	2063	2450	142500	1026	1633	2118	2515	146600	1054	1675	2172	2579
134400	972	1549	2010	2387	138500	1000	1591	2064	2451	142600	1027	1634	2119	2516	146700	1054	1676	2174	2581
134500	973	1550	2011	2388	138600	1000	1592	2066	2453	142700	1028	1635	2120	2518	146800	1055	1677	2175	2582
134600	974	1551	2012	2390	138700	1001	1593	2067	2455	142800	1028	1636	2122	2519	146900	1056	1678	2176	2584
134700	974	1552	2014	2392	138800	1002	1594	2068	2456	142900	1029	1637	2123	2521	147000	1056	1679	2178	2586
134800	975	1553	2015	2393	138900	1002	1595	2070	2458	143000	1030	1638	2124	2522	147100	1057	1680	2179	2587
134900	976	1554	2016	2395	139000	1003	1596	2071	2459	143100	1030	1639	2126	2524	147200	1058	1681	2180	2589
135000	976	1555	2018	2396	139100	1004	1597	2072	2461	143200	1031	1640	2127	2526	147300	1058	1683	2182	2590
135100	977	1556	2019	2398	139200	1004	1598	2074	2463	143300	1032	1641	2128	2527	147400	1059	1684	2183	2592
135200	978	1557	2020	2399	139300	1005	1599	2075	2464	143400	1032	1642	2130	2529	147500	1060	1685	2184	2593
135300	978	1558	2022	2401	139400	1006	1600	2076	2466	143500	1033	1643	2131	2530	147600	1060	1686	2186	2595
135400	979	1559	2023	2403	139500	1006	1602	2078	2467	143600	1034	1644	2132	2532	147700	1061	1687	2187	2597
135500	980	1560	2024	2404	139600	1007	1603	2079	2469	143700	1034	1645	2134	2533	147800	1062	1688	2188	2598
135600	980	1561	2026	2406	139700	1008	1604	2080	2470	143800	1035	1646	2135	2535	147900	1062	1689	2190	2600
135700	981	1562	2027	2407	139800	1008	1605	2082	2472	143900	1036	1647	2136	2537	148000	1063	1690	2191	2601
135800	982	1563	2028	2409	139900	1009	1606	2083	2474	144000	1036	1648	2138	2538	148100	1064	1691	2192	2603
135900	982	1564	2030	2410	140000	1010	1607	2084	2475	144100	1037	1649	2139	2540	148200	1064	1692	2194	2604
136000	983	1565	2031	2412	140100	1010	1608	2086	2477	144200	1038	1650	2140	2541	148300	1065	1693	2195	2606
136100	984	1566	2032	2414	140200	1011	1609	2087	2478	144300	1038	1651	2142	2543	148400	1066	1694	2196	2608
136200	984	1567	2034	2415	140300	1012	1610	2088	2480	144400	1039	1652	2143	2545	148500	1066	1695	2198	2609
136300	985	1568	2035	2417	140400	1012	1611	2090	2481	144500	1040	1653	2144	2546	148600	1067	1696	2199	2611
136400	986	1569	2036	2418	140500	1013	1612	2091	2483	144600	1040	1654	2146	2548	148700	1068	1697	2200	2612
136500	986	1570	2038	2420	140600	1014	1613	2092	2485	144700	1041	1656	2147	2549	148800	1068	1698	2202	2614
136600	987	1571	2039	2421	140700	1014	1614	2094	2486	144800	1042	1657	2148	2551	148900	1069	1699	2203	2616
136700	988	1572	2040	2423	140800	1015	1615	2095	2488	144900	1042	1658	2150	2552	149000	1070	1700	2204	2617
136800	988	1573	2042	2425	140900	1016	1616	2096	2489	145000	1043	1659	2151	2554	149100	1070	1701	2206	2619
136900	989	1575	2043	2426	141000	1016	1617	2098	2491	145100	1044	1660	2152	2556	149200	1071	1702	2207	2620
137000	990	1576	2044	2428	141100	1017	1618	2099	2492	145200	1044	1661	2154	2557	149300	1072	1703	2208	2622
137100	990	1577	2046	2429	141200	1018	1619	2100	2494	145300	1045	1662	2155	2559	149400	1072	1704	2210	2623
137200	991	1578	2047	2431	141300	1018	1620	2102	2496	145400	1046	1663	2156	2560	149500	1073	1705	2211	2625
137300	992	1579	2048	2433	141400	1019	1621	2103	2497	145500	1046	1664	2158	2562	149600	1074	1706	2212	2627
137400	992	1580	2050	2434	141500	1020	1622	2104	2499	145600	1047	1665	2159	2563	149700	1074	1707	2214	2628
137500	993	1581	2051	2436	141600	1020	1623	2106	2500	145700	1048	1666	2160	2565	149800	1075	1708	2215	2630
137600	994	1582	2052	2437	141700	1021	1624	2107	2502	145800	1048	1667	2162	2567	149900	1076	1709	2216	2631
137700	994	1583	2054	2439	141800	1022	1625	2108	2504	145900	1049	1668	2163	2568	150000	1076	1711	2218	2633
137800	995	1584	2055	2440	141900	1022	1626	2110	2505	146000	1050	1669	2164	2570					
137900	996	1585	2056	2442	142000	1023	1627	2111	2507	146100	1050	1670	2166	2571					

Income/ Revenu ($)	Monthly Award/Paiement mensuel ($)			
	one child/ un enfant	two children/ deux enfants	three children/ trois enfants	four children/ quatre enfants
For income over $150,000	**1076** plus 0.67% of income over $150,000	**1711** plus 1.04% of income over 150,000	**2218** plus 1.33% of income over $150,000	**2633** plus 1.58% of income over $150,000
Pour revenu dépassant 150 000$	**1076** plus 0,67% du revenu dépassant 150 000$	**1711** plus 1,04% du revenu dépassant 150 000$	**2218** plus 1,33% du revenu dépassant 150 000$	**2633** plus 1,58% du revenu dépassant 150 000$

Note: This table shows amounts of child support based on income to the nearest $100. There is a mathematical formula for calculating specific child support amounts between the $100 levels. For more information, please contact the Department of Justice.

Nota: La présente table indique le montant de la pension alimentaire pour enfants à verser d'après le revenu (aux 100 $ près). Il existe une formule mathématique pour calculer le montant exact de la pension alimentaire pour enfants dans le cas des revenus qui se situent entre les tranches de 100 $. Pour plus de renseignements, veuillez communiquer avec le ministère de la Justice.

Index

A-I

access	49, 89
adultery	21
Affidavit (No Appeal)	72
assets	27
Blue Backer	67
Canada Pension Plan	36
Certificate of Divorce	72
Certificate of Marriage	63
child custody	47-48
Child Support Fact Sheet	81
cohabitation	37
credit splitting	38
cruelty	22
custodial parent	89
debts and liabilities	39
defended divorce	11
disclaimer	41
Divorce Judgment	68, 72
documents	56-57
equitable distribution	33
family home	35
Financial Statement	67
grounds	19
health coverage	47
insurance policies	88

J-O

Joint Affidavit	63
joint charge cards	88
joint checking accounts	87
joint credit accounts	87
joint custody	48
joint loans	88
Joint Petition for Divorce	57
Joint Waiver of Financial Statements	68
lawyer	
advantages of using	14
finding a	15
legal separation	19
lenders	88
licensure	39
Lis Pendens	28
marital property	34
Marriage Registration Certificate	57
minor children	12
Motion Record and Index	66
non-custodial parent	89
Notice of Motion	66
Order (with children)	82
Order (without children)	82
Order for Substituted Service	67

P-W

pension 36
personal property 34
Petition for Divorce 66
Petitioner's Affidavit 67
post-divorce checklist 87
Praecipe 83
profit-sharing plans 36
property 12, 33-41
real estate 88
refund 88
remarriage 87
Respondent's Affidavit 67
restraining order 28
savings accounts 87
Separation Agreement 20
sole custody 48
support 13, 45-46, 50-51
Support Deduction Order 68-69
Support Deduction Order
    Information Form 68, 70
tax returns 88
title 88
undefended divorce 11
visitation 49, 89
wills 89

NOTES

NOTES

NOTES

NOTES

NOTES

NOTES